DISCOVERING THE
TWENTIETH-CENTURY WORLD

DISCOVERING THE TWENTIETH-CENTURY WORLD

A LOOK AT THE EVIDENCE

Merry E. Wiesner
University of Wisconsin—Milwaukee

Julius R. Ruff
Marquette University

William Bruce Wheeler
University of Tennessee

Franklin M. Doeringer
Lawrence University

Kenneth R. Curtis
California State University Long Beach

HOUGHTON MIFFLIN COMPANY   Boston   New York

Senior Sponsoring Editor: Nancy Blaine
Development Editor: Julie Dunn
Associate Project Editor: Reba Libby
Editorial Assistant: Rachel Zanders
Production/Design Coordinator: Sarah Ambrose
Manufacturing Manager: Florence Cadran
Senior Marketing Manager: Sandra McGuire

Printed in the U.S.A.

Library of Congress Catalog Card Number: 2003105548

ISBN: 0-618-37931-2

2 3 4 5 6 7 8 9-MV-10 09 08 07

CONTENTS

CHAPTER FIVE
Lands of Desire: Department Stores, Advertising, and the New Consumerism (1920s)   129

CHAPTER SIX
The Industrial Crisis and the Centralization of Government (1924–1939)   151

CHAPTER NINE
Berlin: The Crux of the Cold War (1945–1990)   254

CHAPTER TWELVE
The New Europeans: Labor, Migration, and the Problems of Assimilation   363

PREFACE

The title of this book begins with a verb, a choice that reflects our basic philosophy about history. History is not simply something one learns about; it is something one does. One discovers the past, and what makes this pursuit exciting is not only the past that is discovered but also the process of discovery itself. This process can be simultaneously exhilarating and frustrating, enlightening and confusing, but it is always challenging enough to convince those of us who are professional historians to spend our lives at it. And our own students, as well as many other students, have caught this infectious excitement.

The recognition that history involves discovery as much as physics or astronomy does is often not shared by students, whose classroom experience of history frequently does not extend beyond listening to lectures and reading textbooks. The primary goal of *Discovering the Twentieth-Century World: A Look at the Evidence* is to allow students enrolled in twentieth-century history courses to *do* history in the same way that we as historians do—to examine a group of original sources to answer questions about the past. The unique structure of this book clusters primary sources around a set of historical questions that students are asked to "solve." Unlike a source reader, this book prompts students to actually *analyze* a wide variety of authentic primary source material, to make inferences, and to draw conclusions in much the same way that historians do.

The evidence in this book is more varied than that in most source collections. We have included such visual evidence as paintings, statues, literary illustrations, historical photographs, maps, cartoons, film stills, advertisements, and political posters. In choosing written evidence we again have tried to offer a broad sample—eulogies, wills, court records, oral testimonies, and statistical data all supplement letters, newspaper articles, speeches, memoirs, and other more traditional sources.

In order for students to learn history the way we as historians do, they must not only be confronted with the evidence but must also learn how to use that evidence to arrive at a conclusion. In other words, they must learn historical methodology. Too often methodology (or even the notion that historians *have* a methodology) is reserved for upper-level majors or graduate students; beginning students are simply presented with historical facts and interpretations without being shown how these were unearthed or formulated. Students may learn that historians hold different interpretations of the significance of an event or individual or different ideas about causation, but they are not informed of how historians come to such conclusions.

Thus, along with evidence, we have provided explicit suggestions about how one might analyze that evidence, guiding students as they reach their own conclusions. As they work through the various chapters, students will discover both that the sources of historical information are wide-ranging and that the methodologies appropriate to understanding and using them are equally diverse. By doing history themselves, students will learn how intellectual historians handle philosophical treatises, economic historians quantitative data, social historians court records, and political and diplomatic historians theoretical treatises and memoirs. They will also be asked to consider the limitations of their evidence, to explore what historical questions it cannot answer as well as those it can. Instead of remaining passive observers, students become active participants.

Each chapter is divided into six parts: The Problem, Background, The Method, The Evidence, Questions to Consider, and Epilogue. Each of the parts relates or builds upon the others, creating a uniquely integrated chapter structure that helps guide the reader through the analytical process. "The Problem" section begins with a brief discussion of the central issues of the chapter and then states the questions students will explore. A "Background" section follows, designed to help students understand the historical context of the problem. The section called "The Method" gives students suggestions for studying and analyzing the evidence. "The Evidence" section is the heart of the chapter, providing a variety of primary source material on the particular historical event or issue described in the chapter's "Problem" section. The section called "Questions to Consider" focuses students' attention on specific evidence and on linkages among different evidence material. The "Epilogue" section gives the aftermath or the historical outcome of the evidence—what happened to the people involved, the results of a debate, and so on.

Within this framework, we have tried to present a series of historical issues and events of significance to the instructor as well as of interest to the student. We have also aimed to provide a balance among political, social, diplomatic, intellectual, and cultural history. In other words, we have attempted to create a kind of historical sampler that we believe will help students learn the methods and skills used by historians. Not only will these skills—analyzing arguments, developing hypotheses, comparing evidence, testing conclusions, and reevaluating material—enable students to master historical content; they will also provide the necessary foundation for critical thinking in other college courses and after college as well.

Because the amount of material for the twentieth century is so vast, we had to pick certain topics and geographic areas to highlight, though here too we have aimed at a balance. Some chapters, such as Chapter 8 on the Suez

Crisis or Chapter 11 on the youth revolts of the 1960s, are narrow in scope, providing students with an opportunity to delve deeply into a single case study. Others, such as Chapter 1 on the idea of modernity or Chapter 10 on feminism and the peace movement, ask students to make comparisons among individuals, events or developments in different cultures across a fairly broad time frame. A few chapters use only visual sources; Chapter 2, for example, uses the works of a group of major painters, including Gauguin and Picasso, to examine transformations in Western thought in the early twentieth century. A few chapters include only written sources, though most combine different types of sources, thus modeling the methods of many historians. We have included some topics that are always part of twentieth-century courses, such as Chapter 7 on the rise of Nazi Germany, and others that are more unusual but represent topics of current interest to both students and historians, including Chapter 5 on trends in popular culture represented by department stores around the world in the 1920s and Chapter 13 on the global expansion of McDonald's in recent decades.

Discovering the Twentieth-Century World is designed to accommodate any course format, from the small lecture/discussion class at a liberal arts or community college to the large lecture with discussions led by teaching assistants at a sizable university. The chapters may be used for individual assignments, team projects, class discussions, papers, and exams. Each is self-contained, so that any combination may be assigned. The book is not intended to replace a standard textbook, and it was written to accompany any text the instructor chooses.

Acknowledgments

In the completion of this book, the authors received assistance from a number of people. Our colleagues and students at the University of Wisconsin-Milwaukee, California State University-Long Beach, Lawrence University, Marquette University, and the University of Tennessee, Knoxville, have been generous with their ideas and time. The authors also wish to extend their thanks to the staff of Houghton Mifflin Company for their enthusiastic support.

M.E.W.
W.B.W.
F.M.D.
J.R.R.
K.R.C.

CHAPTER ONE

MODERNITY: FROM PROMISE TO

THREAT (1790–1930)

In his 1921 poem "The Second Coming," the Irish poet William Butler Yeats voiced the dread that many felt as the violence of twentieth-century war and upheaval overtook their lives:

Turning and turning in the widening
    gyre
The falcon cannot hear the falconer;
Things fall apart; the center cannot
    hold;
Mere anarchy is loosed upon the
    world,
The blood-dimmed tide is loosed, and
    everywhere
The ceremony of innocence is
    drowned;
The best lack all conviction, while the
    worst
Are filled with passionate intensity.[1]

1. Reprinted with the permission of Scribner, an imprint of Simon & Schuster Adult Publishing Group, from *The Collected Works of W. B. Yeats, Volume I: The Poems*, Revised, edited by Richard J. Finneran. Copyright © 1924 by The Macmillan Company; copyright renewed © 1952 by Bertha Georgie Yeats.

Part of a growing chorus of intellectual discontent, Yeats's lines reflected a widespread fear in the early decades of the twentieth century that the modern world was heading toward some dire catastrophe. This apprehension stood in sharp contrast to the views prevailing in the previous two centuries, at least in the West, where most people welcomed the modern age as the dawn of a better time. With this change in attitude, the characteristic features of this new era, features that had once been associated with improvement and progress, came to be seen as menacing. What had been once exalted as a promise of better life now seemed a threat to many people.

This chapter explores what lay behind this shift in attitudes. It does so by looking at some classic statements about the nature of modern identity, or "modernity," that date from the late eighteenth to the early twentieth century. The earlier pieces reveal a very optimistic view of modern change. The later ones, in contrast, are more critical and even pessimistic. Your task is to trace the change in opinion that they show and to ask what direction it took. In doing so, think about the following three questions. First, what does each document consider to be the most important or defining features of modernity? Second, which of these features initially seemed to promise improvement, and of what? Third, which proved to have effects other than those predicted? That is, what changes either failed to bring the anticipated benefits or led to unexpected problems?

In analyzing how people of the past understood modernity, you will be playing the role of an intellectual historian who studies how certain views or ideas developed over time and influenced society. In this case, of course, the concept in question was special, for it shaped people's perception of a key historical period. By looking at what people took to be the characteristic traits of modernity, you should gain some insight into what they thought gave the modern era a distinct identity and distinguished it from other times.

The concept of a unique modern character or identity did more than just shape people's perception of a single age. It played an important role in the way modern Western historians "periodized" history, or divided it into meaningful eras for study. Convinced that distinct new trends in their own times marked the end of antiquity, early modern historians began to divide the study of history into two broad periods, ancient and modern, and view it in terms of a development from one to the other. Later historians, finding the centuries between these periods largely intermediate or medial in nature, named these centuries the Middle or Medieval Age. Thus the idea of a unique, modern identity not only influenced the way moderns looked at themselves and their own time, but inspired a broad historical framework that affects the way we view the whole of the past. Clearly, then, the idea of modernity holds a special place in the study of history.

BACKGROUND

Though aspects of modernity can be traced back to Renaissance Europe, it was the Scientific Revolution in the sixteenth and seventeenth centuries that nurtured a distinctly modern outlook. Intellectuals in Western Europe began to question traditional knowledge and the ways it had been acquired. Convinced that they had found a new "mode" of experiencing reality, they began to call themselves "moderns" (i.e., those in the new mode), in contrast to the more traditionally minded, whom they termed "ancients." From the start, then, *modernity* implied a special historical outlook, one assuming a sharp break with the past caused by a unique perspective.

The work of Isaac Newton proved decisive to the new outlook. In his *Mathematical Principles of Natural Philosophy* of 1684, this Englishman provided a new, mathematical model of the universe, portraying it as a materialistic world of mindless bodies coursing in regular motions according to inflexible laws of nature. Even more important, he claimed to have developed this model through a new "scientific method" of interpreting nature based on inductive empiricism, a system of inferring knowledge from evidence that can be seen or touched through the senses. Together his model and his method laid the foundation for modern science. They also inspired a broader intellectual shift, for thinkers outside the natural sciences began to believe that the scientific method could disclose social and ethical truths as well as natural facts. A burst of speculation thus followed the Scientific Revolution, and after another Englishman, John Locke, adapted Newton's method for social analysis in his 1690 *Essay Concerning Human Understanding*, new "social sciences" arose as potential tools for improving humanity.

Europe's educated elite quickly embraced both the new sciences and the scientific method. With them, many concluded, reason could unlock Nature's secrets and enhance life materially while improving social conditions. Many Europeans thus welcomed the start of the eighteenth century with great optimism, convinced that a new "age of reason" was dawning—that, as Immanuel Kant was to put it in 1784, "an age of enlightenment" had begun. Fear of change, which had been nearly universal in other eras, now gave way to welcoming change, for in a constantly improving world, the future would always be better. From this view came the idea of "progress" based on the belief that humans were advancing in a continuous process of improvement. Where earlier people had looked to the past for inspiration, moderns now began to exalt the future.

The confidence of the age inspired intellectual leaders, known by the French term *philosophes,* to advocate an ambitious program of social and political reform. François Marie de Voltaire (1694–1778), boldly pronounced humans to be inherently good. Crime and poverty, he said, arose from social and economic circumstances that blighted good impulses, not from inborn sin. To do away with evil, society had only to eliminate the underlying causes: sickness, poverty, and injustice. Thus the *philosophes* called for a reform of harsh laws, an end to cruel punishments, morecharity for the poor, and more compassion for the lower social strata and less advantaged groups like women and children.

In presuming that people would take responsibility for their own improvement, Enlightenment hopes inspired new interest in the self, which eventually led to a doctrine of individualism. Appreciation of individual uniqueness and worth led logically to the idea that all people deserved respect. From this idea evolved a doctrine of rights asserting that *all* humans had claims—such as to life, liberty, and property—that none could deny. John Locke had pioneered this view in 1690, arguing that because people formed governments to secure civil rights, no government could rescind those rights. The *philosophes* developed the idea further, claiming that all people were endowed by nature with inalienable "human rights" that no one could legitimately violate. This belief in equality of endowment in turn encouraged the idea that wealth and power should be more evenly distributed in society to ensure that all people had the opportunity to realize their birthright. Politically, these ideas promoted interest in democratic governments in which the whole populace would have a say in public decisions, leading to demands for constitutional protection of rights and for elected assemblies.

By the end of the eighteenth century, Enlightenment ideas had crystallized into classical liberalism, a system of thought—and eventually a political movement—dedicated to social betterment through the liberation of individual potential. Deeming individuals the basic unit of society, liberals called for more personal freedom and pressed for constitutional curbs on arbitrary power. Their ideal was a society of autonomous citizens in which the pursuit of rational self-interest brought about the good of all. Adam Smith (1723–1790) adapted these ideas to economic life with a parallel vision of free markets in which the pursuit of individual profit secured the most gain for all. Though at first hopeful that rulers would voluntarily enact their program, liberals grew increasingly frustrated by the indifference and opposition they encountered.

In the last third of the eighteenth century, pent-up popular frustrations exploded, sending tides of revolution across much of the Western world, from Poland to Europe's new American colonies. Initial stirrings in Geneva in 1768 and England's North American colonies in 1776 were followed by the French Revolution in 1789, an event that rocked the foundations of the Western world. Under Republican and then Napoleonic leadership, the French armies spread radical ideas across Europe, unleashing decades more of secondary revolutions until these ended with a final round of violence in 1848. Eighty years of revolutionary change and warfare altered Western Europe socially and politically, leaving most of its new leaders committed to Enlightenment ideals and the liberal agenda of making a better world through human emancipation and material improvement.

While political revolution was sweeping across the West, a parallel economic revolution was also taking place. Known as the Industrial Revolution, it entailed the rise of mechanized industries capable of pouring out a vast supply of cheap goods and opening mass markets. Begun in England in the late 1700s with the mechanization of textile making, it soon spread across Western Europe and North America. By the early 1800s, the introduction of steam-driven ships and then of railroads propelled it to a new phase, stimulating growth in coal and steel production while lowering transport costs for all goods. By 1850 England was far enough along in this revolution to gain the title "workshop of the world" and win recognition as the first truly industrial nation. But by then other countries like the United States, France, and Belgium were catching up with it, and basic mechanization was spreading to central and northern Europe. And by the end of the nineteenth century, Japan and Russia were also industrializing.

Industrial growth dramatically altered social patterns. Millions left agriculture for the towns where the new industries were located, bringing rapid urbanization and the rise of huge new cities. These cities provided unprecedented opportunities for advancement, and successful men of business joined traditional commercial and professional groups in an affluent new middle class or *bourgeoisie*, as the French termed it. But most migrants into the cities did not do as well; they joined the industrial working class as mill hands, transport workers, or domestic servants. Wages for such people stayed low and working conditions poor, because their numbers made replacement easy. Women and children especially suffered, for they were paid less and often worked harder than men. The laboring poor, like the unemployed and destitute, often lived in appalling conditions that fostered violence and crime. Yet industrial cities continued to attract newcomers from the countryside because they inspired hope for advancement.

Such cities came to be identified with change. Political revolutions and legal reform had shattered the old corporate, hierarchical nature of Western society, in which people derived their roles, identity, and security from hereditary status in closed groups. In doing so, they eliminated many barriers to geographic and social mobility, freeing people to move in search of better lives. This shift to an open society made the massive migrations into the industrial cities possible in the first place. Then, because people found greater freedom to choose residences, work, and mates in the anonymity of the cities, they seemed less restrictive than the countryside and came to be associated closely with change and modernity. Heightened personal freedom in the new cities also encouraged newly emerging urban groups to press for a greater political say in their societies.

The middle class was the first to succeed. By the early 1830s, as the upper bourgeoisie assumed dominance in a restored French monarchy and the Whig party won control of the British Parliament, a new era of middle-class rule began in Western Europe. Adopting liberalism as their own, middle-class leaders in these countries launched ambitious reforms, inspiring a slow spread of the liberal program across Europe during the mid-nineteenth century. These reforms helped to deflect the rival challenge of working-class groups that arose with the revolutions of 1848 and the cries of radical new thinkers like Karl Marx urging workers to overthrow the existing order. Under pressure from middle-class reformers, rudimentary poor relief and welfare programs were begun and free public schools started. Combined with falling prices made possible by technological advances in the decades after the 1870s, these reforms eased the worst of working-class conditions and afforded workers, too, real hope for a better life. Led by the moderate socialist and labor parties to which they then turned, they also broadened the political franchise; there was universal male suffrage in nearly all industrial states by the early twentieth century.

By then the industrial world was becoming home to "mass society." Expanded manufacturing and agricultural output, improved material conditions, and enhanced public health brought a surge in population that came to be concentrated in the new industrial centers. This trend led in turn to new levels of mass activity in all spheres of modern life. Sprawling plants and towering office buildings replaced small workplaces, requiring the development of mass transit to move large numbers of people between their homes and work. Huge department stores and giant markets crowded out family shops, laying the foundation of a new mass consumerism. Burgeoning popular amusements, from cheap newspapers and dime novels to dance halls and theaters, nurtured the growth of new mass media. And unions and political parties mobilized millions into new mass organizations. But what distinguished mass society more than its numbers was the lack of distinction between its members. The changes that had freed and leveled individuals had also homogenized them into an indistinguishable mass of ordinary or "common men."

Although most concentrated in the industrial nations of the West, these changes had begun to have an effect on the rest of the world by the second half of the nineteenth century. Many industrial nations lacked the domestic resources to sustain their new economies and had to export manufactured goods to obtain needed foodstuffs and raw materials. To increase the supply of such imports, they invested in agricultural and extractive industries abroad, drawing nonindustrial areas into a new integrated and interdependent world economy. This trend increased after the 1880s, when many industrial nations sought to demonstrate their new national power by annexing territories and seizing distant lands as colonies, justifying this on the grounds that they were helping the people of these lands advance. Thus, those outside the industrialized West who failed to embrace "modern civilization" quickly, like the Japanese, soon found it imposed upon them as colonial subjects. Where it was imposed from above, however, modernity conveyed a sense of bondage and despair rather than the emancipation and hope with which it was originally associated.

The devastating wars and economic dislocation of the early twentieth century created an even greater disillusionment with modernity in the West. The Great War—as World War I was then called—proved especially upsetting. During that conflict, which raged from 1914 to 1918, mechanized mass warfare first came of age, and the millions of ordinary citizens drafted to fight were deeply disturbed by the carnage that resulted. At the war's end, many tried to escape in the gaiety of the cabarets and speakeasies associated with the short-lived Jazz Age of the 1920s. But the aftertremors of the war, which took the form of revolutions and political reversals in all the advanced industrial countries, made it impossible to regain lost confidence. Once again change seemed uncertain and threatening.

Works as diverse as Oswald Spengler's postwar treatise *The Decline of the West* and T. S. Eliot's 1922 poem "The Waste Land" portrayed modern culture as a decadent final stage of Western civilization. Their authors found its machines and masses emblems of despair, not hope. Out of such views developed a radically new approach to art and literature called *modernism*. Despite its name, this movement rejected modern optimism concerning progress. Its vision of a fragmented and shallow society instead reflected a profound sense of pessimism and a disillusionment with Enlightenment beliefs about human perfectibility. The growing mood of despair also nurtured the rise of radical political movements that promised a return to security through drastic political and economic programs. Many of these, like the Fascists in Europe, the Communists in Russia, and the ultra-nationalists of Japan, openly assailed liberalism and its doctrines of individualism and democracy, denouncing them as sources of decay and collapse.

Yet some found new freedom in the postwar era. Western youth took advantage of the uncertainty of the time to reject long-standing age constraints and launch a revolution in sexuality. Women in the West also benefited from the growing distrust of authority, winning the vote for themselves and beginning a feminist revolution aimed at breaking down old gender barriers. And in colonial lands, new leaders began to challenge imperial rule and talk of national liberation. These groups infused new vitality into the promise of modernity. But their efforts were soon eclipsed by the worldwide economic collapse that ushered in the Great Depression of the 1930s and the subsequent rise of authoritarian movements in key industrial states like Germany and Japan. By the time World War II erupted at the decade's end, life appeared to be growing morally and materially grimmer by the day, making modernity seem more menace than promise.

THE METHOD

The problem posed here requires you to think about both what modernity originally seemed to promise and what went wrong with that promise. So first look through the evidence for statements in praise of specific aspects of modernity, and then review it for negative comments. The initial sources generally view modernity in positive terms, whereas later ones become increasingly harsh. But guard against the simple assumption that they embrace or reject modernity outright. Many who have looked long and carefully at the idea of modernity

[7]

have remarked on its ambiguity. As one writer notes, modernity is inherently paradoxical:

> There is a mode of vital experience— experience of space and time, of the self and others, of life's possibilities and perils—that is shared by men and women all over the world today. I will call this body of experience "modernity." To be modern is to find ourselves in an environment that promises adventure, power, joy, growth, transformation of ourselves and the world—and, at the same time, that threatens to destroy everything we have, everything we know, everything we are.[2]

Rather than just asking whether a given source extols or denounces modernity, see what aspects of modernity it regards as most important and how it reacts to each of these. Jot these down along with some notes about why the source deems each a promise or a threat—or both. See how many of the same features reappear in different sources: They will provide a rough list of what people of the past understood modernity to entail. Then review your notes, paying attention to how each source reacted to these different aspects. Does any pattern emerge? Are some aspects universally deplored and others universally praised? Or are reactions to them mixed?

A number of defining traits, like a scientific outlook, will be easy to find because they will be explicitly cited.

2. Marshall Berman, *All That Is Solid Melts into Air: The Experience of Modernity* (London: Verso, 1982), p. 53.

But others that are less obvious may be of equal significance. Notice in the above quotation the reference to a unique modern experience of space and time and of the self and others. Being modern involves accepting certain assumptions about time and history; without knowing them, you cannot fully understand what such modern words as *revolution* and *progress* imply. Modernity also entails spatial connotations. Certain places seem more modern than others, inducing people to see landscapes and even the world itself as structured in special ways. Pay attention to which locales, globally and regionally, are presumed to be modern and which are not. Modern ideas of self and society similarly entail unspoken assumptions. Note how concern for individualism affects attitudes about personal and community values. In short, look beyond the obvious features of modernity for underlying beliefs and assumptions associated with it.

The Progress of the Human Mind (Source 1) is an excellent one to begin with for this purpose. Written in 1794 in the midst of the French Revolution by Jean Antoine Nicholas de Condorcet, it reveals the basic beliefs of the Enlightenment. In it, Condorcet presents the idea of history as a process of development and describes what he expects the final stage to be: an age of science and reason, during which humanity frees itself from Nature and folly alike. In doing so, he reveals key Enlightenment assumptions about time, progress, and the world as well as its optimism about the inevitability of attaining human perfection through intellectual and ethical improvement. Contrast this view of progress with that in Source 2, an editorial from the British journal *The Economist*. Inspired by a great world fair held in London in 1851 to celebrate Britain's new industrial status, it shifts the focus of progress to technical and material gains.

Source 3, "Years of the Modern," a poem written by Walt Whitman around 1865, also lauds technology. But it does so on the grounds that machines have freed the "average man" to reach hitherto unattainable goals, giving a distinctly American, democratic coloring to the idea of progress. A very different view appears in Source 4, a pamphlet called *Socialism: Utopian and Scientific*, written by Karl Marx's colleague and patron, Friedrich Engels, and first published in 1880. Critiquing modern industrial society from a Marxist perspective, Engels stresses the "crying social abuses" of early industrialization, claiming that, far from benefiting ordinary men, mechanization led to their subjugation and exploitation by the bourgeois class.

The next two sources offer even more caustic views of modernity from the vantage point of other disaffected groups. Source 5, Gandhi's *Hind Swaraj* or *Indian Self-rule*, written in 1909 while he was experimenting with passive resistance against British rule in South Africa, gives a scathing critique of modern civilization from the perspective of those under colonial dominion. But in seeking a better civilization that would revere morality and intellect rather than materialism—while emancipating millions from unjust rule—Gandhi echoes some of the cherished goals of the Enlightenment. *Woman and Labour*, Source 6, looks at modern civilization from a feminist point of view. The author, Olive Schreiner, was a South African novelist of European descent who became active in what she termed the "Woman's Movement," seeking equality between men and women. Deep concerns about the social and psychological costs of modernity led her in this 1911 book to attribute women's plight not to men but rather to the "social disco-ordination" of modern life, which left both "tortured" amid material plenty.

Source 7, "A Declaration of Beliefs by the *New Youth*," shows, however, that others outside the West remained enthusiastic about modernity as the new century began. A radical periodical founded in 1915 by students at Beijing University, *New Youth* sought to introduce modern ideas and values into China. Many contributors became leading intellectuals and revolutionaries in the struggle to modernize China, including those who founded the Chinese Communist Party in 1921. But as this 1919 article indicates, its editors espoused a liberal, not Marxist, agenda in their efforts "to cultivate a new spirit for our times, a spirit more conducive to the creation of a new society."

Postwar European intellectuals, by contrast, were losing interest in this agenda. Source 8, stills from a famous early German film, *Metropolis*, illustrates one direction this disillusionment took. Directed by Fritz Lang, who was influenced by German Expressionist art and socialist ideals, this 1927 film projects a sinister view of modern urban life. It depicts a fictional city as a dehumanized world in which a small technocratic elite uses machines to keep the masses subject to their will. An equally negative view colors Source 9, from José Ortega y Gasset's 1930 book, *The Revolt of the Masses.* A liberal intellectual and leader of the Spanish Republican movement, Ortega also decries modern mass, technocratic society. But in his case, it is because he thinks it allows ordinary people to dominate, not because it enslaves them. Deeming popular culture shallow and the values of the "common man" cowardly, he fears that mass, industrial society has abandoned Enlightenment ideals and marks a decline rather than an advance in historical development.

THE EVIDENCE

Source 1 from Introduction to Contemporary Civilization in the West *(New York: Columbia University Press, 1946), pp. 1059–1067. Copyright 1946 by Columbia University Press. Reprinted by permission of the publisher.*

1. From Jean Antoine Nicholas de Condorcet, *The Progress of the Human Mind*

TENTH EPOQUE: FUTURE PROGRESS OF MANKIND

Will not every nation one day arrive at the state of civilization attained by those people who are most enlightened, most free, most exempt from prejudices, as the French, for instance, and the Anglo-Americans? Will not the slavery of countries subjected to kings, the barbarity of African tribes, and the ignorance of savages gradually vanish? Is there upon the face of the globe a single spot the inhabitants of which are condemned by nature never to enjoy liberty, never to exercise their reason? . . .

In a word, will not men be continually verging towards that state, in which all will possess the requisite knowledge for conducting themselves in the common affairs of the life by their own reason, and of maintaining that reason uncontaminated by prejudices; in which they will understand their rights, and exercise them, according to their opinion and their conscience; in which all will be able, by the development of their faculties, to procure the certain means of providing for their wants; lastly, in which folly and wretchedness will be accidents, happening only now and then, and not the habitual lot of a considerable portion of society?

In fine, may it not be expected that the human race will be meliorated by new discoveries in the sciences and the arts, and, as an unavoidable consequence, in the means of individual and general prosperity; by farther progress in the principles of conduct, and in moral practice; and lastly, by the real improvement of our faculties, moral, intellectual and physical, which may be the result either of the improvement of the instruments which increase the power and direct the exercise of those faculties, or of the improvement of our natural organization itself? . . .

The advantages that must result from the state of improvement, of which I have proved we may almost entertain the certain hope, can have no limit but the absolute perfection of the human species, since, in proportion as different kinds of equality shall be established as to the various means of providing for our wants, as to a more universal instruction, and a more entire liberty, the more real will be this equality, and the nearer will it approach towards embracing everything truly important to the happiness of mankind. . . .

By applying these general reflections to the different sciences, we might exhibit, respecting each, examples of this progressive improvement, which would remove all possibility of doubts as to the certainty of the further improvement that may be expected. . . .

If we pass to the progress of the arts, those arts particularly the theory of which depends on these very same sciences, we shall find that it can have no inferior limits; that their processes are susceptible of the same improvement, the same simplifications, as the scientific methods; that instruments, machines, looms, will add every day to the capabilities and skill of man—will augment at once the excellence and precision of his works, while they will diminish the time and labour necessary for executing them. . . .

In short, does not the well-being, the prosperity, resulting from the progress that will be made by the useful arts, in consequence of their being founded upon a sound theory, resulting, also, from an improved legislation, built upon the truths of the political sciences, naturally dispose men to humanity, to benevolence, and to justice? Do not all the observations, in fine, which we proposed to develop in this work prove, that the moral goodness of man, the necessary consequence of his organization, is, like all his other faculties, susceptible of an indefinite improvement? and that nature has connected, by a chain which cannot be broken, truth, happiness, and virtue?

Among those causes of human improvement that are of most importance to the general welfare, must be included, the total annihilation of the prejudices which have established between the sexes an inequality of rights, fatal even to the party which it favours. In vain might we search for motives by which to justify this principle, in difference of physical organization, of intellect, or of moral sensibility. It had at first no other origin but abuse of strength, and all the attempts which have since been made to support it are idle sophisms.

The people being more enlightened, and having resumed the right of disposing for themselves of their blood and their treasure, will learn by degrees to regard war as the most dreadful of all calamities, the most terrible of all crimes. . . .

The organic perfectibility or deterioration of the classes of the vegetable, or species of the animal kingdom, may be regarded as one of the general laws of nature.

This law extends itself to the human race; and it cannot be doubted that the progress of the sanative art, that the use of more wholesome food and more comfortable habitations, that a mode of life which shall develop the physical powers by exercise, without at the same time impairing them by excess; in fine, that the destruction of the two most active causes of deterioration, penury and wretchedness on the one hand, and enormous wealth on the other, must necessarily tend to prolong the common duration of man's existence, and secure him a more constant health and a more robust constitution. It is manifest that the improvement of the practice of medicine, become more efficacious in consequence of the progress of reason and the social order, must in the end put a period to transmissible or contagious disorders, as well as to those general maladies resulting from climate, ailments, and the nature of certain occupations. Nor would it be difficult to prove that this hope might be extended to almost every other malady, of which it is probable we shall hereafter discover the most remote causes. . . .

Lastly, may we not include in the same circle the intellectual and moral faculties? May not our parents, who transmit to us the advantages or defects of their conformation, and from whom we receive our features and shape, as well as our propensities to certain physical affections, transmit to us also that part of organization upon which intellect, strength of understanding, energy of soul or moral sensibility depend? Is it not probable that education, by improving these qualities, will at the same time have an influence upon, will modify and improve this organization itself? Analogy, an investigation of the human faculties, and even some facts appear to authorise these conjectures, and thereby to enlarge the boundary of our hopes.

Such are the questions with which we shall terminate the last division of our work. And how admirably calculated is this view of the human race, emancipated from its chains, released alike from the dominion of chance, as well as from that of the enemies of its progress, and advancing with a firm and indeviate step in the paths of truth, to console the philosopher lamenting the errors, the flagrant acts of injustice, the crimes with which the earth is still polluted? It is the contemplation of this prospect that rewards him for all his efforts to assist the progress of reason and the establishment of liberty. . . .

Source 2 from The Economist, *Vol. IX, (January 18, 1851), pp. 57–58.*

2. "The First Half of the Nineteenth Century Progress of the Nation, and the Race"

The close of one half-century and the commencement of another offer to us one of those resting places in the march of time which, whenever they occur, at shorter or longer intervals, impressively summon us to the task of retrospect and reflection. "The poorest moment that passes over us is the conflux of two eternities;" we are, it is true, at every moment standing on the narrow isthmus that divides the great ocean of durations ground that, even as we name it, is washed from beneath our feet; but it is only at the termination of the longer epochs by which our life is told off into the past, that we fully feel this truth. At such times it is well to pause for a brief space amid the struggle and the race of life, to consider the rate of our progress and the direction of our course, to measure our distance from the starting-post in relation to the advantages with which we set out and the time we have spent upon the road, and to calculate, as far as may be, the probable rapidity of our future advance in a career to which there is no goal.

Too many of us are disposed to place our Golden Age in the Past: this is especially the tendency of the imaginative, the ignorant, the indolent, and the old. To such it is soothing to turn from the dry and disappointing labours of the present and the hot and dusty pathways of the actual world, and to speculate on that early spring-time of our Race in which Fancy, without toil or hindrance, can construct a Utopia of which History affords us no trace, and which Logic assures us could have had no existence. Another and a larger class are ever prone to seek a refuge from baffled exertions, disappointed hopes, and dissatisfied desires, in a distant Future in which all expectations, reasonable or unreasonable, are to have their fulfilment: But nearly everybody agrees by common consent to undervalue and abuse the present. We confess that we cannot share their disappointment, nor echo their complaints. We look upon the Past with respect and affection as a series of steppingstones, to that high and advanced position which we actually hold and from the Future we hope for the realisation of those dreams, almost of perfectibility, which a comparison of the Past with the present entitles us to indulge in. But we see no reason to be discontented either with our rate of progress or with the actual stage which we have reached; and we think that man must be hard to please who, with due estimate of human powers and human aims, and a full knowledge of the facts which we propose concisely to recall to the recollection of our readers, can come to a different conclusion.

Economists are supposed to be, by nature and occupation, cold, arithmetical, and unenthusiastic. We shall not, we hope, do discredit to this character when we say that we consider it a happiness and a privilege to have had our lot cast in the first fifty years of this century. For not only has that period been rich beyond nearly all others in political events of thrilling interest and mighty moments, but in changes and incidents of moral and social significance it has had no parallel since the Christian era. It has witnessed the most tremendous war and the most enduring peace which we have known for centuries. It has beheld the splendid career and the sad retribution reverses of the greatest conqueror, scourge, and upsetter of old arrangements, since the days of Gengis-Khan, Attila, or Charlemagne. It has witnessed a leap forward in all the elements of material well-being such as neither scientific vision nor poetic fancy ever pictured. It is not too much to say that, in wealth, in the arts of life, in the discoveries of science and their application to the comfort, the health, the safety, and the capabilities of man, in public and private morality, in the diffusion if not in the advancement of knowledge, in the sense of social charity and justice, in religious freedom, and in political wisdom, the period of the last fifty years has carried us forward faster and further than any other half-century in modern times. It stands at the head, *facile princeps,* unrivalled and unapproached, of all epochs of equal duration. Nay, more; it is scarcely too much to say that, in many of the particulars we have enumerated, it has witnessed a more rapid and astonishing progress than all the centuries which have preceded it. In several vital points the difference between the 18th and the 19th century, is greater than between the first and the 18th, as far as civilized Europe is concerned.

As we proceed we shall have occasion to justify this statement in several particulars; but if in the meantime it should seem too startling to any reader, we would ask him to compare Macaulay's celebrated picture of the state of England under the Stuarts with its condition at the close of the last century; and then to compare this last with its condition now; and he will be amazed to find how nearly all those details of its astonishing advance which most bear upon the comforts and welfare of his daily life, are the produce of the last fifty years. The fact is, that the 18th and the last half of the 17th centuries, being a period of nearly incessant war or of perpetual internal strife, were not marked by any decided progress in the arts of civilization, though during the latter portion of the time wealth appears to have increased faster than population, and comfort and plenty to have been, in consequence, more widely diffused. Compare the year 1800 with the year 1650, and we shall find the roads almost as bad everywhere, except near the metropolis; the streets nearly as ill-lighted and not much more safe at night; sanitary matters as much neglected; prisons only less pestilential and ill-arranged; the criminal law as sanguinary, vindictive, and inconsistent; bull and bear-baiting nearly as favourite amusements, and intemperance among the higher classes almost as prevalent; locomotion scarcely more rapid or more pleasant, and the transmission of letters not much less tedious and not at all less costly.

But perhaps the best way of realising to our conceptions the actual progress of the last half-century would be to fancy ourselves suddenly transported back to the year 1800, with all our habits, expectations, requirements and standard of living formed upon the luxuries and appliances collected round us in the year 1850. In the first year of the century we should find ourselves eating bread at 1s 10-½d the quartem loaf, and those who could not afford this price driven to short commons, to entire abstinence, or to some miserable substitute. We should find ourselves grumbling at heavy taxes laid on nearly all the necessaries and luxuries of life—even upon salt; blaspheming at the high prices of coffee, tea, and sugar, which confined these articles, in any adequate abundance, to the rich and the easy classes of society; paying twofold for our linen shirts, threefold for our flannel petticoats, and above fivefold for our cotton handkerchiefs and stockings; receiving our newspapers seldom, poverty-stricken, and some days after date; receiving our Edinburgh letters in London a week after they were written, and paying thirteenpence halfpenny for them when delivered; exchanging the instantaneous telegraph for the slow and costly express by chaise and four; travelling with soreness and fatigue by the "old heavy," at the rate of seven miles an hour, instead of by the Great Western at fifty; and relapsing from the blaze of light which gas now pours along our streets, into a perilous and uncomfortable darkness made visible by a few wretched oil lamps scattered at distant intervals.

But these would by no means comprise the sum total, nor the worst part of the descent into barbarism. We should find our criminal law in a state worthy of Draco; executions taking place by the dozen; the stealing of five shillings punishable and punished as severely as rape or murder; slavery and the slave trade flourishing in their palmiest atrocity. We should find the liberty of the subject at the lowest ebb; freedom of discussion and writing always in fear and frequently in jeopardy; religious rights trampled under foot; Catholics, slaves and not citizens; Dissenters still disabled and despised. Parliament was unreformed; public jobbing flagrant and shameless; gentlemen drank a bottle where they now drink a glass, and measured their capacity by their cups; and the temperance medal was a thing undreamed of. Finally, the *people* in those days were little thought of, where they are now the main topic of discourse and statesmanship; steam-boats were unknown, and a voyage to America occupied eight weeks instead of ten days; and while in 1850, a population of nearly 30,000,000 paid 50,000,000 £ of taxes, in 1801 a population of 15,000,000 paid not less than 63,000,000 £.

Source 3 from Walt Whitman: Complete Poetry and Collected Prose *(New York: Library of America, 1982), pp. 597–598.*

3. Walt Whitman, "Years of the Modern"

Years of the modern! years of the unperform'd!
Your horizon rises, I see it parting away for more august dramas,
I see not America only, not only Liberty's nation but other nations preparing,
I see tremendous entrances and exits, new combinations, the solidarity of races,
I see that force advancing with irresistible power on the world's stage,
(Have the old forces, the old wars, played their parts? are the acts suitable to
   them closed?)
I see Freedom, completely arm'd and victorious and very haughty, with Law
   on one side and Peace on the other,
A stupendous trio all issuing forth against the idea of caste;
What historic denouements are these we so rapidly approach?
I see men marching and countermarching by swift millions,
I see the frontiers and boundaries of the old aristocracies broken,
I see the landmarks of European kings removed,
I see this day the People beginning their landmarks, (all others give way;)
Never were such sharp questions ask'd as this day,
Never was average man, his soul, more energetic, more like a God,
Lo, how he urges and urges, leaving the masses no rest!
His daring foot is on the land and sea everywhere, he colonizes the Pacific, the
   archipelagoes,
With the steamship, the electric telegraph, the newspaper, the wholesale
   engines of war,
With these and the world-spreading factories, he interlinks all geography,
   all lands:
What whispers are these O lands, running ahead of you, passing under
   the seas?
Are all nations communing? is there going to be but one heart to the globe?
Is humanity forming en-masse? for lo, tyrants tremble, crowns grow dim,
The earth, restive, confronts a new era, perhaps a general divine war,
No one knows what will happen next, such portents fill the days and nights;
Years prophetical! the space ahead as I walk, as I vainly try to pierce it, is full
   of phantoms,
Unborn deeds, things soon to be, project their shapes around me.
This incredible rush and heat, this strange ecstatic fever of dreams O years!
Your dreams O years, how they penetrate through me! (I know not whether I
   sleep or wake;)

The perform'd America and Europe grow dim, retiring in shadow behind me.
The unperform'd, more gigantic than ever, advance, advance upon me.

Source 4 from Friedrich Engels, Socialism: Utopian and Scientific *(New York: International Publishers, 1982), pp. 40, 51–53, 62–64, 69, 71–72, 75. Reprinted by permission of International Publishers, New York.*

4. From Friedrich Engels, *Socialism: Utopian and Scientific*

Whilst in France the hurricane of the revolution swept over the land, in England a quieter, but not on that account less tremendous, revolution was going on. Steam and the new toolmaking machinery were transforming manufacture into modern industry, and thus revolutionising the whole foundation of bourgeois society. The sluggish march of development of the manufacturing period changed into a veritable storm and stress period of production. With constantly increasing swiftness the splitting-up of society into large capitalists and non-possessing proletarians went on. Between these, instead of the former stable middle class, an unstable mass of artisans and small shopkeepers, the most fluctuating portion of the population, now led a precarious existence.

The new mode of production was, as yet, only at the beginning of its period of ascent; as yet it was the normal, regular method of production—the only one possible under existing conditions. Nevertheless, even then it was producing crying social abuses—the herding together of a homeless population in the worst quarters of the large towns; the loosening of all traditional moral bonds, of patriarchal subordination, of family relations; overwork, especially of women and children, to a frightful extent; complete demoralisation of the working class, suddenly flung into altogether new conditions, from the country into the town, from agriculture into modern industry, from stable conditions of existence into insecure ones that changed from day to day. . . .

. . . The class struggle between proletariat and bourgeoisie came to the front in the history of the most advanced countries in Europe, in proportion to the development, upon the one hand, of modern industry, upon the other, of the newly-acquired political supremacy of the bourgeoisie. Facts more and more strenuously gave the lie to the teachings of bourgeois economy as to the identity of the interests of capital and labour, as to the universal harmony and universal prosperity that would be the consequence of unbridled competition. . . .

. . . The socialism of earlier days certainly criticised the existing capitalistic mode of production and its consequences. But it could not explain them, and, therefore, could not get the mastery of them. It could only simply reject them as bad. The more strongly this earlier socialism denounced the exploitation of the working class, inevitable under capitalism, the less able was it clearly to show in what this exploitation consisted and how it arose. But for this it was necessary 1) to present the capitalistic method of production in its historical connection and its inevitableness during a particular historical period, and therefore, also, to present its inevitable downfall; and 2) to lay bare its essential character, which was still a secret. This was done by the discovery of *surplus value*. . . .

These two great discoveries, the materialistic conception of history and the revelation of the secret of capitalistic production through surplus value, we owe to Marx. With these discoveries socialism became a science. The next thing was to work out all its details and relations.

But the perfecting of machinery is making human labour superfluous. If the introduction and increase of machinery means the displacement of millions of manual, by a few machine workers, improvement in machinery means the displacement of more and more of the machine workers themselves. It means, in the last instance, the production of a number of available wage workers in excess of the average needs of capital, the formation of a complete industrial reserve army, as I called it in 1845, available at the times when industry is working at high pressure, to be cast out upon the street when the inevitable crash comes, a constant dead weight upon the limbs of the working class in its struggle for existence with capital, a regulator for the keeping of wages down to the low level that suits the interests of capital. Thus it comes about, to quote Marx, that machinery becomes the most powerful weapon in the war of capital against the working class; that the instruments of labour constantly tear the means of subsistence out of the hands of the labourer; that the very product of the worker is turned into an instrument for his subjugation. . . . Thus it comes about that overwork of some becomes the preliminary condition for the idleness of others, and that modern industry, which hunts after new consumers over the whole world, forces the consumption of the masses at home down to a starvation minimum, and in doing thus destroys its own home market. . . .

As a matter of fact, since 1825, when the first general crisis broke out, the whole industrial and commercial world, production and exchange among all civilised peoples and their more or less barbaric hangers-on, are thrown out of joint about once every ten years. Commerce is at a standstill, the markets are glutted, products accumulate, as multitudinous as they are unsaleable, hard cash disappears, credit vanishes, factories are closed, the mass of the workers are in want of the means of subsistence, because they have produced too much of the means of subsistence; bankruptcy follows upon bankruptcy, execution upon execution. The stagnation lasts for years; productive forces and products are wasted and destroyed wholesale, until the accumulated mass of commodities finally filter off, more or less depreciated in value, until

[19]

production and exchange gradually begin to move again. Little by little the pace quickens. It becomes a trot. The industrial trot breaks into a canter, the canter in turn grows into the headlong gallop of a perfect steeplechase of industry, commercial credit and speculation, which finally, after breakneck leaps, ends where it began—in the ditch of a crisis. And so over and over again. . . .

In these crises, the contradiction between socialised production and capitalist appropriation ends in a violent explosion. The circulation of commodities is, for the time being, stopped. Money, the means of circulation, becomes a hindrance to circulation. All the laws of production and circulation of commodities are turned upside down. The economic collision has reached its apogee. *The mode of production is in rebellion against the mode of exchange.* . . .

Whilst the capitalist mode of production more and more completely transforms the great majority of the population into proletarians, it creates the power which, under penalty of its own destruction, is forced to accomplish this revolution. Whilst it forces on more and more the transformation of the vast means of production, already socialized, into state property, it shows itself the way to accomplish this revolution. *The proletariat seizes political power and turns the means of production into state property.* . . .

. . . The socialised appropriation of the means of production does away not only with the present artificial restrictions upon production, but also with the positive waste and devastation of productive forces and products that are at the present time the inevitable concomitants of production, and that reach their height in the crises. Further, it sets free for the community at large a mass of means of production and of products by doing away with the senseless extravagance of the ruling classes of today, and their political representatives. The possibility of securing for every member of society, by means of socialised production, an existence not only fully sufficient materially, and becoming day by day more full, but an existence guaranteeing to all the free development and exercise of their physical and mental faculties. . . .

To accomplish this act of universal emancipation is the historical mission of the modern proletariat. To thoroughly comprehend the historical conditions and thus the very nature of this act, to impart to the now oppressed proletarian class a full knowledge of the conditions and of the meaning of the momentous act it is called upon to accomplish, this is the task of the theoretical expression of the proletarian movement, scientific socialism.

Source 5 from Sources of Indian Tradition *(New York: Columbia University Press, 1958),* *pp. 803–809. Copyright © 1958 by Columbia University Press. Reprinted by permission of the publisher.*

5. From Mohandis K. Gandhi,
Hind Swaraj

Those who are intoxicated by modern civilization are not likely to write against it. Their care will be to find out facts and arguments in support of it, and this they do unconsciously, believing it to be true. A man whilst he is dreaming, believes in his dream; he is undeceived only when he is awakened from his sleep. A man laboring under the bane of civilization is like a dreaming man. What we usually read are the works of defenders of modern civilization, which undoubtedly claims among its votaries very brilliant and even some very good men. Their writings hypnotize us. And so, one by one, we are drawn into the vortex. . . .

Let us first consider what state of things is described by the word "civilization." Its true test lies in the fact that people living in it make bodily welfare the object of life. We will take some examples. The people of Europe today live in better-built houses than they did a hundred years ago. This is considered an emblem of civilization, and this is also a matter to promote bodily happiness. Formerly, they wore skins, and used spears as their weapons. Now, they wear long trousers, and, for embellishing their bodies, they wear a variety of clothing, and, instead of spears, they carry with them revolvers containing five or more chambers. If people of a certain country, who have hitherto not been in the habit of wearing much clothing, boots, etc., adopt European clothing, they are supposed to have become civilized out of savagery. Formerly, in Europe, people plowed their lands mainly by manual labor. Now, one man can plow a vast tract by means of steam engines and can thus amass great wealth. This is called a sign of civilization. Formerly, only a few men wrote valuable books. Now, anybody writes and prints anything he likes and poisons people's minds. Formerly, men traveled in wagons. Now, they fly through the air in trains at the rate of four hundred and more miles per day. This is considered the height of civilization. It has been stated that, as men progress, they shall be able to travel in airships and reach any part of the world in a few hours. Men will not need the use of their hands and feet. They will press a button, and they will have their clothing by their side. They will press another button, and they will have their newspaper. A third, and a motor-car will be in waiting for them. They will have a variety of delicately dished up food. Everything will be done by machinery. Formerly, when people wanted to fight with one another, they measured between them their bodily strength; now it is possible to take away thousands of lives by one man working behind a gun from a hill. This is civilization. Formerly, men worked

[21]

in the open air only as much as they liked. Now thousands of workmen meet together and for the sake of maintenance work in factories or mines. Their condition is worse than that of beasts. They are obliged to work, at the risk of their lives, at most dangerous occupations, for the sake of millionaires. Formerly, men were made slaves under physical compulsion. Now they are enslaved by temptation of money and of the luxuries that money can buy. There are now diseases of which people never dreamt before, and an army of doctors is engaged in finding out their cures, and so hospitals have increased. This is a test of civilization. Formerly, special messengers were required and much expense was incurred in order to send letters; today, anyone can abuse his fellow by means of a letter for one penny. True, at the same cost, one can send one's thanks also. Formerly, people had two or three meals consisting of home-made bread and vegetables; now, they require something to eat every two hours so that they have hardly leisure for anything else. What more need I say? All this you can ascertain from several authoritative books. These are all true tests of civilization. And if anyone speaks to the contrary, know that he is ignorant. . . .

This civilization is irreligion, and it has taken such a hold on the people in Europe that those who are in it appear to be half-mad. They lack real physical strength or courage. They keep up their energy by intoxication. They can hardly be happy in solitude. Women, who should be the queens of households, wander in the streets or they slave away in factories. For the sake of a pittance, half a million women in England alone are laboring under trying circumstances in factories or similar institutions. This awful fact is one of the causes of the daily growing suffragette movement. This civilization is such that one has only to be patient and it will be self-destroyed. According to the teaching of Mahomed this would be considered a Satanic Civilization. Hinduism calls it the Black Age. I cannot give you an adequate conception of it. It is eating into the vitals of the English nation. It must be shunned. Parliaments are really emblems of slavery. If you will sufficiently think over this, you will entertain the same opinion and cease to blame the English. They rather deserve our sympathy. . . .

Civilization is that mode of conduct which points out to man the path of duty. Performance of duty and observance of morality are convertible terms. To observe morality is to attain mastery over our mind and our passions. So doing, we know ourselves. The Gujarati equivalent for civilization means "good conduct."

If this definition be correct, then India, as so many writers have shown, has nothing to learn from anybody else, and this is as it should be. We notice that the mind is a restless bird; the more it gets the more it wants, and still remains unsatisfied. The more we indulge our passions the more unbridled they become. Our ancestors, therefore, set a limit to our indulgences. They saw that happiness was largely a mental condition. A man is not necessarily happy because he is rich, or unhappy because he is poor. The rich are often seen to be unhappy, the poor to be happy. Millions will always remain poor. Observing all this, our ancestors dissuaded us from luxuries and pleasures. We have managed with the same kind of plow as existed thousands of years ago. We have retained the same kind of cottages that we had in former times and our indigenous education remains the same as before. We have had no system of life-corroding competition. Each followed his own occupation or trade and charged a regulation wage. It was not that we did not know how to invent machinery, but our forefathers knew that, if we set our hearts after such things, we would become slaves and lose our moral fibre. They, therefore, after due deliberation decided that we should only do what we could with our hands and feet. They saw that our real happiness and health consisted in a proper use of our hands and feet. They further reasoned that large cities were a snare and a useless encumbrance and that people would not be happy in them, that there would be gangs of thieves and robbers, prostitution, and vice flourishing in them and that poor men would be robbed by rich men. They were, therefore, satisfied with small villages. They saw that kings and their swords were inferior to the sword of ethics, and they, therefore, held the sovereigns of the earth to be inferior to the Rishis and the Fakirs. A nation with a constitution like this is fitter to teach others than to learn from others. This nation had courts, lawyers, and doctors, but they were all within bounds. Everybody knew that these professions were not particularly superior; moreover, these *vakils and vaids*[3] did not rob people; they were considered people's dependents, not their masters. Justice was tolerably fair. The ordinary rule was to avoid courts. There were no touts to lure people into them. This evil, too, was noticeable only in and around capitals. The common people lived independently and followed their agricultural occupation. They enjoyed true Home Rule.

And where this cursed modern civilization has not reached, India remains as it was before. The inhabitants of that part of India will very properly laugh at your newfangled notions. The English do not rule over them, nor will you ever rule over them. Those in whose name we speak we do not know, nor do they know us. I would certainly advise you and those like you who love the motherland to go into the interior that has not yet been polluted by the railways and to live there for six months; you might then be patriotic and speak of Home Rule. Now you see what I consider to be real civilization.

3. Lawyers and doctors.

Source 6 from Olive Schreiner, Woman and Labour *(London: T. Fisher Unwin, 1911), pp. 41–53, 64–67, 252, 258, 264–273.*

6. Olive Schreiner, *Woman and Labour* (1911)

CHAPTER I

[W]e find that wherever that condition which we call modern civilisation prevails, and in proportion as it tends to prevail—wherever steam-power, electricity, or the forces of wind and water, are compelled by man's intellectual activity to act as the motor-powers in the accomplishment of human toil, wherever the delicate adaptions of scientifically constructed machinery are taking the place of the simple manipulation of the human hand—there has arisen, all the world over, a large body of males who find that their ancient fields of labour have slipped or are slipping from them, and who discover that the modern world has no place or need for them. At the gates of our dockyards, in our streets, and in our fields, are to be found everywhere, in proportion as modern civilisation is really dominant. . . .

Yet it is only upon one, and a comparatively small, section of the males of the modern civilised world that these changes in the material conditions of life have told in such fashion as to take all useful occupation from them and render them wholly or partly worthless to society. If the modern man's field of labour has contracted at one end (the physical), at the other (the intellectual) it has immeasurably expanded! If machinery and the command of inanimate motor forces have rendered of comparatively little value the male's mere physical motor-power, the demand upon his intellectual faculties, the call for the expenditure of nervous energy, and the exercise of delicate manipulative skill in the labour of human life, have immeasurably increased.

In a million new directions forms of honoured and remunerative social labour are opening up before the feet of the modern man, which his ancestors never dreamed of; and day by day they yet increase in numbers and importance. The steamship, the hydraulic lift, the patent road-maker, the railway-train, the electric tram-car, the steam driven mill, the Maxim gun and the torpedo boat, once made, may perform their labours with the guidance and assistance of comparatively few hands but a whole army of men of science, engineers, clerks, and highly-trained workmen is necessary for their invention, construction, and maintenance. . . .

In our woman's field of labour, matters have tended to shape themselves wholly otherwise! The changes which have taken place during the last centuries, and which we sum up under the compendious term "modern civilisation," have tended to rob woman, not merely in part but almost wholly, of the more valuable of her ancient domain of productive and social labour;

and, where there has not been a determined and conscious resistance on her part, have nowhere spontaneously tended to open out to her new and compensatory fields.

It is this fact which constitutes our modern "Woman's Labour Problem." . . .

Even the minor domestic operations are tending to pass out of the circle of woman's labour. In modern cities our carpets are beaten, our windows cleaned, our floors polished, by machinery, or extra domestic, and often male labour. Change has gone much farther than to the mere taking from us of the preparation of the materials from which the clothing is formed. Already the domestic sewing-machine, which has supplanted almost entirely the ancient needle, begins to become antiquated, and a thousand machines driven in factories by central engines are supplying not only the husband and son, but the woman herself, with almost every article of clothing from vest to jacket; while among the wealthy classes, the male dress designer with his hundred male-milliners and dressmakers is helping finally to explode the ancient myth, that it is woman's exclusive sphere, and a part of her domestic toil, to cut and shape the garments she or her household wear.

Year by year, day by day, there is a silently working but determined tendency for the sphere of woman's domestic labours to contract itself, and the contraction is marked exactly in proportion as that complex condition which we term "modern civilisation" is advanced.

It manifests itself more in England and America than in Italy and Spain, more in great cities than in country places, more among the wealthier classes than the poorer, and is an unfailing indication of advancing modern civilisation. . . .

Further, owing partly to the diminished demand for child-bearing, rising from the extreme difficulty and expense of rearing and education, and to many other complex social causes, to which we shall return later, millions of women in our modern societies are so placed as to be absolutely compelled to go through life not merely childless, but without sex relationship in any form whatever; while another mighty army of women is reduced by the dislocations of our civilisation to accepting sexual relationships which practically negate childbearing, and whose only product is physical and moral disease.

Thus, it has come to pass that vast numbers of us are, by modern social conditions, prohibited from child-bearing at all; and that even those among us who are child-bearers are required, in proportion as the class of race to which we belong stands high in the scale of civilisation, to produce in most cases a limited number of offspring; so that even for these of us, child-bearing and suckling, instead of filling the entire circle of female life from the first appearance of puberty to the end of middle age, becomes an episodal occupation, employing from three or four to ten or twenty of the threescore-and-ten-years which are allotted to human life. . . .

It is this great fact, so often and so completely overlooked, which lies as the propelling force behind that vast and restless "Woman's Movement" which marks our day. It is *this* fact, whether clearly and intellectually grasped, or, as is more often the case, vaguely and painfully *felt*, which awakes in the hearts of the ablest modern European women their passionate, and at times it would seem almost incoherent cry for new forms of labour and new fields for the exercise of their powers. . . .

CHAPTER VI

Our material environment differs in every respect from that of our grandparents, and bears little or no resemblance to that of a few centuries ago. Here and there, even in our civilised societies in remote agricultural districts, the old social conditions may remain partly undisturbed; but throughout the bulk of our societies the substitution of mechanical for hand-labour, the wide diffusion of knowledge through the always increasing cheap printing-press; the rapidly increasing gathering of human creatures into vast cities, where not merely thousands but millions of individuals are collected together under physical and mental conditions of life which invert every social condition of the past; the increasingly rapid means of locomotion; the increasing intercourse between distant races and lands, brought about by rapid means of intercommunication, widening and changing in every direction the human horizon—all these produce a society, so complex and so rapidly altering, that social coordination between all its parts is impossible; and social unrest and the strife of ideals of faiths, of institutions and consequent human suffering is inevitable.

If the ancient guns and agricultural implements which our fathers taught us to use are valueless in the hands of their descendants, if the samplers our mothers worked and the stockings they knitted are become superfluous through the action of the modern loom, yet more are their social institutions, faiths, and manners of life become daily and increasingly unfitted to our use; and friction and suffering inevitable, especially for the most advanced and modified individuals in our societies. This suffering, if we analyse it closely, rises from three causes.

Firstly, it is caused by the fact that mere excessive rapidity of change tends always easily to become painful, by rupturing violently already hardened habits and modes of thought, as a very rapidly growing tree ruptures its bark and exudes its internal juices.

Secondly, it arises from the fact that individuals of the same human society, not adapting themselves at the same rate to the new conditions, or being exposed to them in different degrees, a wide and almost unparalleled dissimilarity has to-day arisen between the different individuals composing our societies; where, side by side with men and women who have rapidly adapted or are so successfully seeking to adapt themselves to the new conditions of knowledge and new conditions of life, that, were they to reappear in future ages in more coordinated societies, they might perhaps hardly appear wholly antiquated, are to be found men and women whose social, religious, and moral ideals would not constitute them out of harmony if returned to the primitive camps of the remote forbears of the human race; while between these extreme classes lies that large mass of persons in an intermediate state of development. . . .

Thirdly, the unrest and suffering peculiar to our age is caused by conflict going on within the individual himself. So intensely rapid is the change which is taking place in our environment and knowledge that in the course of a single life a man may pass through half a dozen phases of growth. Born and reared in possession of certain ideas and manners of action, he or she may, before middle life is reached, have had occasion repeatedly to modify, enlarge, and alter, or completely throw aside those traditions. Within the individuality itself of such persons goes on, in an intensified form, that very struggle, conflict and disco-ordination which is going on in society at large between its different members and sections; and agonising moments must arise, when the individual, seeing the necessity for adopting new courses of action, or for accepting new truths, or conforming to new conditions, will yet be tortured by the hold of traditional convictions. . . .

Thus, social disco-ordination, and subjective conflict and suffering, pervade the life of our age, making themselves felt in every division of human life, religious, political, and domestic; and, if they are more noticeable, and make themselves more keenly felt in the region of sex than in any other, even the religious, it is because when we enter the region of sex we touch, as it were, the spinal cord of human existence. Its great nerve centre, where sensation is most acute, and pain and pleasure most keenly felt. It is not sex disco-ordination that is at the root of our social unrest; it is the universal disco-ordination which affects even the world of sex phenomena. . . .

. . . The sexual tragedy of modern life lies, not in the fact that woman as such is tending to differ fundamentally from man as such; but that, in the unassorted confusion of our modern life, it is continually the modified type of man or woman who is thrown into the closest personal relations with the antiquated type of the opposite sex; that between father and daughter, mother and son, brother and sister, husband and wife, may sometimes be found to intervene not merely years, but even centuries of social evolution. . . .

Source 7 from Dun J. Li, The Road to Communism: China Since 1912 *(New York: Van Nostrand Reinhold Company, 1969), vol. II, pp. 40–41.*

7. A Declaration of Beliefs by the *New Youth*

We believe that the world's traditional, conventional concepts in politics, economics, and ethics have in them reactionary and irrational elements. To promote social progress, we have to destroy prejudices camouflaged as "law of Heaven and Earth" or "eternal practice" of all times. We, on our part, have decided not only to discard all these traditional or conventional concepts but also to create new ideas that synthesize old and contemporary philosophies in addition to those of our own. We wish to cultivate a new spirit for our times, a spirit more conducive to the creation of a new society.

The new society we have in mind is characterized by honesty, progress, positivity, liberty, equality, creativity, beauty, goodness, peace, love, mutual assistance, joyful labor, and devotion to the welfare of mankind. . . .

The youths in our new society will of course honor and glorify labor. But the labor they perform should be proportional to their ability and in accordance with their personal interest.

. . . Though we do not think that politics can solve every problem, it is nevertheless an important form of public life. We believe in true democracy, a kind of government where political power is in the hands of all the people.

. . . We believe that all activities—political, ethical, scientific, aesthetic, religious, and educational—should have as their point of emphasis the actual need of social progress, either of today or in the future.

. . . We believe in natural science and pragmatic philosophy. To eliminate superstition and irrational thinking is the prerequisite to social progress.

We regard the respect for women's rights and personal dignity as a necessary ingredient in social progress. We also hope that women should be thoroughly aware that they, too, have responsibilities towards the society in which they live.

8. Still Shots from Fritz Lang's Film *Metropolis*

(a) Towering skyscrapers of the upper city

(b) The "Moloch" machine sustaining the city

(c) Workers before the master clock

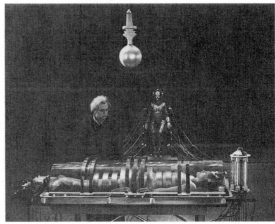

(d) Transferring a human psyche into a robot

9. José Ortega y Gasset, *The Revolt of the Masses*

1

There is one fact which, whether for good or ill, is of utmost importance in the public life of Europe at the present moment. This fact is the accession of the masses to complete social power. As the masses, by definition, neither should nor can direct their own personal existence, and still less rule society in general, this fact means that actually Europe is suffering from the greatest crisis that can afflict peoples, nations, and civilisation. Such a crisis has occurred more than once in history. Its characteristics and its consequences are well known. So also is its name. It is called the rebellion of the masses. . . .

The concept of the multitude is quantitative and visual. Without changing its nature, let us translate it into terms of sociology. We then meet with the notion of the "social mass." Society is always a dynamic unity of two component factors: minorities and masses. The minorities are individuals or groups of individuals which are specially qualified. The mass is the assemblage of persons not specially qualified. By masses, then, is not to be understood, solely or mainly, "the working masses." The mass is the average man. . . .

No one, I believe, will regret that people are to-day enjoying themselves in greater measure and numbers than before, since they have now both the desire and the means of satisfying it. The evil lies in the fact that this decision taken by the masses to assume the activities proper to the minorities is not, and cannot be, manifested solely in the domain of pleasure, but that it is a general feature of our time. Thus—to anticipate what we shall see later—I believe that the political innovations of recent times signify nothing less than the political domination of the masses. The old democracy was tempered by a generous dose of liberalism and of enthusiasm for law. By serving these principles the individual bound himself to maintain a severe discipline over himself. Under the shelter of liberal principles and the rule of law, minorities could live and act. Democracy and law—life in common under the law—were synonymous. To-day we are witnessing the triumphs of a hyperdemocracy in which the mass acts directly, outside the law, imposing its aspirations and its desires by means of material pressure. . . .

The same thing is happening in other orders, particularly in the intellectual. I may be mistaken, but the present day writer, when he takes his pen in hand to treat a subject which he has studied deeply, has to bear in mind that the average reader, who has never concerned himself with this subject, if he reads does so with the view, not of learning something from the writer, but rather, of pronouncing judgment on him when he is not in agreement with the commonplaces that the said reader carries in his head. If the individuals who make up the mass believed themselves specially qualified, it would be a case merely of personal error, not a sociological subversion. *The characteristic of the hour is that the commonplace mind, knowing itself to be commonplace, has the assurance to proclaim the rights of the commonplace and to impose them wherever it will.* . . .

3

. . . The desires so long in conception, which the XlXth Century seems at last to realise, is what it named for itself in a word as "modern culture." The very name is a disturbing one; this time calls itself "modern," that is to say, final, definitive, in whose presence all the rest is mere preterite, humble preparation and aspiration towards this present. Nerveless arrows which miss their mark! . . .[4]

4

The rule of the masses and the raising of the level, the height of the time which this indicates, are in their turn only symptoms of a more complete and more general fact. This fact is almost grotesque and incredible in its stark and simple truth. It is just this, that the world has suddenly grown larger, and with it and in it, life itself. . . .

. . . But what I wanted to make clear just now was the extent to which the life of man has increased in the dimension of potentiality. It can now count on a range of possibilities fabulously greater than ever before. In the intellectual order it now finds more "paths of ideation," more problems, more data, more sciences, more points of view. Whereas the number of occupations in primitive life can almost be counted on the fingers of one hand—shepherd, hunter, warrior, seer—the list of possible avocations today is immeasurably long. Something similar occurs in the matter of pleasures, although (and this is a phenomenon of more importance than it seems) the catalogue of pleasures is not so overflowing as in other aspects of life. Nevertheless, for the man of the middle classes who lives in towns—and towns are representative of modern existence—the possibilities of enjoyment have increased, in the course of the present century, in fantastic proportion. . . .

4. The primary meaning of the words "modern," "modernity," with which recent times have baptised themselves, brings out very sharply "the height of time" which I am at present analyzing. "Modern" is what is in fashion, that is to say, the new fashion or modification which has arisen over against the old. The word "modern" then expresses a consciousness of a new life, superior to the old one, and at the same time an imperative call to be at the height of one's time. For the "modern" man not to be "modern" means to fall below the historic level. [Note in original]

[31]

. . . We are, in fact, confronted with a radical innovation in human destiny, implanted by the XIXth Century. A new stage has been mounted for human existence, new both in the physical and the social aspects. Three principles have made possible this new world: liberal democracy, scientific experiment, and industrialism. The two latter may be summed up in one word: technicism. Not one of those principles was invented by the XIXth Century; they proceed from the two previous centuries. The glory of the XIXth Century lies not in their discovery, but in their implantation. No one but recognises that fact. But it is not sufficient to recognise it in the abstract, it is necessary to realise its inevitable consequences.

The XIXth Century was of its essence revolutionary. This aspect is not to be looked for in the scenes of the barricades, which are mere incidents, but in the fact that it placed the average man—the great social mass—in conditions of life radically opposed to those by which he had always been surrounded. It turned his public existence upside down. Revolution is not the uprising against pre-existing order, but the setting up of a new order contradictory to the traditional one. Hence there is no exaggeration in saying that the man who is the product of the XIXth Century is, for the effects of public life, a man apart from all other men. The XVIIIth-Century man differs, of course, from the XVIIth-Century man, and this one in turn from his fellow of the XVIth Century, but they are all related, similar, even identical in essentials when confronted with this new man. For the "common" man of all periods "life" had principally meant limitation, obligation, dependence; in a word, pressure. Say oppression, if you like, provided it be understood not only in the juridical and social sense, but also in the cosmic. For it is this latter which has never been lacking up to a hundred years ago, the date at which starts the practically limitless expansion of scientific technique—physical and administrative. Previously, even for the rich and powerful, the world was a place of poverty, difficulty and danger.

The world which surrounds the new man from his birth does not compel him to limit himself in any fashion, it sets up no veto in opposition to him: on the contrary, it incites his appetite, which in principle can increase indefinitely. Now it turns out—and this is most important—that this world of the XIXth and early XXth Centuries not only has the perfections and completeness which it actually possesses, but furthermore suggests to those who dwell in it the radical assurance that tomorrow it will be still richer, ampler, more perfect, as if it enjoyed a spontaneous, inexhaustible power of increase. . . .

10

. . . The principles on which the civilised world—which has to be main-tained—is based, simply do not exist for the average man of to-day. He has no interest in the basic cultural values, no solidarity with them, is not prepared to place himself at their service. How has this come about? For many reasons, but for the moment I am only going to stress one. Civilisation becomes more complex and difficult in proportion as it advances. The problems which it sets before us to-day are of the most intricate. The number of people whose minds are equal to these problems becomes increasingly smaller. The post-war period offers us a striking example of this. The reconstruction of Europe—as we are seeing—is an affair altogether too algebraical, and the ordinary European is showing himself below this high enterprise. . . .

Hence, Bolshevism and Fascism, the two "new" attempts in politics that are being made in Europe and on its borders, are two clear examples of essential retrogression. . . . Typical movements of mass-men, directed, as all such are, by men who are mediocrities, improvised, devoid of a long memory and a "historic conscience," they behave from the start as if they already belonged to the past, as if, though occurring at the present hour, they were really fauna of a past age. . . .

11

. . . The civilisation of the XlXth Century is, then, of such a character that it allows the average man to take his place in a world of superabundance, of which he perceives only the lavishness of the means at his disposal, nothing of the pains involved. He finds himself surrounded by marvellous instruments, healing medicines, watchful governments, comfortable privileges. On the other hand, he is ignorant how difficult it is to invent those medicines and those instruments and to assure their production in the future; he does not realise how unstable is the organisation of the State and is scarcely conscious to himself of any obligations. This lack of balance falsifies his nature, vitiates it in its very roots, causing him to lose contact with the very substance of life, which is made up of absolute danger, is radically problematic. The form most contradictory to human life that can appear among the human species is the "self-satisfied man." Consequently, when he becomes the predominant type, it is time to raise the alarm and to announce that humanity is threatened with degeneration, that is, with relative death. . . .

12

. . . There can be no doubt that it is technicism—in combination with liberal democracy—which has engendered mass-man in the quantitative sense of the expression. But these pages have attempted to show that it is also responsible for the existence of mass-man in the qualitative and pejorative sense of the term.

By mass—as I pointed out at the start—is not to be specially understood the workers; it does not indicate a social class, but a kind of man to be found today in all social classes, who consequently represents our age, in which he is the predominant, ruling power. We are now about to find abundant evidence for this.

Who is it that exercises social power today? Who imposes the forms of his own mind on the period? Without a doubt, the man of the middle class. Which group, within that middle class, is considered the superior, the aristocracy of the present? Without a doubt, the technician: engineer, doctor, financier, teacher, and so on. Who, inside the group of technicians, represents it at its best and purest? Again, without a doubt, the man of science. . . .

And now it turns out that the actual scientific man is the prototype of the mass-man. Not by chance, not through the individual failings of each particular man of science, but because science itself—the root of our civilisation—automatically converts him into mass-man, makes of him a primitive, a modern barbarian. . . .

QUESTIONS TO CONSIDER

Condorcet's *The Progress of the Human Mind* reveals most of the Enlightenment's ideals. Pay particular attention to the title. A key assumption here, as in all modernity, is the belief that humans advance over time "with a firm and indeviate step" toward perfection. Note how this renders history a story of *progress*. Think about the motion implied and the relationship it sets up between past, present, and future. Are all equal? What about people? Why are some more "advanced"? Who are they? Reason and science, Condorcet says, play key roles in progress. Draw up a list of the gains, both material and immaterial, they are said to bring. Which matter most? Finally, note his concern for liberty. What view of self and society does this imply?

The *Economist* editorial recalls Condorcet's work but offers a somewhat different vision of progress. It extolls the present era, which it deems "unrivalled and unapproached." List the advances it celebrates most. How do they compare with those you found before? In this context, note the talk of concrete gains in public health and material well-being—and the claim that the people have become "the main topic of discourse and statesmanship." Whitman, too, stresses this aspect in "Years of the Modern," though as an American he lauds "Liberty's nation" over Europe as the true center of the "unperform'd." For him, machines have created a "new era" in which the "average man" assumes control of advanced societies and "interlinks all geography." But what is his view of the future? Does he welcome the "space ahead," so "full of phantoms," or dread it? Engels, by contrast, sees the immediate impact of industrialization as disastrous to workers. But is it because of the historical process itself or because of those who misdirected it? Given his faith in an ultimate socialist revolution and his optimism about emancipation, is Engels perhaps truer to the beliefs of the Enlightenment than Whitman? What about his view of science?

Gandhi shares no such faith in Western progress. At the time he wrote *Hind Swaraj*, he was encouraging Indians to reaffirm the value of their own tradition in preparation to challenge British rule. Here Gandhi refutes European claims to cultural advancement, deriding modern civilization as "Satanic" and dismissing the modern era as a Black Age. Note that he finds modern life destructive to the colonizers as well as the colonized. Why? What are his grounds for repudiating modernity? He clearly recognizes the benefits Westerners claim to derive from modern life—compare his list of them with those from the other documents. Yet he faults all of them. The modern focus on material welfare and "bodily happiness" bothers him most. Why? What does he rank as a better mark of civilization? Note his special disdain for modern cities and machines and his view that industrial society debases women and enslaves people. Nonetheless, his belief in the importance of human freedom and dignity is not unlike that of Enlightenment writers. Has he accepted at least this part of the modern agenda?

The emancipation of repressed groups, of course, was one of the constant goals of modern reformers. In *Women and Labour*, Olive Schreiner analyzes the constraints that modernity placed on women. Like many feminists, she advocates equal political rights and economic opportunities for women. But she is unusual

in arguing that the "Woman's Movement" is a response to the "social disco-ordination" of industrial society, with its labor-saving machinery, social unrest, and "strife of ideals." Men and women alike, she warns, suffer from "conflict . . . within the individual." Why? To what aspects of modernity does she attribute this conflict? "The Declaration of Beliefs from *New Youth*" addresses another group pressing for change: youth. As a call to young Chinese, it shows how modern values and ideas, especially the identification of modernity with youth, were spreading beyond the West at the start of the twentieth century, even as Europeans were starting to doubt them. Compare the list of reforms it seeks for China with those in other documents. The pledge to embrace "positivity" and avoid skepticism hints at growing disillusionment with the modern agenda elsewhere. What may have induced such concern in this 1919 editorial?

The darkening mood of post–World War I Europe clearly colors Fritz Lang's film *Metropolis* and its grim portrayal of the modern city. Lang used the new popular medium to challenge almost all the old assumptions about progress. Science and technology still produce wonders, but not to the benefit of ordinary people. Note the vast scale of the city, with its looming towers and labyrinthine ways. Look how human figures cower before the huge and bewildering machines that control their lives. What has become of the promise of a better world through technology—or the hope for a freer, more creative life in modern urban society? The shot of a scientist transferring the psyche of a woman into a robot dramatically portrays the dehumanization of industrial society, which Lang, like Gandhi, deplored. What is the image of science here?

Ortega y Gasset's condemnation of modernity has points in common with Lang's. His view that "technicism" has produced a regimented mass society closely parallels Lang's vision of a technocratic tyranny. And he, too, seems to believe that modern urban life represents a lapse in human development. But whereas Lang

laments common people's enslavement to machines and technocracy, Ortega y Gasset worries over their political dominance in "hyperdemocracy." Why? How does his concern contrast with earlier expectations about democracy, egalitarianism, and the value of the "average man"? Like Gandhi, Ortega y Gasset denounces the material abundance of modern society. Why? Compare his view of social fragmentation with Yeats's claim that "things fall apart." Does he, too, expect a similar catastrophic end of modern civilization?

EPILOGUE

The insecurity of the Great Depression in the 1930s followed by the bloodbath unleashed in World War II confirmed the interwar generation's worst fears that modernity posed a threat rather than a promise to humanity. The specter of death camps and devastated cities, of ruined nations and impoverished populations, undermined belief in rationality and discredited the idea of inevitable advancement. Only in America did a semblance of the old confidence in progress survive into the immediate postwar era. And even there, hopes for a better life focused more on material gains and increased consumption than on the improvement of "the intellectual and moral faculties" that *philosophes* like Condorcet regarded as the highest measures of progress.

The rebuilding of Europe after World War II and the East Asian economic "miracle" of the last quarter of the twentieth century helped these areas catch up with America in prosperity. Combined with the stable order created by the cold war balance of power, affluence in these regions made the second half of the twentieth century less turbulent and insecure than the first. But optimism about humanity's perfectibility did not revive. Material growth, once hailed for its transforming power, seemed a source of problems, from urban sprawl to pollution. Science and technology, formerly viewed as tools for remaking humanity, were now associated with war or environmental degradation. Furthermore, faith in reason and rational efforts to shape a better society were eroded by mounting public cynicism and the rise of contentious interest groups. Instead of a better time, the future increasingly appeared a threshold to one catastrophe or another, whether nuclear war, overpopulation, or global warming. And modern "centers" lost their former luster as decolonization and the rise of the Third World ended Western supremacy while urban blight drove the affluent middle class out of the cities.

The widespread loss of public faith in the values of modernity in the early twentieth century makes some historians see this period as the end of the modern age. They thus locate the start of a new "postmodern" era sometime in the middle decades of the century. But because of its closeness, few are able to define the new period in its own terms. Instead, as the term *post-modern* indicates, they conceive of it in contrast with the prior modern period. The idea of modernity, then, not only affects the way we have periodized and viewed the distant past, it provides the backdrop against which many are presently attempting to delineate a new age. What it meant to be modern and how the meaning of modernity changed in the early twentieth century are thus crucial to any understanding of current approaches to history.

CHAPTER TWO

TO THE AGE ITS ART[1] (1870–1920)

THE PROBLEM

During World War I, a small group of writers and artists came together in Zurich, Switzerland, to form the core of a movement they called Dada.[2] They chose the name intentionally, precisely because it is a meaningless, nonsensical word conveying their reaction to a West capable of the

1. "To the age its art": Part of the inscription on the façade of the House of the Secession in Vienna, Austria, built in 1898 as a gallery home for the work of the group of artists calling themselves the Secession because of their break with artistic conventions of the late nineteenth century. The full inscription is: "To the age its art. To the art its freedom."

2. Dada: the precise origin of this term has been explained in various ways. It means "hobbyhorse" in French, and one version of its origin holds that it was selected by a random opening of a French dictionary at the word dada. Others explain "Dada" as the "Da, Da," that is "Yes, Yes," of the Romanian conversation of one of its founders. Whatever its actual origins, the term was nonsensical to most Europeans in 1918. The original Dada *Manifesto* issued in Berlin in 1918 is reprinted in Hans Richter, *Dada: Art and Anti-Art*, trans. David Britt (New York: Oxford University Press, 1978), pp. 104–107.

carnage of the Great War. Dadaists saw everything in Western civilization as absurd and futile, the products of a world become increasingly mechanistic, and they gave form to their vision in startling literary and artistic innovations designed to mock conventional modes of expression. A dadaist poet cut words randomly from newspapers, dropped them into a bag and shook them up, then drew them out and assembled them in the order they emerged as a nonsensical poem.[3] A dadaist artist displayed his version of Leonardo da Vinci's *Mona Lisa*, faithful to the original save for a mustache added, an act that at the time appeared shockingly disrespectful of artistic conventions.[4] In such ways did dadaists call into question all traditional values and modes of expression.

Although the Dada movement had spent itself by 1924, it was nonetheless a highly significant cultural phenomenon, marking the culmina-

3. Tristan Tzara (1896–1963).

4. Marcel Duchamp (1887–1968).

[38]

tion of a number of developments in Western thought that, taken together, represented for many an intellectual crisis, a real challenge to traditional values and beliefs during the period from about 1870 to 1920.

By the early decades of the twentieth century, the patterns of nineteenth-century Western thought seemed under assault on every front. Old ways of thinking fell to new discoveries in the physical and social sciences, and Western artistic expression cast off old norms as well, often with provocative results. To take the example of music, a number of composers of the early twentieth century abandoned traditional harmonies in their compositions, producing a new dissonant sound. The first performance in 1913 of a ballet, *The*

Rite of Spring, by one of these composers, Igor Stravinsky (1882–1971), almost provoked a Paris audience to riot. To composers like Stravinsky, harmony no longer seemed appropriate in a world of discord.

Reflecting the trends of the period 1870 to 1920, another art form, painting, also abandoned traditional conventions during this time of intellectual crisis. Your goal in this chapter is to examine the magnitude of the transformations in Western thought of this period by analyzing the works of a group of major painters. How do the paintings reflect a break with traditional artistic standards? What trends can be traced from each artist's work? How did artists reveal the intellectual currents of the period in their works?

BACKGROUND

The traditional values and beliefs of most nineteenth-century Westerners were founded on the tenets of Judeo-Christian religion and the legacy of the eighteenth-century Enlightenment. From the Bible, most Westerners derived their faith in a Creator. From the Enlightenment, they drew a belief in the rational nature of humans and their ability to use their intellectual gifts to understand and master the physical world. In the last years of the nineteenth century and the first years of the twentieth century, however, the findings of physical and social scientists called traditional values and beliefs into question while failing to advance an

alternative faith. At the same time, as we will see, the art of the age reflected an increasing knowledge of the physical world and the diminished authority of old standards of thought and behavior. We will note here only the more important late-nineteenth-century developments in Western knowledge that contradicted traditional thought, some aspects of which continue to stir controversy a century later.

Western religious beliefs met challenges on several fronts after 1870. The pioneering English biologist Charles Darwin (1809–1882) had presented his theory of evolution as it applied to animals in his 1859 classic, *On the Origin of Species*. In 1871 Darwin published what was for many a more disturbing work, *Descent of Man*, in which he applied his evolutionary theories to mankind.[5] Educated Westerners suddenly found that their religious beliefs, grounded on the story of the Creation in the Bible's book of Genesis, conflicted with the rational framework of the natural science in which they also put great stock. The result was a crisis of belief that still manifests itself in parts of the West in struggles over the content of public school biology courses.

At the same time that Darwin's work challenged one basic article of the Judeo-Christian faith, archaeological and biblical studies diminished the uniqueness of the Judeo-Christian heritage. Increasing Western knowledge of ancient Middle Eastern civilization, for example, revealed a great cultural kinship between the Hebrews of the Old Testament and the Babylonians and other ancient peoples. Similarly, scholars of the New Testament period found remarkable parallels to the story of the life of Christ in non-Christian cultures. Was the Judeo-Christian heritage, based on a belief in the Jews as God's chosen people and in a Savior of humankind, as unique as it had previously seemed? The debate still continues between religious fundamentalists and those who accept an increasing body of knowledge founded on scholarship and not faith.

As modern scholarship challenged traditional religious thought, it also raised doubts about the intellectual legacy of the eighteenth century. A

5. The full titles of these works were *On the Origin of Species by Means of Natural Selection or the Preservation of Favored Races in the Struggle for Life* and *The Descent of Man in Relation to Sex.*

central tenet of the Enlightenment held that reason was the supreme and exclusive achievement of humankind. The work by psychological and biological researchers in the late nineteenth and early twentieth centuries, however, cast increasing doubt on the validity of that belief. Wilhelm Wundt (1832–1920) opened the first experimental psychology laboratory at the University of Leipzig in 1870. His purpose was to conduct experiments on animal subjects to demonstrate that the animal mind and the human mind were fundamentally similar. The Russian physiologist Ivan Pavlov (1849–1936), conducting similar laboratory experiments with dogs in the 1890s, determined that certain responses in his subjects could be conditioned—that is, learned and unlearned. The emerging behaviorist school of psychology to which Pavlov's experiments contributed held that most human actions and emotions, like those of the laboratory dogs, could be similarly conditioned. The human mind suddenly seemed quite similar to that of the animal. Such a concept did not accord with the Enlightenment belief in human rationality. Even more destructive of reason as the cornerstone of human behavior was the work of the Austrian physician Sigmund Freud (1856– 1939).

Freud began his pioneering work in mental disorders in the 1880s, achieving success with a therapeutic process in which he allowed his patients to talk freely about their childhood memories, their emotions, and their fantasies. The result of his work was the modern school of psychoanalysis and a very unsettling view of the human mind. Freud and other psychological researchers posited the existence of the human unconscious, an irrational and inaccessible portion of the psyche that exerted tremendous influence, through feelings and impulses repressed from consciousness, on human behavior. Indeed, for Freud, the unconscious was a virtual battleground of conflicting inner forces. The *id* embodied base and instinctual drives, such as sex and violence, which demanded immediate, hedonistic gratification. The *superego*, on the other hand, embraced the conventions of society and the strictures of religion that aimed at repressing such impulses. Between these two extremes was the *ego*, the mediating point of consciousness in which some sort of balance between the hedonistic drives of the id and the repressive tendencies of the superego had to be achieved for the well-balanced mind. The goal of Freud's psychoanalysis was to defuse potentially dangerous unconscious impulses by making them conscious, that is, drawing them into the patient's field of awareness, where they could then be examined and treated.

After Freud, reason could no longer be upheld as the motivating principle of human behavior. The optimistic view of progress—that is, that history and human development moved toward better and better forms—also declined as a result of the work of two pioneering sociologists, the Frenchman Emile Durkheim (1858–1917) and the German Max Weber (1864–1920). In examining his

society, Durkheim found that modern times in the West were not necessarily an improvement over the past. In medieval and early modern Europe, social station was determined at birth and traditional social values and religious strictures dictated the individual's comportment within his or her station. In the modern Western world, however, the individual enjoyed greater freedom at the same time that the force of traditional religious and social controls waned. Anarchy threatened society, and *anomie*, a loss of personal direction resulting from the collapse of moral guidelines, afflicted the individual and contributed, Durkheim said, to the West's high rate of suicide. Consequently, he believed, the modern world required a new, secular moral order.

Max Weber examined the results of the Enlightenment effort to explain the physical world scientifically and to organize governments rationally around constitutions and bureaucratic procedures. The results had been high scientific accomplishment and stable government won at the cost of human creativity and personal freedom. The modern institutions of the state and corporations aim at domination of the individual. Thus Weber pessimistically concluded his essay "Politics as a Vocation" with the words: "Not summer's bloom lies ahead of us, but rather a polar night of icy darkness and hardness . . ."[6]

6. Quoted in H. H. Gerth and C. Wright Mills, editors and translators, *From Max Weber: Essays in Sociology* (New York: Oxford University Press, 1946), p. 128.

[41]

Progress, for Weber and others, was a mixed blessing.

Other social theorists advanced a different but equally disturbing view of the world, one marked by strife, violence, and conflict. Marxists found human existence to be dominated by class conflict; other thinkers advanced equally unsettling visions of human conflict. An important tenet of Enlightenment thought was the basic equality of all humans. Yet some nineteenth-century thinkers, in their enthusiasm for the new scientific discoveries of the age, applied Darwin's biological theory of evolution to society as a whole. Emphasizing the struggle for existence that they found in Darwin's work, they claimed that a process of "survival of the fittest" characterized modern human society. All people were not created equal; rather, the stronger or more intelligent had a right to triumph and survive in life's struggle, whereas others did not. Such an application of Darwin's ideas, known as Social Darwinism, could be used, for example, to justify imperialism on the grounds that a "superior" people had a right to rule an "inferior" people. According to this view, despite the progressive improvement predicated by Enlightenment thinkers, human beings still were engaged in a primal struggle for existence.

Philosophers, too, joined in the criticism of the Christian tradition, the Enlightenment, and the modern world. Indeed, the German philosopher Friedrich Nietzsche (1844–1900) offered the most thoroughgoing rebuttal of Enlightenment thought and everything associated with it. Nietzsche saw the modern world in decay because its elevation of reason had undermined the capacity to feel passionately, to will, and to be creative. But if he attacked the Enlightenment tradition, Nietzsche was equally hostile to Christianity. An atheist, he proclaimed that "God is dead," people's belief in the supernatural having been effectively destroyed by generations of rational scientific thinking. And yet, Nietzsche maintained, Christianity continued to exert a large and harmful influence, and its moral dictates still inhibited people's will to act spontaneously and creatively. Nietzsche also deplored the growth of democratic government, which in his view subjected the creative few to the authority of the mediocre majority—the common herd. Nietzsche advocated instead the leadership of a few superior persons, or *Übermenschen* ("overmen" or "higher men"), philosopher-rulers whose wills would be unencumbered by the controls of rational thought, Christianity, or democratic rule.

Even the work of the Scientific Revolution, which formed the basis for the Enlightenment, came under attack in the half-century from 1870 to 1920. Nineteenth-century science was based on Newtonian physics, which held that the human intellect could discern the basic laws that structured the physical world. With such knowledge, scientists confidently believed that they could ultimately predict the development of the physical world. The result of scientific research in our period, however, has proved instead the existence of a highly unpredictable world.

In classical physics, the atom was considered a solid, indivisible particle and the basis of all matter. In a number of scientific breakthroughs, however, this concept, along with certain laws of Newtonian physics, was disproved. In 1897 Joseph John Thomson (1856–1940), an English physicist, discovered that the atom is not solid but composed of electrons revolving around a nucleus. Niels Bohr (1855– 1962), a Danish physicist, found in 1913 that the electrons do not adhere to Newton's laws of motion. The German physicist Werner Heisenberg (1901–1976) summed up this and other work in modern atomic physics shortly after 1920 in his *uncertainty principle*, which posited that modern physicists could only attempt to describe what occurrences were probable in subatomic matter. Nothing was absolutely certain, some people concluded. Heisenberg's principle prompted one distinguished traditional scientist of the era to exclaim in disbelief, "I refuse to believe that God plays dice with the world!"

The work of Albert Einstein (1879–1955) marked the culmination of research in the physical sciences in our period. Einstein dislodged another cornerstone of traditional science, the notion that time, space, and matter were absolute and measurable phenomena. In Einstein's *relativity theory*, time and space became relative, not absolute concepts. Moreover, energy and matter might be converted into each other. Expressed in the famous equation E (energy) = m (mass) $\times$ c^2 (speed of light squared), this concept was to have literally earth-shattering results when the splitting of the atom allowed the conversion of matter into vast and potentially destructive amounts of energy. Einstein's work brought the world to the threshold of the atomic age while discrediting the long-held tenets of absolute time and space.

The greatest challenge to the world view of nineteenth-century Westerners, however, came not as abstract theory but as devastating reality: World War I. Many intellectuals and artists initially joined their fellow citizens in welcoming a war that they believed would revitalize the West. In that conflagration, however, every belligerent government harnessed modern science and industry to its war effort. The result was bloodletting on an unprecedented scale that caused intellectuals and artists to despair of traditional values—the mood represented by the Dada movement. As the Dada *Manifesto* declared: "After the carnage, we keep only the hope of a purified humanity."

THE METHOD

This chapter introduces you to a primary source historians traditionally have used in studying a past era—its art. Analysis of a period's works of art can provide the historian with an excellent entry into the intellectual life of that epoch because art often reflects the thought of its age. But we must be clear about what is and is not part of the analytical process you must carry out with this chapter's evidence.

The evidence should not be the object of your aesthetic analysis, that is, your attempt to determine which paintings express your individual concept of beauty. We all have opinions and preferences regarding art, especially the modern art this chapter presents. Consequently, you might be inclined simply to dismiss some of the paintings reproduced here as "strange looking" because they do not accord with your individual taste.

You should, however, analyze the paintings in the context of their times. To help focus your analysis, the paintings selected all have a common subject, the human form, to enable you to appreciate the different visions artists brought to the problem of portraying their fellow humans. They also are arranged roughly chronologically to show you both traditional nineteenth-century art before 1870 and some of its main trends over the half-century from 1870 to 1920. You should attempt to assess the impact that these works would have had on their contemporary viewers. Try to imagine yourself as an educated Western European born about 1850 and living until 1920. You would have reached maturity about 1870 and, in the course of your lifetime, would have experienced tremendous change. Materially, you would have been born in an age in which most people traveled by foot or horse and carriage and would have lived to see people traveling by train, automobile,

and airplane. Your messages in later life would be carried by telephone and telegraph, and the diseases that threatened your parents would be only a memory by your middle years. In the course of your lifespan of seventy years, then, your material world would have been totally transformed. So, too, would have been your culture's art. Would you have found this transformation unsettling? To supplement your analysis, a brief introduction to the artists whose work this chapter presents is necessary.

Sources 1 and 2, representing two conventional styles of nineteenth-century art, are works whose style would have seemed familiar to their viewers. They are the starting point for your analysis of artistic trends. The French painter Jean-Auguste Dominique Ingres (1780–1867) was an exponent of the neoclassical style of painting. Art historians apply the label "neoclassical" to Ingres and other artists of his period who found much of their inspiration in classical subjects. In the execution of their works, these artists sought to duplicate the harmony, balance, and realism they found in Greek and Roman art. They also often presented classical themes in their works. Source 1, *The Apotheosis of Homer*, is an example of such a work and of the techniques of many early-nineteenth-century artists. In Source 1 Ingres presents his vision of the reception of the Greek poet Homer into the ranks of the gods, symbolized in the painting by his coronation. What do you notice about Ingres's conception of this scene that illustrates classical values of harmony and balance? What in the artist's technical execution of this mythical scene would lead you to characterize his efforts as almost photographic in detail?

Source 2, *Greece Expiring on the Ruins of Missolonghi*, by Eugène Delacroix (1798–1863), is an example of nineteenth-century romanticism. Romanticism arose in large part as a reaction to the Enlightenment with its emphasis on a rational interpretation of the human experience. In literature and art, exponents of the romantic impulse sought to recover the emotion and drama of life. In thus approaching art, many romantic artists were in conscious revolt against the formalism of neoclassical artists like Ingres. The Greek rebellion of the 1820s against Turkey excited European romantics because it was the war for independence of the land of Homer and Plato; and one English romantic poet, Lord Byron, died in Greece seeking to join the rebel cause. Delacroix's painting shows a Greek fighter crushed in the ruins of the city of Missolonghi, where the Greek defenders succumbed in 1826 to a long siege by the Turks. (Missolonghi, not inconsequentially, was the site of Byron's death.) The woman's gesture of defenseless resignation reflects Greek martyrdom. What view of the world and the role of human beings in it did Delacroix convey? What view of the individual does the image of "Greece" convey to you? Compare the paintings of Delacroix and Ingres. Certainly the artists reflected two very different philosophies. Nevertheless, what similarities do you find in their portrayal of the human form?

As your analysis moves beyond Source 2, you must be careful to assess the paintings in light of the intellectual breakthroughs we have just examined. Remember, too, that by 1850 the invention of the camera, with its ability to produce accurate images, obliged artists to make a serious reevaluation of the function of their art. What was the purpose of the labor involved in re-creating the details in Sources 1 and 2 in portraits when a photograph would capture an even more accurate image?

In Source 3 we encounter the work of an artistic movement that reflected the late nineteenth century's interest in science and the reassessment of the artistic function prompted by the camera. With the impressionist artists who flourished especially in France in the 1870s and 1880s, we see a reconsideration of the whole function of painting that relegated portraiture to the photographer. We also find a systematic attempt, much in the vein of modern science, to portray the artist's subjects with an accuracy that would convey to the viewer the subtle effects of light and shadow as they actually appeared to the human eye.

Some impressionists executed their works with large splashes of color. Georges Seurat (1859–1891) moved beyond this technique to a postimpressionism that he called pointilism in which he created pictures with intricate arrangements of tiny dots of color, the result of his study of scientific theories of color perception. *A Sunday Afternoon on the Island of La Grande Jatte* shows excursioners on an island in the river Seine near Paris. What was the artist's purpose in this painting? Why did he pay so little apparent attention to developing the individual characteristics of the persons in his painting? How would you characterize the figures in *La Grande Jatte*?

In the 1870s many viewed impressionism and the work of Seurat as a dramatic revolt against artistic conventions, but far more was to come.

The Dutchman Vincent van Gogh (1853–1890) studied the impressionists and moved beyond them. He gloried in the use of broad brush strokes to express his excitement and emotions in a picture, distorting images in that quest. His work thus makes him an early exponent of another style of art, expressionism. A deeply religious man, van Gogh sought to express his personal vision of his subjects while also seeking in them what he called "that something of the eternal which the halo used to symbolize."[7] Source 4, his portrait *La Berceuse* (The Cradle Rocker), employs startling colors: The woman's hair is orange, her dress green, the wallpaper background green and pink flowers, and the floor red. What feelings did the artist seek to express here? Compare La Berceuse with the work of Ingres. Why did van Gogh engage in such obvious distortions of the human shape?

Paul Gauguin (1848–1903) also emerged from the impressionists to create a style called symbolism. Gauguin had two careers, first as a successful Parisian stockbroker, then as an impoverished artist. Indeed, he

left his family and business for his art in 1883. In rejecting his middle-class past, he also rejected much of modern industrial society. Gauguin found that Westerners had lost much of life's emotions and mystery in their progress toward the industrial age with its concern for material gain. Western art, he believed, reflected this loss, and he sought to reinfuse the missing emotion into his paintings by studying the art of non-Western peoples. Gauguin spent most of his last years in the South Pacific trying to capture the spirit of non-Western art. A number of artists followed Gauguin's lead in exploring non-Western art, especially after World War I, which convinced them of the bankruptcy of Western culture and values. Indeed, later artists sought non-Western inspiration more widely than Gauguin; many, for example, incorporated African art forms in their work. In Source 5, Gauguin's painting *Manao Tupapau—The Spirit of the Dead Watches*, how has he added non-Western elements in achieving his artistic goal? How did he inject a fantastic element into Western art?

Source 6, *The Dream*, is the work of Frenchman Henri Rousseau (1844–1910). A self-taught artist, Rousseau spent the first half of his adulthood as a government customs inspector, and his paintings reflect his lack of traditional training. *The Dream* is a fantastic, impossible, and highly detailed scene that conveys Rousseau's view of life. What does the choice of a dream as his subject tell you about the artist's outlook? Does the artist present a realistic group of figures in the nude, the lions, and the snake

7. Quoted in H. W. Janson, *History of Art: A Survey of the Major Visual Arts from the Dawn of History to the Present Day* (New York: Harry N. Abrams and Prentice-Hall, 1962), p. 507.

charmer? Why might you think that Rousseau sought to paint the same natural and non-Western settings that Gauguin did?

The work of the Norwegian artist Edvard Munch (1863–1948) reflected the influence of van Gogh, Gauguin, and the philosophical thought of his day. His *The Scream*, Source 7, is an expressionist work. Even more than van Gogh, however, Munch subordinated detail and character study to a strong message. What sentiments does the central figure convey in *The Scream*? How does the artist's treatment of the background magnify the feelings of the central character? What might the artist be saying about the central figure's relationships with other people?

The work of van Gogh and Gauguin influenced other artists as well. Exhibits of their works in Paris during the first years of the twentieth century inspired a group of young artists to break so much with artistic conventions that their contemporaries called them *les Fauves*, or "The Wild Beasts." And in Vienna, a group of artists calling themselves "The Secession" to reflect their abandonment of traditional modes of artistic expression flourished in the last decades of the nineteenth century and in the twentieth century prior to World War I. The leading artist in this group was Gustav Klimt (1862–1918), a contemporary of Freud, in whom we can plainly see the intellectual and artistic turmoil of this period. Like other artists, Klimt challenged stylistic convention. But what really made his work especially controversial was his apparent rejection of the norms of morality and good taste embraced by late-nineteenth- and early-twentieth-century middle- and upper-class Europeans and his negation of that group's faith in the eventual triumph of liberal ideas and scientific progress.

Controversy engulfed Klimt when he was commissioned by the government to provide paintings for the ceremonial hall ceilings of the new University of Vienna building. Klimt's commission was to portray "Philosophy," "Medicine," and "Jurisprudence," and his work was expected to have reflected the nineteenth century's scientific and intellectual triumphs and the growth of political liberalism with its concern for justice for all. Instead, Klimt provided paintings, controversial in the extreme because they were to have been paid for with public funds, that offered primitive sexuality and death, the expression of all the dark forces that questioned the very idea of progress. The government rejected the paintings, for not only did they question the progress of the age, they also caused many in the public to charge Klimt with creating pornography.

Source 8 presents one of Klimt's best-known paintings, *The Kiss*, a work completed in 1907–1908 after the university controversy. This painting reflects Klimt's rebellion in several ways. Its background color is gold, demonstrating Klimt's interest in pre-twentieth-century media, especially Byzantine gold mosaics. What else do you notice about it? Why would its divorce from reality lead you to consider this abstract art? The painting contains a great deal of symbolism, too. How do you think many in early-twentieth-century audiences responded to the rectangles on the cloak of the male figure and the ovals on that of the female when you understand that these forms were generally taken to symbolize the genital organs of each figure? Why do you think Klimt's art might have been the most controversial of all?

A young Spanish artist, Pablo Picasso (1881–1973), moved to Paris in 1900 and immediately reflected in his work the influence of many of the artists we have discussed. Yet Picasso went beyond them in the extent of his break with artistic tradition. Source 9, *Les Demoiselles d'Avignon*, shocked Picasso's audiences in several ways in 1907. First, its subject is a group of prostitutes on Avignon Street in Barcelona. Second, it is an early expression of the cubist style in art, in which the artist used a variety of wedges and angles to create his picture.

In *Les Demoiselles d'Avignon*, Picasso abandoned traditional rules of perspective as well as any effort to portray the human form accurately. Some found his cubism almost an attempt to portray his subjects geometrically; others remarked that Picasso's women looked like arrangements of broken pieces of glass. Certainly, too, this work represents Picasso's exploration of forms of artistic expression from Africa and parts of the non-Western world. Why do you think Picasso abandoned artistic conventions? Can you discern any parallels between Picasso's art and the physical science of Einstein and others? What trend in modern art is reflected in the two faces on the picture's right?

Picasso was one of a number of abstract artists at work early in the twentieth century. Abstract art puts primary emphasis on the structure, not the subject, of the picture. Another abstract artist was the German George Grosz (1893–1959), who joined the Dada movement after World War I. Grosz's works show cubist influences in a type of collage technique; they also frequently have a social message, as in Source 10, *Germany, A Winter's Tale*. Completed amid the famine and defeat that overtook Germany in the last days of World War I, this painting presents Grosz's views on the war and the society that produced it. The central figure is an "average" German surrounded by a kaleidoscope of Berlin scenes. What do you notice about the plate in front of him? What comment does this make on the Germany of 1918? What social groups do the three figures at the bottom represent? What roles did they play in pre-1918 German society, according to the artist? What vision of German society in 1918 does the background convey?

The final artist whose work appears in our evidence is the Frenchman Marcel Duchamp (1887–1968). Duchamp joined the Dada movement in despair after World War I, and it was he who created the "*Mona Lisa*" with the mustache that we described earlier in this chapter. Even before the war, however, his work challenged all artistic conventions. Source 11, *Nude Descending a Staircase, Number 1*, challenged traditionalists, who found little here resembling a human being. It also challenged the artistic rebels of the day; cubists, accustomed to presenting static forms, rejected the obvious motion of Duchamp's figure. Cubists forced the picture's removal from the major modern art exhibit in Paris in 1912, and traditionalists were scandalized when the picture appeared at the Armory Show of modern art in New York in 1913. Why do you think the artist rejected any attempt to portray the human form accurately? What manner of comment on the machine age might this work be making? How and why were artists like Duchamp striving for a new and more subjective reality?

Using this background on the painters, turn now to the evidence. As you look at the paintings, seek to assess the magnitude of the changes in Western thought in the period 1870–1920. How do the paintings reflect a break with traditional artistic standards? What trends can be traced from each artist's work? How did the artists reveal the intellectual currents of the period in their works?

THE EVIDENCE

Sources 1 and 2 copyright Réunion des Musées Nationaux/Art Resource, NY.

1. Jean-Auguste Dominique Ingres, *The Apotheosis of Homer*, 1827

2. Eugène Delacroix, *Greece Expiring on the Ruins of Missolonghi, 1827*

3. Georges Seurat, *A Sunday Afternoon on the Island of La Grande Jatte*, 1884–1886

Source 4 from the Stichting Kröller-Müller, Otterlo.

4. Vincent van Gogh, *La Berceuse*, 1889

Source 5 from the Albright-Knox Art Gallery, Buffalo, New York (A. Conger Goodyear Collection). Oil on burlap mounted on canvas, 28½" × 38⅜".

5. Paul Gauguin, *Manao Tupapau—The Spirit of the Dead Watches,* 1892

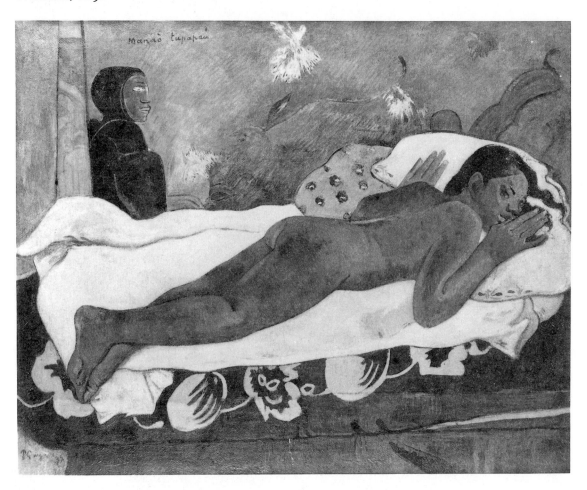

6. Henri Rousseau, *The Dream,* **1910**

7. Edvard Munch, *The Scream,* **1893**

Source 8 from Galerie Welz, Salzburg, reprinted in Carl E. Schorske, Fin-de-Siècle Vienna: Politics and Culture *(New York: Vintage Books, 1981), Plate viii. Photograph: Erich Lessing/ Art Resource, NY.*

8. Gustav Klimt, *The Kiss*, 1907–1908

9. Pablo Picasso, *Les Demoiselles d'Avignon*, 1907

Source 10 formerly from the Collection Garvens, Hanover, Germany (painting has been lost).

10. George Grosz, *Germany, A Winter's Tale*, 1918

[59]

11. Marcel Duchamp, *Nude Descending a Staircase, Number 1, 1911*

QUESTIONS TO CONSIDER

Free public education was becoming more widely available in Western Europe by the late nineteenth century. The number of people with sufficient education to understand intellectual trends grew rapidly in the years before 1920. Consequently, the shifts in thinking we are examining in this chapter were evident to a considerably larger audience than that of the Enlightenment. Many in this growing educated class must have found the upheavals in the natural sciences, philosophy, and art of their day unpredictable and disturbing.

At the most basic level, consider the changes in art in the period 1870 to 1920. Contrast Sources 1 and 2 with the art that follows. How do you think nineteenth-century audiences would have received the impressionists' offerings after a steady diet of works like Sources 1 and 2? How would you account for the following reaction in 1876 by one French journalist to an early impressionist exhibit?

The Rue le Peletier is a road of disasters. After the fire at the Opera, there is now yet another disaster there. An exhibition has just been mounted at Durand-Ruel [gallery] which allegedly contains paintings. I enter and my horrified eyes behold something terrible. Five or six lunatics, among them a woman, have joined together and exhibited their works. I have seen people rock with laughter in front of these pictures, but my heart bled when I saw them. These would-be artists call themselves revolutionaries, "Impressio-

nists." They take a piece of canvas, colour and brush, daub a few patches of colour on them at random, and sign the whole thing with their name. It is a delusion of the same kind as if the inmates of Bedlam picked up stones from the wayside and imagined they had found diamonds.[8]

But the art of the period was the result of an aesthetic impulse far more significant than change for the sake of change, and perhaps all the more significant for that reason. Art reflected a new view of the world and the place of the individual in it. You must now examine the paintings reproduced here in light of the emerging intellectual outlook we examined at the outset of this chapter. How did the impressionists respond to the great faith in science that characterized their age? Why do you find in the work of the postimpressionist Seurat far less emphasis on the individual than in the work of Ingres and Delacroix? What vision of life does Seurat express? What philosophical changes (and responses by educated persons to those changes) might this diminished importance have represented? How does Seurat's view of the individual contrast with that of later artists like Picasso?

Van Gogh's portrait *La Berceuse* offered its viewers an expression of the artist's sentiments. Why was van Gogh expressing his own feelings through the medium of another individual rather than creating a photolike replica of that person?

8. Quoted in E. H. Gombrich, *The Story of Art* (New York: Phaidon, 1971), pp. 392–393. Bedlam: the early English institution for the insane.

What developments in nineteenth-century thought did he reflect in this study of his subject?

In the works of Gauguin we find a search for an art with more meaning than that produced by Western civilization, which the artist found sterile. How would those familiar with the work of Nietzsche, Durkheim, Weber, and perhaps Marx have interpreted Gauguin's work? Remember, too, that Gauguin painted during the age of imperialism. How does his art stand in relation to his age's avowed belief in the superiority of Western civilization, the rallying point of the Social Darwinists?

Munch's *The Scream* brings together in one work of art many tendencies in late-nineteenth- and early-twentieth-century thought. Recall the ideas of Durkheim and Weber. Why did Munch portray his subject as a solitary individual? What do you think provoked the agonized scream? Although Munch's work predated most of Freud's great writings, why might you think that Munch and Freud shared a common view of the human psyche?

Consider next Klimt's *The Kiss*. Why do you think Freud's work on the human mind might have influenced Klimt? Many viewers of Klimt's work would have seen it as an attack. What was the artist attacking? George Grosz satirized the world in which he lived. Recall particularly the ideas of the pioneering German sociologist Max Weber and the sterility he found in an increasingly bureaucratized world. What elements of Weber's thought do you find embodied in Grosz's response to German society?

You may find that Picasso's *Les Demoiselles d'Avignon* reflects several trends in Western thought. What is the significance of mathematical and geometric relationships in the cubist approach to the human form? What contrasting message is given by the masklike faces on the right of the picture? How do they reflect some of the same influences Gauguin experienced? What was the effect of the age's ideas on Picasso?

Consider Rousseau's *The Dream*. In one of his most significant works, *The Interpretation of Dreams* (1900), Freud sought to understand the irrational side of the human psyche, the unconscious, by explaining the psychological meaning of dreams. How does Rousseau's vision of reality coincide with Freud's? What significance might you ascribe to the nude and the powerful lions in the context of Freud's work?

The final painting is Duchamp's nude. Review our findings on the paintings that precede his chronologically. Why are you probably not surprised to find in his work a painting totally devoid of anything resembling the human form? What trends in art culminate in Duchamp's work? Remember that he eventually became a dadaist. Can you detect in the nude a message about the machine age and its impact on the individual?

As you answer these questions, you should gain a better understanding of the sweeping intellectual changes that overtook the late-nineteenth- and early-twentieth-century Western world. The dadaist outlook on Western civilization, described in the introduction to this chapter, embodied one extreme reaction to those changes, and the art we have studied presents other responses. You should now be able to answer the central questions of this chapter: How did the paintings reflect a break from traditional artistic standards? What trends can be identified in each artist's work? Finally, how did the artists collectively reveal the intellectual currents of the period?

EPILOGUE

In a sense, this chapter presents a turning point in the history of Western civilization. The West after 1920 was in many ways a far less secure place than the West of the eighteenth and nineteenth centuries, when Europe had been equally secure in its world power and its world view. The nineteenth century in particular had produced a standard of living in the West higher than ever before enjoyed by people anywhere. Westerners were convinced of their primacy.

As the nineteenth century drew to a close, however, many Europeans looked to a disturbing future. Certainly the trends in art we have observed here continued. Dadaism gave way to surrealism, which drew on the artist's unconscious. Later, abstract expressionism and other styles would also develop to present viewers with even greater challenges to their interpretive skills. Other undercurrents were even more distressing, however. Intellectually, the authority of the old faiths and tenets that long had guided Westerners eroded for many persons, and the consequent questioning of traditional values and practices invaded every area of human endeavor. Internationally, the strength of the European powers was challenged by the rise of non-European nations like the United States and Japan. Politically, the nineteenth-century faith in democracy would be challenged by twentieth-century totalitarian movements that reminded many of the threat Max Weber saw in an irrational but charismatic leader. Technologically, humankind's progress meant that it had developed unprecedented ability to destroy life. Economically, nineteenth-century bourgeois capitalism faced the challenge of communist revolution. The art of the period 1870–1920 reflected all these disturbing developments.

Indeed, the art produced after 1920 by surrealist, abstract expressionist, and other modern artists mirrored the changes in the West that came with accelerating speed after the period we have examined in this chapter. Einstein's work unlocked the destructive possibilities of the atom, and Western science was to create technologies of war far in excess of those employed in World War I. In the giant corporations that came to dominate the Western economy, the individual's significance diminished still further. Using the analytical technique you have mastered in this chapter, you may wish to continue exploring the ideological messages of modern art beyond the period 1870–1920.

[63]

CHAPTER THREE

TOTAL WAR: THE COST OF

UNLIMITED CONFLICT (1914–1945)

Appalled by the terrible slaughter that occurred during the Battle of the Somme in World War I, one of the British soldiers who survived, Edmund Blunden, asked himself if anyone could claim victory in such warfare. In the end, he decided, "[B]oth sides had seen, in a sad scrawl of broken earth and murdered men, the answer to the question. . . . Neither race had won, nor could win, the War. The War had won, and would go on winning."[1] Like countless others to come, Blunden discovered that in twentieth-century mass warfare, winners and losers alike paid a high price.

War, of course, has always been destructive. But until the late eighteenth century, practical constraints limited its scale and the devastation it caused. The emergence of modern

society, which allowed nations to overcome so many traditional limitations, freed them from most of the old constraints on warfare as well. Beginning with the French Revolution, the scope and violence of warfare increased steadily, reaching new levels of potential destructiveness in the nineteenth century. But because Europe, then the most developed part of the world economically and technologically, remained free of major wars toward the century's end, many people concluded that modern warfare between "advanced" countries would be like the Franco-Prussian War of 1870: quick and without great loss of life or property. When World War I erupted in 1914, people were unprepared for what was to follow— over four exhausting years of carnage in the very heart of the "advanced" world. Destructive as that conflict proved, it was soon eclipsed by the greater violence that exploded a generation later in World War II. By the close of that war in 1945, Europe and the rest of the world had to face the

1. Quoted in Paul Fussell, *The Great War and Modern Memory* (New York: Oxford University Press, 1975), p. 13.

fact that modern nations had unleashed a new kind of unlimited and extremely destructive warfare that had the potential to destroy all of humanity.

As their names imply, World Wars I and II raged across the entire globe. Yet it was in their intensity more than in their geographic extension that they stood out from earlier conflicts. They overwhelmed all aspects of life in the countries involved. Truly "nations in arms," the combatants struggled not just for material gain or even victory itself, but ultimately for national survival. They sought every advantage that modern technology and industry could give them to wage unrestrained warfare. To sustain such warfare, they had not only to draft huge numbers of their citizenry into arms but organize most of the rest for war-related work. They had to intervene in their economies, diverting production from peacetime goods to the manufacture of an unending supply of armaments and military equipment. And they had to curtail many ordinary pursuits and freedoms, imposing general rationing, enforcing widespread cen-

sorship, and often suspending normal laws and civil liberties. This nearly complete disruption of civilian life as much as the fury of modern combat earned this type of conflict a new name: total war.

This chapter takes a look at the nature of such warfare. It asks you to consider what made total war so all-encompassing and, perhaps more importantly, what the consequences were. The focus here, however, is not just on the immediate cost to the losers—or the winners—for the impact of total war cannot be measured solely by the number of the dead and the defeated. Total war deeply affected the living and the victors, too, and in ways far beyond their immediate losses. The economic, social, psychological, and moral effect these wars had on those who survived them must be taken into account, along with the legacy they left to all who came after them later in the twentieth century. In asking you to consider the consequences of total war, then, this chapter asks you to think about the broader impact this new form of combat had on the modern world.

BACKGROUND

Prussian General Carl von Clausewitz, the great European authority on modern combat, warned in his classic work, *On War*, that warfare should always be seen as a means to a higher end and never allowed to become an end in itself. Clausewitz considered war "an extension of policy," a

calculated use of violence to compel others to political objectives. Combat, he felt, should be a limited affair that in its ideal form approached what he called "absolute war": the elimination of all the "friction" or obstacles of warfare in order to allow the delivery of a single swift stroke that renders enemy forces powerless and willing to accept terms. How to achieve such a sudden, telling blow

[65]

Chapter 3

Total War: The

Cost of

Unlimited

Conflict

(1914–1945)

thereafter became the goal of most modern Western military planners.

The great social and economic changes of late eighteenth- and nineteenth-century Europe, however, confounded the efforts to attain this ideal. First, the French Revolution and Napoleonic Wars encouraged the use of citizen armies. Though individually less capable than professionals, patriotic citizen soldiers made effective fighters when deployed in large numbers and equipped with weapons that compensated for their inexperience. Industrialization provided a way to supply such weapons at low cost, and also provided new forms of transport and communication that allowed large armies to be moved and managed in battle. By the mid-nineteenth-century, therefore, a new kind of mass warfare had emerged whose scale and complexity defied efforts to gain sudden, telling victories. Success depended increasingly on the efficient mobilization of huge citizen armies and their deployment in battle. It also required constant replenishment of the equipment and weaponry that such troops needed in order to maintain their fighting strength. Production, transportation, and supply thus began to eclipse tactical brilliance as factors determining victory. The changing nature of combat could already be seen in the American Civil War of the 1860s, but most Europeans dismissed this conflict as a distant affair between unprofessional forces, and few paid it much mind. Further evidence of change appeared in the Franco-Prussian War of the early 1870s, but the speed with which this conflict ended again kept most observers from noticing it.

The lack of any big wars in Europe in the last decades of the nineteenth century further obscured the transformation of warfare. So when World War I broke out in August 1914, most Europeans thought that the conflict would be a short-lived one, decided by a few battles in which the valor of fighting men would win the day. Many naively assumed that the troops would be back home by Christmas. But during the more than four years that the war raged, people slowly awoke to the fact that the limited combat of the past had given way to a new kind of unrestrained war. Ultimately, as the scope and intensity of the war mounted beyond anything previously known, they paid it an off-handed compliment, naming it "the Great War" to distinguish it from all earlier conflicts. And it was this Great War that first revealed to the combatants what made war total.

Their first insight came with the discovery that an all-out conflict would not be brief. At the start, Germany planned for a quick war and tried to attain it by mounting a rapid, massive invasion of France through neutral Belgium, hoping then to turn its attention to helping its ally, Austria-Hungary, defeat Russia in the east. But when French and British troops halted the German offensive in northern France, the contending forces dug into fixed positions in a long line of trenches running from Switzerland to the English Channel. This became the infamous western front. After two years of inconclusive fighting, both sides attempted massive breakouts in 1916, leading to the battles of Verdun and the Somme, in which first the Germans and then the British went on the offensive. In these battles, great masses of men charged and counter-charged across "no man's land" between opposing trench systems; because of the destructiveness of new weaponry, the losses were incredible. But despite casualties in the hundreds of thousands over a few days—with a high point of 60,000 in one day at the Somme—neither side could win a significant victory.

Gradually generals and other national leaders realized that the technological advances in warfare had favored defense over offense. Improved rifles, grenades, machine guns, and explosive artillery shells, along with abundant barbed wire and mines, made frontal assault ruinous in casualties. Efforts at outflanking positions also failed, because railroads and trucks allowed defenders to rush reserve forces forward in sufficient numbers to launch huge counteroffensives. Governments thus enlisted scientists and engineers to come up with new weapons and devices that would improve offensive capability. All sides experimented with battlefield innovations from gas warfare to tanks, submarines, and airplanes. Science was thus mobilized as never before to turn out ever more deadly weapons in the interest of narrow national goals, ignoring the larger human costs. The result was the development on both sides of what came to be called the "killing machine," a form of warfare designed to wear out and exhaust the enemy through mass slaughter.

Although they gave neither side a decisive edge, these innovations constantly increased the material and economic cost of the war, demanding ever greater sacrifices from civilians and overstraining industrial production. As the conflict lengthened into a grim war of mass attrition, the strength and will of civilians and the resilience of the combatants' political and economic systems became as important to victory as their military forces. By 1917 the German decision to use unrestricted submarine warfare to blockade Britain threatened the British with mass starvation, a possibility already haunting Germany as a result of an Allied naval blockade. Struggling to keep up flagging morale under worsening conditions at home as well as on the battlefields, all the belligerents increasingly used modern mass media to disseminate propaganda and make patriotic appeals. But beginning in Russia in 1917, and then in most of the Central Powers in 1918, over-strained populations revolted, toppling governments and leaving their armies stranded in the field. Peace came not from defeat in battle but from failures on the home front, failures prompted by the collapse of political and economic institutions under the stress of prolonged wartime conditions. Such defeat entailed not just the frustration of war aims, but almost total national breakdown.

World War I thus revealed the deadly nature of total war, in which whole nations rather than just their

Chapter 3

Total War: The

Cost of

Unlimited

Conflict

(1914–1945)

armies were locked in conflict. In 1935, General Eric von Leudendorf, who had served on the German general staff during the Great War, analyzed the new form of combat in a book called *Total War*. Such warfare, he noted, could no longer be confined to battlefields. Because of the ease and speed of modern transportation, it would spread everywhere, erasing the distinction between the front lines and other areas. Belligerents would thus have to mobilize their entire civilian populations to wage war. This effort, in turn, would require constant propaganda campaigns and government control over media to sustain national morale. In short, total war demanded total national readjustment. And to make this occur smoothly, plans for mobilization and a wartime economy must be made well in advance to ensure their swift implementation once war erupted. Finally, he warned, leadership in a total war must be vested in a single authority, preferably a military one, to prevent dissent and confusion from weakening the all-out national effort.

Analyses of this sort suggested that disrupting an enemy's home front would be as effective as defeating its armies. Strategists thus began to consider ways to strike behind enemy lines, either to demoralize populations or to destroy crucial support systems, ignoring traditional distinctions between combatants and noncombatants in war. Small-scale experiments in World War I of attacking enemy cities with long-range guns and bomb-laden Zeppelins had not been very effective. But younger military planners felt confident that newer weapons would make this tactic more feasible and spoke of the need to organize "civilian defense" to protect populations from it. In a struggle for all-out victory, they warned, countries could not expect any quarter—nor could they give any in turn. The alternative to total triumph would be total annihilation.

Many postwar leaders, particularly in liberal, democratic states like Britain and France, recoiled from such ideas, fearing that their people would refuse to enter another bloodbath like World War I, and so sought other options. French military leaders responded by fortifying the entire Franco-German frontier to create an impregnable front line. Built at great expense, this Maginot line, as it was called, was supposed to make another invasion of France too costly to contemplate. More forward-looking military men, however, realized that such a defensive solution invited a return to deadly fixed fronts. So they looked for new offensive strategies based on highly technical weapons that would allow small, professional forces to strike deeply into enemy territory without the static battlefields and high attrition associated with World War I.

British planners, taking advantage of their country's island nature and its large navy, which protected it from immediate attack, grew interested in a new offensive form of air power called strategic bombing. Fleets of airplanes, they said, could be used to strike directly at the enemy's critical home front and either destroy its inhabitants outright or cripple their ability to support a war.

They thus lobbied for a force of long-range planes that could bomb the continental cities of their most likely enemies. For a while in the 1920s and early 1930s, Britain's efforts in this direction made its Royal Air Force the world's first significant form of air power. But the primitive nature of planes through the 1930s and the lack of experienced pilots made this a risky approach to national defense, especially for land-locked nations with potential enemies all around their borders.

Continental European innovators thus took another tack, focusing on mechanized, mobile forces that could rapidly penetrate an enemy's front lines and strike at its home territory. Charles de Gaulle, later head of the Free French forces in World War II, advocated this approach. In his 1934 book *Army of the Future*, he argued for a "completely motorized" professional army that would move on "caterpillar wheels."[2] But France had already committed its defense to the Maginot line and ignored his ideas. It was thus left to German generals to develop similar ideas into what came to be called *blitzkrieg*, or "lightning war." *Blitzkrieg* was a form of combat using a relatively small and highly mechanized army designed to fight a short, limited war. Instead of a mass infantry of conscript riflemen, it relied on a well-trained force of professional soldiers organized around tanks and other motorized units and provided with air cover by squadrons of accompa-

nying airplanes. Ready at all times, such an army could be launched instantly into the heart of an enemy nation before that nation had time to mobilize and deploy a more traditional mass army of citizen soldiers. German strategists initially favored this approach because postwar agreements severely limited the size of Germany's army. But once they were convinced of its merits, they held to it even after Hitler came to power in 1933 and began a major military buildup. Germany's rearmament thus focused on building a mechanized army with the most up-to-date equipment then known. Hitler's air minister, Hermann Goering, also used this opportunity to press for advanced airplanes, and by 1935 his *Luftwaffe* or air force approached Britain's Royal Air Force in both design and numbers.

The world got its first glimpse of this new weaponry when Germany intervened in the Spanish civil war. During the fighting there in 1937, the German Condor Legion staged the world's first major air raid against civilians, dropping incendiary and high-explosive bombs on the small Spanish town of Guernica. The act brought a loud outcry from across the world against the killing of civilians (and occasioned Pablo Picasso's famous painting in protest). But the effectiveness of the tactic convinced the Germans to add more bombers to their air force and increase its size.

The ability of air power to disrupt and demoralize enemy defenses was further shown in Germany's invasion of Poland in 1939 and then in its "lightning war" against France in the

2. Charles de Gaulle, *The Army of the Future* (New York and Philadelphia: J. B. Lippincott Co., 1941), p. 100.

Chapter 3

Total War: The

Cost of

Unlimited

Conflict

(1914–1945)

spring of 1940. German air strikes against cities and strategic centers behind the lines terrorized civilians and confused defense measures, creating a mood of helplessness that hastened surrender. In the fall of 1940, however, when the German military machine turned its might against Britain, it faced a nation with air power of its own. Before Germany could risk an invasion across the English Channel, it had to destroy the Royal Air Force. Determined RAF resistance in the air and effective "civilian defense" on the ground to help people survive air raids allowed the British eventually to win the Battle of Britain. In the process, they became even more appreciative of air power. Once they had achieved mastery in the air, they realized, they could use bombers to attack the industrial base on which Germany's highly mechanized army depended for resupply. When the United States joined the war on Britain's side at the end of 1941 following the Japanese attack on Pearl Harbor, British leaders accordingly called for fleets of English and American bombers to strike directly at German cities.

American military men were already familiar with the idea of strategic bombing, because U.S. Army General William "Billy" Mitchell had been one of its earliest proponents in the interwar period. A veteran of World War I, Mitchell tried to convince his countrymen that airplanes could form a first line of defense for North America, especially if they were based on specially designed ships stationed at sea. Such a force, he argued, could also be sent to strike directly at a distant enemy's home-

land. Technological problems and economic constraints kept the U.S. Army from taking his ideas seriously during the interwar period. But with the outbreak of war in Europe and the rapid advance of aircraft it inspired, American war planners began to reevaluate them.

One of the attractive features of strategic bombing was that it allowed the Americans and British to strike back at Germany at a time when they felt unable to launch a land assault against its heavily fortified European base. It also provided a way to aid the beleaguered Russian forces. Drawn into the war in mid-1941 by a German surprise attack, the Soviet Union was initially unable to halt the advance of German forces. Appealing to Britain and the United States, with whom it soon allied, it asked them to attack Germany in the west to relieve German pressure on Soviet forces. Unwilling to commit to an all-out invasion of Europe, the combined chiefs of staff coordinating the British and American forces instead announced their decision in February of 1943 to begin what they called the Combined Bomber Offensive to destroy Germany's ability to remain in the war by demolishing its industrial base and terrorizing its people.

Inasmuch as Germany had pioneered air attacks against nonmilitary targets, the offensive was not a new idea. But the scale and intensity of these air raids dramatically changed the nature of modern warfare. Fleets of hundreds of aircraft, many specially designed for the task like the American B-29 bomber, attacked German cities around the clock. Attempts at precision bombing, or hitting select targets, proved too costly and soon gave way to "saturation bombing," or indiscriminate attacks on urban areas. Occasionally bombers equipped with special incendiary bombs even attempted to set large sections of cities aflame. These attacks brought the war directly to German civilians and destroyed much of German industry. Allied land offensives from Russia, Africa, and then France were ultimately required in order to defeat the German military forces, but the Anglo-American air offensive contributed greatly to their defeat. A postwar U.S. government survey concluded that "Allied air power was decisive in the war in Western Europe," noting:

> It brought the economy which sustained the enemy's armed forces to virtual collapse, although the full effects of this collapse had not reached the enemy's front lines when they were overrun by Allied forces. It brought home to the German people the full impact of modern war with all its horror and suffering. Its imprint on the German nation will be lasting.[3]

Strategic bombing proved so effective in Europe that the United States used it in the Pacific theater, too, once American forces pushed past the outer Japanese defenses to secure bases within air range of Japan itself. Japan began to experience this new form of warfare late in 1944. By March of the next year, air raids against Tokyo and other Japanese cities had escalated into massive attacks that unleashed thousands of tons of incendiary bombs, burning large portions of these cities to the ground. When Japanese resistance continued despite this destruction, U.S. leaders decided to introduce the world's first atomic bombs into the air campaign. Originally developed to deter a German nuclear threat, the atomic bomb proved the ultimate weapon for total war. For as the two dropped on Hiroshima and Nagasaki in August 1945 showed, a single atom bomb could obliterate an entire city. Armed with such weapons, nations could now truly annihilate one another. Realizing that fact, the Japanese government offered unconditional surrender, even though most of its armies in Asia remained undefeated and no invasion of its home territories had yet begun. Again, defeat on the home front made resistance on the battlefield futile.

THE METHOD

Each of the sources in the Evidence section deals with one or more aspects of total war. Try first to determine which characteristic features of this warfare each source reveals. Then look within the source for hints or suggestions about the likely consequences of these features. You may find it helpful to make a written list of both as you proceed, not only to provide a reminder later of what you found, but also to obtain a broad overview from which to

3. *The United States Strategic Bombing Survey, Summary Report (European War)*, Sept. 30, 1945 (Washington, D.C.: U.S. Government Printing Office, 1945), pp. 15–16.

Chapter 3

Total War: The

Cost of

Unlimited

Conflict

(1914–1945)

attempt some final generalizations about the nature and cost of total war.

The first source, excerpted from Carl von Clauswitz's 1832 classic study *On War*, offers a definition of limited war against which to contrast the concept of total war. A veteran of the Napoleonic Wars, Clausewitz was a career officer in the Prussian army whose views on strategy dominated nineteenth-century military thought and continued to exert an influence throughout the twentieth century. By World War I, however, the shift in modern war that he feared had reached a new level, as Source 2, a passage from the memoirs of David Lloyd George, illustrates. A liberal reformer with pacifist leanings who became British prime minister in the midst of the war, Lloyd George was appalled by the mounting casualties of 1916. Not only did enlistment fail to keep pace with them, but they threatened the stability and structure of society, as he hints here.

The war consumed unprecedented quantities of funds, too, and hard-pressed governments appealed to their people for wartime loans to finance soaring budgets. France, known for its artists, benefited from their help in launching poster campaigns in 1915 to bring this appeal to the masses. Soon other governments followed suit, using propaganda posters like those depicted here as Source 3 to raise funds, solicit enlistment, and boost morale. Source 4 helps to explain why such measures were needed in order to sustain popular support for the war. Taken from the final dispatch written by the head of the British Expeditionary Forces on the western front, Field Marshal Sir

Douglas Haig, at the war's end, it outlines the overall scope and nature of the conflict. Often called "the butcher of the Somme" because of his willingness to expend so many forces in that battle, Haig here details the enormous needs of an army fighting a modern mass war of attrition.

The next two documents represent assessments of the conflict's postwar impact. Source 5 comes from an essay called "The Crisis of the Spirit" written in 1919 by Paul Valéry, one of France's most outstanding poets. His focus is not just on France but on the entire European world, for in his view the war had fatally damaged Europe's "spirit" to the detriment of its intellectual and cultural standing. Veterans had special problems after the war, for its carnage left most of them deeply disillusioned with all ideals and authority. Source 6, excerpts from a popular novel of 1929 called *All Quiet on the Western Front*, indicates why. Based on the experiences of its German author, Erich Maria Remarque, it portrays the numbing effect of the war on the soldiers and how it made survivors view themselves as a "lost generation," without hopes or dreams. Their demoralization helps to explain why the world was soon plunged into the even more costly Second World War.

This apathy encouraged authoritarian leaders to seize power in Italy, Germany, and Japan, and then to risk limited conflicts against disillusioned neighbors that were unwilling to engage in more fighting. Indeed, leaders of other countries often had difficulty arousing their citizens to oppose such aggression until directly attacked. Thus Source 7, President

Roosevelt's first address to Congress in January 1942, shows him trying to rally the American people for what he warns will be another "all-out" war to counter the aggression of the Axis nations. Source 8, a government poster and popular song featuring a fictitious "Rosie the Riveter," illustrates one consequence of the massive mobilization of the home front that followed: the effort to engage women in the national war effort. The escalating nature of the conflict can also be seen in Source 9, the transcript of a radio broadcast delivered to the German public in October 1942 by Hermann Goering, Hitler's second in command, who was then trying to mobilize his nation's economy more fully to match the growing demands of the war. Any Axis hope for limiting the scale and intensity of the war was dashed at the Casablanca Conference between Roosevelt and British Prime Minister Winston Churchill in January 1943. For as Source 10, a subsequent radio announcement by Roosevelt, reveals, he and Churchill there decided that they would accept nothing less than a total victory over their enemies.

It was also at Casablanca that the two Allied leaders agreed to mount the full-scale Combined Bombing Offensive against German cities. Source 11, an official U.S. government survey, made in 1946, of the damage inflicted upon Japan by the American strategic bombing offensive there, provides a detailed description of the devastation this new form of total war inflicted upon enemy home fronts. Like a similar survey conducted on Germany, it reveals that massive air strikes nearly leveled entire cities. Its final remarks about the atomic bomb, however, reveal how this new weapon introduced near the war's end approached the "untrammeled, absolute manifestation of violence" that Clauswitz warned might come of unrestrained warfare. What this weapon meant in human terms can be seen in Source 12, a recollection of the Hiroshima atomic blast by a Japanese schoolboy, Astuko Tsujioka, taken from a collection of Japanese children's accounts compiled in 1951. It poignantly illustrates the ultimate consequences of total war between modern nations.

Chapter 3

Total War: The

Cost of

Unlimited

Conflict

(1914–1945)

Source 1 from Carl von Clausewitz, On War *(Princeton, N.J.: Princeton University Press, 1976), pp. 86, 588–593. Copyright © 1976 by Princeton University Press. Reprinted by permission of Princeton University Press.*

1. Carl von Clausewitz, *On War*, 1832

When whole communities go to war—whole peoples, and especially *civilized* peoples—the reason always lies in some political situation, and the occasion is always due to some political object. War, therefore, is an act of policy. Were it a complete, untrammeled, absolute manifestation of violence (as the pure concept would require), war would of its own independent will usurp the place of policy the moment policy had brought it into being; it would then drive policy out of office and rule by the laws of its own nature. . . .

. . . The end of the seventeenth century, the age of Louis XIV, may be regarded as that point in history when the standing army in the shape familiar to the eighteenth century reached maturity. . . .

The conduct of war thus became a true game, in which the cards were dealt by time and by accident. In its effect it was a somewhat stronger form of diplomacy, a more forceful method of negotiation, in which battles and sieges were the principal notes exchanged. Even the most ambitious ruler had no greater aims than to gain a number of advantages that could be exploited at the peace conference. . . .

This was the state of affairs at the outbreak of the French Revolution. . . . Suddenly war again became the business of the people—a people of thirty millions, all of whom considered themselves to be citizens. We need not study in detail the circumstances that accompanied this tremendous development; we need only note the effects that are pertinent to our discussion. The people became a participant in war; instead of governments and armies as heretofore, the full weight of the nation was thrown into the balance. The resources and efforts now available for use surpassed all conventional limits; nothing now impeded the vigor with which war could be waged, and consequently the opponents of France faced the utmost peril. . . .

Since Bonaparte, then, war, first among the French and subsequently among their enemies, again became the concern of the people as a whole, took on an entirely different character, or rather closely approached its true character, its absolute perfection. There seemed no end to the resources mobilized; all limits disappeared in the vigor and enthusiasm shown by governments and their subjects. Various factors powerfully increased that vigor: the vastness of available resources, the ample field of opportunity, and the depth of feeling generally aroused. The sole aim of war was to overthrow the opponent. Not until he was prostrate was it considered possible to pause and try to reconcile the opposing interests.

War, untrammeled by any conventional restraints, had broken loose in all its elemental fury. This was due to the peoples' new share in these great affairs of state; and their participation, in turn, resulted partly from the impact that the Revolution had on the internal conditions of every state and partly from the danger that France posed to everyone.

Will this always be the case in the future? From now on will every war in Europe be waged with the full resources of the state, and therefore have to be fought only over major issues that affect the people? Or shall we again see a gradual separation taking place between government and people? Such questions are difficult to answer, and we are the last to dare to do so. But the reader will agree with us when we say that once barriers—which in a sense consist only in man's ignorance of what is possible—are torn down, they are not so easily set up again. At least when major interests are at stake, mutual hostility will express itself in the same manner as it has in our own day.

Source 2 from David Lloyd George, War Memoirs of David Lloyd George, 1915–1916 *(Boston: Little, Brown, 1933), pp. 9–10. Reprinted by permission of AMS Press, Brooklyn, NY.*

2. Lloyd George on the Battle of the Somme, July 1, 1916

So, much to the secret satisfaction of General Joffre, we turned our backs on Salonika and our faces once more to the Somme. It ranks with Verdun as one of the two bloodiest battles ever fought on this earth up to that date. The casualties on both sides were well over a million. It was not responsible for the failure of the German effort to capture Verdun. It was only an element in slackening up a German offensive which had already slowed down and was by now a practical and almost an acknowledged failure. The French Commander-in-Chief said in May that the Germans had already been beaten at Verdun. Had the battle continued to rage around the remaining forts which held up the German Army we could have helped to reinforce the hard-pressed French Army either by sending troops to the battle area or by taking over another sector of the French Front. The Somme campaign certainly did not save Russia. That great country was being rapidly driven by the German guns towards the maelstrom of anarchy. You could even then hear the roar of the waters. That is, we might have heard it had it not been for the thunders of the Somme. These deafened our ears and obscured our vision so that we could not perceive the approaching catastrophe in Russia and therefore did not take measures to avert it. One-third of the Somme guns and

Chapter 3

Total War: The

Cost of

Unlimited

Conflict

(1914–1945)

ammunition transferred in time to the banks of another river, the Dnieper, would have won a great victory for Russia and deferred the Revolution until after the war.

It is claimed that the Battle of the Somme destroyed the old German Army by killing off its best officers and men. It killed off far more of our best and of the French best. The Battle of the Somme was fought by the volunteer armies raised in 1914 and 1915. These contained the choicest and best of our young manhood. The officers came mainly from our public schools and universities. Over 400,000 of our men fell in this bullheaded fight and the slaughter amongst our young officers was appalling. The "Official History of the War," writing of the first attack, says:

> For the disastrous loss of the finest manhood of the United Kingdom and Ireland there was only a small gain of ground to show. . . .

Summing up the effect on the British Army of the whole battle it says:

> Munitions and the technique of their use improved, but never again was the spirit or the quality of the officers and men so high, nor the general state of the training, leading and, above all, discipline of the new British armies in France so good. The losses sustained were not only heavy but irreplaceable.

Source 3: Photo (a): Hoover Institution Archives, #FR 793; Photo (b): The Imperial War Museum, London.

3. French and British World War I Posters

(a) French Loan Poster

(b) British Recruiting Poster

"We'll get them!
Second National Defense Loan
Subscribe"

Chapter 3

Total War: The

Cost of

Unlimited

Conflict

(1914–1945)

Source 4 from Field Marshal Sir Douglas Haig, "Features of the War," U.S. War Department Document No. 952 (Washington, D.C.: U.S. Government Printing Office, 1919). Obtained from The World War I Document Archive, *http://www. lib.byu.edu/~rdh/wwi/1918p/ haigdesp.html.*

4. Field Marshal Sir Douglas Haig, "Features of the War," Fourth Supplement to *The London Gazette*, Tuesday, April 8, 1919

(10) If the operations of the past four and a half years are regarded as a single continuous campaign, there can be recognized in them the same general features and the same necessary stages which between forces of approximately equal strength have marked all the conclusive battles of history. There is in the first instance the preliminary stage of the campaign in which the opposing forces seek to deploy and maneuver for position, endeavoring while doing so to gain some early advantage which might be pushed home to quick decision. This phase came to an end in the present war with the creation of continuous trench lines from the Swiss frontier to the sea.

Battle having been joined, there follows the period of real struggle in which the main forces of the two belligerent armies are pitted against each other in close and costly combat. Each commander seeks to wear down the power of resistance of his opponent and to pin him to his position, while preserving or accumulating in his own hands a powerful reserve force with which he can maneuver, and when signs of the enemy becoming morally and physically weakened are observed, deliver the decisive attack. . . .

In former battles this stage of the conflict has rarely lasted more than a few days, and has often been completed in a few hours. When armies of millions are engaged, with the resources of great Empires behind them, it will inevitably be long. It will include violent crises of fighting which, when viewed separately and apart from the general perspective, will appear individually as great indecisive battles. To this stage belong the great engagements of 1916 and 1917 which wore down the strength of the German armies.

Finally, whether from the superior fighting ability and leadership of one of the belligerents, as the result of greater resources or tenacity, or by reason of higher morale, or from a combination of all these causes, the time will come when the other side will begin to weaken and the climax of the battle is reached. . . . In this World War the great sortie of the beleaguered German armies commenced on March 21, 1918, and lasted for four months, yet it represents a corresponding stage in a single colossal battle. . . .

(12) Obviously the greater the length of a war the higher is likely to be the number of casualties incurred in it on either side. The same causes, therefore,

which served to protract the recent struggle are largely responsible for the extent of our casualties. There can be no question that to our general unpreparedness must be attributed the loss of many thousands of brave men whose sacrifice we deeply deplore, while we regard their splendid gallantry and self-devotion with unstinted admiration and gratitude.

. . . The total British casualties in all theaters of war, killed, wounded, missing, and prisoners, including native troops, are approximately three millions (3,076,388). Of this total some two and a half millions (2,568,834) were incurred on the western front. The total French losses, killed, missing, and prisoners, but exclusive of wounded, have been given officially as approximately 1,831,000. If an estimate for wounded is added, the total can scarcely be less than 4,800,000, and of this total it is fair to assume that over four millions were incurred on the western front. The published figures for Italy, killed and wounded only, exclusive of prisoners, amount to 1,400,060, of which practically the whole were incurred in the western theater of war.

Figures have also been published for Germany and Austria. The total German casualties, killed, wounded, missing, and prisoners, are given at approximately six and a half millions (6,485,000), of which the vastly greater proportion must have been incurred on the western front, where the bulk of the German forces were concentrated and the hardest fighting took place. In view of the fact, however, that the number of German prisoners is definitely known to be considerably understated, these figures must be accepted with reserve. The losses of Austria-Hungary in killed, missing, and prisoners are given as approximately two and three-quarter millions (2,772,000). An estimate of wounded would give a total of over four and a half millions. . . .

During the second half of the war, and that part embracing the critical and costly period of the wearing out battle, the losses previously suffered by our Allies laid upon the British Armies in France an increasing share in the burden of attack. From the opening of the Somme Battle in 1916 to the termination of hostilities the British armies were subjected to a strain of the utmost severity which never ceased, and consequently had little or no opportunity for the rest and training they so greatly needed.

In addition to these particular considerations, certain general factors peculiar to modern war made for the inflation of losses. The great strength of modern field defenses and the power and precision of modern weapons, the multiplication of machine guns, trench mortars, and artillery of all natures, the employment of gas, and the rapid development of the aeroplane as a formidable agent of destruction against both men and material, all combined to increase the price to be paid for victory.

If only for these reasons, no comparisons can usefully be made between the relative losses incurred in this war and any previous war. There is, however, the further consideration that the issues involved in this stupendous struggle were far greater than those concerned in any other war in recent history. Our existence as an Empire and civilization itself, as it is understood by the free

Chapter 3

Total War: The

Cost of

Unlimited

Conflict

(1914–1945)

western nations, were at stake. Men fought as they have never fought before in masses. . . .

(16) A remarkable feature of the present war has been the number and variety of mechanical contrivances to which it has given birth or has brought to a higher state of perfection.

Besides the great increase in mobility made possible by the development of motor transport, heavy artillery, trench mortars, machine guns, aeroplanes, tanks, gas, and barbed wire have in their several spheres of action played very prominent parts in operations, and as a whole have given a greater driving power to war. The belligerent possessing a preponderance of such mechanical contrivances has found himself in a very favorable position as compared with his less well provided opponent. The general superiority of the Allies in this direction during the concluding stages of the recent struggle undoubtedly contributed powerfully to their success. In this respect the army owes a great debt to science and to the distinguished scientific men who placed their learning, and skill at the disposal of their country. . . .

(19) The immense expansion of the army, from 6 to over 60 infantry divisions, combined with the constant multiplication of auxiliary arms, called inevitably for a large increase in the size and scope of the services concerned in the supply and maintenance of our fighting forces.

As the army grew and became more complicated the total feeding strength of our forces in France rose until it approached a total of 2,700,000 men. The vastness of the figures involved in providing for their needs will be realized from the following examples. For the maintenance of a single division for one day, nearly 200 tons dead weight of supplies and stores are needed, representing a shipping tonnage of nearly 450 tons. In an army of 2,700,000 men, the addition of 1 ounce to each man's daily ration, involves the carrying of an extra 75 tons of goods. . . .

(20) . . . No survey of the features of the war would be complete without some reference to the part played by women serving with the British Armies in France. . . . Women in the British Red Cross Society and other organizations have driven ambulances throughout the war, undeterred by discomfort and hardship. Women have ministered to the comfort of the troops in huts and canteens. Finally, Queen Mary's Auxiliary Army Corps, recruited on a wider basis, responded with enthusiasm to the call for drafts, and by the aid they gave to our declining man power contributed materially to the success of our arms.

5. Paul Valéry, "The Crisis of the Spirit," 1919

The military crisis is perhaps over. The economic crisis is visible in all of its force; but the intellectual crisis, more subtle, and by nature more deceptive in appearances (because it takes place in the very realm of deception)—this crisis renders its full extent or stage difficult to grasp.

No one can say what will be dead or alive tomorrow in literature, in philosophy, or in aesthetics. No one knows yet which ideas and modes of expression will be inscribed in the list of things lost, or what novelties will be proclaimed. . . .

. . . The facts, however, are clear and unrelenting. Millions of young writers and young artists are dead. There is the lost illusion of European culture and proof of the powerlessness of knowledge to save anything whatsoever; there is science, fatally stricken in its moral ambitions, and seemingly dishonored by the cruelty of its applications; there is idealism, enduring with difficulty, profoundly maimed, and liable to its dreams; deluded realism, beaten down, overwhelmed with crimes and mistakes; covetousness and renunciation equally scorned; beliefs confounded between camps: cross against cross, crescent against crescent; there are skeptics who themselves, unhinged by events so sudden, so violent, and so moving, toy with our thinking like a cat with a mouse—skeptics who shed their doubts, rediscover them, and shed them again, but no longer know how to make use of the workings of the spirit.

The boat has been so forcibly rocked that even the most securely hung lamps have in the end been overturned. . . .

The storm has just ended, and yet we are as disquieted, as anxious, as if the storm were still to break upon us. Nearly all things human remain in terrible uncertainty. We look at what has vanished—we are almost destroyed by what is destroyed; we do not know what will come forth: still we can reasonably fear it. We hope in vagueness; we dread with precision. Our fears are infinitely more precise than our hopes; we admit that the best of life is behind us, that fullness is behind us, but disarray and doubt are in us and with us. There is no thinking mind, however wise or educated we imagine it, that can flatter itself with control over this affliction, or escape from this impression of darkness, or measure the likely duration of this troubled period in the vital exchanges of humanity.

We are a very unfortunate generation to whom it has fallen to see the moment of its passage through life coincide with the arrival of great and frightful events whose reverberations will fill all of our lives.

Chapter 3

Total War: The

Cost of

Unlimited

Conflict

(1914–1945)

We can say that all the essential things of this world have been affected by the war, or more exactly, by the circumstances of the war. The erosion ate away something deeper than the renewable parts of the being. You know what the trouble is in the general economy, the politics of states, and even in the lives of individuals: the constraint, the hesitation, the universal apprehension. *But among all these wounded things is the spirit.* The spirit in truth is cruelly stricken. The heart of man laments over the spirit and sadly judges itself. It doubts itself profoundly.

Source 6 from All Quiet on the Western Front, *Erich Maria Remarque. "Im Westen Nichts Neues", copyright 1928 by Ullstein A. G.; Copyright renewed © 1956 by Erich Maria Remarque. "All Quiet on the Western Front", copyright 1929, 1930 by Little, Brown and Company; Copyright renewed © 1957, 1958 by Erich Maria Remarque. All rights reserved.*

6. Erich Maria Remarque, *All Quiet on the Western Front*, 1929

All day the sky is hung with observation balloons. There is a rumour that the enemy are going to put tanks over and use low flying planes for the attack. But that interests us less than what we hear of the new flame throwers.

We wake up in the middle of the night. The earth booms. Heavy fire is falling on us. We crouch into corners. We distinguish shells of every caliber. . . .

Every man is aware of the heavy shells tearing down the parapet, rooting up the embankment and demolishing the upper layers of concrete. When a shell lands in the trench, we note how the hollow, furious blast is like a blow from the paw of a raging beast of prey. Already by morning a few of the recruits are green and vomiting. They are too inexperienced. . . .

Suddenly the nearer explosions cease. The shelling continues but it has lifted and falls behind us, our trench is free. We seize the hand grenades, pitch them out in front of the dug-out and jump after them. The bombardment has stopped and a heavy barrage now falls behind us. The attack has come. . . .

We have become wild beasts. We do not fight, we defend ourselves against annihilation. It is not against men that we fling our bombs, what do we know of men in this moment when Death with hands and helmets is hunting us down—now, for the first time in three days we can see his face, now, for the first time in three days we can oppose him; we feel a mad anger. No longer do we lie helpless, waiting on the scaffold, we can destroy and kill, to save ourselves, to save ourselves and be revenged.

We crouch behind every corner, behind every barrier of barbed wire, and hurl heaps of explosives at the feet of the advancing enemy before we run. The blast of the hand-grenades impinges powerfully on our arms and legs; crouching like cats we run on, overwhelmed by this wave that bears us along, that fills us with ferocity, turning us into thugs, into murderers, into God only knows what devils; this wave that multiplies our strength with fear and madness and greed of life, seeking and fighting for nothing but our deliverance. If your own father came over with them you would not hesitate to fling a bomb into him. . . .

Bombardment, barrage, curtain-fire, mines, gas, tanks, machine-guns, hand-grenades—words, words, but they hold the horror of the world.

Our faces are encrusted, our thoughts are devastated, we are weary to death; when the attack comes we shall have to strike many of the men with our fists to waken them and make them come with us—our eyes are burnt, our hands are torn, our knees bleed, our elbows are raw. . . .

How long has it been? Weeks—months—years? Only days. We see time pass in the colourless faces of the dying, we cram food into us, we run, we throw, we shoot, we kill, we lie about, we are feeble and spent, and nothing supports us but the knowledge that there are still feebler, still more spent, still more helpless ones there who, with staring eyes, look upon us as gods that escape death many times. . . .

I am young, I am twenty years old; yet I know nothing of life but despair, death, fear, and fatuous superficiality cast over an abyss of sorrow. I see how peoples are set against one another, and in silence, unknowingly, foolishly, obediently, innocently slay one another. I see that the keenest brains of the world invent weapons and words to make it yet more refined and enduring. And all men of my age, here and over there, throughout the whole world, see these things; all my generation is experiencing these things with me. What would our fathers do if we suddenly stood up and came before them and proffered our account? What do they expect of us if a time ever comes when the war is over? Through the years our business has been killing;—it was our first calling in life. Our knowledge of life is limited to death. What will happen afterwards? And what shall come of us? . . .

From a mockery the tanks have become a terrible weapon. Armoured they come rolling on in long lines, and more than anything else embody for us the horror of war.

We do not see the guns that bombard us; the attacking lines of the enemy infantry are men like ourselves; but these tanks are machines, their caterpillars run on as endless as the war, they are annihilation, they roll without feeling into the craters, and climb up again without stopping, a fleet of roaring, smoke-belching armour-clads, invulnerable steel beasts squashing the dead and the wounded—we shrivel up in our thin skin before them against their colossal weight, our arms are sticks of straw, and our hand grenades matches.

Shells, gas clouds, and flotillas of tanks—shattering, starvation, death.

Dysentery, influenza, typhus—murder, burning, death.

Trenches, hospitals, the common grave—there are no other possibilities. . . .

Had we returned home in 1916, out of the suffering and the strength of our experiences we might have unleashed a storm. Now if we go back we will be weary, broken, burnt out, rootless, and without hope. We will not be able to find our way any more.

[83]

Chapter 3

Total War: The

Cost of

Unlimited

Conflict

(1914–1945)

Source 7 from President Roosevelt's 1942 Annual Message to Congress. Obtained from http://www.ibiblio.org/pha/policy/1942/420106a.html.

7. President Franklin D. Roosevelt, Annual Message to Congress, January 6, 1942

Exactly one year ago today I said to this Congress: "When the dictators are ready to make war upon us, they will not wait for an act of war on our part. . . They—not we—will choose the time and the place and the method of their attack."

We now know their choice of the time: a peaceful Sunday morning—December 7, 1941.

We know their choice of the place: an American outpost in the Pacific.

We know their choice of the method: the method of Hitler himself. . . .

With Hitler's formation of the Berlin-Rome-Tokyo alliance, all of these plans of conquest became a single plan. Under this, in addition to her own schemes of conquest, Japan's role was to cut off our supply of weapons of war to Britain, Russia, and China—weapons which increasingly were speeding the day of Hitler's doom. The act of Japan at Pearl Harbor was intended to stun us—to terrify us to such an extent that we would divert our industrial and military strength to the Pacific area or even to our own continental defense.

The plan failed in its purpose. We have not been stunned. We have not been terrified or confused. This reassembling of the Seventy-seventh Congress is proof of that; for the mood of quiet, grim resolution which here prevails bodes ill for those who conspired and collaborated to murder world peace. . . .

Plans have been laid here and in the other capitals for coordinated and cooperative action by all the United Nations—military action and economic action. Already we have established unified command of land, sea, and air forces in the southwestern Pacific theater of war. There will be a continuation of conferences and consultations among military staffs, so that the plans and operations of each will fit into a general strategy designed to crush the enemy. . . .

But modern methods of warfare make it a task not only of shooting and fighting, but an even more urgent one of working and producing. . . .

The superiority of the United Nations in munitions and ships must be overwhelming—so overwhelming that the Axis nations can never hope to catch up with it. In order to attain this overwhelming superiority the United Nations must build planes and tanks and guns and ships to the utmost limit of our national capacity. We have the ability and capacity to produce arms not only for our own forces but also for the armies, navies, and air forces fighting on our side. . . .

This production of ours in the United States must be raised far above its present levels, even though it will mean the dislocation of the lives and occupations of millions of our own people. We must raise our sights all along the production-line. Let no man say It cannot be done. It must be done—and we have undertaken to do it.

I have just sent a letter of directive to the appropriate departments and agencies of our Government, ordering that immediate steps be taken:

1. To increase our production rate of airplanes so rapidly that in this year, 1942, we shall produce 60,000 planes, 10,000 more than the goal set a year and a half ago. This includes 45,000 combat planes—bombers, dive bombers, pursuit planes. The rate of increase will be continued, so that next year, 1943, we shall produce 125,000 planes, including 100,000 combat planes.

2. To increase our production rate of tanks so rapidly that in this year, 1942, we shall produce 45,000 tanks; and to continue that increase so that next year, 1943, we shall produce 75,000 tanks.

3. To increase our production rate of anti-aircraft guns so rapidly that in this year, 1942, we shall produce 20,000 of them; and to continue that increase, so that next year, 1943, we shall produce 35,000 anti-aircraft guns.

4. To increase our production rate of merchant ships so rapidly that in this year, 1942, we shall build 8,000,000 deadweight tons as compared with a 1941 production of 1,100,000. We shall continue that increase so that next year, 1943, we shall build 10,000,000 tons. . . .

Our task is hard—our task is unprecedented—and the time is short. We must strain every existing armament-producing facility to the utmost. We must convert every available plant and tool to war production. That goes all the way from the greatest plants to the smallest—from the huge automobile industry to the village machine shop.

Production for war is based on men and women—the human hands and brains which collectively we call labor. Our workers stand ready to work long hours; to turn out more in a day's work; to keep the wheels turning and the fires burning 24 hours a day and 7 days a week. They realize well that on the speed and efficiency of their work depend the lives of their sons and their brothers on the fighting fronts.

Production for war is based on metals and raw materials—steel, copper, rubber, aluminum, zinc, tin. Greater and greater quantities of them will have to be diverted to war purposes. Civilian use of them will have to be cut further and still further—and, in many cases, completely eliminated.

War costs money. So far, we have hardly even begun to pay for it. We have devoted only 15% of our national income to our national defense. As will appear in my budget message tomorrow, our war program for the coming

Chapter 3

Total War: The

Cost of

Unlimited

Conflict

(1914–1945)

fiscal year will cost 56 billion dollars, or, in other words, more than one-half of the estimated annual national income. This means taxes and bonds, and bonds and taxes. It means cutting luxuries and other non-essentials. In a word, it means an "all-out" war by individual effort and family effort in a united country. . . .

We must, on the other hand, guard against defeatism. That has been one of the chief weapons of Hitler's propaganda machine—used time and again with deadly results. It will not be used successfully on the American people. . . .

When our enemies challenged our country to stand up and fight, they challenged each and every one of us. And each and every one of us has accepted the challenge—for himself and for the Nation. . . .

That is the conflict that day and night now pervades our lives. No compromise can end that conflict. There never has been—there never can be—successful compromise between good and evil. Only total victory can reward the champions of tolerance and decency and freedom and faith.

8. Rosie the Riveter, American Propaganda Icon

"Rosie the Riveter"
by Redd Evans and John Jacob Loeb

All the day long,
Whether rain or shine,
She's a part of the assembly line.
She's making history,
Working for victory,
Rosie the Riveter.
Keeps a sharp lookout for sabotage,
Sitting up there on the fuselage.
That little girl will do more than a male will do.
Rosie's got a boyfriend, Charlie.
Charlie, he's a Marine.
Rosie is protecting Charlie,
Working overtime on the riveting machine.
When they gave her a production "E,"
She was as proud as she could be.
There's something true about,
Red, white, and blue about,
Rosie the Riveter.

9. Reichsmarschal Hermann Goering, German Radio Broadcast, October 4, 1942

National comrades, men and women! Germans on the land! We are at the beginning of the fourth year of the war, and today we celebrate the German harvest thanksgiving. Today we cannot celebrate the nation's festivals in the scope and manner to which we were formerly accustomed.

Today great masses of the German country folk cannot appear before the Fuehrer through their deputations, to bring him a harvest wreath and fruits of

Chapter 3

Total War: The

Cost of

Unlimited

Conflict

(1914–1945)

the last harvest, because we are in a war, in the most difficult war of the German people, and in this war there is only one thing: work, work, fighting and work, and again fighting and work.

The last three harvest years, in particular the first two of them, were by no means favorable. Quite unexpectedly, three terribly hard and severe winters broke upon us and destroyed much of the labor that had previously been put into the ground.

But, nevertheless, it was possible, first of all, to guarantee nourishment of the people absolutely; for at that time, when I spoke in this same hall on taking over the responsibility of carrying out the Four-Year Plan, many a compatriot will still be able to remember how, right at that time, I laid very strong emphasis on the concept and the term "enemy blockade." . . .

Now that the future is clearer, the meat ration is to be increased by another fifty grammes in the raid-threatened areas. . . .

By no means let us forget that when it is a question of raw materials for armament, there are two raw materials which are just as fundamental for feeding our people as for their subsistence as a whole. And these raw materials are coal and iron, and both raw materials we ourselves possess in sufficient quantities, and we have also—thank God—won enormous additional quantities by conquest.

Bear in mind, therefore, that since we do not have a sufficient surplus of this valuable material, coal, we should not waste it unnecessarily. And every one who turns on a single light or other electrical appliance unnecessarily, or who leaves it on longer than necessary, is committing a sin. Any one who uses too much gas should remember that this gas comes from coal, and that a worker has to slave for it by the sweat of his brow hundreds of meters underground. Any one who uses too much power, should also consider that fact.

But, my dear German comrades, one thing more I should like to say here quite plainly. When a national community is being created, and when an entire nation, as a totality and a single entity, must win a victory and must secure its freedom, then the individual, too, must be ready to submit to more or less stringent limitations on his personal freedom.

This limitation of personal freedom is necessary even in peacetimes. In democracy, to be sure, there is always one thing only—freedom of the individual. That is what we National Socialists call license. If every one may do as he likes, if no one has to have any consideration for his neighbors or his relatives, and even gets ahead by doing so, then you can imagine how such a community gets along. . . .

I should like now to broach a topic that indeed concerns me very especially as the Commander in Chief of the air force and Reich Air Minister. It is about the heavy enemy air attacks on German cities. Here, too, my dear fellow countrymen, there must often be a very great restriction of personal freedom.

I am far from belittling these attacks or anything like that. I know how it is. I am an expert. I know what it means when a hundred or two hundred planes drop their bomb load. I know that many innocent people must die, in this way, absolutely to no purpose.

The Fuehrer told our enemies in his Reichstag speech some time ago that one should at least stop attacking absolutely harmless people where there is no war industry. And today they cannot get out of it by saying that they just accidentally missed, they were aiming at industrial plants, because we are in possession of their original orders.

Mr. British Air General instructed his fliers that war industry was not the important thing to destroy, but residential sections . . . terrorizing the German population, dropping bombs on children and women. That is the main thing for these gentlemen, even though a few decent fliers have protested against being assigned again and again to this slaughter.

So I know how hard all this is and how terrible and how senseless this destruction of cultural values. If that fool would reflect on the virtues of German culture, and that German culture exists not only for Germans—it has made endless contributions to Europe and the world—that simple respect for it should keep the wretches from destroying German seats of culture. . . .

You may be sure—I am now speaking to our fellow countrymen of those regions that are subject to the threat of air raids—that everything humanely possible is being done in my efforts to alleviate the situation and to prevent such attacks, first of all by active counter defense. . . .

I shall see to it myself that steadily increasing and additional camps shall be prepared that will take care of the victims of the air raids. I have purchased supplies in all countries to which I had access, on a tremendously large scale. . . .

And, my dear fellow-citizens, everything is in our favor when we consider the situation. Just how are our enemies going to be able to carry out their continued assertions and declarations that they are going to win this war?

They have some hope or other in the astronomical figures of American production. Now, I would be the last person to underestimate American production. In certain fields the Americans have made colossal achievements in technique and in production.

We know they have done a stupendous amount with the auto. They have also won special merit with the radio and the razor blade. In these three fields they have undoubtedly wrought ever colossally, but these things are, nevertheless, something else yet than what one needs for war. . . .

And even in America nothing gets done faster than with us, but slower rather, and even in America raw materials are necessary, workers are necessary. You can't at the same time build up an army of several million, and on the other hand triple the number of workers. That doesn't work in America, either.

Chapter 3

Total War: The

Cost of

Unlimited

Conflict

(1914–1945)

Source 10 from The Public Papers of F. D. Roosevelt, *vol. 12, p. 71. This version obtained from* World War II Resources, Words of Peace. Words of War, *http://www.ibiblio.org/pha /policy/1943/430212a.html.*

10. President Roosevelt's Radio Address on Casablanca Conference, February 12, 1943

The decisions reached and the actual plans made at Casablanca were not confined to any one theater of war or to any one continent or ocean or sea. Before this year is out, it will be made known to the world—in actions rather than words—that the Casablanca Conference produced plenty of news; and it will be bad news for the Germans and Italians and the Japanese. . . .

In an attempt to ward off the inevitable disaster, the Axis propagandists are trying all of their old tricks in order to divide the United Nations. They seek to create the idea that if we win this war, Russia, England, China, and the United States are going to get into a cat-and-dog fight.

This is their final effort to turn one nation against another, in the vain hope that they may settle with one or two at a time—that any of us may be so gullible and so forgetful as to be duped into making "deals" at the expense of our Allies.

To these panicky attempts to escape the consequences of their crimes we say—all the United Nations say—that the only terms on which we shall deal with an Axis government or any Axis factions are the terms proclaimed at Casablanca: "Unconditional Surrender." In our uncompromising policy we mean no harm to the common people of the Axis nations. But we do mean to impose punishment and retribution in full upon their guilty, barbaric leaders. . . .

In the years of the American and French revolutions the fundamental principle guiding our democracies was established. The cornerstone of our whole democratic edifice was the principle that from the people and the people alone flows the authority of government.

It is one of our war aims, as expressed in the Atlantic Charter, that the conquered populations of today be again the masters of their destiny. There must be no doubt anywhere that it is the unalterable purpose of the United Nations to restore to conquered peoples their sacred rights.

Source 11 from United States Strategic Bombing Survey (Pacific War) *(Washington, D.C.: U.S. Government Printing Office, 1946), pp. 15–17, 21–22, 29–30.*

11. United States Strategic Bomb Survey (Pacific War), 1946

Basic United States strategy contemplated that the final decision in the Japanese war would be obtained by an invasion of the Japanese home islands. The long-range bombing offensive from the Marianas was initiated in November 1944, with that in mind as the primary objective. As in Europe prior to D-day, the principal measure of success set for strategic air action was the extent to which it would weaken enemy capability and will to resist our amphibious forces at the time of landings. This led, originally, to somewhat greater emphasis on the selection of targets such as aircraft factories, arsenals, electronics plants, oil refineries, and finished military goods, destruction of which could be expected to weaken the capabilities of the Japanese armed forces to resist at the Kyushu beachheads in November 1945, than on the disruption of the more basic elements of Japan's social, economic, and political fabric. . . .

On 9 March 1945, a basic revision in the method of B-29 attack was instituted. It was decided to bomb the four principal Japanese cities at night from altitudes averaging 7,000 feet. Japanese weakness in night fighters and antiaircraft made this program feasible. Incendiaries were used instead of high explosive bombs and the lower altitude permitted a substantial increase in bomb load per plane. One thousand six hundred and sixty-seven tons of bombs were dropped on Tokyo in the first attack. The chosen areas were saturated. Fifteen square miles of Tokyo's most densely populated area were burned to the ground. The weight and intensity of this attack caught the Japanese by surprise. No subsequent urban area attack was equally destructive. Two days later, an attack of similar magnitude on Nagoya destroyed 2 square miles. In a period of 10 days starting 9 March, a total of 1,595 sorties delivered 9,373 tons of bombs against Tokyo, Nagoya, Osake, and Kobe destroying 31 square miles of those cities at a cost of 22 airplanes. The generally destructive effect of incendiary attacks against Japanese cities had been demonstrated. . . .

A striking aspect of the air attack was the pervasiveness with which its impact on morale blanketed Japan. Roughly one quarter of all people in cities fled or were evacuated, and these evacuees, who themselves were of singularly low morale, helped spread discouragement and disaffection for the war throughout the islands. This mass migration from the cities included an estimated 8,500,000 persons throughout the Japanese islands, whose people had always thought themselves remote from attack. United States planes crisscrossed the skies with no effective Japanese air or antiaircraft opposition.

Chapter 3

Total War: The

Cost of

Unlimited

Conflict

(1914–1945)

That this was an indication of impending defeat became as obvious to the rural as to the urban population. . . .

The interrelation of military, economic and morale factors was complex. To a certain extent each reacted on the other. In the final analysis the Japanese military machine had lost its purpose when it could no longer protect the Japanese people from destruction by air attack. General Takashima when asked by the Survey as to his reaction to the Imperial Rescript, stated that surrender had become unavoidable; the Army, even should it repel invasion, could no longer protect the Japanese people from extermination. . . .

On 6 August and 9 August 1945, the first two atomic bombs to be used for military purposes were dropped on Hiroshima and Nagasaki respectively. One hundred thousand people were killed, 6 square miles or over 50 percent of the built-up areas of the two cities were destroyed. The first and crucial question about the atomic bomb thus was answered practically and conclusively; atomic energy had been mastered for military purposes and the overwhelming scale of its possibilities had been demonstrated. . . .

Does the existence of atomic bombs invalidate all conclusions relative to air power based on pre-atomic experience? It is the Survey's opinion that many of the pre-existing yardsticks are revolutionized, but that certain of the more basic principles and relationships remain. The atomic bomb, in its present state of development, raises the destructive power of a single bomber by a factor of somewhere between 50 and 250 times, depending upon the nature and size of the target. The capacity to destroy, given control of the air and an adequate supply of atomic bombs, is beyond question. Unless both of these conditions are met, however, any attempt to produce war-decisive results through atomic bombing may encounter problems similar to those encountered in conventional bombing.

The problem of control of the air, primarily of our own air, and should we be attacked, of the enemy's air as well becomes of even greater significance. The most intense effort must be devoted to perfecting defensive air control both by day and night, through the improvement of early warning and fighter control apparatus, anti-aircraft ordnance and defensive fighters, not only from the standpoint of technological improvement and volume, but also of disposition and tactics. It would be rash, however, to predict an increase in the effectiveness of defensive control sufficient to insure that not a single enemy plane or guided missile will be able to penetrate. It therefore behooves us to accept the possibility that at least a small number of enemy planes or guided missiles may be able to evade all our defenses and to attack any objective within range. . . .

If we are not to be overwhelmed out of hand, in the event we are nevertheless attacked, we must reduce materially our vulnerability to such attack. The experience of both the Pacific and European wars emphasizes the extent to which civilian and other forms of passive defense can reduce a country's vulnerability to air attack. Civilian injuries and fatalities can be reduced, by presently known techniques, to one-twentieth or less of the casualties which would be suffered were these techniques not employed. This does not involve moving everything underground, but does involve a progressive evacuation, dispersal, warning, air-raid shelter, and postraid emergency assistance program, the foundations for which can only be laid in peacetime. The analysis of the effects of the atomic bombs at Hiroshima and Nagasaki indicates that the above statement is just as true and much more terrifyingly significant in an age of atomic bombs than it was in an age of conventional weapons. Similarly, economic vulnerability can be enormously decreased by a well worked out program of stockpiles, dispersal and special construction of particularly significant segments of industry. Such a program in the economic field can also be worked out satisfactorily only in peacetime.

In the strictly military field the impact of atomic weapons and guided missiles on strategy and tactics can only be developed by specialists. It is the Survey's opinion, however, that mature study by such specialists will support the conclusion that dispersal of military forces, and therefore space and distance in which to effect such dispersal will be significant considerations; that heavy bombers similar to those used in this war will not be able to operate effectively and on a sustained basis much beyond the range of protective fighters, and that newer types of offensive weapons and new tactics must be developed to do so; that forward air bases will have to be defended or more advanced bases acquired step by step in actual combat; and that the basic principles of war, when applied to include the field of the new weapons, will be found to remain. If such be the case, atomic weapons will not have eliminated the need for ground troops, for vessels, for air weapons, or for the full coordination among them, the supporting services and the civilian effort, but will have changed the context in which they are employed to such a degree that radically changed equipment, training and tactics will be required.

Source 12 from Arata Osada, Children of Hiroshima *(London: Taylor and Francis, 1981), pp. 265–269.*

12. Iwao Nakamura,
Recollections of August 6, 1945

In an instant it became dark as night, Hiroshima on that day. Flames shooting up from wrecked houses as if to illuminate this darkness. Amidst this, children aimlessly wandering about, groaning with pain, their burned faces twitching and bloated like balloons. An old man, skin flaking off like the skin of a potato, trying to get away on weak, unsteady legs, praying as he went. A man frantically calling out the names of his wife and children, both hands to his forehead from which blood trickled down. Just the memory of it makes my

Chapter 3

Total War: The

Cost of

Unlimited

Conflict

(1914–1945)

blood run cold. This is the real face of war. To those who knew nothing of the pitiful tragedies of Hiroshima's people, the scene would seem like a world of monsters, like Hades itself. A devil called war swept away the precious lives of several hundred thousand citizens of Hiroshima. . . .

The five of us [Nakamura, his two brothers, and his parents] left our burning home and hurried toward Koi. Around us was a sea of flames. The street was filled with flames and smoke from the burning wreckage of houses and burning power poles which had toppled down blocked our way time after time, almost sending us into the depths of despair. . . . This narrow passage was covered with seriously burned and injured people, unable to walk, and with dead bodies, leaving hardly any space for us to get through. At places, we were forced to step over them callously, but we apologized in our hearts as we did this. Among them were old people pleading for water, tiny children seeking help, students unconsciously calling for their parents, brothers, and sisters, and there was a mother prostrate on the ground, moaning with pain but with one arm still tightly embracing her dead baby.

QUESTIONS TO CONSIDER

The important thing to remark in the first selection is Clausewitz's view that war must be limited in order to avoid its "tendency to extreme." Notice how he credits seventeenth- and eighteenth-century European rulers with success in this task. In their hands, he claims, war served to gain advantages in negotiations, making it a "somewhat stronger form of diplomacy." What does he say limited the scope and devastation of these rulers' wars? The dramatic change in war, according to Clausewitz, came with the French Revolution, which revealed "all its elemental fury." What did he think brought about this change? Note his remarks about the role of "the people" in war and how a popular war affects the nature of conflict and of peacemaking. Keep his views in mind as you look over later sources. Could total war be a consequence of increasing democratization?

In Source 2, Lloyd George addresses the most obvious cost of unrestrained combat: high casualties. How does he assess British losses in the Battle of the Somme, both in size and in significance? What advantages did he think the deaths of so many gained the nation? Observe his general attitude toward what he calls "this bullheaded fight." Is it what you would expect of a prime minister recalling a great battle? His claim that "the losses sustained were . . . irreplaceable" hints at more than just concern over the number of battlefield deaths. What social implications does he seem to find in them— and perhaps even more in the losses

that Britain's ally Russia was suffering on the eastern front? As Lloyd George points out, the original British Expeditionary Army was a volunteer force. Recruitment required intensive enlistment drives. These campaigns, and the loan appeals made by the French government, prompted the use of new propaganda tools like Source 3, public posters. At whom were these posters aimed? What view of warfare do they project? How does this view compare with the tone of Lloyd George's comments?

Source 4, Field Marshal Haig's final dispatch as commander of the British Expeditionary Force, offers a broad assessment of the first total war. As Haig explains, by 1916 and 1917 the war had lapsed into a series of "indecisive battles" waged only to "wear down" the enemy through attrition. What did he find so unique about this war, leading him to think that Britain's "existence as an empire and civilization itself . . . were at stake?" Think about the "factors peculiar to modern war" that he lists, as well as his comments on the "mechanical contrivances" introduced in the war and the complications occasioned by the size of the armies. His remark about the way women bolstered "our declining man power" merits attention, too. Woman gained the vote in England and other democratic nations right after the war. How might total war have hastened this change?

Sources 5 and 6 show aspects of the conflict's effect on postwar Europe. Valéry's essay alludes to the financial crisis then threatening European nations faced with vast war debts and

Chapter 3

Total War: The

Cost of

Unlimited

Conflict

(1914–1945)

reparation payments. But something else bothers him more. What is it? Note his talk of darkness and overturned lamps. Consider these metaphors in the context of the European Enlightenment. Valéry speaks of the failure of knowledge, science, and idealism. But what is the "spirit" that he says has been so "cruelly stricken?" Think about the war's effect on European claims to worldwide intellectual and cultural leadership. Valéry speaks on behalf of intellectuals, but Remarque's novel voices the alienation and despair that ordinary people felt in the war's aftermath. Notice the young protagonist's claim that the war made him and his fellows "wild beasts." What does he say led them to this extreme? And what does he say they have lost? His lament that they are "weary, broken, burnt out, rootless, and without hope" is chilling. What do these works suggest about the war's psychological and intellectual impact on Europeans—and their future actions in the world?

Although the war affected Americans far less, it led them to retreat into isolationism. The United States thus refrained from helping its former allies sustain the collapsing world order in the 1930s or coming to their aid when Germany attacked them. But once aroused by Japan's surprise attack on Pearl Harbor late in 1941, it quickly resolved on an all-out fight. Source 7, President Roosevelt's 1942 Annual Message to Congress, shows this determination. Notice how he links "modern methods of warfare" with "working and producing" as well as "shooting and fighting" and calls for all-out economic mobilization, conceding that "it will mean the dislocation of the lives and occupations of millions." How much diversion of national labor and income does he say the war will require? Pay attention to his final call for "total victory." Do either the means he proposes for fighting the war or this end suggest concern with limiting the war? Source 8, the poster and song dealing with Rosie the Riveter, represents one effect of this all-out effort: To compensate for the fifteen million people, mostly men, who were drafted into the armed forces, six million American women were drawn into war work. According to these materials, what were they asked to do? How might such work have affected conventional ideas about gender roles and women's rights?

Source 9, Hermann Goering's address to the German people, reveals how the American entry into the war and its escalation into a total conflict began to affect Germany. Despite having control over most of Europe and eastern Russia, Germany was beginning to suffer from scarcities by late 1942. What seems to have been most lacking? Observe how Goering reminds the Germans that in the face of such hardships, they must set aside personal interests and fight as "an entire nation, as a totality." What does he say they must be prepared to give up, and why? His comments on "enemy air attacks" are also worth noting. How does he characterize them? What does he claim they will destroy along with "harmless people?" Do his remarks suggest that the air raids were having a significant effect? What about his reaction to the American threat to wage an all-out economic war against the Axis? Source 10, part of a radio address by President Roosevelt on his return from Casablanca, first revealed the Allied demand for "unconditional surrender," a term derived from the Union terms for ending the American Civil War. What did "unconditional" imply in this older context? How might it have affected enemy fighting in World War II? Notice in this regard the call for "punishment and retribution."

The Allied refusal to negotiate terms of surrender may have prolonged Japanese resistance despite the vast loss of civilian lives to American bomb raids. Source 11, the bomb survey, assesses the impact of those raids. What specific areas did they target, and why? How effective do they seem to have been—and in what ways? The survey acknowledges that atomic bombs were a significant new weapon. Note its shift from reporting their effect on Japan to discussing how they may have changed the nature of warfare in general. What does it conclude? Specifically, how does it react to the fact that nuclear warfare focuses on the destruction of cities and civilians rather than armies? Source 12, the account of the Hiroshima blast, gives a personal view of what this fact means. Compare the way the two documents assess the significance of nuclear weapons. Were they merely a means of making total war truly total or an unjustifiable new weapon?

EPILOGUE

Atomic bombs may have provided the United States with the ultimate weapon for waging total war in 1945, when it had a monopoly of such weapons, but the further development and spread of nuclear arms in the postwar era soon made them problematic. When the rivalry between the Soviet Union and the United States, the two principal victors of World War II, erupted into the Cold War in the late 1940s, further conflict seemed likely. But after the Soviet Union perfected an atomic bomb in 1949 and began to build a nuclear arsenal of its own, neither side could hope to benefit from a future total war. Even a limited exchange of these highly destructive weapons, particularly after both nations developed hydrogen bombs in the 1950s, could mean mutual annihilation. The spread of these weapons to other powers in the ensuing decade further complicated the problem. So, too, did the development of new delivery systems based upon rockets rather than manned bombers. Because of the speed with which such missiles could move and the ability of their nuclear warheads to obliterate most of a nation's cities in a first strike, they ruled out long wars of attrition. All-out nuclear war would probably end in a few hours, leaving both sides totally destroyed—thus raising total war to an absolute but absurd level.

After nearly two decades of a vain

Chapter 3

Total War: The

Cost of

Unlimited

Conflict

(1914–1945)

arms race and a close brush with a full-scale nuclear war between the Soviet Union and the United States at the time of the Cuban missile crisis in 1962, both sides sought ways to reduce the danger of a nuclear war. Unable to negotiate an effective ban on nuclear weapons or reduce their number, they eventually settled for a rough parity of enough destructive power to annihilate each other. Termed MAD or mutually assured destruction, this policy helped to reduce tensions between the United States and the Soviet Union. In essence, it marked their recognition that total war was no longer a rational option for enemies armed with nuclear weapons. If they were to fight each other, they could only do so in limited wars or through nonnuclear client states. Ironically, then, weapons of total destruction may have rendered total war between major powers obsolete in the late twentieth century.

CHAPTER FOUR

BEYOND SUFFRAGE: FOUR "NEW

WOMEN" OF THE 1920s

Beginning in the nineteenth century, women's rights movements in many parts of the world began to pressure governments and other institutions for improvements in women's opportunities for education and employment, for their right to own property and control their own wages, and for access to an expanded public role for women. These movements were extremely diverse, with varying bases for their arguments in favor of women's emancipation. Some women's rights advocates, especially those in central and western Europe, argued that women and men had complementary roles and natures, but that these gender differences did not mean that there should be a gender hierarchy in the family or society. Both sexes, they argued, had important contributions to make to the improvement of society, and expanded rights for women would allow them to better shoulder their

responsibilities. Women's rights advocates in England, the United States, and Russia tended to put more emphasis on the fundamental equality of men and women, stressing the importance of women's legal and political independence and self-determination. Expanded rights for women would allow them to develop as autonomous persons, able to claim "life, liberty, and the pursuit of happiness" as their natural rights in the way that men had for centuries.

Acceptance of these ideas came very slowly, which led some women's rights advocates to concentrate their attention completely on suffrage in the early twentieth century. Through their efforts, women gained the vote in Norway in 1913, in Iceland and Denmark in 1915, in Russia in 1917, and in Germany and Britain in 1918. Women's being given the vote did not end the debate about women's proper role in society, however. This debate continued, but now in a world that was very different from that of the era before World War I. As we saw in Chapters 2 and 3 economic changes and the shock of the war itself had led many people to question traditional values and assumptions and recommend more modern attitudes, beliefs, and behaviors. Women who advocated new ideas or broke with older standards of behavior were often dubbed "New Women" as they fought restrictions on women's lives and debated the proper balance between individual fulfillment and social responsibility for both men and women. Your task in this chapter will be to analyze works by four women who might be seen as examples of the "New Woman" of the 1920s in order to answer the following questions: What do these authors see as essential for women? How do they see the "New Woman" as differing from the women of the past?

BACKGROUND

The movement for women's rights in the nineteenth century—now often termed the "first wave" of the feminist movement, the foundation for the "second wave" of feminism that began in the 1960s and the "third wave" that began in the 1990s—involved a large number of groups with a broad range of ideas.

The division between complementary and individualistic arguments for women's rights was accompanied by a class split within the women's movement, between socialist feminists who concentrated more on working conditions and political rights for all workers and a more middle-class feminist movement that put greater stress on women's education, property rights, and suffrage. The two lines of division among women's rights advocates were not the same, so that there were some socialist feminists who developed individualistic arguments while others concentrated on complementary ones, and some middle-class feminists who stressed responsibilities while others focused on natural rights. Within any of the many groups that worked for women's rights, there was often a spectrum of opinion on these questions.

This diversity of opinion continued throughout the nineteenth century as the advocates for women's rights slowly gained some of their goals. A few European universities began admitting women in the 1870s, and some medical schools reluctantly joined them. Married women in England gained the right to control their own earnings in 1878 and their property in 1882; by the early twentieth century, they could sit on town councils and school boards and vote in local elections if they owned a certain amount of property. Beginning in the 1880s, women in most European nations gained some maternity benefits: up to eight weeks off with pay at the time of childbirth and free medical care. The hours they could work each day were limited, which slowly led to limitations on the hours of work for men.

In the early twentieth century, both middle- and working-class women joined suffrage organizations in great numbers. Especially in England, some of these groups began to use militant tactics such as hunger strikes, mass rallies, and attacks against property, which often led to harsh reprisals such as imprisonment and forced feedings. Others continued more traditional pressure tactics, such as petitioning Parliament. All of this activity ended abruptly when England entered World War I in 1914, and most supporters of suffrage became patriotic supporters of the war. This support, plus women's work in the war effort (as discussed in Chapter 3), led most people to support votes for women, and women over the age of thirty in England were given the right to vote in 1918. (Men could vote at twenty-one, and women's age for voting was lowered to twenty-one in 1928.) Most of the women who had worked so long for this cause—some for more than fifty years—regarded their victory as final, as one that would lead to complete equality between men and women. This sentiment was shared to some degree by women's rights advocates in other European countries.

Other women were not so sure. Many women's groups, especially those not in England, had never put as much emphasis on suffrage. As it became clear that, despite the arguments of both the opponents and the supporters of women's suffrage, women voted very much like the men of their families, some women's groups continued to work for better access to training and employment and more egalitarian economic structures. They pointed out that achieving suffrage, and even achieving the right to own property or to work, was only a small part of achieving emancipation, and they turned their attention to fundamental social institutions such as the family and motherhood. Others picked up the new psychological ideas about human nature and impulses drawn from Sigmund Freud that we traced in Chapter 2, and began to discuss women's emotional and physical desires along with their rational capacity. Others expanded on older ideas about women's responsibility to the community to discuss women's role in shaping the future of the human race through selective breeding, a movement termed *eugenics*. Thus, in the 1920s, the debate about women's proper role did not disappear, but became more complex, with economic and sexual issues joining political ones as matters of discussion.

THE METHOD

The sources for this chapter were all written by women who lived through the 1920s and whose lives are usually seen as very "modern," but the sources themselves differ significantly in terms of their genre, purpose, and audience, and thus must be read somewhat differently. Sources 1 and 4 are memoirs, autobiographical accounts of the author's life that were written and published later. (Sources 5 and 6 are two photographs of the author of Source 4.) Like all autobiographies, they are one person's view of events and reflect the personality and aims of the author. Memories are not always accurate, and people may have reasons to vary their stories from what actually happened. Because we are interested in the authors' attitudes and beliefs as well as the events of their lives, however, memoirs such as these may be more revealing than more objective biographical accounts written by others and based on a range of materials. Source 2 is a brief selection from a longer best-selling book, written both to inform and to persuade readers. Source 3 is part of a brief essay that began life as two speeches to women's colleges, designed to entertain as well as to influence listeners. These sources speak more directly to the issues at hand than the memoirs, but you will also need to read them carefully in order to assess their authors' views on women of the 1920s. You may discover that the four authors agree on some points but disagree on others, so it will be helpful if you make notes on their ideas as you go along.

In order to assess the ideas of these four "new women," it will be useful to know some of the details of their lives. Source 1 was written by Alexandra Kollontai (1872–1952). Born into a liberal aristocratic family in Russia, Kollontai became a socialist and connected with socialist feminists throughout Europe. She began organizing working-class women in the Russian Social Democratic Party after

the 1905 revolution, then spent many years in exile before the 1917 revolution. She was appointed commissar for public welfare by Lenin, arranged the first Congress of Women Workers and Peasants in 1917, and from 1920 to 1922 headed the Zhenodtel, the Communist Women's Bureau. The first five years after the Russian Revolution were a time of many legal changes regarding women and the family: Women were given the right to vote and to hold office; a new marriage law was passed that made marriage a civil ceremony between equals, instead of a religious ceremony in which the husband was given legal power over his wife; divorce was made legal; state protection for mothers and children was mandated. Source 1 is a selection from Kollontai's autobiography, written in 1926, describing events in her life up to that point and giving her opinions about the significance of her accomplishments. Between the time Kollontai wrote her autobiography and the time it was published, she changed her mind about what she wanted to include, and the published version omitted many sections, which appear here in italics. Read this selection carefully. How does Kollontai see her life as reflecting new opportunities for women? What does she see as the most important issues facing women in Russia?

Source 2 is a brief selection from one of the best-selling books of the 1920s, Marie Stopes's (1880–1958) *Married Love*, first published in 1918. Although Stopes initially had difficulty finding a publisher, Married

Love eventually went into more than twenty editions in English and sold over a million copies. It was translated into French, German, Spanish, Danish, Swedish, Dutch, Polish, Hungarian, Czech, and Rumanian; an American edition was also published, but the book was judged obscene and banned until 1931. Stopes was born in Scotland, the daughter of a father who was a scientist and a mother who was the first woman in Scotland to attain a university certificate. (Women were not allowed to receive university degrees in Scotland at this time.) Stopes herself studied science at the University of London and became Britain's youngest Doctor of Science in 1905, with a specialty in paleobotany. Along with her mother, she joined the suffrage campaign. She also began to write about issues that brought together her interests in science and women's rights; *Married Love*, dedicated to "young husbands and all those who are betrothed in love," was her first such work. Stopes's language may at first seem a bit flowery and old-fashioned, but as you read the selection, you will also learn what she saw as essential to both women's and men's happiness. How, in her eyes, should marriage and childbearing be changed to avoid the problems of the past?

Source 3 comes from one of the best-known works in the history of feminism, Virginia Woolf's (1882–1941) *A Room of One's Own*, first presented as two lectures at women's colleges and then published in 1929. Woolf was born in London to a well-to-do family; her father was a statesman and scholar. Her mother died when Virginia was thirteen, and Virginia had the first of many mental breakdowns; she had a second breakdown and attempted suicide when her father died in 1904. Her mental state did not keep her from writing, however, and she began writing essays and book reviews for the *Times Literary Supplement*, and also teaching at an evening college for working men and women. In 1912, she married Leonard Woolf, and shortly thereafter they began a small publishing firm, Hogarth Press, on a second-hand printing press in their basement. Hogarth Press later published many important modern authors, including T. S. Eliot, Katherine Mansfield, Sigmund Freud, and Virginia Woolf's own works. Throughout the 1920s and 1930s, Woolf wrote a number of novels, essays, and short stories, including *A Room of One's Own*. Woolf had been asked by those sponsoring her lectures to speak on the issue of "women and fiction," and used the occasion for a broader consideration of issues facing women. What does Woolf see as essential to her own career as a writer, and, by extension, to the careers of other women? What does she view as the chief obstacles facing women writers of the past? How are the opportunities for young women of the 1920s, her audience at these lectures, different?

Source 4 differs from the other sources in this chapter in that it was written and published long after the 1920s, although it describes earlier events. Its author, Vicki Baum (1888–1960), was born into a middle-class Jewish family in Vienna; she learned to play the harp at an early age and worked professionally as a harpist as a young woman. She married a journalist in 1914, but divorced him shortly afterwards, and in 1916 married a conductor, Richard Lert. In 1926 she went to Berlin and worked as an editor for the Ullstein publishing company. Baum began writing when she was a child and published her first book in 1919. In 1929 she published two highly successful books, *Menschen im Hotel (People in the Hotel)* and *Stud. Chem. Helene Willfüer (Chemistry Student Helene Willfüer)*. The former relates the intertwined stories of various people who passed through a hotel in one weekend; it became the Oscar-winning film *Grand Hotel*, starring Joan Crawford and Greta Garbo. (This is the movie in which Garbo, cast as the aging prima ballerina Grusinskaya, uttered her famous line "I want to be alone.") The latter tells the story of a young chemistry student, Helene Willfüer, who becomes pregnant through an affair with a suicidal fellow-student, contemplates an illegal abortion, but decides to keep the child; she later becomes wealthy by discovering an elixir of youth and marries her much older professor. Baum emigrated to the United States with her husband and two children in 1932, worked for the film studios for a

decade, and then returned to writing novels. In the late 1950s she wrote her memoirs, *It Was All Quite Different*, which were published in 1964, several years after her death. Source 4 is a selection from these memoirs, and Sources 5 and 6 are two photographs of Baum, one from the early 1900s when she was a teenager and one from Berlin in the 1920s. You may find the style of Baum's memoirs very different from that of Kollontai's, as Baum was an experienced novelist and screenwriter and designed her book for a popular audience. What does Baum describe as influential in her early life and development? How were these influences different from those of the past? What does she do in Berlin during the 1920s that might not have been possible for women living in earlier times? Thinking of the changes in women's lives that she discusses, why might she have chosen to include these two photographs of herself in her autobiography?

At this point you no doubt have a significant list of points that the authors have made in considering women's past, present, and future. What role does the newly won right to vote play in their ideas? Do any of their ideas appear to contradict one another or to contain radically different emphases?

Source 1 from Alexandra Kollontai, The Autobiography of a Sexually Emancipated Communist Woman, *edited by Iring Fetscher (New York: Herder and Herder, 1971), pp. 3, 5–7, 10–11, 13, 30, 35, 37–38, 40, 42, 43, 47–48.*

1. Autobiography of Alexandra Kollontai, 1926

Nothing is more difficult than writing an autobiography. What should be emphasized? Just what is of general interest? It is advisable, above all, to write honestly and dispense with any of the conventional introductory protestations of modesty. For if one is called upon to tell about one's life so as to make the events that made it what it became useful to the general public, it can mean only that one must have already wrought something positive in life, *accomplished a task that people recognize. . . .*

. . . I managed to become a member of a government cabinet, of the first Bolshevik cabinet in the years 1917/18. I am also the first woman ever to have been appointed ambassadress, a post which I occupied for three years and from which I resigned of my own free will. *This may serve to prove that woman certainly can stand above the conventional conditions of the age. The World War, the stormy, revolutionary spirit now prevalent in the world in all areas has greatly contributed to blunting the edge of the unhealthy, overheated double standard of morality. We are already accustomed not to make overly taxing demands, for example, on actresses and women belonging to the free professions in matters relating to their married life. Diplomacy, however, is a caste which more than any other maintains its old customs, usages, traditions, and, above all, its strict ceremonial. The fact that a woman, a "free," a single woman was recognized in this position without opposition shows that the time has come when all human beings will be equally appraised according to their activity and their general human dignity. When I was appointed as Russian envoy to Oslo, I realized that I had thereby achieved a victory not only for myself, but for women in general and indeed, a victory over their worst enemy, that is to say, over conventional morality and conservative concepts of marriage. When on occasion I am told that it is truly remarkable that a woman has been appointed to such a responsible position, I always think to myself that in the final analysis, the principal victory as regards women's liberation does not lie in this fact alone. Rather, what is of a wholly special significance here is that a woman, like myself, who has settled scores with the double standard and who has never concealed it, was accepted into a caste which to this very day staunchly upholds tradition and pseudo-morality. Thus the example of my life can also serve to dispel the old goblin of the double standard also from the lives of other women. And this is a most crucial point of my own existence, which has a certain social-psychological worth and* contributes to the liberation struggle of working women. To avoid any misunderstanding, however, it should be said here that I am still far from being the type of the positively new women who take their experience as females with a relative lightness. . . .

. . . My first bitter struggle against these traditions revolved around the idea of marriage. I was supposed to make a good match and mother was bent upon marrying me off at a very early age. My oldest sister, at the age of nineteen, had contracted marriage with a highly placed gentleman who was nearly seventy. I revolted against this marriage of convenience, this marriage for money and wanted to marry only for love, out of a great passion. Still very young, and against my parents' wishes, I chose my cousin, an impecunious young engineer whose name, Kollontai, I still bear today. My maiden name was Domontovich. The happiness of my marriage lasted hardly three years. I gave birth to a son. Although I personally raised my child with great care, motherhood was never the kernel of my existence. A child had not been able to draw the bonds of my marriage tighter. I still loved my husband, but the happy life of a housewife and spouse became for me a "cage." More and more my sympathies, my interests turned to the revolutionary working class of Russia. I read voraciously. I zealously studied all social questions, attended lectures, and worked in semi-legal societies for the enlightenment of the people. . . .

In 1905, at the time the so-called first revolution in Russia broke out, after the famous Bloody Sunday, I had already acquired a reputation in the field of economic and social literature. And in those stirring times, when all energies were utilized in the storm of revolt, it turned out that I had become very popular as an orator. Yet in that period *I realized for the first time how little our Party concerned itself with the fate of the women of the working class and how meager was its interest in women's liberation. To be sure a very strong bourgeois women's movement was already in existence in Russia. But my Marxist outlook pointed out to me with an illuminating clarity* that women's liberation could take place only as the result of the victory of a new social order and a different economic system. . . .

. . . I had above all set myself the task of winning over women workers in Russia to socialism and, at the same time, of working for the liberation of woman, for her equality of rights. . . .

One of the most burning questions of the day was the high cost of living and the growing scarcity of vital necessities. Thus the women of the poverty-stricken strata had an indescribably hard time of it. *Precisely this situation prepared the terrain in the Party for "work with women" so that very soon we were able to accomplish useful work.* Already in May of 1917 a weekly called "The Women Workers" made its debut. *I authored an appeal to women against the high cost of living and the war. . . .*

The Soviet Government was formed. I was appointed People's Commissar (Minister) of Social Welfare. I was the only woman in the cabinet *and the first woman in history* who had ever been recognized as a member of a government. When one recalls the first months of the Workers' Government, months which were so rich in *magnificent illusions*, plans, ardent initiatives to improve life, to organize the world anew, months of the real romanticism of the Revolution, one would in fact like to write about all else save about one's self. . . .

. . . In my opinion the most important accomplishment of the People's Commissariat, however, was the legal foundation of a Central Office for Maternity and Infant Welfare. The draft of the bill relating to this Central Office was signed by me in January of 1918. A second decree followed in which *I* changed all maternity hospitals into free Homes for Maternity and Infant Care, in order thereby to set the groundwork for a comprehensive government system of pre-natal care. I was greatly assisted in coping with these tasks by Dr. Korolef. We also planned a "Pre-Natal Care Palace," a model home with an exhibition room in which courses for mothers would be held *and, among many other things*, model day nurseries were also to be established. We were just about completing preparations for such a facility in the building of a girls' boarding school at which formerly young girls of the nobility had been educated and which was still under the direction of a countess, when a fire destroyed our work, which had barely begun! Had the fire been set deliberately? . . . I was dragged out of bed in the middle of the night. I rushed to the scene of the fire; the beautiful exhibition room was totally ruined, as were all the other rooms. Only the huge name-plate "Pre-Natal Care Palace" still hung over the entrance door.

My efforts to nationalize maternity and infant care set off a new wave of insane attacks against me. All kinds of lies were related about the "nationalization of women," *about my legislative proposals which assertedly ordained that little girls of 12 were to become mothers.*

Now began a *dark time* of my life which I cannot treat of here since the events are still too fresh in my mind. *But the day will also come when I will give an account of them.*

There were differences of opinion in the Party. I resigned from my post as People's Commissar *on the ground of total disagreement with the current policy. Little by little I was also relieved of all my other tasks. I again gave lectures and espoused my ideas on "the new woman" and "the new morality."* The Revolution was in full swing. The struggle was becoming increasingly irreconcilable and bloodier, *much of what was happening did not fit in with my outlook.* But after all there was still the unfinished task, women's liberation. Women, of course, had received all rights but in practice, of course, they still lived under the old yoke: without authority in family life, enslaved by a thousand menial household chores, bearing the whole burden of maternity, even the material cares, because many women now found life alone as a result of the war and other circumstances.

A serious illness tore me away from the exciting work for months. Hardly having recovered—at that time I was in Moscow—I took over the direction of the Coordinating Office for Work among Women and again a new period of intensive, grueling work began. A communist women's *newspaper* was founded, conferences and congresses of women workers were convoked. The foundation was laid for work with the women of the East (Mohamme-dans). Two world conferences of communist women took place in Moscow. The law liberalizing abortion was put through and a number of regulations of benefit to women were introduced by our Coordinating Office and legally confirmed. *At this time I had to do more writing and speaking than ever before. . . .*

A heated debate flared up when I published my thesis on the new morality. *For our Soviet marriage law, separated from the Church to be sure, is not essentially more progressive than the same laws that after all exist in other progressive democratic countries. Marriage, civil marriage and* although the illegitimate child *was* placed on a legal par with the legitimate child, in practice a great deal of hypocrisy and injustice still exists in this area. When one speaks of the "immorality" which the Bolsheviks purportedly propagated, it suffices to submit our marriage laws to a close scrutiny to note that in the divorce question we are on a par with North America whereas in the question of the illegitimate child we have *not yet even* progressed as far as the Norwegians. . . .

If I have attained something in this world, it was not my personal qualities that originally brought this about. Rather my achievements are only a symbol of the fact that woman, after all, is already on the march to general recognition. It is the drawing of millions of women into productive work, which was swiftly effected especially during the war and which thrust into the realm of possibility the fact that a woman could be advanced to the highest political and diplomatic positions. Nevertheless it is obvious that only a country of the future, such as the Soviet Union, can dare to confront woman without any prejudice, to appraise her only from the standpoint of her skills and talents, and, accordingly, to entrust her with responsible tasks. Only the fresh revolu-tionary storms were strong enough to sweep away hoary prejudices against woman and only the productive-working people is able to effect the complete equalization and liberation of woman by building a new society.

As I now end this autobiography, I stand on the threshold of new missions and life is making new demands upon me. . . .

No matter what further tasks I shall be carrying out, it is perfectly clear to me that the complete liberation of the working woman and the creation of the foundation of a new sexual morality will always remain the highest aim of my activity, and of my life.

Source 2 from Marie Carmichael Stopes, Married Love *(New York: G.P. Putnam's Sons, 1931), pp. 8–9, 24, 25, 96–99, 105–106, 118–119, 124–125, 128–129, 136. Copyright 1931, 1939 by Marie C. Stopes. Renewed 1966 by Dr. H. V. Stopes-Roe. Used by permission of G. P. Putnam's Sons, a division of Penguin Putnam Inc.*

2. Selections from Marie Stopes, *Married Love*, 1918

In this world our spirits not only permeate matter but find their only expression through its medium. So long as we are human we must have bodies, and bodies obey chemical and physiological, as well as spiritual laws.

If our race as a whole set out to pursue an ideal which must ultimately eliminate bodies altogether, it is clear that very soon we should find the conditions of our environment so altered that we could no longer speak of the human race.

In the meantime, we *are* human. We each and all live our lives according to laws, some of which we have begun to understand, many of which are completely hidden from us. The most complete human being is he or she who consciously or unconsciously obeys the profound physical laws of our being in such a way that the spirit receives as much help and as little hindrance from the body as possible. A mind and spirit finds its fullest expression thwarted by the misuse, neglect or gross abuse of the body in which it dwells.

By the ignorant or self-indulgent breaking of fundamental laws endless harmonies are dislocated. The modern, small-minded ascetic endeavors to grow spiritually by destroying his physical instincts instead of by using them. But I would proclaim that we are set in the world so to mold matter that it may express our spirits; that it is presumption to profess to fight the immemorial laws of our physical being, and that he who does so loses unconsciously the finest flux in which wondrous new creations take their rise. . . .

Many writers, novelists, poets and dramatists have represented the uttermost tragedy of human life as due to the incomprehensible contrariness of the feminine nature. The kindly ones smile, perhaps a little patronizingly, and tell us that women are more instinctive, more childlike, less reasonable than men. The bitter ones sneer or reproach or laugh at this in women they do not understand, and which, baffling *their* intellect, appears to them to be irrational folly. . . .

Vaguely, perhaps, men have realized that much of the charm of life lies in the sex-*differences* between men and women; so they have snatched at the easy theory that women differ from themselves by being capricious. Moreover, by attributing to mere caprice the coldness which at times comes over the most ardent woman, man was unconsciously justifying himself for at any time coercing her to suit himself.

Circumstances have so contrived that hitherto the explorers and scientific investigators, the historians and statisticians, the poets and artists have been

[109]

mostly men. Consequently woman's side of the joint life has found little or no expression. Woman, so long coerced by economic dependence, and the need for protection while she bore her children, has had to be content to mold herself to the shape desired by man wherever possible, and she has stifled her natural feelings and her own deep thoughts as they welled up.

Most women have never realized intellectually, but many have been dimly half-conscious, that woman's nature is set to rhythms over which man has no more control than he has over the tides of the sea. . . .

[Stopes then includes a long discussion of cycles in women's sexual desires and techniques that husbands can use to stimulate their wives' desire.]

From their mutual penetration into the realms of supreme joy the two lovers bring back with them a spark of that light which we call life.

And unto them a child is born.

This is the supreme purpose of nature in all her enticing weft of complex factors, luring the two lovers into each other's arms. Only by the fusion of two can the new human life come into being, and only by creating a new life in this way can we hand on the torch which lights our consciousness in the sphere of matter.

This mystical and wonderful fact has never yet found the poet to sing its full glory. But in the hearts of all who have known true love lies the realization of the sacredness that is theirs when they are in the very act of creation. . . .

It is utterly impossible, organized as our bodies are at present, for us to obey the dictates of theologians and refrain from the destruction of potential life. The germ-cells of the woman, though immeasurably less numerous than the male germ-cells (the sperm), yet develop uselessly over and over again in every celibate as well as in every married woman; while myriads of sperm-cells are destroyed even in the process of the act which does ensure fertilization of the woman by the single favored sperm. If the theologians really mean what they say, and demand the voluntary effort of complete celibacy from all men, save for the purpose of procreation, this will *not* achieve their end of preventing the destruction of all potential life; and the monthly loss of unfertilized egg-cell by women is beyond all the efforts of the will to curb. Nature, not man, arranged the destruction of potential life against which ascetic Bishops rage.

If then, throughout the greater part of their lives the germinal cells of both sexes inevitably disintegrate without creating an embryo, there can be nothing wrong in selecting the most favorable moment possible for the conception of the first of these germinal cells to be endowed with the supreme privilege of creating a new life.

For many reasons it is more ideal to have the children spontaneously and early; but if economic conditions are hard, as they so often are in "civilized" life, it may be better to marry and defer the children rather than not to marry.

If the pair married very young, and before they could afford to support children, they might wait several years with advantage. An exceptional case is one of the happiest marriages I know. The pair married while they were young students in the University, and fourteen years later they had their first child, a splendidly healthy boy. Though such a long interval is certainly not to be universally recommended, as it is said that it may result in sterility, in this instance it was triumphantly better for the two to have lived normally satisfied happy lives than to have waited for marriage for fourteen years and risked the man's "fall."

There are many reasons, both for their own and for the child's sake, why the potential parents should take the wise precaution of delay, unless owing to special circumstances they cannot expect to live together uninterruptedly.

The child, conceived in rapture and hope, should be given every material chance which the wisdom and love of the parents can devise. And the first and *most* vital condition of its health is that the mother should be well and happy and free from anxiety while she bears it.

The tremendous and far-reaching effects of marriage on the woman's whole organism makes her less fitted to bear a child at the very commencement of marriage than later on, when the system will have adjusted itself to its new conditions.

It is generally (though perhaps not always) wise thoroughly to establish their relation to each other before introducing the inevitable dislocation and readjustment necessitated by the wife's pregnancy and the birth of a child.

In this book I am not speaking so much of the universal sex-relation as to those who find themselves to-day in the highly civilized, artificial communities of English-speaking people. . . .

After the birth of the first child the health of the mother and of the baby both demand that there should be no hurried beginning of a second. *At least* a year should pass before the second little life is allowed to begin its unfolding, so that *a minimum* of about two years should elapse before the second child is born.

The importance of this, both for the mother and for the child, is generally adequately recognized by medical specialists, and some distinguished gynecologists advocate as much as three or five years between the births of successive children. While in the whole human relation there is no slavery or torture so horrible as coerced, unwilling motherhood, there is no joy and pride greater than that of a woman who is bearing the developing child of a man she adores. It is a serious reflection on our poisoned "civilization" that a pregnant woman should feel shame to appear in the streets. Never will the race reach true health till it is cured of its prurient sickness, and the prospective mother can carry her sacred burden as a priestess in a triumphal procession. . . .

It is important to observe that Holland, the country which takes *most* care that children shall be well and voluntarily conceived, has increased its survival-rate, and has thereby, not diminished, but increased its population, and has the lowest infant mortality in Europe. While in America, where the outrageous "Comstock Laws"[1] confuse wise scientific prevention with illegal abortion and label them both as "obscene," thus preventing people from obtaining decent hygienic knowledge, horrible and criminal abortion is more frequent than in any other country.

To those who protest that we have no right to interfere with the course of nature, one must point out that the whole of civilization, everything which separates man from animals, is an interference with what such people commonly call "nature." Nothing in the cosmos can be against nature, for it all forms part of the great processes of the universe.

Actions differ, however, in their relative positions in the scale of things. Only those actions are worthy which lead the race onwards to a higher and fuller completion and the perfecting of its power, which steer the race into the main current of that stream of life and vitality which courses through us and impels us forward.

It is a sacred duty of all who dare to hand on the awe-inspiring gift of life, to hand it on in a vessel as fit and perfect as they can fashion, so that the body may be the strongest and most beautiful instrument possible in the service of the soul they summon to play its part in the mystery of material being. . . .

In marriage each one dreams that he will find the Understander—the one from whom he may set out into the world in search of treasures of knowledge and experience, and before whom the spoils may be exhibited without thought of rivalry, and with the certainty of glad apprisal. Treasures, dear to our own hearts but of no value to others, should here find appreciation, and here the tender supersensitive germ of an idea may be watered and tended till its ripe beauty is ready to burst upon the world.

As marriage is at present, such tenderness and such stimulating apprecia-tion is much more likely to come from the woman to the man and his work than from the man to the woman. For too long have men been accustomed to look upon woman's views, and in particular on her intellectual opinions, as being something demanding, at the most, a bland humoring beneath the kindest smiles.

Even from the noblest man, the woman of sensitive personality to-day feels an under-current as of surprised congratulation when she has anything to say worth his *serious* attention outside that department of life supposed to belong to her "sphere." Thus man robs his wedded self of a greatness which the dual unity might reach.

But in marriage the mutual freedom and respect for opinion, vitally important though it be, is not sufficient for the full development of character. Life demands ever-widening interests. . . .

1. **Comstock Laws:** a general term for the federal Comstock Act of 1873 and various state laws that banned or restricted the dissemination of contraceptive devices and birth control information in the United States.

While modern marriage is tending to give ever more and more freedom to each of the partners, there is at the same time a unity of work and interest growing up which brings them together on a higher plane than the purely domestic one which was so confining to the women and so dull to the men. Every year one sees a widening of the independence and the range of the pursuits of women; but still, far too often, marriage puts an end to woman's intellectual life. Marriage can never reach its full stature until women possess as much intellectual freedom and freedom of opportunity within it as do their partners.

That at present the majority of women neither desire freedom for creative work, nor would know how to use it, is only a sign that we are still living in the shadows of the coercive and dwarfing influences of the past.

In the noblest society love will hold sway. The love of mates will always be the supremest life-experience, but it will no longer be an experience exclusive and warped.

The love of friends and children, of comrades and fellow-workers, will but serve to develop every power of the two who are mates. By mingling the greatness of their individual stature they can achieve together something that, had both or either been dwarfed and puny individuals, would have remained forever unattainable.

Source 3 from Virginia Woolf, A Room of One's Own *(New York: Harcourt Brace, 1929), pp. 37–38, 43–44, 48–50, 52–53, 112, 116–117. Copyright 1929 by Harcourt, Inc., and renewed 1957 by Leonard Woolf. Reprinted by permission of the publisher.*

3. Selections from Virginia Woolf, *A Room of One's Own*

My aunt, Mary Beton, I must tell you, died by a fall from her horse when she was riding out to take the air in Bombay. The news of my legacy reached me one night about the same time that the act was passed that gave votes to women. A solicitor's letter fell into the post-box and when I opened it I found that she had left me five hundred pounds a year for ever.[2] Of the two—the vote and the money—the money, I own, seemed infinitely the more important. Before that I had made my living by cadging odd jobs from newspapers, by reporting a donkey show here or a wedding there; I had earned a few pounds by addressing envelopes, reading to old ladies, making artificial flowers, teaching the alphabet to small children in a kindergarten. Such were the chief occupations that were open to women before 1918. I need not, I am afraid, describe in any detail the hardness of the work, for you know perhaps women

2. Five hundred pounds a year was enough for Woolf to live independently in an apartment (what she terms a "room") of her own.

who have done it; nor the difficulty of living on the money when it was earned, for you may have tried. But what still remains with me as a worse infliction than either was the poison of fear and bitterness which those days bred in me. To begin with, always to be doing work that one did not wish to do, and to do it like a slave, flattering and fawning, not always necessarily perhaps, but it seemed necessary and the stakes were too great to run risks; and then the thought of that one gift which it was death to hide—a small one but dear to the possessor—perishing and with it myself, my soul—all this became like a rust eating away the bloom of the spring, destroying the tree at its heart. However, as I say, my aunt died; and whenever I change a ten-shilling note a little of that rust and corrosion is rubbed off; fear and bitterness go. Indeed, I thought, slipping the silver into my purse, it is remarkable, remembering the bitterness of those days, what a change of temper a fixed income will bring about. No force in the world can take from me my five hundred pounds. Food, house and clothing are mine for ever. Therefore not merely do effort and labour cease, but also hatred and bitterness. I need not hate any man; he cannot hurt me. I need not flatter any man; he has nothing to give me. So imperceptibly I found myself adopting a new attitude towards the other half of the human race. It was absurd to blame any class or any sex, as a whole. Great bodies of people are never responsible for what they do. They are driven by instincts which are not within their control. . . .

For it is a perennial puzzle why no woman [in Elizabethan times] wrote a word of that extraordinary literature when every other man, it seemed, was capable of song or sonnet. What were the conditions in which women lived, I asked myself; for fiction, imaginative work that is, is not dropped like a pebble upon the ground, as science may be; fiction is like a spider's web, attached ever so lightly perhaps, but still attached to life at all four corners. Often the attachment is scarcely perceptible; Shakespeare's plays, for instance, seem to hang there complete by themselves. But when the web is pulled askew, hooked up at the edge, torn in the middle, one remembers that these webs are not spun in midair by incorporeal creatures, but are the work of suffering human beings, and are attached to grossly material things, like health and money and the houses we live in. . . .

. . . I thought of that old gentleman, who is dead now, but was a bishop, I think, who declared that it was impossible for any woman, past, present, or to come, to have the genius of Shakespeare. He wrote to the papers about it. He also told a lady who applied to him for information that cats do not as a matter of fact go to heaven, though they have, he added, souls of a sort. How much thinking those old gentlemen used to save one! How the borders of ignorance shrank back at their approach! Cats do not go to heaven. Women cannot write the plays of Shakespeare.

Be that as it may, I could not help thinking, as I looked at the works of Shakespeare on the shelf, that the bishop was right at least in this; it would have been impossible, completely and entirely, for any woman to have written the plays of Shakespeare in the age of Shakespeare. Let me imagine, since facts are so hard to come by, what would have happened had Shakespeare had a wonderfully gifted sister, called Judith, let us say. Shakespeare himself went, very probably—his mother was an heiress—to the grammar school, where he may have learnt Latin—Ovid, Virgil and Horace—and the elements of grammar and logic. He was, it is well known, a wild boy who poached rabbits, perhaps shot a deer, and had, rather sooner than he should have done, to marry a woman in the neighborhood, who bore him a child rather quicker than was right. That escapade sent him to seek his fortune in London. He had, it seemed, a taste for the theatre; he began by holding horses at the stage door. Very soon he got work in the theatre, became a successful actor, and lived at the hub of the universe, meeting everybody, knowing everybody, practising his art on the boards, exercising his wits in the streets, and even getting access to the palace of the queen. Meanwhile his extraordinarily gifted sister, let us suppose, remained at home. She was as adventurous, as imaginative, as agog to see the world as he was. But she was not sent to school. She had no chance of learning grammar and logic, let alone of reading Horace and Virgil. She picked up a book now and then, one of her brother's perhaps, and read a few pages. But then her parents came in and told her to mend the stockings or mind the stew and not moon about with books and papers. They would have spoken sharply but kindly, for they were substantial people who knew the conditions of life for a woman and loved their daughter—indeed, more likely than not she was the apple of her father's eye. Perhaps she scribbled some pages up in an apple loft on the sly, but was careful to hide them or set fire to them. Soon, however, before she was out of her teens, she was to be betrothed to the son of a neighbouring wool-stapler. She cried out that marriage was hateful to her, and for that she was severely beaten by her father. Then he ceased to scold her. He begged her instead not to hurt him, not to shame him in this matter of her marriage. He would give her a chain of beads or a fine petticoat, he said; and there were tears in his eyes. How could she disobey him? How could she break his heart? The force of her own gift alone drove her to it. She made up a small parcel of her belongings, let herself down by a rope one summer's night and took the road to London. She was not seventeen. The birds that sang in the hedge were not more musical than she was. She had the quickest fancy, a gift like her brother's, for the tune of words. Like him, she had a taste for the theatre. She stood at the stage door; she wanted to act, she said. Men laughed in her face. The manager—a fat, loose-lipped man— guffawed. He bellowed something about poodles dancing and women acting—no woman, he said, could possibly be an actress. He hinted—you can imagine what. She could get no training in her craft. Could she even seek her dinner in a tavern or roam the streets at midnight? Yet her genius was for fiction and lusted to feed abundantly upon the lives of men and women and the study of their ways. At last—for she was very young, oddly like

[115]

Shakespeare the poet in her face, with the same grey eyes and rounded brows—at last Nick Greene the actor-manager took pity on her; she found herself with child by that gentleman and so—who shall measure the heat and violence of the poet's heart when caught and tangled in a woman's body?—killed herself one winter's night and lies buried at some cross-roads where the omnibuses now stop outside the Elephant and Castle.

That, more or less, is how the story would run, I think, if a woman in Shakespeare's day had had Shakespeare's genius. But for my part, I agree with the deceased bishop, if such he was—it is unthinkable that any woman in Shakespeare's day should have had Shakespeare's genius. For genius like Shakespeare's is not born among labouring, uneducated, servile people. It was not born in England among the Saxons and the Britons. It is not born today among the working classes. How, then, could it have been born among women whose work began, according to Professor Trevelyan, almost before they were out of the nursery, who were forced to it by their parents and held to it by all the power of law and custom? Yet genius of a sort must have existed among women as it must have existed among the working classes. . . .

That woman, then, who was born with a gift of poetry in the sixteenth century, was an unhappy woman, a woman at strife against herself. All the conditions of her life, all her own instincts, were hostile to the state of mind which is needed to set free whatever is in the brain. But what is the state of mind that is most propitious to the act of creation, I asked. Can one come by any notion of the state that furthers and makes possible that strange activity? . . .

. . . To write a work of genius is almost always a feat of prodigious difficulty. Everything is against the likelihood that it will come from the writer's mind whole and entire. Generally material circumstances are against it. Dogs will bark; people will interrupt; money must be made; health will break down. Further, accentuating all these difficulties and making them harder to bear is the world's notorious indifference. It does not ask people to write poems and novels and histories; it does not need them. . . .

Nobody could put the point more plainly. "The poor poet has not in these days, nor has had for two hundred years, a dog's chance . . . a poor child in England has little more hope than had the son of an Athenian slave to be emancipated into that intellectual freedom of which great writings are born." That is it. Intellectual freedom depends upon material things. Poetry depends upon intellectual freedom. And women have always been poor, not for two hundred years merely, but from the beginning of time. Women have had less intellectual freedom than the sons of Athenian slaves. Women, then, have not had a dog's chance of writing poetry. That is why I have laid so much stress on money and a room of one's own. However, thanks to the toils of those obscure women in the past, of whom I wish we knew more, thanks, curiously enough, to two wars, the Crimean which let Florence Nightingale out of her drawing-room, and the European War[3] which opened the doors to the average woman some sixty years later, these evils are in the way to be bettered. Otherwise you would not be here tonight, and your chance of earning five hundred pounds a year, precarious as I am afraid that it still is, would be minute in the extreme. . . .

How can I further encourage you to go about the business of life? Young women, I would say, and please attend, for the peroration is beginning, you are, in my opinion, disgracefully ignorant. You have never made a discovery of any sort of importance. You have never shaken an empire or led an army into battle. The plays of Shakespeare are not by you, and you have never introduced a barbarous race to the blessings of civilisation. What is your excuse? It is all very well for you to say, pointing to the streets and squares and forests of the globe swarming with black and white and coffee-coloured inhabitants, all busily engaged in traffic and enterprise and love-making, we have had other work on our hands. Without our doing, those seas would be unsailed and those fertile lands a desert. We have borne and bred and washed and taught, perhaps to the age of six or seven years, the one thousand six hundred and twenty-three million human beings who are, according to statistics, at present in existence, and that, allowing that some had help, takes time.

There is truth in what you say—I will not deny it. But at the same time may I remind you that there have been at least two colleges for women in existence in England since the year 1866; that after the year 1880 a married woman was allowed by law to possess her own property; and that in 1919—which is a whole nine years ago—she was given a vote? May I also remind you that the most of the professions have been open to you for close on ten years now? When you reflect upon these immense privileges and the length of time during which they have been enjoyed, and the fact that there must be at this moment some two thousand women capable of earning over five hundred a year in one way or another, you will agree that the excuse of lack of opportunity, training, encouragement, leisure and money no longer holds good. Moreover, the economists are telling us that Mrs. Seton has had too many children. You must, of course, go on bearing children, but, so they say, in twos and threes, not in tens and twelves.

Thus, with some time on your hands and with some book learning in your brains—you have had enough of the other kind, and are sent to college partly, I suspect, to be uneducated—surely you should embark upon another stage of your very long, very laborious and highly obscure career. A thousand pens are ready to suggest what you should do and what effect you will have.

3. **European War:** World War I.

4. Selections from Vicki Baum, *It Was All Quite Different*

If my lover had wanted me, I wouldn't have given a fig for that confounded virginity of mine. I was constantly in a swooning "take-me-I-am-yours" state. I've often thought since that it would have been better for my libido not to have been kept steaming in an emotional pressure cooker. We, lucky pre-Freudians, didn't know we had a libido; all we knew was passion, love. But he refrained carefully from seducing me. Instead, we sublimated like crazy.

Whatever I became later, this first man in my life shaped and developed it in me. With a born teacher's or gardener's care he raised every sleeping seed in me to bud and flower. He brought order and sense into my haphazard reading, guided me through all kinds of literature, from Andersen's fairy tales up to and including Huysmans, whose Satanism was the latest cry, or Otto Weininger and Karl Kraus whose pessimism put them into the dark niche more or less inhabited today by Sartre and his school. He took me to the great Russian and French authors, and, not only had he read Ibsen's plays, but he knew them almost by heart. No longer was I alone and lonely, happily I gave up my hard, proud solitude. We shared our treasures as children swap colored marbles, searched and found more, holding hands on secret strolls.

Not quite so secret, though. It could not fail that somebody saw us or that we were caught in Father's espionage nets. Earth-shaking scenes were the consequence, strictest prohibition to see that scoundrel again, Mama's tears and screams, once more the house smelled of paraldehyde, it got so bad that I fainted once or twice. I was submitted to some awful, debasing examinations by young Dr. Popper and declared intact but gravely undernourished. If I had not had my job with the symphony and my career as a soloist, Father would have put me under house arrest. He did not realize, the poor boob, that all this necessarily only strengthened my resistance. I reared up on my hind legs, I broke out, I kicked; to myself I had become the tragic heroine in a great drama, battling against a world filled with dust and ashes, the blind stupid world of old people. Not grownups any longer, for by now I was grown up myself, just old, old and stinking with convention and corruption, the corruption of their minds.

One Sunday morning Father put on his top hat and went forth to have a serious man-to-man discussion with the alleged scoundrel. He was going to ask him point-blank either to marry me or keep his hands off. The scoundrel, I was informed, squirmed and stalled. I can picture him; confronted with Father's dry and stern common sense, he must have tried to sound equally reasonable. He gave his word of honor that he never had, and never would have, anything but the purest friendship for me and interest in my talent. He talked about my career that came first, and about his obligations—two sisters to support on a musician's limited earnings, one a spinster, the other a widow in poor health and with several children. He wisely refrained from mentioning the fiancée in the background. He wished nothing but to help me in my career; he had some influence, hadn't had? After all, he had placed me as soloist in several concerts; how could he do that if he was told "hands off," he concluded, with a neat excursion into polite blackmail.

The outcome was a short reprieve, a kind of armistice, a short-term truce. Father muttered that perhaps the man wasn't quite such a fool as my rantings made him out to be; maybe not an absolute scoundrel either, taking care of his sisters, working hard. . . .

This was the Twentieth Century at last. It was called the Children's Century; and observing today the results of sixty years of progressive, permissive, and pragmatic education I often want to shout: And look at the mess you made of it! But, leaving the Freudians to one side and the pragmatists to the other, we, the young people of this young century, felt a brisk breeze blowing around our noses. We kicked out the cluttered bourgeois tastes and musty, cumbersome precepts and the untenable political ideas of the nineteenth-century class society. We looked around. We coagulated in small lumps of similar goals and tastes. By an almost automatic reflex I landed in a little group that called itself no less than The Young People's Society for Music, Literature, and the Fine Arts, the same circle where I had, a few years before, made a mild sensation in our maid's black uniform. We discovered that we were not so alone as we had believed, not outsiders, each individual involved in his or her own private revolution—we were a generation.

Life was easy, we had a good time, much fun, plenty to entertain and interest us. The key to our apartment door was always under the mat, friends would drop in at all hours, the entire Young People's Society for Music, Literature, and the Fine Arts wandered in and out. There was laughter and wit and serious discussions deep into the night, much unveiling of sensitive souls and coarse ribbing of same. Fiestas were held over mountains of bread and butter and sardines at financial high tide or, when the money ran out, margarine and cottage cheese.

But after a while our crowd trooped back to its native habitat, the *Kaffeehaus.* There the young intellectuals would heatedly proclaim new theories about art, sex, politics, and the world in general, exactly as similar young people were doing on the Left Bank and in Bloomsbury. . . .

Those were good years, from 1921 to 1923. Good years in spite of the runaway inflation, the return of hunger and cold, worse than ever. Niedecken[4] and Lert[5] made a fine avant-garde team; together they launched a mighty Handel revival, and created a new style, the first time in many years, for staging opera in general, precursor of present Bayreuth. Mary Wigman left some of her best young dancers with us—Kreutzberg, Georgi, Hanya Holm. Terpis[6] became choreographer, and around this nucleus there was an explosion of painters, composers, singers, writers. Soon they all made a name for themselves, went on to the Metropolitan Opera, to international fame. To me it seemed that for the first time life and art were marching together, the one not just an ornament, but a direct expression of the other. Cubism, futurism, expressionism, whatever name you put on the label, this was how we were, *our* world, so shaken up that the walls wouldn't stand straight, the colors and lights we saw were born of fevers, hunger, nightmares, everything of a clarity more real than reality. Surrealism, of course. We were yearning for the sharply pointed angles, the cut-up forms, the dissonances, the gall-bitter humor of our young poets. Perhaps we were the first generation to tell the truth about war, every war, whether won or lost. We had the courage to say Bunk! to war's glories, to hero worship pounded into malleable youth in all the history classes of the globe. In our total disillusion we threw away insipid beauty and discovered the magic of ugliness.

In Hanover, Lert clamored for singers less covered with flab and blubber, whose moving and acting would put less of a strain upon the imagination of the audience. Terpis obliged by establishing dance classes for them and for any enthusiasts who would like to take part. And would I like it!

We were ordered to come in shorts and loose tunics and—there was the rub—barefoot. A few years later it was discovered that females had legs, but meanwhile a heavy load of shame, secrecy, and chaste covers were appended to those limbs, in spite of all the new freedom. In one of the dressing rooms I changed into my homemade outfit, and I felt outrageously nude. Bare feet, all right, but those chilly, goose-pimpled bare calves, bare knees, shivering stretch of bare thighs! It took me at least five minutes before I found the courage to wade out into the bottomless cold of the ballet hall. (Decent bathing suits of that vintage covered the knees, and decent girls wore stockings and sandals for swimming. Chicest outfit you ever saw!)

After five minutes of fundamental calisthenics I was at white heat, I had forgotten my legs, I left myself behind, which is the ever-new miracle of dancing, for me, at least. And when at the end of class I was allowed to improvise, express whatever I wanted, I felt as though my life had begun only that afternoon. . . .

4. **Hanns Niedecken:** a stage director.

5. **Richard Lert:** an opera conductor and Baum's husband.

6. **Max Terpis:** a choreographer.

I think our marriage has kept some of its pleasant freshness by the frequent stretches of having had to live apart. I shudder when I observe some of those Siamese-twin marriages, those clinging, clutching couples who never draw apart except when they're at last so sick and tired of each other than nothing but divorce will help. Like every girl, I had packed a good load of illusions into my hope chest, the main one being that our marriage was to be like no other, something unique, exemplary, perfect. It's a stale truism to say that no marriage ever is. Our marriage had been founded on the firm understanding that we were not to stand in each other's way, particularly in professional matters. I thoroughly respected Lert—still do—as a musician, a conductor. For several years I didn't think he really noticed that I had found myself a new profession. What I did during my evenings was of no great concern to him, and it was many more years before he ever glanced through a book of mine. That's as it should be. The fictions of women writers are not attractive to men. Musicians, especially, are locked away in their own abstract world. Men, at best, read for instruction, for philosophies, ideas, history. At the worst, they read for the little tickle that descriptions of violence and sexual intercourse so amply provide in certain paperbacks. When my older son was about ten he put his arms around my neck and announced sweetly: "Now I've read all your books, Mum." At which I swelled up a bit and asked, "Well, and how do you like them?" He stroked my cheeks and answered in a condescending tone of consolation, "Well, my poor little Mum, they're stupid and boring."

Need I say that I was delighted with this thoroughly masculine reaction? . . .

Berlin was wonderfully gay, full of a strange electricity. Night clubs—I had never seen a night club until I came to Berlin. We are getting Americanized; too bad, our middle-aged conservatives grumbled, cocktails instead of the noble wines that had been consumed before. "Before," that always meant before the war. Now costume balls in private homes, costumes exposing skin and flesh, and wild goings-on. A little too free for our taste, our doddering elders would snort. But this freedom was precisely what we wanted and needed. . . .

Sabri Mahir was another original who did great things for me and for many others. A former prize fighter known for his astuteness, he was a stocky, barrel-chested man near forty. Born in Turkey, the son of a well-to-do family, he showed the indelible imprint of a good background. As a young boy, he had run away from home and worked his way to Paris: he wanted to become an artist, a painter. When I knew him he was still painting, very dramatic and very awful pictures. I think he was communicating his passion for the well-built body to all his disciples at the training gym near Tauentzienstrasse. He had one ostentatious feather in his cap—he had trained the German heavyweight champion Franz Diener. There were, of course, some lesser stars among the young professionals he put mercilessly through their paces in that invigorating atmosphere of sweat and rubbing alcohol and leather, and its incongruous mixture of sadism and affectionate loyalties. I have never been to

Stillman's, but I assume that Sabri's stable was smaller, more refined, if the word can be applied to a boxing ring. That place, the office and massage rooms upstairs, the gym in the basement, was distinctly Sabri Mahir. In the street, in a restaurant, at a première with his beautiful, soft-spoken blond wife, he was a gentleman; at work, in his gym, he was a roaring tiger, a slave-driver, a Simon Legree made of stone and iron.

As is usual, a few boxing fans, sportsmen, writers, actors handed themselves over to Sabri to be kept in shape. I don't know how the feminine element sneaked into those masculine realms, but in any case, only three or four of us were tough enough to go through with it (Marlene Dietrich was one).

The funny thing about Sabri was that he was incapable of distinguishing between the training of professionals and those who only wanted a good workout. He was relentless. Stamping, cursing, shouting, screaming his commands, he made you keep up his speed, he wouldn't let you off when you felt you had no more breath, no feet, no arms, not an ounce of strength left. A heart attack would be the next step. Roaring in four or five languages, a sort of circus catch-as-catch-can lingo, you were told to take your junk and get out and never show your face again—and maybe your junk would be thrown into your face. At that moment, miraculously, you found the strength to do another ten knee-bends or push-ups. What Sabri gave me, and what I could well use in those years, at the verge of turning forty, was the feeling of my own strength. Each workout was a bout for me, reviving my old war cry "I can take it!" He was in my corner, giving out an almost tangible stream of energy to his warrior—me, five-foot-three, one hundred and four pounds. I had never done any sport; my teachers, both the Professors Zamara, hadn't even permitted me to carry as much as an umbrella for fear I'd ruin my hands. Besides, I'm the most unsportive person possible. The idea of competition, of wanting to win, has been left out of my construction. But win against myself?—ah, that is another matter. In Sabri's basement I lived through a few failures and some glorious victories, such as the time I matched Franz Diener's rope-skipping routine, a champion's test of speed, wind, and endurance. Sabri put one limitation on women—no sparring in the ring, no black eyes, no bloody noses. Punching the ball was okay, though, to develop a pretty mean straight left, a quick one-two; a woman never knew when she might have to defend herself, right?

The self-assurance he carefully planted into me, as if I'd have to fight and be sure to win any day, and the habit of not giving in under any circumstances, did me a heap of good in those years. Even now, in my seventies, I occasionally detect traces of Sabri-instilled endurance, and then I go through with digging another flower bed or writing for another hour. . . .

I believe there are two fortunate conditions for a writer: to be in total revolt against, or ahead of, the times or to be intensely at home in them. I was certainly not at home in the overstuffed times of my childhood and adolescence. Not at home in the times of war, fiery patriotism and swindle, or in the times of Spartakists or the opposite fanatics, the ultrareactionary and militaristic free corps. In Berlin, in those brief years, I was at home for the first time in my own times. I thought, lived, talked, felt the same as most people did; I had the cadence of their speech in my ear and their problems on my mind. I had shared their experiences, so their memories were mine, too.

That's why it was easy for me to write about them, and as easy for them to read my tales. They found in my books what even the most choosy reader likes best, whether he knows it or not, self-identification.

Sources 5 and 6 from Vicki Baum, It Was All Quite Different: The Memoirs of Vicki Baum *(New York: Funk and Wagnalls, 1964). Reprinted with permission from HarperCollins Company.*

5. Vicki Baum in Vienna in the 1900s

6. Vicki Baum in Berlin in the 1920s

Historians have a tendency to pay more attention to change than to continuity in the past; change is often more interesting, and it also tends to create more sources. Focusing only on change may be misleading, however, for it leads us to ignore the power of continuity, and to expect dramatic alterations to occur more quickly and easily than they do. It may also lead us to expect advocates of change to be more consistent than they are, for established ways of thinking and acting are often very hard to shake, even among radicals. This is particularly true when the changes involve sexual relations, family structures, or women's roles, and many revolutionary thinkers had very traditional ideas when it came to gender roles.

The women whose writings are included here provide excellent examples of both the external and the internal force of tradition, and it is important to consider this part of their lives and ideas as well. Kollontai provides the most dramatic example of both external opposition and internal self-censorship. The changes in Russian family structures and women's roles that she proposed were too sweeping for many people—including Lenin—and by the middle of the 1920s there was opposition to both Kollontai and many of her ideas. She was denounced by communist and socialist leaders, male and female; Lenin dismissed her as head of the Zhenodtel and sent her away from the Soviet Union on diplomatic missions. She returned for debates on the marriage laws and other policies during the 1920s, and was viciously opposed. Can you find evidence of this opposition in her autobiography? The reaction to Kollontai's ideas may have been one of the reasons she changed her mind about what she would include in her published autobiography, thus intentionally altering

her recollections of the past to fit her current purposes. The sections she deleted are those in italics; how does leaving them out change the story of her life? How does it alter your view of her sense of her accomplishments and her relations with other party leaders?

Opposition to Marie Stopes was even more vociferous than opposition to Kollontai. *Married Love* was attacked—and banned in the United States—because of both its discussion of women's sexual needs and its advocacy of birth control. Stopes wrote a number of other books on contraception, and in 1921 she opened the first birth control clinic in England, providing information to poor and working-class women. In 1923, the English government prevented the distribution of a pamphlet about contraception to poor women in East London on the grounds that it was obscene, and a Roman Catholic physician, Halliday Sutherland, charged Stopes with experimenting on the poor. She sued him for libel and won her case in a spectacular and widely reported trial, but the decision was later overturned by the House of Lords. As you read Source 2, are there indications that Stopes knew about the opposition to her ideas? Is there evidence that she had any doubts about what she was advocating, like those reflected in Kollontai's revisions of her autobiography?

Finding specific evidence of external opposition or internal self-doubt is more difficult in Sources 3 and 4. Virginia Woolf continued to write and publish after the publication of

A Room of One's Own, and became increasingly concerned about the threat of war in Europe during the 1930s. In 1941, she suffered another mental breakdown and committed suicide by drowning herself in the River Ouse, though there is no evidence this was in any way a reaction to her ideas about women. Looking again at the final section of Source 3, how would you describe Woolf's view of the prospects for young women of the 1920s? How does she assess the recent improvements in educational and legal opportunities for women? How have these made the situation for women writers more favorable?

Vicki Baum's career might be viewed as evidence that Woolf was right, that young women with talent and perseverance could by the 1920s make their living as writers rather than killing themselves as Judith Shakespeare had. Like her fictional creation Helene Willfüer and the satisfied women Stopes describes in *Married Love*, Baum had both a career and a family. Look carefully at the brief section discussing her marriage in Source 4. How does Baum describe her relationship with her husband and sons? How do they react to her writing? Does her response to their reaction surprise you?

You are now ready to summarize what you have found. Drawing both on the sources and on the details of the authors' lives provided for you, what separated the "New Woman" of the 1920s from the women of the past? Now that women in many parts of Europe could vote, what else was viewed as essential for women's satisfaction and fulfillment? What impact would these changes in women's lives have on the men around them?

EPILOGUE

In some ways, the "New Woman" of the 1920s was a very short-lived phenomenon. The economic expansion of that decade was replaced by a worldwide depression in the 1930s, and women who worked were viewed as taking men's jobs away. Married women were subject to being fired from their jobs, and the percentage of women in the paid labor force remained constant or went down. The short skirts and boyish haircuts of the 1920s were replaced by longer and fuller clothing. The ideal woman now was the wife and mother whose domestic activities saved the family money rather than the fit and witty woman who danced, learned to box, and spent time in nightclubs. The expansion of women's suffrage largely stopped. Women in Spain gained the right to vote in 1931, but women in France and Italy would not gain this until after World War II.

Changes such as those advocated by Kollontai ended in Stalinist Russia. The Zhenodtel was abolished in 1930, divorce was made more difficult, and abortion was outlawed. Expansion of education for women continued, as women were expected to be part of the paid labor force, but women were also expected to do all of the work at home, for Kollontai's plans for communal child-care centers and kitchens were never realized. Thus the ideal Soviet woman in the 1930s was both a worker and a mother, which for many women meant an actual workday double that of men. Nazi Germany and Fascist Italy placed an even stronger emphasis on women's roles as wife and mother, with motherhood becoming a patriotic duty. Mothers of many children were rewarded with medals, birth control was outlawed, and the "sexual freedom" of women during the 1920s was described as a cause of national decline.

This rejection of new roles for women did not turn back the clock completely, however. Women's rights to own property and to retain their wages were not seriously challenged, nor was their right to vote (although their votes, like those of men, were largely meaningless in the totalitarian regimes of the 1930s). Women's participation in the paid labor force shrank only slightly, in large part because economic changes necessitated women's work. Although litera-

ture on birth control continued to be difficult to obtain in many countries, in a few it became more readily available. In England, for example, both the Labour government and the Church of England came to approve contraception in certain cases and to allow the distribution of contraceptive information.

The ideas essential to New Women of the 1920s were also not forgotten. When a new women's rights movement began again in Europe (and elsewhere in the world) during the 1960s, it built not only on the socialist and middle-class women's rights movements of the nineteenth century, pushing for civil rights and equity in employment, but also on the thoughts and plans of the 1920s. Economic independence, personal fulfillment, self-knowledge, choice in childbirth, and shared parental responsibilities all joined political rights as appropriate goals, although, as in the first women's rights movement, the tactics for achieving these goals and their ultimate meaning for individual women and society at large were hotly debated.

CHAPTER FIVE

LANDS OF DESIRE: DEPARTMENT

STORES, ADVERTISING, AND THE NEW

CONSUMERISM[1] (1920s)

The response to the death of American department store magnate John Wanamaker on December 12, 1922, was one normally reserved for important heads of state. In Wanamaker's native Philadelphia, public schools and the stock exchange were closed, the city council suspended its meetings, and thousands filed by the casket to pay their respects as Wanamaker's body lay in state in the Bethany Presbyterian Church. Condolences poured in from around the world and included expressions of sympathy from United States president Warren Harding and the secretary of state, Charles Evans Hughes. Graveside services were attended by inventor Thomas Edison, Chief Justice of the United States William

1. We are happy to attribute this chapter's title to William Leach, from his excellent book *Land of Desire: Merchants, Power, and the Rise of a New American Culture* (New York: Pantheon Books, 1993), p. 3.

Howard Taft, soup and ketchup king Howard Heinz, politician William Jennings Bryan, and a host of U.S. senators and governors. Indeed, John Wanamaker was as honored in death as he had been powerful and influential in life.

Wanamaker and men like him throughout the world were products of the Industrial Revolution that swept through much of Europe, the Americas, and Japan in the nineteenth century. Mass production made a host of consumer goods available to the middle and skilled working classes for the first time at reasonable prices. In order to distribute these goods, the institution of the department store was born, the first one opening in Paris in 1852. By 1900, department stores were important in bringing consumer goods to the people in France, England, Germany, Japan, the United States, Canada, Brazil, Mexico, Australia, South Africa, New Zealand, Switzerland, Sweden, Norway, Belgium, and Denmark. Wherever they were founded,

Chapter 5

Lands of Desire:

Department

Stores,

Advertising, and

the New

Consumerism

(1920s)

department stores bore remarkable similarities; from country to country they looked the same: a mammoth retail emporium selling a myriad of consumer items reasonably priced and grouped together in "departments."

Department store founders like John Wanamaker, however, could not simply open their establishments and expect masses of customers automatically to flock in. Wage earners had to be convinced that they actually *needed* these goods, that owning a felt fedora or a silk chemise would improve their status and happiness. Led by pioneer John Wanamaker, department store owners spent lavishly on newspaper advertising in order to *create* desire for the consumer goods they sold. As Wanamaker himself was fond of saying, "The time to advertise is all the time," and almost all department store owners did precisely that. So dependent did urban newspapers become on department store advertising that by 1904 one observer did not overstate the case when he remarked that the "newspaper of today is largely the creation of the department store." And, spurred by the spectacular success of department store advertising, other businesses began to adver-

tise their products and services as well, especially the manufacturers of what became "brand name" products.

In this chapter, you will be examining and analyzing a series of department store advertisements from six countries: the United States, Brazil, France, Canada, Australia, and the Union of South Africa. All of these promotions appeared in the 1920s, which was probably the height of the downtown department store phenomenon. Your task in this chapter is to determine the types of appeals department stores used to convince potential customers that they needed the goods the stores offered. What can these advertisements tell us about middle and skilled working classes' values, fears, aspirations, and visions of "the good life"? Keep in mind that each advertisement may have more than one appeal. Also be aware that appeals can be overt and obvious or may be quite subtle. Finally, note that various advertisements may be directed at particular demographic groups—middle-class women, for instance. In all, how did department store advertisements create what historian William Leach calls the "land of desire"?

BACKGROUND

Several interrelated factors were responsible for the rise of mass consumerism in the late nineteenth and early twentieth centuries in Europe, the Americas, Japan, and elsewhere. To begin with, the Industrial Revolu-

tion and the evolution of the modern factory system made possible staggering increases in the production of manufactured goods. Traditional methods such as the "putting out system" and the apprenticeship system were fairly quickly replaced by mechanized factories where, until the rise of the trade union movement, men, women, and children worked for slim wages with little hope of advancement or in a piece-work system that paid workers, not for their time, but for the amount of goods their machines produced. Beginning in the textile, clothing, shoe, and stick furniture industries, the factory system rapidly spread to most areas of production. Between 1890 and 1900 alone, the production of ready-to-wear clothing doubled; by 1914, factories were turning out almost four times the numbers of cheap glassware, lamps, and tableware as they had in 1890.

Several demographic trends also help to explain mass consumerism's advent. For one thing, Europe and the Americas both experienced rapid population increases between 1750 and 1900. Britain's population alone surged from approximately 8 million people in 1750 to over 40 million in 1900. The number of people in what became Germany in 1871 more than doubled between 1800 and 1900, and France's population growth, while somewhat less dramatic, was also impressive (from over 25 million in 1800 to around 39 million by 1900). Thanks to immigration and high natural increases, the Americas' population increases were even more incredible. At the same time, the birthrate in Europe actually was declining. Population increases, therefore, were largely the result of a higher survival rate, which can be explained primarily by greater food supplies and to a lesser extent by improvements in medicine. Life expectancy in France went from an average of around twenty-one years

in 1660 to approximately thirty-eight years by 1832.

A growing number of these people made their livings in nonagricultural occupations, increasingly in urban factories. Manchester, England, once described by an observer as a "sewer of gold" because of the wealth its factories generated while many lived in horrible conditions, surged from 50,000 people in 1780 to 100,000 in 1801 to 400,000 by 1850. Most of these people had migrated from the countryside as part of a rural-to-urban population shift that took place throughout most of Europe and the Americas during the late eighteenth and nineteenth centuries. In Paris and London in 1850, over one-half of those cities' populations had not been born there. Without these demographic changes, it is questionable whether mass consumerism would have appeared where and when it did.

Finally, in spite of the fact that nineteenth-century writers and thinkers like Charles Dickens, Émile Zola, Karl Marx, Friedrich Engels, and others concentrated their attention on the seamier sides of the Industrial Revolution, for many people the factory system—and the accompanying agricultural and demographic changes—brought better and longer lives.[2] In England, real wages (that is, wages adjusted to take into account the cost of living) actually doubled between 1850 and 1906, and the average per capita consumption of food and goods in Great Britain increased by 75 percent between 1780 and 1851.

2. Zola did call the department store the "cathedral of modern commerce."

Chapter 5

Lands of Desire:

Department

Stores,

Advertising, and

the New

Consumerism

(1920s)

Other nations in Europe and the Americas could boast of equally impressive gains. Therefore, while the new industrial age meant frightful working and living conditions for many, on the whole the standard of living actually improved during the nineteenth century wherever industrialism had triumphed.

Thus the Industrial Revolution increased the ability to produce goods and, at the same time, increased people's ability to consume them. But how were these products to be distributed (sold), and how would the middle and skilled working classes come to perceive that they actually needed them? Small specialty stores that sold only one type of product (like shoes, for example) and street vendors would be insufficient, and mail-order distribution was far better suited to rural regions than to cities. It was at that point that department stores arose to bridge the chasm between producers and potential consumers.

Most of the nineteenth-century department store barons (including John Wanamaker himself) credited Frenchman Aristide Boucicaut with originating the department store concept. In 1852 in Paris, Boucicaut opened Bon Marché, a huge building that contained several merchandise departments. Markups from the wholesale prices were small, meaning that Bon Marché could sell items from 15 to 20 percent cheaper than single-line specialty shops. All items had fixed, marked prices, something of a revolution in retail trade: Before then, no goods were labeled and prices were negotiated through individual bargaining. Boucicaut opened his doors to everyone and began the practice of free returns and exchanges, equally revolutionary for their time. In 1852 (the year it opened), Bon Marché sold 500,000 francs worth of goods. By 1860 it was selling over 5 million francs annually (20 million by 1870), and the modern department store was born. Bon Marché was soon followed by Galeries Lafayette and Le Printemps in Paris; Whiteley's, Harrod's, and Selfridges in London; Wertheim in Berlin; Magasin du Nord in Copenhagen; Steen and Strom in Oslo; Magazine zum Globus in Zurich; Nordiska Kompaniet in Stockholm; Mitsukoshi in Tokyo; Stuttafords in South Africa; A. T. Stewart in New York; and John Wanamaker's in Philadelphia. Aided by architectural innovations (the escalator, of which there were twenty-seven in New York's Gimbel's when that department store opened in 1927) and by technological improvements (electric lighting in 1878, cash registers in the 1880s, the pneumatic tube by the 1890s), department stores became retailing palaces that (as Wanamaker manager Robert Ogden once observed) "added to the sum of human happiness by increasing the power of money to supply the comforts of life."

To entice customers, department stores spent millions on newspaper advertising. In the United States alone, the total spent on newspaper advertising mushroomed from $40 million in 1880 to over $140 million in 1904. John Wanamaker, the bricklayer's son become merchant, opened his first department store in 1877 and is generally credited with being the first to appreciate the value of mass advertising. Wanamaker quickly recognized that mass-circulation newspapers reached tens of thousands of his potential customers every day, and he immediately capitalized on that opportunity. Technological improvements like photoengraving made large "display" advertisements with pictures not only inexpensive but eye-catching. Largely because of his advertising, over 70,000 people swarmed into Wanamaker's Philadelphia department store on its opening day in 1877. As L. Frank Baum (an advertising pioneer who abandoned that field when his enormously popular *The Wonderful Wizard of Oz* was published in 1900) remarked, "Without advertising, the modern merchant sinks into oblivion." Wanamaker and his fellow retail giants recognized the wisdom of Baum's pithy observation. At his death in 1922, Wanamaker's wealth was estimated at well over $25 million.

What appeals did Wanamaker and other department store owners make to their potential middle- and working-class customers? How did their newspaper advertisements create a "land of desire"? What do those advertisements reveal about popular values, fears, aspirations, and visions of "the good life"?

THE METHOD

No historian would suggest that newspaper advertisements of the past (or today's ads, for that matter) simply announce the availability of particular goods for sale. In addition to such announcements, advertisements are created with the intention of making people want to buy those products. Therefore, advertisements contain messages telling consumers why these purchases are desirable. Some of these messages are blatant, whereas others are remarkably subtle—so subtle that readers may not even recognize that a powerful message is being communicated. Yet even though the potential consumers of the past may have been oblivious to their advertising vulnerability, historians can analyze those same advertisements in order to detect those underlying appeals.

Messages communicated in advertisements can be divided into two general categories: *positive* messages and *negative* ones. Positive advertisements show the benefits—direct or indirect, explicit or implicit—that would come from purchasing the advertised product. For example, a *direct* benefit of owning a hat would be to keep rain or excessive sunlight off the head; an *indirect* benefit would be that wearing such a hat would communicate to others that the hat's owner was chic, fashionable, modern, or even affluent. In contrast, negative advertisements demonstrate the disastrous consequences of *not* purchasing the advertised product. And, like positive messages, negative messages

Chapter 5

Lands of Desire:

Department

Stores,

Advertising, and

the New

Consumerism

(1920s)

can be direct or indirect. Returning to our advertisement for hats, a direct negative consequence would be a wet head (cold, flu, ruined coiffure) or a sunburned head. An indirect negative consequence would be to be thought of as unfashionable, frumpy, or even poor. Most effective advertisements combine positive and negative approaches, thereby evoking strong emotional responses that almost compel consumers to purchase the products being advertised.

By 1900, manufacturers, advertising agencies (an infant industry), and department store owners had developed a number of extremely sophisticated and effective appeals that were used in newspaper and magazine advertisements. As you examine and analyze department store advertisements from the United States, Brazil, France, Canada, Australia, and South Africa, make a list of the ways in which department stores appealed to potential customers. Keep in mind that each advertisement can contain several types of appeals, or messages. Also remember that neither the very rich nor the very poor did their shopping in department stores. Elite men and women would have been horrified to have been seen in a department store, and the very poor clearly were not welcome. Department stores were primarily for the urban middle and working classes, and all advertising appeals would have been directed at them.[3]

3. A possible exception might have been department stores in Brazil, where there was a comparatively smaller middle class and where the wealthy did patronize department stores.

In addition, it might be interesting to compare and contrast advertisements from different nations. Were the appeals to the urban middle and working classes in the United States, Brazil, France, Canada, Australia, and South Africa similar or different? How would you explain your findings?

Finally, what comparisons can be made between the advertisements of the early twentieth century included here and the advertisements that fill today's newspapers and magazines? If the appeals are similar, how would you explain this consistency? If they are different, does that signify a change in popular values, fears, aspirations, and visions of "the good life"?

The twelve advertisements in the Evidence section of this chapter are fairly representative of department store advertisements during the 1920s. Sources 1 and 2 are from the United States—Strawbridge & Clothier and Bonwit Teller, respectively. The majority of all department store advertisements emphasized women's clothing, with children's clothing and toys ranking next in advertising space expended. Why do you think this was so?

Sources 3 and 4 are advertisements from the Mappin Stores, Brazil's largest department store chain (they even sold major appliances, like refrigerators). Source 3 concentrates exclusively on men's clothing, whereas Source 4 reveals the very popular market for women of silks and fabrics—for those who made their own clothes. Are appeals to men and women different or similar?

Sources 5 and 6 are from France, the former promoting Bon Marché, generally believed to have been the world's first department store (*bon marché* can be translated as "good deal"). These two advertisements do not contain as much written copy as the advertisements from other nations. Therefore, you will have to interpret from the artwork (as the original viewers of these advertisements had to do) what messages are being communicated. For a clue to the message, look closely at how the figures are drawn.

Sources 7 and 8 are from the Hudson's Bay Company of Canada. Chartered as a fur trading company by King Charles II of England on May 2, 1670, it is perhaps the oldest still extant company in the Western Hemisphere. Are the Hudson's Bay Company's appeals different from or similar to the advertisements you have analyzed so far?

Sources 9 and 10 are from Australia, and Sources 11 and 12 are from Garlick's Department Store in Capetown, South Africa. Garlick's was founded in 1875, and by the 1920s it contained over fifty "departments." What special appeals did these department stores make to customers who clearly felt they were far removed geographically from the latest trends and fashions?

Chapter 5

Lands of Desire:

Department

Stores,

Advertising, and

the New

Consumerism

(1920s)

THE EVIDENCE

Source 1: Philadelphia Inquirer, December 1, 1922. Courtesy of the Center for Research Libraries.

1. Strawbridge & Clothier, Philadelphia, 1922

This Great Store is Gloriously Ready to Take Care of School and College Girls To-day

Daughter home from college and little sister with an extra holiday to enjoy, usually, we have discovered, plan this day for the greatest pleasure they can think of —selecting new clothes: A great coat or a darling of a fur neck scarf for that next big sports event; a dance frock to take back to college, or one of the new costume suits to wear on the return trip, or one of the new mannish sweaters—"all the girls are wearing them, mother, indeed they are—they're all the fashion." Oh! They'll all be here to-day, and we are gloriously ready for them.

Source 2: Philadelphia Bulletin, *November 14, 1923. Courtesy of the Atwater Kent Museum #85.7.15.*

2. Bonwit Teller & Co., Philadelphia, 1923

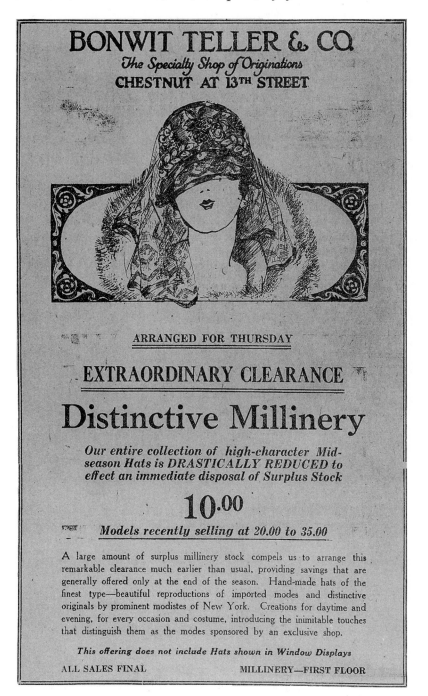

3. Mappin Stores, Brazil

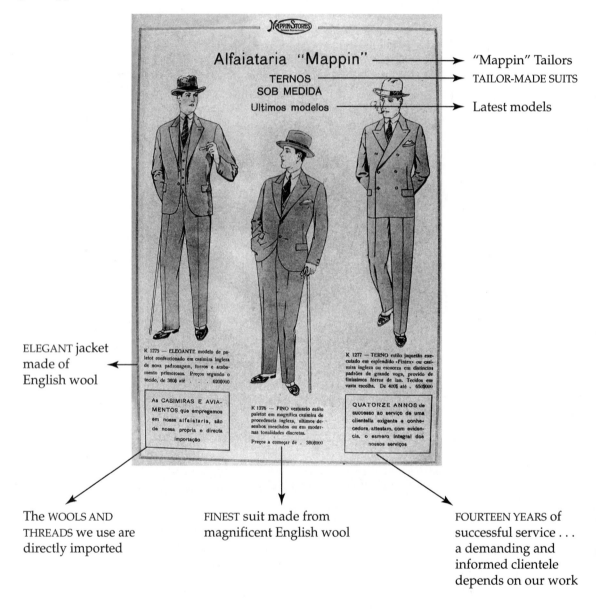

"Mappin" Tailors

TAILOR-MADE SUITS

Latest models

ELEGANT jacket made of English wool

The WOOLS AND THREADS we use are directly imported

FINEST suit made from magnificent English wool

FOURTEEN YEARS of successful service . . . a demanding and informed clientele depends on our work

Source 4: Courtesy of Zuleika Alvim/Grifo.

4. Mappin Stores, Brazil

Silks ←

The finest products from Lyon, Como and Milan ←

COTTON from Manchester →

THREADS →
HARRIS THREADS for dresses. New colors. →

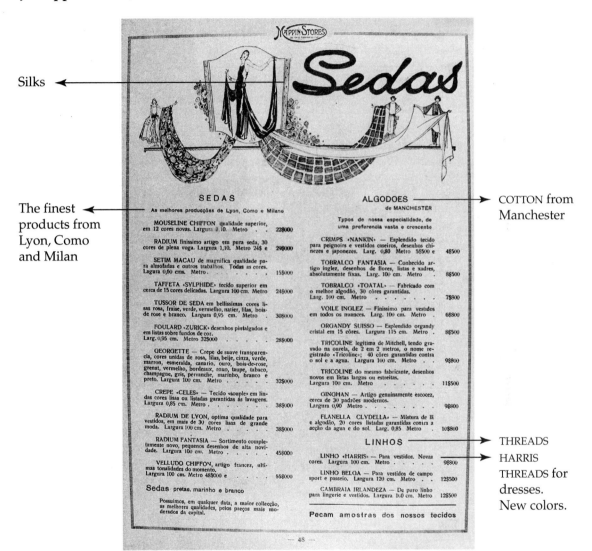

[139]

5. Bon Marché, Paris, 1923

Summer Outfits

Source 6: Kharbine/Tapabor, Paris.

6. Galeries Lafayette, Paris, 1924

General Display
OF THE SEASON'S
NEW FASHION LINE ←

Sources 7 and 8: Manitoba Free Press, April 3, 1926; April 19, 1926. Legislative Library of Manitoba. Prints courtesy of Hudson's Bay Company Archives, Provincial Archives of Manitoba.

7. Hudson's Bay Company, Canada, 1926

Easter Promenade

Last Minute Easter News

Fashion's Smartest Frocks, Suits Coats, Millinery and the Rest

Saturday's Prices Are Decidedly Favorable to You

—Daily arrivals during the past week or two have brought our assemblage up to, and even beyond, the high mark we had aimed for.

—Come, assured of delightful choice among fashion-right apparel for Easter and a service that will garment you completely for the world's greatest fashion season—Easter.

The Sparkling Spirit of Youth in These

Model Easter Frocks at $15.95

—Unusual indeed are their values. Printed silk crepes in newest colors, beautifully patterned.

—Flare and straight line models.

—Georgette combinations and contrasting color effects.

—New sleeves, tuckings and flares.

Easter Coats

Choose From Five Ultra Smart Groups All New Arrivals Here

The "Amhat"
A New York Model

—Exclusive with the Hudson's Bay Company, in chief fon felts with new folded and creased crowns.

—Gay colors of bois-de-rose, blue, sand, green and grey.

—Moderately priced at $6.50

The Beret

—First cousin to the tam, is new in Spring millinery fashions, as are folded crowns. Fisk hats of taffeta silk. Chiefly off-the-face styles. Quilted cording and embroidery for embellishment.

—Newest pastel colors and navy and black. Priced at $8.50

[142]

8. Hudson's Bay Company, Canada, 1926

Sources 9 and 10: Courtesy of the Coles Myer Archives.

9. Myer's, Australia, 1929

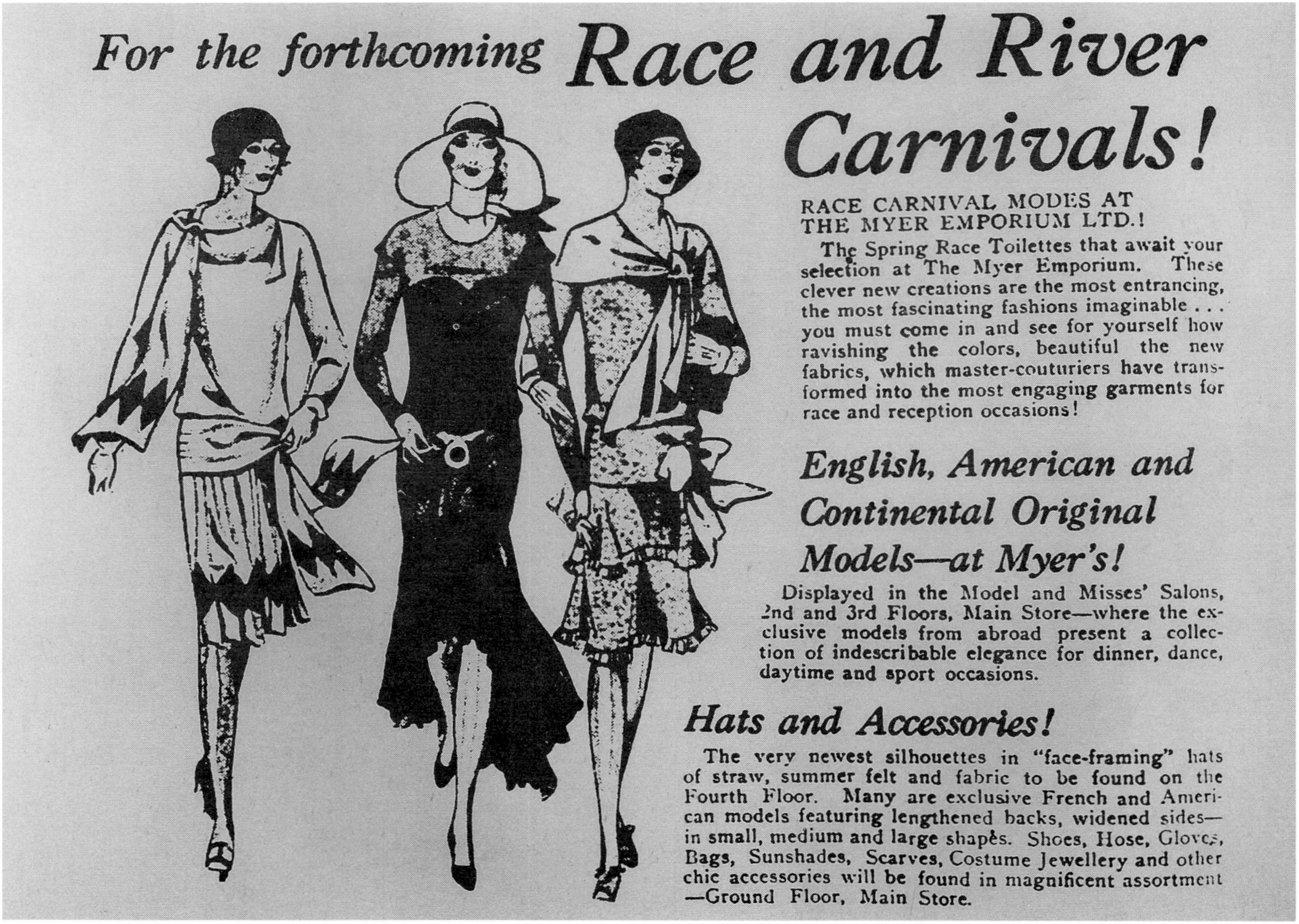

10. Myer's, Australia, 1922

FREIGHT FREE ——— FROM MYER'S. ——————— FREIGHT FREE ——— FROM MYER'S.

A wonderful shipment comes to Myer's !
Daintiest Swiss wovenwear for women!

Unique concessions secured in purchase by Myer Buyer !

JUST OPENED, BY MYER'S! A shipment the Myer buyer journeyed expressly from Melbourne to Switzerland to buy. No looms in the world turn out such perfect woven garments as Swiss looms. The Swiss weaver displays a remarkable aptitude in spinning, weaving, bleaching, and finishing—hence the world-wide reputation for quality that his products have won. For cool comfort, for service and value, the lots listed here would be difficult to surpass. Come, Monday, and see the attractive displays on the 3rd floor!

[The remainder of the text describes the seven items pictured at left, together with their "usual" prices and Myer's "special" prices.]

Sources 11 and 12: Capetown (South Africa) Cape Times, November 4, 1926; December 1, 1926.
Courtesy of the Center for Research Libraries.

11. Garlick's, South Africa, 1926

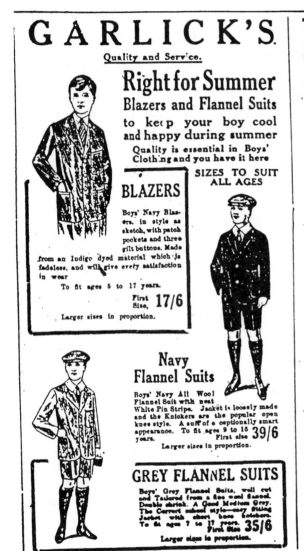

GARLICK'S
Quality and Service.

Right for Summer
Blazers and Flannel Suits

to keep your boy cool and happy during summer

Quality is essential in Boys' Clothing and you have it here

BLAZERS

SIZES TO SUIT ALL AGES

Boys' Navy Blazers, in style as sketch, with patch pockets and three gilt buttons. Made from an Indigo dyed material which is fadeless, and will give every satisfaction in wear

To fit ages 5 to 17 years.

First Size, **17/6**

Larger sizes in proportion.

Navy Flannel Suits

Boys' Navy All Wool Flannel Suit with neat White Pin Stripe. Jacket is loosely made and the Knickers are the popular open knee style. A suit of exceptionally smart appearance. To fit ages 9 to 15 years. First size **39/6**

Larger sizes in proportion.

GREY FLANNEL SUITS

Boys' Grey Flannel Suits, well cut and Tailored from a fine wool flannel. Double shrink. A Good Medium Grey. The Correct school style—easy fitting Jacket with short hose knickers. To fit ages 7 to 17 years. First Size **35/6**

Larger sizes in proportion.

THE SECRET OF HER LOVELY SKIN

SHE ALWAYS VISITS GARLICK'S BEAUTY PARLOUR

A special offer for THURSDAY and FRIDAY ONLY.

MADAME VANN says —

"Do coarse pores or blackheads mar your Beauty—let me clear your skin, clear the ugly distended pores, correct their laxness and keep your skin healthy and fine textured."

FOR THURSDAY AND FRIDAY ONLY

Usually 21.- **5/-**

Madame Vann is expert in all Beauty Culture Arts— Electrolysis, Violet Ray Massage and all Facial Treatments.

PARIS, LONDON & NEW YORK FASHION LEADERS SAY

"No Long Hair, Shingled Heads must remain

and so Garlick's make this very special offer for Thursday and Friday. Mr. ALBERT—who

12. Garlick's, South Africa, 1926

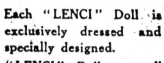

Chapter 5

Lands of Desire:

Department

Stores,

Advertising, and

the New

Consumerism

(1920s)

QUESTIONS TO CONSIDER

Your task in this chapter is to analyze department store advertisements of the early twentieth century to determine what types of appeals these advertisements utilized and what those appeals reveal about popular values, fears, aspirations, and visions of "the good life."

As you examine the twelve advertisements presented as Evidence, keep in mind that department stores for the most part catered to the middle and skilled working classes, not to the elite or the very poor. In London, most upper-class men and women went to tailoring establishments where their clothes were specially fitted—some had their measurements "on file" at exclusive shops. Similarly, the very poor did not shop in department stores either, mainly because even prices this low were beyond their means. Hence department stores tailored their advertisements to middle- and skilled working-class potential customers. In what ways did they do that?

As you examine each advertisement, you will find it helpful to make notes. First, try to determine the *message* of each advertisement. To what emotions is the advertisement appealing?

As late as the seventeenth century, it was illegal in much of Europe and in some of the English colonies in North America for people to "dress above their station"—that is, to wear clothes normally worn by the elite. People were fined for wearing lace at their wrists and necks! By the nineteenth century, democratic revolutions in Europe and America had done away with such distinctions, and many people in the middle and skilled working classes purposely tried to imitate their "betters" in dress. Which advertisements attempt to play upon such yearnings? For example, in the 1920s it was extremely rare for a young woman not from the elite to go to college, and very few college women would have patronized department stores. How, then, can we understand the advertisement from Strawbridge and Clothier (Source 1)?

Middle-class shoppers also were extremely fashion conscious and wanted to purchase only the most up-to-date goods. Indeed, it seems that the farther a department store was from one of the world's centers of fashion, the more advertisements sought to emphasize that these stores carried the latest goods from these fashion meccas. Which advertisements play upon that desire, and how do they do so?

But above all, the middle-class shoppers were interested in value. In addition to the positive messages (be stylish) and the negative messages (don't be ordinary), middle-class shoppers above all were concerned with price. How did the advertisements emphasize savings?

Many middle-class shoppers deferred buying things for themselves, choosing to help their children leapfrog over humble parents into the upper-middle class. How do these advertisements demonstrate this? How does this fit in with middle-class assumptions of "the good life"?

What is remarkable about these advertisements (from the United States,

Brazil, France, Canada, Australia, and South Africa) is not how different they were, but how similar. Indeed, mass consumption in department stores (the "lands of desire") had conquered much of the world. The Industrial Revolution had embraced the world's new middle class.

EPILOGUE

At their peak in the 1920s, urban department stores were important institutions in the industrialized world. To begin with, and as noted above, the department store served as a major way to distribute the goods that industrialism's factories continued to churn out. But in order to perform this function, department stores needed to convince a new generation of consumers, many of whom had been used to making their own clothing, tools, furniture, and toys, that it actually *needed* the goods that department stores offered for sale. This they did by newspaper advertising, using appeals to the middle and working classes to be smart, up-to-date, and stylish, to be generous parents—and all of this at affordable prices and in giant consumer palaces in which they were treated like royalty.

As you can see by the advertisements from these six countries, mass production and mass consumption through the department store led to a homogenization of dress, furniture, and other goods. Accounting for climate, the middle and working classes in the industrial nations (as well as those in other nations who could afford imported goods) began to dress alike, something they had not done previously when they made most of their own clothes and accessories. Regional variations began to fade as department stores constantly urged the up-and-coming to buy the latest goods from Paris, London, or New York.

The department store was a major factor in the return of middle-class women to the center city, a place they had abandoned in the period from the 1830s to the 1850s as dirty, dangerous, and dominated by males. But department stores, realizing that middle-class women often controlled the homes' purse strings, made every effort to draw middle-class women back downtown. To assist these women with their purchases, department stores offered employment to female salesclerks, albeit at wages considerably lower than those of their male counterparts. By 1907, Germany boasted of approximately 200 department stores, where 80 percent of the clerks were women. In the United States, department stores in 1920 gave employment to 350,000 women salesclerks. A few women rose from salesclerks to buyers, positions considerably elevated in both pay and status. On the other hand, the proliferation of women shoppers also led to an increase in female shoplifters who could operate more boldly amid the new thousands of women shoppers and staff. Thus department stores added employment opportunities—both legal

Chapter 5

Lands of Desire:

Department

Stores,

Advertising, and

the New

Consumerism

(1920s)

and illegal—for women in industrialized nations.[4]

Although no one could have predicted it, John Wanamaker's death in 1922 came at about the peak of the center-city department store. The Great Depression of the 1930s and World War II (in Europe 1939–1945) severely curtailed consumption, although American journalist James Rorty maintains that the "advanced system of dream-manufacture" survived these periods of cutbacks in the manufacture of civilian consumer goods. At war's end, led by the United States, the industrialized world experienced the profound demographic shift known as *suburbanization,* in which people from the cities and the rural areas took up residence in the rimlands surrounding the urban centers. In the United States, in 1900 a bare 5.8 percent of Americans lived in suburbs. By 1990 that figure had exploded to 46.2 percent, and fourteen of the nation's most populous states had suburban populations over 50 percent.

In the United States and elsewhere, suburbanites often did not return to the city center to shop. By 1978, the United States had over 117 million registered automobiles, which would have created massive congestion and parking problems had shoppers wished to do so. Increasingly suburbanites made their purchases at massive shopping malls, which offered convenience, ample parking, and a variety of retail stores. In the United States, in 1945 only eight shopping malls existed; by 1960, almost 4,000 catered to consumers. Suburbanization proceeded at slower paces in other nations, but the demographic shifts were nonetheless significant. Within a half-century of the department store's peak in the 1920s, the massive downtown palaces of consumer desire were either closed or on the wane. Their own branch establishments in the shopping malls were pale imitations of the center-city retail jewels.

Nevertheless, in its comparatively brief lifetime the department store performed a number of important economic and social functions for the industrialized world. Perhaps most important was its impact on the value systems of the industrialized nations. As middle and skilled working-class people began to shift their self-definition and their definitions of others from who we (they) *are* to what we (they) *own,* a major upheaval in world-views was taking place, both in the industrialized nations and elsewhere.[5] People might continue to tell themselves that money does not buy happiness, but judging by their actions, a decreasing number of men and women actually believed it.

4. On women shoplifters in the United States, see Elaine B. Abelson, *When Ladies Go A-Thieving: Middle-Class Shoplifters in the Victorian Department Store* (New York: Oxford University Press, 1989).

5. According to *The New York Times* (Dec. 27, 1991, and Aug. 15, 1992), the Nike Corporation, manufacturers of athletic shoes and sportswear, recorded a 1991 profit of $3 billion, while paying its Indonesian sneaker-makers $1.03 a day.

CHAPTER SIX

THE INDUSTRIAL CRISIS AND THE

CENTRALIZATION OF GOVERNMENT

(1924–1939)

On August 7, 1931, Britain's Chancellor of the Exchequer Philip Snowden wrote an alarming letter to Prime Minister Ramsay MacDonald; in part, it read,

> I have been thinking seriously and constantly about the whole situation these last few days, and the more I think the more I am convinced of the terrible gravity of it. . . . We cannot allow matters to drift into utter chaos, and we are perilously near that.[1]

The complete letter makes it clear that Snowden was referring to the Great Depression, the economic catastrophe that struck Europe, the Americas, and portions of Africa, Asia, the Middle East, and Oceania in the late 1920s and 1930s. By 1931 it had become evident that recovery was not in the

1. Snowden to MacDonald, August 7, 1931, quoted in David Marquand, *Ramsay MacDonald* (London: Jonathan Cape, 1977), p. 613.

immediate future. Rather, the situation was growing increasingly grave. Prices of both industrial and agricultural products had collapsed, with world crop prices (which still represented 40 percent of all world trade) only 38.9 percent of what they had been in 1923–1925. Unemployment in the industrialized nations was staggering, creating severe social problems and making millions of men and women potentially easy targets for anyone who promised a return to prosperity. Investments and savings were wiped out as securities markets collapsed around the world and bank failures and bankruptcies mounted. The failure of the Austrian State Bank (Credit Anstalt) in May 1931 dragged other banks, in Germany and in central Europe, down with it, while in the United States the banking system was in a shambles. Bankruptcies of private businesses reached record proportions in Germany and the United States. In Great Britain, the government was in the process of defaulting on its annual debt payment

Chapter 6

The Industrial

Crisis and the

Centralization of

Government

(1924–1939)

to the United States. Indeed, Snowden did not exaggerate the bleakness of the economic situation.

The economic collapse caused tremors in the political arena as well. In Great Britain, the Labour Party government was near extinction and would be succeeded at the end of 1931 by a National Coalition government. And in the United States, the Democratic Party made healthy gains in the 1930 off-year elections and appeared poised to chase President Herbert Hoover and the Republicans from the White House in 1932. More ominously, in Germany, the September 1930 elections increased the number of Reichstag seats held by Adolf Hitler's National Socialist (Nazi) Party from 12 to 107. In Japan, parliamentary government found the military to be increasingly out of control. And where there was not political instability, there were other grim repercussions: harsh authoritarian governments in Portugal, Austria, and Spain; the Great Purge in the Soviet Union in 1936–1937; and a rise in militarism in Italy under Benito Mussolini.

Whether unstable or not, all of these governments had to devise methods to respond to the economic catastrophe, the longest and deepest industrial depression the world ever had seen.

Your task in this chapter is twofold. First, you must read and analyze selections from the speeches of four government leaders during the Great Depression: Ramsey MacDonald (prime minister of Great Britain, 1924, 1929–1935), Franklin Roosevelt (president of the United States, 1933–1945), Adolf Hitler (chancellor of Germany, 1933–1945), and Hashimoto Kingoro (prominent Japanese army officer, expansionist, and politician). Then, having analyzed those speeches, you should examine the sets of statistics that follow the speeches to see how the proposals you read about in the speeches were put into effect. How did each of the four major industrialized nations (Great Britain, the United States, Germany, and Japan) choose to combat the Great Depression? What were the principal similarities between their approaches? the differences?

BACKGROUND

In order to understand the gravity of the worldwide depression of the 1930s, we should begin by examining the long-term structural changes in the world economy that led to this depression. For most of the nineteenth century, Great Britain had been the world's industrial leader and as such had played a crucial role in the international economy. As the

birthplace of the Industrial Revolution in the late 1700s, Britain had taken an early lead in the manufacturing of textiles, clothing, and iron products, all of which were exported to Britain's empire and elsewhere. Profits from manufacturing, shipping, and insurance services had made London a world financial center that directed the extraction and importation of raw materials, the production of finished goods from those raw materials, and the shipment of manufactured products throughout the world.

The gradual spread of the Industrial Revolution not only challenged Great Britain's economic and financial dominance but also resulted in profound dislocations in the international economy. By the end of the nineteenth century, both Germany and the United States equaled Britain's industrial capacity; Japan was offering aggressive rivalry for Asian markets; and France, Italy, Russia, and nations in Latin America were industrializing as well, albeit more slowly. Therefore, nations that once had been primarily importers of industrial products were now beginning to produce these products themselves, thereby decreasing their dependence on the older industrial powers and even generating industrial surpluses that they were able to export into a vastly more competitive market. Inevitably, this industrial proliferation resulted in intense competition between nations for raw materials, fuel, and (most importantly) markets for manufactured goods. The imperialistic scramble for colonies that gripped the West in the late nineteenth century was a direct product of that competition. Some historians believe that the outbreak of war in Europe in 1914 was another.

At the same time that widespread industrialization was altering the traditional structure of the world economy, the industrial nations were faced with a major agricultural crisis. Worldwide overproduction (in some crops caused by mechanization of farms) drove agricultural prices down until farmers and agricultural workers could no longer afford to buy the manufactured goods pouring off world assembly lines. Those farmers who raised wheat and coffee were especially hard hit, in part because they had mortgaged their farms to buy more land to take advantage of high crop prices in the 1920s. Faced with ruin, millions of farmers abandoned rural regions for the cities, hoping to find jobs in factories. In Japan alone, the urban population went from 12 percent in 1895 to over 45 percent by 1935. And in the United States, the 1920 federal census revealed for the first time over 50 percent of Americans living in cities and towns. But factories, forced to compete with their counterparts throughout the world, could not sell all they were able to produce and therefore could not even hope to employ the horde of rural-to-urban migrants.

Thus, even before the Great War erupted in Europe in 1914, the world economy was undergoing some fundamental structural changes that hinted at some rather frightening consequences. Increased international industrial competition, the collapse of world agricultural prices, and the rural-to-urban migration into already troubled industrial cities all spelled difficulties ahead.

The Great War (World War I, 1914–1918) brought further dislocations and world economic instability. The chief beneficiary of the conflict was the United States, already the world's most potent industrial nation before the outbreak of war (by 1913 the United States was producing one-third of the world's manufactured goods). Emerging from the war virtually unscathed, the United States immediately became

Chapter 6
The Industrial
Crisis and the
Centralization of
Government
(1924–1939)

the world's creditor, with billions of dollars of wartime and postwar reconstruction loans owed by the other participants.[2] Almost overnight, New York replaced London as the world's financial center (by 1930 the U.S. Federal Reserve held over half of the world's stock of gold), and American manufacturing, stimulated by massive production and consumption of automobiles, steel, rubber, and electrical products (radios, vacuum cleaners, refrigerators, and the like) and extensive housing construction, experienced a sustained boom almost unmatched in the history of the Industrial Revolution.

The postwar world was not so pleasant for other nations. After a brief postwar recovery, Great Britain slumped into a sustained recession for most of the 1920s, with never fewer than a million workers unemployed after March 1921. To combat hard times, British leaders were forced to keep wages down in order to keep production costs down (this made British exports cheaper but precipitated the General Strike of 1926) and to raise interest rates (this restored value to the British pound, but choked off borrowing). Once the world's industrial leader, Great Britain in the 1920s was slipping rapidly.

In Germany, the situation was even more distressing. Led by a vengeful France, the victorious nations of World War I demanded that Germany pay huge reparations to compensate for wartime damages it had

inflicted. Outraged by German non-payment, in 1923 French and Belgian forces marched into the Ruhr (Germany's industrial heartland) to force payments or, failing that, to seize anything of value. The Germans responded with passive resistance and printed money to assist the Ruhr's residents. The German currency, already seriously inflated, simply became worthless and the entire economy collapsed, only to be propped up later by continued loans from the United States.[3] By the late 1920s, Germany was borrowing money from the United States in order to make reparation payments to France, Britain, and Belgium, which in turn were repaying their own loans to the United States. These practices were extremely dangerous, since the whole system rested on funding by the United States. Moreover, the cry for reparations left a feeling of extreme bitterness in Germany. Even the French recognized this, as General Ferdinand Foch remarked of the Treaty of Versailles, "This is not a Peace. It is an Armistice for twenty years." Foch's dire prediction was off the mark by only two months.[4]

Japan had profited immensely from World War I, as it had been able to gain access to markets in Asia that were traditionally controlled by Eur-

2. Even the majority of wartime and postwar relief deliveries by the United States were not gifts but loans—63 percent, as opposed to 29 percent cash sales and only 8 percent outright gifts.

3. Germany's wholesale price index (1913 = 100) was 245 in 1918, 800 in 1919, 1,400 in 1920, and had reached 126 *trillion* by December 1923.

4. Germany was forced to sign the Treaty of Versailles ending World War I on June 28, 1919; in response to Hitler's invasion of Poland, Britain and France declared war on Germany on September 3, 1939, thus beginning World War II.

ope and the United States. Between 1914 and 1919, the Japanese merchant fleet doubled in size, and some corporations experienced such enormous windfalls that they declared dividends of 100 percent of par value on their stock. But at the close of World War I Europe and the United States returned to Asia and shoved the Japanese out of their recently won markets. The Japanese economy collapsed in 1920, and many banks were forced to close. In addition, rapid population growth (from 44 million people in 1900 to 73 million by 1940) meant that for the first time Japan would have to become an importer of food rather than an exporter. Partial recovery came with a drop in the value of the yen in 1924, which made Japanese exports somewhat more attractive. But Japan still faced massive problems: How was the nation to secure access to raw materials for its industries (especially oil to fuel the factories) and markets for its manufactured goods?

The New York stock market crash of October 1929 was the push that toppled the whole unstable mechanism. American banks and investors, forced to absorb massive losses incurred because they had been speculating in the market, cut off loans to Europe and tried to call back money they already had loaned. In an effort to keep out foreign manufactured goods and thereby protect its own industries, the United States also raised tariffs, setting off a wave of retaliatory increases in other nations. It was as if each nation was trying to seal itself up, like a watertight compartment, so as to solve its own economic troubles—an isolationist policy that was both shortsighted and ultimately disastrous.[5]

Great Britain's economy, already paralyzed, sickened even more, with unemployment gradually climbing to 2,725,000 by December 1930. Prime Minister Ramsay MacDonald mourned, "Is the sun of my country sinking?" Dependent on foreign loans, Germany's economy simply fell apart. The government tried to cut the budget, with the result that by the beginning of 1932 one-third of Germany's work force was unemployed and another third was working only part-time. By late 1932, 25 percent of U.S. workers were unemployed and banks were totally closed or only partially operating in forty-seven of the nation's forty-eight states. In Japan, as elsewhere, production and prices both plummeted, while unemployment crept up. For those who had jobs, wages were but 69 percent of what they had been in 1926 (rural cash incomes were only 33 percent), and exports by 1931 had dropped 50 percent. Thus virtually all nations that sought to become participants in the world economic network saw their national economies spiral downward, almost out of control. Worldwide production of manufactured goods (by long-time and newly industrialized nations) outpaced consumers' abilities to purchase these goods. As surplus items piled up in warehouses, manufacturers were forced to discharge or

5. Over thirty nations had formally protested to U.S. President Herbert Hoover about the tariff, and a thousand economists had urged him not to sign the bill.

Chapter 6

The Industrial

Crisis and the

Centralization of

Government

(1924–1939)

lay off workers, who then could buy even less than they had before. Farmers and agricultural workers, faced with declining prices, tried to produce even more, which in turn drove farm prices even lower. The world's worst industrial depression had begun.

The worldwide economic collapse had serious political ramifications in virtually every industrial nation. In Britain and the United States, the party in power when the Depression finally struck saw its power dramatically erode. In Great Britain, MacDonald (of the Labour Party) was able to stay on as prime minister, but he was forced to preside over a National Coalition government of Conservatives, Labourites, and Liberals. In the United States, Republican Herbert Hoover was ousted from the presidency by Democrat Franklin Roosevelt, who offered the vague promise of a "new deal" to the American people. In Germany, voters turned to the National Socialists and Adolf Hitler, who preached a message of

recovery, national pride, attacks on the struggling Weimar government, and a virulent anti-Semitism. In January 1933, backed by his own party as well as by powerful non-Nazi right-wing politicians and businessmen, Hitler was named chancellor of the German Republic. In Japan, the military increasingly appeared to be the best hope to lead the rapidly industrializing nation out of its economic doldrums as well as to counteract what many Japanese saw as an unhealthy embrace of Western culture (films, clothing, cigarette smoking, Western alcoholic beverages, Western dancing, and more) by middle-class young people.[6]

Each nation ultimately devised a plan for rescuing itself. By examining and analyzing the speeches of four prominent leaders of Great Britain, the United States, Germany, and Japan, respectively, you will be able to determine how the leaders of each of the major industrialized powers proposed to battle the Great Depression.

THE METHOD

This problem contains two types of evidence: (1) speeches by national leaders of Great Britain, the United States, Germany, and Japan concerning how the nation ought to combat the worldwide economic depression of the 1930s, and (2) statistics that will help you see how the proposals you read about in the speeches were put into effect.

Begin by examining and analyzing the four speeches. What does each

speaker see as the principal problems his nation faces? How does each speaker propose that his nation approach those problems? Be careful to read between the lines for more subtle messages. For example, in his speech to the Nazi *Parteitag* (party convention) on September 10, 1936, Hitler brags of the "roaring and

6. The 1920s saw the advent in Japan of that nation's version of the "flaming youth" of the West. In the United States, women of this group were nicknamed flappers, and in Japan, such a woman was referred to as a *modan garu*, a Japanese variation of the English words "modern girl"; a male was called a *modan boi*.

hammering of the machines of the German resurrection" in the Krupp factories. What did Krupp manufacture primarily? Make notes as you go along.

Keep in mind that the *purpose* of a speech most often is *not* to present an objective picture of the topic at hand, in this case how to deal with economic disaster. Rather, the purpose of a speech is to convince, to exhort, to "sell" a particular idea or program. Thus these speeches are better classified as *propaganda* than as objective analyses of a situation.

Even so, both the speaker's analysis of the problems and the proposed solutions must resonate with his listeners. Otherwise, the speech—and the particular approach—might well be rejected by its audience.

After you have read, examined, and analyzed the four speeches, move on to the sets of statistics that follow them. Many students greet statistics with a mixture (to borrow from writer Hunter S. Thompson) of "fear and loathing." And yet, understanding and being able to work with statistics is as critical to today's men and women as their ability to use computers, operate cellular telephones, or order products over the Internet. Once having learned the skills of analyzing and even generating sets of statistics, many people come to understand how indispensable they are to our knowledge. Indeed, a good number of people have even confessed that they enjoy working with statistics.

As you examine any set of statistics, ask three questions: (1) What variable is being measured in this set?

(2) How does this variable change over time? (3) How does this set relate to the other sets and to the economic picture as a whole? Think of each set as a piece of a picture puzzle; by answering question 3 for each set, you will be able to see where that set fits into the overall picture. Whenever you begin to analyze any set of statistics, ask those three questions.

The first statistical set you will confront (Source 5) is an *index*. An index is a statistical measure designed to show changes in a variable (such as industrial production) *over time*. A *base year* is selected and given the value of 100. The index for other years is then expressed as a percentage of the base year level.

Look at the index of industrial production for Germany between 1929 and 1938 (Source 5). How does Germany's industrial production change over time? How can you account for that change? Germany's industrial production did rise significantly (more than doubling between 1933 and 1938) and unemployment (Source 6) did fall, to around 2.0 percent by 1938. How was Germany able to accomplish this impressive feat? Do any of the other statistical sets help you to answer that question?

As you can see, each of the statistical sets is related to all the others. Taking one nation-state at a time, link the sets together like links in a chain. In this way, you will be able to assess the economic problems that each nation faced and to observe how each nation attempted to overcome its economic difficulties. Note that we

Chapter 6
The Industrial
Crisis and the
Centralization of
Government
(1924–1939)

do not have all the statistical evidence we would like to have—historians rarely do. Let's use Germany again as an example. If you look at the expenditures of the German government from 1924 on (Source 7), you will notice that no statistics are available after 1934; can you guess why? By looking at the government's revenues, however, you can see that from 1924 to 1934 the German government's expenditures almost always exceeded revenues (1933 was the lone exception). Since we do have revenue figures after 1934, and since expenditures in documented years almost always exceeded those revenues, it is reasonable for us to suppose that the German government's expenditures after 1934 were roughly equal to (or greater than) revenues. With this kind of logic, historians can fill in some of the blanks where statistics are missing.

A *tariff* is a tax on *imports* from other nations. Governments may enact tariffs to raise revenues, or they may raise tariff duties so high in order to discourage imports—thus helping native industries. What does Source 8 tell you?

Finally, there are some sets of statistics dealing with military expenditures (Sources 9 to 11). Why are they included in this problem? How (if at all) do they relate to the speeches?

How did each of the four major industrialized nations (Great Britain, the United States, Germany, and Japan) choose to combat the Great Depression? What were the principal similarities between their approaches? the differences?

THE EVIDENCE

Source 1 from Parliamentary Debates: House of Commons, *Fifth Series (London: H.M. Stationery Office, 1931), vol. 248 HC, pp. 646–660.*

1. Prime Minister Ramsay MacDonald, February 12, 1931

[*On February 12, 1931, a motion was introduced in the House of Commons calling for the government to "formulate and to present to Parliament an extensive policy" to provide work for the unemployed on public works projects, to be funded by borrowing. The prime minister rose to respond to that motion.*]

There is nothing the country can do with greater wisdom at this moment than to develop its resources, and make them effective as the soil from which our people are going to draw their life-blood, and to find capital for that development.

That is all the truer because the unemployment which we are now facing is not ordinary unemployment. It is not the unemployment we had to face two, three, or four years ago. . . . That was unemployment from day to day, from month to month, from season to season, unemployment of a normally operating capitalist system. The unemployment which we are facing to-day is partly that, undoubtedly. It was that when we came in. But now we are undergoing an industrial revolution. Economic conditions are changing. For instance, in order to face the extraordinarily increased severity of competition which this country has now to meet in the markets of the world, we have to economise our economic and our material power in the shape of machinery and in the shape of works. By that economy we cheapen production. But at the same time we are discharging men and women. In order to increase our efficiency, we are reducing employment, at any rate, for the time being.

But, after all, the men and women who live to-day have to face the problem to-day. They cannot be consoled by the fact that perhaps 10 or 12 years after this, owing to the expansion made possible by the cheapening of production, their sons or daughters will be absorbed in the expanded industry. That is not good enough for the men and women who are living to-day. Therefore, on account of the increasing efficiency, and on account of the reconditioning of our industry which is going on, thousands of men and women are being turned out of employment with a very, very small percentage of chance of ever being called upon again to engage in that industry. . . .

These are very important considerations. You are dealing with a body of unemployment which is not merely temporary. Between 2,500,000 and 2,750,000 of people now ranked as unemployed are not people who are out because there has been a breakdown of machinery in some factory, nor because there has been a seasonal change, nor because there has been a fluctuation in fashion, nor because there is a temporary cessation of the free flow of exchange; they are out on account of the reconditioning of the economic world, and, whoever faces the problem of unemployment now, has to face, not only the problem of public works to give temporary relief, but the problem of how to bring back people into contact with the raw material from which they were making their living. . . . The biggest part of the responsibility is not mentioned in this Motion at all, and that is, direct industrial stimulation so that labour may be absorbed not into work provided because of this unemployment, but that labour may be absorbed into normal industry.

We are asked if we can afford money for the relief of the unemployed. I say we can, but I am much more concerned with what, I think, is the more apposite question—Can we afford to have so many unemployed in existence? We cannot. That is the problem we really have to face. As regards public work, we have, first of all, to provide temporary work. Do remember that it is temporary. When the right hon. Gentleman makes an observation about the millions that have been spent on insurance having produced nothing, I

Chapter 6

The Industrial

Crisis and the

Centralization of

Government

(1924–1939)

disagree with him. If you had not spent a pound of that money, you would have found that you would have had to spend it on something else. If the money had been spent on public works, how many people would have been put to employment? By now these people would have been out of work because the work would have been finished. What struck me most in producing these schemes was how very limited and temporary that kind of work is bound to be. That is the first thing that has to be done. We have to provide it. I am not condemning it at all. I am only trying to impart to the House the kind of problem we are up against when we sit down, not to take part in a Debate in this House, but when we sit down in a committee-room facing the actual details of the problem, and struggling to meet and overcome the whole lot of them.

The second thing that has to be done is, by using neglected resources, the putting of men into permanent ways of earning a living. . . .

[*MacDonald goes on to remind Parliament of the "lag time" that exists between the appropriation and the actual spending of public funds. He then speaks of programs for slum clearance and new industrial cities and new industries, and of the necessity of the government's maintaining a good credit rating.*]

The problem to be tackled is the provision of public works of a temporary character, the opening up of the land to the people of the country, giving them rights upon the soil and, finally, giving to industry vigilance, activity and adventure to enable it to carry on its production and back up this production by marketing. That is the problem we have to face, and that is the spirit and energy in which the Government are facing it and carrying it through. I appeal for a great national effort to enable us to carry on this work, to increase the programme of public works, to enable us to put more and more men upon them, to put more and more work in hand. I appeal to the country to stop the sort of pessimism to which a great contribution was made by the right hon. Gentleman who opened the Debate yesterday, and which I see is already being used with considerable effect. I appeal to the whole country to see that the prospects of this country are good, that we still have resources, that we still have the command of capital, that we still have the power of production and the energy that has made this country so great and powerful and splendid, and that by mobilising it, and only by mobilising it, to carry out the programme of the Government with energy and resource this problem will solve itself. This problem will be solved, a new source of power and wealth will be created in this nation, and we shall go on facing the world with its new problems even more successfully, on account of the experience of social organisation and the application of Socialist ideas, than has been possible in past generations.

Source 2 from B. D. Zevin, ed., Nothing to Fear: The Selected Addresses of Franklin Delano Roosevelt, 1932–1945 *(Boston: Houghton Mifflin Co., 1946), pp. 132–143.*

2. President Franklin Roosevelt, April 14, 1938[7]

Five years ago we faced a very serious problem of economic and social recovery. For four and a half years that recovery proceeded apace. It is only in the past seven months that it has received a visible setback.

And it is only within the past two months, as we have waited patiently to see whether the forces of business itself would counteract it, that it has become apparent that government itself can no longer safely fail to take aggressive government steps to meet it.

This recession has not returned us to the disasters and suffering of the beginning of 1933. Your money in the bank is safe; farmers are no longer in deep distress and have greater purchasing power; dangers of security speculation have been minimized; national income is almost 50 per cent higher than in 1932; and government has an established and accepted responsibility for relief.

But I know that many of you have lost your jobs or have seen your friends or members of your families lose their jobs, and I do not propose that the government shall pretend not to see these things. I know that the effect of our present difficulties has been uneven; that they have affected some groups and some localities seriously, but that they have been scarcely felt in others. But I conceive the first duty of government is to protect the economic welfare of all the people in all sections and in all groups. I said in my message opening the last session of Congress that if private enterprise did not provide jobs this spring, government would take up the slack—that I would not let the people down. We have all learned the lesson that government cannot afford to wait until it has lost the power to act.

Therefore, I have sent a message of far-reaching importance to the Congress. I want to read to you tonight certain passages from that message, and to talk with you about them. . . .

[*Here Roosevelt explains what he believes were the causes of the collapse of 1929—chief among them, the underconsumption of manufactured goods.*]

I then said this to the Congress:

"But the very vigor of the recovery in both durable goods and consumers' goods brought into the picture early in 1937 certain highly undesirable

7. The April 14, 1938, address was delivered "live" over the radio, one of President Roosevelt's so-called Fireside Chats. In early 1937, Roosevelt had tried to remove government supports of the economy, but, unable to stand without those supports, the economy began to deteriorate once again. This selection is from the printed release of the speech. Roosevelt deviated slightly from the printed text as he spoke to his radio audience. See Russell D. Buhite and David W. Levy, *FDR's Fireside Chats* (Norman: University of Oklahoma, 1992), pp. 111–123.

Chapter 6

The Industrial

Crisis and the

Centralization of

Government

(1924–1939)

practices, which were in large part responsible for the economic decline which began in the later months of that year. Again production outran the ability to buy.

"There were many reasons for this overproduction. One was fear—fear of war abroad, fear of inflation, fear of nationwide strikes. None of these fears has been borne out.

". . . Production in many important lines of goods outran the ability of the public to purchase them. For example, through the winter and spring of 1937 cotton factories in hundreds of cases were running on a three-shift basis, piling up cotton goods in the factory and in the hands of middle men and retailers. For example, also, automobile manufacturers not only turned out a normal increase of finished cars, but encouraged the normal increase to run into abnormal figures, using every known method to push their sales. This meant, of course, that the steel mills of the Nation ran on a twenty-four hour basis, and the tire companies and cotton factories speeded up to meet the same type of abnormally stimulated demand. The buying power of the Nation lagged behind.

"Thus by the autumn of 1937 the Nation again had stocks on hand which the consuming public could not buy because the purchasing power of the consuming public had not kept pace with the production. . . ."

I went on to point out to the Senate and the House of Representatives that all the energies of government and business must be directed to increasing the national income, to putting more people into private jobs, to giving security and a feeling of security to all people in all walks of life.

I am constantly thinking of all our people—unemployed and employed alike—of their human problems of food and clothing and homes and education and health and old age. You and I agree that security is our greatest need; the chance to work, the opportunity of making a reasonable profit in our business—whether it be a very small business or a larger one— the possibility of selling our farm products for enough money for our families to live on decently. I know these are the things that decide the well-being of all our people.

Therefore, I am determined to do all in my power to help you attain that security, and because I know that the people themselves have a deep conviction that secure prosperity of that kind cannot be a lasting one except on a basis of business fair dealing and a basis where all from top to bottom share in prosperity, I repeated to the Congress today that neither it nor the Chief Executive can afford "to weaken or destroy great reforms which, during the past five years, have been effected on behalf of the American people. In our rehabilitation of the banking structure and of agriculture, in our provisions for adequate and cheaper credit for all types of business, in our acceptance of national responsibility for unemployment relief, in our strengthening of the credit of State and local government, in our encouragement of housing, slum clearance and home ownership, in our supervision of stock exchanges and public utility holding companies and the issuance of new securities, in our provision for social security, the electorate of America wants no backward steps taken. . . .

"I came to the conclusion that the present-day problem calls for action both by the Government and by the people, that we suffer primarily from a failure of consumer demand because of lack of buying power. It is up to us to create an economic upturn.

"How and where can and should the Government help to start an upward spiral?"

I went on to propose three groups of measures and I will summarize the recommendations.

First, I asked for certain appropriations which are intended to keep the Government expenditures for work relief and similar purposes during the coming fiscal year at the same rate of expenditures as at present. That includes additional money for the Works Progress Administration; additional funds for the Farm Security Administration; additional allotments for the National Youth Administration, and more money for the Civilian Conservation Corps, in order that it can maintain the existing number of camps now in operation.

These appropriations, made necessary by increased unemployment, will cost about a billion and a quarter more than the estimates which I sent to the Congress on the third of January.

Second, I told the Congress that the Administration proposes to make additional bank reserves available for the credit needs of the country. About one billion four hundred million dollars of gold now in the Treasury will be used to pay these additional expenses of the Government, and three-quarters of a billion dollars of additional credit will be made available to the banks by reducing the reserves now required by the Federal Reserve Board.

These two steps, taking care of relief needs and adding to bank credits, are in our judgment insufficient by themselves to start the Nation on a sustained upward movement.

Therefore, I came to the third kind of Government action which I consider to be vital. I said to the Congress:

"You and I cannot afford to equip ourselves with two rounds of ammunition where three rounds are necessary. If we stop at relief and credit, we may find ourselves without ammunition before the enemy is routed. If we are fully equipped with the third round of ammunition, we stand to win the battle against adversity."

The third proposal is to make definite additions to the purchasing power of the Nation by providing new work over and above the continuing of the old work.

First, to enable the United States Housing Authority to undertake the immediate construction of about three hundred million dollars of additional slum clearance projects.

Chapter 6

The Industrial

Crisis and the

Centralization of

Government

(1924–1939)

Second, to renew a public works program by starting as quickly as possible about one billion dollars worth of needed permanent public improvements in states, counties and cities.

Third, to add one hundred million dollars to the estimate for federal aid [to] highways in excess of the amount I recommended in January.

Fourth, to add thirty-seven million dollars over and above the former estimate of sixty-three million dollars for flood control and reclamation.

Fifth, to add twenty-five million dollars additional for federal buildings in various parts of the country.

In recommending this program I am thinking not only of the immediate economic needs of the people of the Nation, but also of their personal liberties—the most precious possession of all Americans. I am thinking of our democracy and of the recent trend in other parts of the world away from the democratic ideal.

Democracy has disappeared in several other great nations—not because the people of those nations disliked democracy, but because they had grown tired of unemployment and insecurity, of seeing their children hungry while they sat helpless in the face of government confusion and government weakness through lack of leadership in government. Finally, in desperation, they chose to sacrifice liberty in the hope of getting something to eat. We in America know that our own democratic institutions can be preserved and made to work. But in order to preserve them we need to act together, to meet the problems of the Nation boldly, and to prove that the practical operation of democratic government is equal to the task of protecting the security of the people.

Not only our future economic soundness but the very soundness of our democratic institutions depends on the determination of our Government to give employment to idle men. The people of America are in agreement in defending their liberties at any cost, and the first line of that defense lies in the protection of economic security. Your Government, seeking to protect democracy, must prove that Government is stronger than the forces of business depression.

History proves that dictatorships do not grow out of strong and successful governments, but out of weak and helpless ones. If by democratic methods people get a government strong enough to protect them from fear and starvation, their democracy succeeds; but if they do not, they grow impatient. Therefore, the only sure bulwark of continuing liberty is a government strong enough to protect the interests of the people, and a people strong enough and well enough informed to maintain its sovereign control over its government. . . .

What I said to the Congress in the close of my message I repeat to you.

"Let us unanimously recognize the fact that the Federal debt, whether it be twenty-five billions or forty billions, can only be paid if the Nation obtains a vastly increased citizen income. I repeat that if this citizen income can be raised to eighty billion dollars a year the national Government and the overwhelming majority of State and local governments will be 'out of the red.'

The higher the national income goes the faster shall we be able to reduce the total of Federal and state and local debts. Viewed from every angle, today's purchasing power—the citizens' income of today—is not sufficient to drive the economic system at higher speed. Responsibility of Government requires us at this time to supplement the normal processes and in so supplementing them to make sure that the addition is adequate. We must start again on a long steady upward incline in national income.

"... And in that process, which I believe is ready to start, let us avoid the pitfalls of the past—the overproduction, the overspeculation, and indeed all the extremes which we did not succeed in avoiding in 1929. In all of this, Government cannot and should not act alone. Business must help. I am sure business will help.

"We need more than the materials of recovery. We need a united national will. . . ."

Source 3 from Norman H. Baynes, ed., The Speeches of Adolf Hitler, April 1922–August 1939 *(London: Oxford University Press for the Royal Institute of International Affairs, 1942), vol. 1, pp. 650–654. Copyright © 1942. Reprinted by permission of the Royal Institute of International Affairs.*

3. Chancellor Adolf Hitler, September 10, 1936[8]

In all spheres of our national life there has been since four years ago an immense advance. The tempo and the scale of the political advance are unique, and above all the inner consolidation of the German nation is unique in history. . . .

On the evening of 30 January 1933 I made known to the German people in a short Proclamation the aims which we had set before us in our battle. I then asked that I might be granted four years: at the end of that time I wished to render account to the German people of the fulfilment or non-fulfilment of that promise.

Our foes were convinced that we should never have an opportunity to ask the nation for such a judgement, for the longest period that they were prepared to allow our Government was barely six to twelve weeks.

And what has National Socialism in these four years made of Germany? Who from amongst our foes would to-day have the effrontery to step forward as our accuser?

What appeared to them then fantastic and incapable of realization in my Proclamation seems to-day the most modest announcement of an achievement which towers above the promises then made. Our opponents thought that we

8. Hitler's speech was intended to answer the question "What has National Socialism made out of Germany in the last four years?"

Chapter 6

The Industrial

Crisis and the

Centralization of

Government

(1924–1939)

could not carry out the programme of 1933 which now seems to us so small an affair. But what would they have said if I had propounded to them *that* programme which the National Socialist Government has as a matter of fact realized in not quite four years? How they would have jeered if on the 30th of January 1933 I had declared that within four years Germany would have reduced its six million unemployed to one million!

That the enforced expropriation of the German peasantry would have been brought to an end.

That the receipts from German agriculture would be higher than in any previous year in time of peace.

That the total national income would be raised from 41 milliards annually to over 56 milliards.[9]

That the German middle classes and German artisans would enjoy a new prosperity.

That trade would once more recover.

That German ports would no more resemble ship grave-yards.

That in 1936 on German wharves alone over 640,000 tons of shipping would be under construction.

That countless manufactories would not merely double but treble and quadruple the number of their workmen. And that in less than four years innumerable others would be rebuilt.

That a Krupp factory would vibrate once again with the roaring and the hammering of the machines of the German resurrection and that over all of these undertakings men would recognize as the supreme law of their effort not the unscrupulous profit of the individual but the service of the nation.

That the silent motor-works would not only spring into life but would be enlarged on an unheard of scale.

That the production of motor-cars would rise from 45,000 in the year 1932 to some quarter of a million.

That in four years the deficits of our States and cities would be wiped out.

That the Reich would gain from taxation an annual increase of nearly five milliards.

That the German Imperial Railway would at length recover, and that its trains would be the quickest in the world.

That to the German Reich would be given roads such that since the beginnings of human civilization they have never had their match for size and beauty: and that of the first 7,000 kilometres which were planned already after not quite four years 1,000 kilometres would be in use and over 4,000 kilometres would be in course of construction.

That enormous new settlements with hundreds of thousands of houses would come into being, while in ancient cities of the Reich mighty new buildings would arise which may be said to be the greatest in the world.

That hundreds upon hundreds of gigantic bridges would be thrown over

9. **milliard:** one billion (marks, in this case).

gorges and valleys.

That German "Kultur" in these and similar new achievements would confirm its eternal value.

That German theatres and concerts of our German music would celebrate their resurrection.

That with all this the German people would take an active share in this revolutionary renewal of the spirit, while not a single Jew would make an appearance in this intellectual leadership of the German people.

If I had prophesied then that in four years the whole German Press would be filled with a new "ethos" and would be in the service of German aims, that for German business life (*Wirtschaft*) the law of a new professional honour would be proclaimed, so that in every sphere the German experiences a renewal of his personality and his action.

If I had at that time foretold that after these four years there would be only one single German people, that no Social Democracy, no Communism, no Centrum, not even a *bourgeois* party would any longer be able to sin against the life of Germany, that no trade union would any longer be able to incite the workers, and no employers' association to ruin the employers, that after these four years no German State would have its separate government, that in Germany there would no longer be any State-parliaments (*Landtage*), that the sixteen flags and the sixteen different traditions which they represented would have ceased to exist and have been brought together as one, and that the whole nation—from the workman to the soldier—would in the future march only in support of a single confession of faith and a single flag.

What would they have said if I had prophesied to them that Germany in these four years would have freed itself from the slave-fetters of Versailles, that the Reich would regain general compulsory military service, that every German, as before the War, would serve two years for the freedom of the country, that a new fleet would be under construction to protect our coasts and our trade, that a mighty new air arm would guarantee the security of our towns, our factories and works, that the Rhineland would be brought under the supremacy of the German nation, and that thereby the sovereignty of the Reich would be restored over the whole of its territory?

What would they have said to my prophecy that the people, at that time so divided, before four years were past would—99 per cent of it—go to the polls and that 99 per cent would say "Yes" in support of the National Socialist policy of reconstruction, of national honour and freedom?

If four years ago I had prophesied this and much else I should have been branded as a madman and the whole world would have laughed at me. But all this is now accomplished fact, and this is the achievement of not quite four years. . . . The National Socialist political leadership of Germany in this short time has wrought a miracle.

Chapter 6

The Industrial

Crisis and the

Centralization of

Government

(1924–1939)

Source 4 from Ryusaku Tsunoda, et al., comp., Sources of Japanese Tradition *by William Theodore de Bary. (New York: Columbia University Press, 1958), vol. 2, pp. 289–291. Copyright © 1942. Reprinted with the permission of the publisher.*

4. Hashimoto Kingoro,
Address to Young Men, 1930s

We have already said that there are only three ways left to Japan to escape from the pressure of surplus population. We are like a great crowd of people packed into a small and narrow room, and there are only three doors through which we might escape, namely emigration, advance into world markets, and expansion of territory. The first door, emigration, has been barred to us by the anti-Japanese immigration policies of other countries. The second door, advance into world markets, is being pushed shut by tariff barriers and the abrogation of commercial treaties. What should Japan do when two of the three doors have been closed against her?

It is quite natural that Japan should rush upon the last remaining door.

It may sound dangerous when we speak of territorial expansion, but the territorial expansion of which we speak does not in any sense of the word involve the occupation of the possessions of other countries, the planting of the Japanese flag thereon, and the declaration of their annexation to Japan. It is just that since the Powers [United States, Britain, France] have suppressed the circulation of Japanese materials and merchandise abroad, we are looking for some place overseas where Japanese capital, Japanese skills and Japanese labor can have free play, free from the oppression of the white race.

We would be satisfied with just this much. What moral right do the world powers who have themselves closed to us the two doors of emigration and advance into world markets have to criticize Japan's attempt to rush out of the third and last door?

If they do not approve of this, they should open the doors which they have closed against us and permit the free movement overseas of Japanese emigrants and merchandise. . . .

At the time of the Manchurian incident [1931], the entire world joined in criticism of Japan. They said that Japan was an untrustworthy nation. They said that she had recklessly brought cannon and machine guns into Manchuria, which was the territory of another country, flown airplanes over it, and finally occupied it. But the military action taken by Japan was not in the least a selfish one. Moreover, we do not recall ever having taken so much as an inch of territory belonging to another nation. The result of this incident was the establishment of the splendid new nation of Manchuria. The Powers are still discussing whether or not to recognize this new nation, but regardless of whether or not other nations recognize her, the Manchurian empire has already been established, and now, seven years after its creation, the empire is further consolidating its foundations with the aid of its friend, Japan.

And if it is still protested that our actions in Manchuria were excessively violent, we may wish to ask the white race just which country it was that sent warships and troops to India, South Africa, and Australia and slaughtered innocent natives, bound their hands and feet with iron chains, lashed their backs with iron whips, proclaimed these territories as their own, and still continues to hold them to this very day?

They will invariably reply, these were all lands inhabited by untamed savages. These people did not know how to develop the abundant resources of their land for the benefit of mankind. Therefore it was the wish of God, who created heaven and earth for mankind, for us to develop these undeveloped lands and to promote the happiness of mankind in their stead. God wills it.

This is quite a convenient argument for them. Let us take it at face value. Then there is another question that we must ask them.

Suppose that there is still on this earth land endowed with abundant natural resources that have not been developed at all by the white race. Would it not then be God's will and the will of Providence that Japan go there and develop those resources for the benefit of mankind?

And there still remain many such lands on this earth. . . .

Chapter 6
The Industrial
Crisis and the
Centralization of
Government
(1924–1939)

Sources 5 and 6 from League of Nations, Monthly Bulletin of Statistics (Geneva: League of Nations, 1939), vol. 20, p. 12; pp. 51–52.

5. Index of Industrial Production, 1929–1938 (1929 = 100)

Year	Germany	Japan	Great Britain	United States
1929	100.0	100.0	100.0	100.0
1930	85.9	94.8	92.3	80.7
1931	67.6	91.6	83.8	68.1
1932	53.3	97.8	83.5	53.8
1933	60.7	113.2	88.2	63.9
1934	79.8	128.7	98.8	66.4
1935	94.0	141.8	105.8	75.6
1936	106.3	151.1	115.9	88.1
1937	117.2	170.8	123.7	92.2
1938 (May)	127.0	174.8	113.4	72.3

6. Unemployment (Numbers Out of Work and Percentage of Civilian Labor Force), 1930–1938

Year	Germany		Japan	
	Number	Percentage	Number	Percentage
1930	3,075,580	—	369,408	5.3%
1931	4,519,704	23.7%	422,755	6.1
1932	5,575,492	30.1	485,681	6.8
1933	4,804,428	25.8	408,710	5.6
1934	2,718,309	14.5	372,941	5.0
1935	2,151,039	11.6	356,044	4.6
1936	1,592,655	8.1	338,365	4.3
1937	912,312	4.5	295,443	3.7
1938 (June)	429,475	2.0	230,262	2.9

Year	Great Britain		United States[10]	
	Number	*Percentage*	*Number*	*Percentage*
1930	1,464,347	11.8%	4,340,000	8.7%
1931	2,129,359	16.7	8,020,000	15.9
1932	2,254,857	17.6	12,060,000	23.6
1933	2,110,090	16.4	12,830,000	24.9
1934	1,801,913	13.9	11,340,000	21.7
1935	1,714,844	13.1	10,610,000	20.1
1936	1,497,587	11.2	9,030,000	16.9
1937	1,277,928	9.4	7,700,000	14.3
1938 (Nov.)	1,529,133	10.8	10,390,000	19.0

10. United States statistics are from U.S. Department of Commerce, Bureau of the Census, *Historical Statistics of the United States* (Washington: Government Printing Office, 1975), vol. 2, p. 135.

Chapter 6

The Industrial

Crisis and the

Centralization of

Government

(1924–1939)

Source 7 from B. R. Mitchell, European Historical Statistics, 1750–1970 (New York: Columbia University Press, 1978), pp. 376–385, and Historical Statistics of the United States, vol. 2, p. 1104.

7. Central Government Revenues and Expenditures in National Currencies, 1924–1940 (in millions)

Year	Germany (mark)			Great Britain (pound)		
	Revenue	Expenditures	Surplus or Deficit	Revenue	Expenditures	Surplus or Deficit
1924	4,650	5,027	–377	799	751	48
1925	4,731	5,683	–952	812	776	36
1926	5,313	6,616	–1,303	806	782	24
1927	6,357	7,168	–811	843	774	69
1928	6,568	8,517	–1,949	836	761	75
1929	6,741	8,187	–1,446	815	782	33
1930	6,634	8,392	–1,758	858	814	44
1931	5,704	6,995	–1,291	851	819	32
1932	4,994	5,965	–971	827	833	–6
1933	6,850	6,270	580	809	770	39
1934	8,220	8,221	–1	805	785	20
1935	9,650	Not available	—	845	829	16
1936	11,492	N/A	—	897	889	8
1937	13,964	N/A	—	949	909	40
1938	17,712	N/A	—	1,006	1,006	0
1939	23,575	N/A	—	1,132	1,401	–269

| Year | United States (dollar) | | |
	Revenue	*Expenditures*	*Surplus or Deficit*
1924	$3,871,214	$2,907,847	$963,367
1925	3,640,805	2,923,762	717,043
1926	3,795,108	2,929,964	865,144
1927	4,012,794	2,857,429	1,155,365
1928	3,900,329	2,961,245	939,083
1929	3,861,589	3,127,199	734,391
1930	4,057,884	3,320,211	737,673
1931	3,115,557	3,577,434	−461,877
1932	1,923,892	4,659,182	−2,735,290
1933	1,996,844	4,598,496	−2,601,652
1934	3,014,970	6,644,602	−3,629,632
1935	3,705,956	6,497,008	−2,791,052
1936	3,997,059	8,421,608	−4,424,549
1937	4,955,613	7,733,033	−2,777,421
1938	5,588,012	6,764,628	−1,176,617
1939	4,979,066	8,841,224	−3,862,158

Chapter 6

The Industrial

Crisis and the

Centralization of

Government

(1924–1939)

Source 8 from Economic Intelligence Service, World Economic Survey, 1931–1932 *(Geneva: League of Nations, 1932), pp. 319–322.*

8. Tariffs, Import Duties, Taxes Imposed

	Import Duties, Taxes Imposed, Consular Fees (etc.)	
	General Increase (All Items)	*Increases on Individual Items*
June 1930		U.S.A.[11]
September 1931		Argentina
		Colombia
		Egypt
		Italy
		Latvia
		Poland
October 1931	India	Argentina
	South Africa	Australia
		Canada
		Czechoslovakia
		Denmark
		Egypt
		Lithuania
		Poland
		Roumania
November 1931	Netherlands	Belgium
		United Kingdom
		Bulgaria
		France
		Persia
December 1931	Brazil	United Kingdom
		Columbia
		Czechoslovakia
		Estonia
		France
		Lithuania
		Switzerland
January 1932	Norway	Austria
		Colombia
		Germany
		Hungary
		Irish Free State
		Italy
		Poland
		Salvador
		Switzerland
February 1932	Australia	Belgium

(continues on next page)

11. For the United States tariff (the Hawley-Smoot Act), see F. W. Taussig, *The Tariff History of the United States,* 8th ed. (New York: G.P. Putnam's Sons, 1931), p. 518.

	Finland	Estonia
	Persia	Germany
	Portugal	Italy
	Siam	Lithuania
		Mexico
		South Africa
		Sweden
		Switzerland
		Venezuela
March 1932	Belgium	Bolivia
	United Kingdom	Brazil
	Poland	Egypt
	South Africa	Estonia
	Venezuela	France
		Guatemala
		India
		Irish Free State
		Mexico
		Netherlands
		Roumania
		Salvador
		Spain
April 1932	France	Belgium
	U.S.A.	United Kingdom
		Canada
		China
		Egypt
		Irish Free State
		Italy
		Mexico
		Netherlands
		Spain
		Sweden
		Uruguay
May 1932	Czechoslovakia	Belgium
	Egypt	United Kingdom
		Chile
		Greece
		Irish Free State
		Italy
		Mexico
		Sweden
June 1932	Japan	United Kingdom
	Estonia	Denmark
	Lithuania	Egypt
		Germany
		Italy
		Norway
		Roumania
July 1932		United Kingdom
		Irish Free State
		U.S.A.

Chapter 6

The Industrial

Crisis and the

Centralization of

Government

(1924–1939)

Source 9 from Paul Kennedy, The Rise and Fall of the Great Powers: Economic Change and Military Conflict from 1500 to 2000 *(New York: Random House, 1987), p. 296. Copyright © 1987 by Paul Kennedy. Used by permission of Random House, Inc.*

9. Defense Expenditures of Great Britain, the United States, Germany, and Japan, 1930–1938 (in millions of current dollars)

Year	Great Britain	United States	Germany	Japan
1930	512	699	162	218
1933	333	570	452	183
1934	540	803	709	292
1935	646	806	1,607	300
1936	892	932	2,332	313
1937	1,245	1,032	3,298	940
1938	1,863	1,131	7,415	1,740

Source 10 from David Chandler, ed., The Oxford History of the British Army *(Oxford: Oxford University Press, 1994), p. 256; Robin Higham,* Armed Forces in Peacetime: Britain, *1918–1940 (Hamden, Conn.: Archon Books, 1962), p. 95; Peter Dennis,* Decision by Default: Peacetime Conscription and British Defense, 1919–1939 *(Durham, N.C.: Duke University Press, 1972), p. 27; U.S. Bureau of the Census,* Historical Statistics of the United States, Colonial Times to 1957 *(Washington, D.C.: Government Printing Office, 1960), p. 736; Matthew Cooper,* The German Army, 1933–1945: Its Political and Military Failure *(New York: Stein and Day, 1978), pp. 50, 130–131.*

10. Sizes of Armies, Great Britain, United States, Germany

Year	Great Britain	United States	Germany
1920	370,000[12]	204,292	100,000[13]
1921	285,300	230,725	
1922	235,000	148,763	
1923		133,243	
1924		142,673	
1925		137,048	
1926		134,938	
1927		134,829	
1928		136,084	
1929		139,118	
1930		139,378	

Year	Great Britain	United States	Germany
1931		140,516	
1932		134,957	
1933	206,000	136,547	100,000
1934	195,845	138,464	240,000
1935	196,137	139,486	450,000
1936	192,325	167,816	
1937	190,830	179,968	
1938		185,488	
1939		189,839	730,000 (1 June)
			3,706,104 (1 Sept)

12. Does not include the British army in India or in the Territories.

13. The Treaty of Versailles limited the size of the German army to 100,000, although there is evidence that even before Hitler became chancellor Germany was evading that limit.

Chapter 6

The Industrial

Crisis and the

Centralization of

Government

(1924–1939)

Source 11 from Paul Kennedy, Rise and Fall of the Great Powers: Economic Change and Military Conflict from 1500 to 2000 (New York: Random House, 1987), p. 300. Copyright © 1987 by Paul Kennedy. Used by permission of Random House, Inc.

11. Armed Services Spending as a Percentage of Total Government Expenditures, Japan, 1931–1938

1931–1932	31%
1936–1937	47%
1937–1938	70%

QUESTIONS TO CONSIDER

Ramsay MacDonald's speech in Parliament is a defense of his approach toward combating unemployment in Great Britain. MacDonald begins by explaining what he believes were the causes of the Great Depression in Britain. What factors does he cite? Note that the prime minister does not see the economic downturn as temporary in Britain. Therefore, his remedy is twofold, the first part consisting of temporary work for the unemployed, but the second involving a permanent restructuring of the British economy. How does MacDonald propose to accomplish phase two? What should government's role be? What should government's role *not* be?

Franklin Roosevelt's Fireside Chat details his strategies and principles for mobilizing the federal government to deal with the sudden economic downturn of 1937–1938. Like MacDonald, Roosevelt also begins with his own analysis of the causes of the Depression, although this time in the United States. How does Roosevelt's analysis differ from MacDonald's? Note that Roosevelt believed that the 1937–1938 downturn was a repeat of what had occurred in 1929–1932. Contrast Roosevelt's suggested solutions with those of MacDonald. How is the role of the central government different? How does each leader approach the notion of "deficit spending" (in which expenditures exceed revenues, the difference to be made up by borrowing, principally through government bonds)? Roosevelt concludes his radio address by insisting that "business must help." What would MacDonald's reaction be to such a statement?

On the surface, Adolf Hitler's speech at the opening of the Nazi Party's 1936 convention is a simple listing of what Germany has accomplished since he became chancellor in

[178]

January 1933. Faintly visible beneath the gloating, however, is an obscure outline of Hitler's plan to end the Depression in Germany (see the Epilogue section for a brief explanation of that plan).

Hitler begins by boasting of Germany's significant reduction in unemployment since the Nazi rise to power (from 6 million to 1 million). Do the statistics (Source 6) confirm his claim (by September 1936 the 1 million figure probably was an accurate one)? The main question is, how were the National Socialists able to bring this about? Hitler gives broad hints when he refers to the Krupp industries, the "silent motor-works," the revival of vehicle production, compulsory military service, the requirement of two years of service "for the freedom of the country" (see Epilogue for an explanation), the production of ships and airplanes, and the freedom "from the slave-fetters of Versailles." He also mentions the Rhineland being "brought under the supremacy of the German nation," a reference to the military occupation of that region in 1936 by Germany's revived half-million-man army. The other world powers did nothing, thereby encouraging Hitler's later aggressions. Finally, look at Hitler's comment regarding labor unions ("that no trade union would any longer be able to incite the workers"). What does Hitler really mean by that (see Epilogue)?

Hashimoto's address is as clear as Hitler's is vague. To Hashimoto, Japan's central problem is overpopulation, and he envisions only three possible resolutions. What were those three potential options? Why, in Hashimoto's opinion, were two of the three not possible? How would territorial expansion, in his view, solve Japan's economic problems? What would that expansion bring to Japan economically? Finally, how many of Japan's economic obstacles does Hashimoto attribute to anti-Japanese attitudes (racism?) on the part of other nations? Explain.

Once you have analyzed the speeches to discern how each national leader proposed to deal with the Great Depression, it would be appropriate to compare and contrast the approaches urged upon Great Britain, the United States, Germany, and Japan. How were these approaches different? In what ways were they similar? For example, how would each nation deal with unemployment? Were Germany and Japan similar in their approaches? Was the United States similar to or different from Germany and Japan, and in what ways? What about Great Britain? How did each nation propose to involve government in ending the Depression?

After you have analyzed, compared, and contrasted the four speeches, examine the sets of statistics (Sources 5 through 11). Some of the dimensions of this decline, the deepest in world history, are revealed in Source 5, the indexes of industrial production for Germany, Japan, Great Britain, and the United States—four major industrialized nations that were affected at somewhat different times. Note that Japan and

Chapter 6

The Industrial

Crisis and the

Centralization of

Government

(1924–1939)

Great Britain did not experience the collapse of production in the 1930s in the same manner as Germany and the United States. How would you explain this? Also, both Germany and the United States "hit bottom" in the same year, 1932, and then began slowly to recover. Can any of the other statistical evidence help you to understand why this was so? At the same time, how can the changing unemployment figures (Source 6) be explained by other statistical sets? How can Source 7 prove helpful (recall the speeches, especially those of MacDonald and Roosevelt)?

As noted above, tariffs can be used both to raise revenue for the government (as a tax on imports) and to assist native industries by raising tariff schedules so high as to discourage imports from elsewhere. How does Source 8 clarify governments'

policies to combat their nations' economic troubles? Most economists—both then and now—criticized such a policy as shortsighted and detrimental. What is your opinion of these economists' assertion?

Sources 9 through 11 concentrate on military expenditures. How are these statistics related to individual governmental policies to combat the Depression? What is your opinion of these policies?

Now put the speeches and the statistics together. How did each of the four major industrial nations choose to combat the Great Depression? What were the principal similarities between their approaches? the differences? Finally, on a larger scale, how would you *evaluate* these policies? What were their immediate effects? their long-range effects?

EPILOGUE

In some ways, the Great Depression of the 1930s was one of the eventual results of the Industrial Revolution. As industrialization expanded into nations and regions that previously had been consumers of the manufactures of others, international markets diminished and the scramble for the remaining markets became fierce. In order to secure raw materials and guarantee markets, in the late nineteenth century almost all Western nations engaged in an almost frantic imperialism. And during the Great Depression of the 1930s, some nations kept a certain level of manufacturing

going by forcing products on their respective empires. Finally, in order to keep exported manufactures as inexpensive as possible (to make them more competitive in world markets), industrial wages had to be kept low, thus making it difficult for domestic workers to increase their own consumption of manufactured goods. In some ways, then, the Industrial Revolution was undermined by its own snowballing success.

As noted earlier, the Depression shook the industrialized nations' political foundations as profoundly as it did their economic ones. Japan suffered a wave of political assassinations and attempted coups (at least two of which were masterminded by

Hashimoto) until the military finally emerged as the controlling force in that nation's politics, a position in part strengthened by the military's uneasy alliance with Japan's giant corporations (*zaibatsu*).[14] In Germany, the National Socialists had garnered 14.5 million votes in the 1932 election, in part a response to Hitler's promise of economic recovery. When prominent industrialists and army officers fell into step, German president Hindenburg was persuaded to name Hitler Germany's chancellor, on January 30, 1933. Within a year, the Nazi leader had turned Germany into a totalitarian state.

Political reactions in Great Britain and the United States were less extreme. In Britain, MacDonald was forced to accept a coalition government but was able to retain his post as prime minister. In the United States, in spite of some dire warnings that capitalism was near death, in 1932 voters elected moderate Democrat Franklin Roosevelt, and government changed hands peacefully in March 1933.

As you might expect after reading the speeches in this chapter, each of the major industrial powers sought to loosen the grip of the Depression in its own way; any international or cooperative efforts were abandoned following the collapse of the World Economic Conference of sixty-six nations in 1933. In some ways, Great Britain was the most fortunate. High

interest rates and the economic slump of the 1920s had created pent-up demand for manufactured products. When Britain abandoned the gold standard[15] in 1931, prices fell and a natural "boomlet" was created. Unemployment remained high, however, and was not eradicated until Britain entered World War II in September 1939. But Britain did not need the massive infusions of government money into the economy that was necessary in other industrialized nations (see Source 7). This was indeed fortunate because the British government could ill afford the deficit financing that Germany and the United States utilized.

Germany's approach to the Depression was considerably more severe. Hitler instituted the compulsory National Labor Service to staff public works projects, tried to drive women out of the work force (to make room for unemployed males), smashed labor unions, and increased government revenues for investment in fresh industrial production. Ominously, much of that industrial production was military goods, a policy that eventually would drive that nation into war (that, along with Hitler's megalomania).

As President Franklin Roosevelt's New Deal gradually took shape, its general philosophy seems to have been to stimulate domestic consumption in a variety of ways. Consumer

---

14. A *zaibatsu* resembles an American holding company, manufacturing several types of products and providing many services as well. In the 1920s, Mitsui was Japan's largest zaibatsu, having assets representing approximately 15 percent of all Japanese business firms.

15. **gold standard:** an international system in which each nation's currency was equal in value to and exchangeable for a specified amount of gold. The system provided monetary stability. Great Britain abandoned the gold standard in order to let the value of the pound fall, thereby instigating an inflationary trend.

Chapter 6

The Industrial

Crisis and the

Centralization of

Government

(1924–1939)

demand, New Dealers reasoned, would bring people back to work to fill that demand. Hence the federal government engaged in deficit financing to put money in the hands of farmers (Agricultural Adjustment Act), the unemployed (Works Progress Administration), the elderly (Social Security), unemployed youth (Civilian Conservation Corps), and other groups. Yet unemployment in the United States remained high (over 10 million in 1938, 19 percent of the civilian labor force) until the nation's entrance into World War II in 1941.

After 1931, recovery in Japan was comparatively rapid. Unemployment dropped steadily and real wages increased. This was partly the result of military expansion into Manchuria, but even more, Japan was able to orchestrate an enviable economic marriage of Western industrial technology and low Asian wages, a union that made Japan's manufactured goods more competitive in Asian markets.

Taken as a whole, the industrial world's varied responses to the Great Depression raises a number of questions. To begin with, we are almost compelled to question whether *any* actions of a central government can *cure* the ills of a depression. Doubtless governments may *alleviate* the worst effects of an economic collapse, but whether they can engineer national economic recovery is more debatable. In Great Britain, a natural economic upturn did more to move that nation toward recovery than all the government's nostrums. In the United States, it appears that the New Deal, although it gave Americans a tremen-

dous psychological lift, had rather anemic results when it came to stimulating permanent recovery, perhaps because (as some economists claim) the extent of government intervention in the United States was too limited to stimulate total restoration. Neither nation experienced full employment until the war. And, of course, it was precisely that military buildup that allowed Germany and Japan to experience comparatively rapid turnarounds. Did it, therefore, take the horrific slaughter of World War II to bring the Depression to an end? What in fact had been the roles of governments and their policies and programs to battle the economic crisis? Were they effective, apart from the war?

Finally, the national responses to the Great Depression show that the refusal of nations to work together can have disastrous consequences, as the almost endless spiral of tariff wars (Source 8) ultimately showed. Speaking of the relationship between the crisis in Britain and the world situation, British government official Sir John Anderson wrote in 1930, "You cannot drain a bog while the surrounding country is still under water." In the nineteenth century, Britain had provided a kind of world leadership that benefited other nations as well as itself. When the world's economic center of gravity shifted to the United States about the time of World War I, that nation lacked the vision and experience to exercise a similar style of world leadership. Instead, the United States started the round of tariff increases in 1930, refused to participate in the

World Economic Conference of 1933 (and actually was a major contributor to the summit's collapse), and followed a path toward recovery that (if it worked) would benefit no one but itself. And yet the United States was hardly alone in pursuing self-serving policies. Indeed, it is likely that the wisdom of King Solomon himself could not have persuaded the industrialized nations to work together.

Overworked and sick, Ramsay MacDonald resigned as prime minister in 1935 and died soon after, in 1937. Franklin Roosevelt won unprecedented third and fourth presidential elections (in 1940 and 1944), but did not live to see Allied victories over Germany and Japan in World War II. He died on April 12, 1945.

Adolf Hitler, driven by his own dark dreams and hatreds, committed suicide in his fortified bunker underneath a decimated Berlin just eighteen days after Roosevelt's death. Of the four speakers excerpted in this chapter, only Hashimoto Kingoro survived the war. Tried as a war criminal by the Americans, he was sentenced to life imprisonment but was released in 1955. He died in 1957.

CHAPTER SEVEN

SELLING A TOTALITARIAN SYSTEM

THE PROBLEM

Hitler's dictatorship differed in one fundamental point from all its predecessors in history. His was the first dictatorship in the present period of modern technical development, a dictatorship which made complete use of all technical means for the domination of its own country.

Through technical devices like the radio and the loud-speaker, eighty million people were deprived of independent thought. It was thereby possible to subject them to the will of one man . . .

Earlier dictators needed highly qualified assistants, even at the lowest level, men who could think and act independently. The totalitarian system in the period of modern technical development can dispense with them; the means of communication alone make it possible to mechanize the lower leadership. As a result of this there arises the new type of the uncritical recipient of orders. . . . Another result was the far-reaching supervision of the citizens of the State and the maintenance of a high degree of secrecy for criminal acts.

The nightmare of many a man that one day nations could be dominated by technical means was all but realized in Hitler's totalitarian system.[1]

This was how Albert Speer, once one of Hitler's most trusted subordinates,

1. Final statement by Albert Speer to the International Military Tribunal for major war criminals at Nuremberg, 1946. Quoted in Alan Bullock, *Hitler: A Study in Tyranny*, rev. ed. (New York: Harper & Row, 1964), p. 380. An architect by training, Speer (1905–1981) first attracted Hitler's attention because of his expertise in that field and talent for orchestrating party rallies. He testified at Nuremberg, "If Hitler had had any friends, I would certainly have been one of his close friends." (*Inside the Third Reich: Memoirs by Albert Speer*, translated by Richard and Clara Winston [New York: Macmillan, 1970], p. 609). Hitler promoted Speer to Minister of Armaments during World War II, and in that capacity, Speer's efforts maintained German war production despite Allied bombing. As it became clear, however, that the war was lost and that Hitler was determined to fight on regardless of the cost to Germany, Speer made an attempt to assassinate the dictator.

sought to answer the question that every student of the Nazi phenomenon must ultimately ask: "How could it have happened?"[2] Because your textbook examines the roots and development of Hitler's doctrines, we will not focus in this chapter on the horrific ideology of the Nazi movement. Rather, we will examine the question that Speer addressed, for in the political history of the West, the Nazi party was the first totalitarian movement to make full use of modern media to gain and maintain power.

To achieve power, the Nazis persuaded substantial numbers of German voters to support their candidates. Certainly in the aftermath of Germany's defeat in 1918, the party's extreme nationalism attracted support, as did its anti-Semitism, which blamed the country's economic and political woes on its tiny Jewish minority. This Nazi political rhetoric of hatred ultimately became govern-

ment policy when Hitler gained power. Anti-Semitism took on brutal form in the Holocaust. Extreme nationalism manifested itself in the Nazi goal of settling Germans in eastern Europe by pushing out the area's Slavic natives. But other German parties in the 1920s and early 1930s also expressed anti-Semitic and nationalistic ideas. Your objective in this chapter is to determine how Nazi use of modern media and techniques, such as propaganda for molding public opinion, allowed Hitler's party to draw the German voter's attention. As you assess the evidence that follows, you should ask yourself what kind of image the Nazis projected. Why did it appeal to German voters? How did the Nazis use media to aid their rise to power? As a result of your analysis, you should be able to answer in some form that most disturbing question, "How could it have happened?"

BACKGROUND

In their use of modern media and campaign techniques to achieve power, Hitler and his followers built on a number of developments in Western politics, technology, and intellectual life. In the late nineteenth century the nature of politics in the West had begun to change. The right to vote in the more advanced European countries expanded to include all men

and, after World War I, women as well. The increased electorate demanded new political techniques. No longer could gentlemen politicians gain power by winning the support of a small, male, socially privileged electorate. A mass audience had to be addressed. Although many politicians at first refused to degrade themselves by appealing for support to such an audience, we can see emerging in late-nineteenth-century campaigns the modern political objective—and the requirement—of swaying large numbers of voters.

In 1879 and 1880, the British statesman William E. Gladstone (1809–1898)

2. See, for example, Richard F. Hamilton, *Who Voted for Hitler?* (Princeton, N.J.: Princeton University Press, 1982), p. 3.

won election to Parliament from Midlothian County, Scotland, following a campaign that became the model for modern ones, especially after Gladstone built his victory into his second term as prime minister. In Midlothian Gladstone delivered numerous public speeches. He presented many of these from the platform of his campaign train at a variety of locations, the first "whistle-stop campaign." Gladstone's campaign style found imitators in other democracies, although they did not always achieve his success. In the U.S. presidential campaign of 1896, the Democratic candidate, William Jennings Bryan (1860–1925), traveled about 18,000 miles and gave more than 600 speeches in an unsuccessful campaign against the Republican candidate, William McKinley (1843–1901). McKinley, who epitomized the old-style campaigner, simply received visitors from the press and public at the front porch of his Ohio home. Other candidates in many democracies would follow the example of Gladstone and Bryan.

Technological advances aided political leaders in their appeals for mass support. By the 1890s, developments like the Linotype machine, which mechanized typesetting, greatly reduced the price of newspapers and other printed materials for an increasingly literate public. Mass-circulation daily newspapers had tremendous potential for shaping public opinion. Political leaders also used other technological developments in delivering their messages. By 1920 the motion picture, photograph, radio, and mi-

crophone and public-address system all represented new media through which to influence the public.

At the same time that new media became available to political leaders, a greater understanding of how to influence public opinion was emerging in the early-twentieth-century West. During World War I, many belligerent countries employed increasingly sophisticated propaganda techniques to sustain the morale of their own citizens or to erode the will to fight among enemy populations. The lessons learned on influencing public opinion were not forgotten, as we will see.[3]

Industrial mass production required mass markets, and in the United States modern advertising techniques developed to stimulate the consumption necessary to sustain production. Advertising had political applications as well. One advertising strategy is to generate interest in a new product by creating suspense about it. When the Nazis launched a new Berlin newspaper, *Der Angriff* (*The Attack*), in 1927, a poster campaign was launched to heighten interest in it. The first posters issued simply stated, "The Attack?" The next group of posters proclaimed, "The Attack takes place on July 4!" The last set of posters was informational, alerting readers that the paper would appear on Mondays, that its

3. Hitler in *Mein Kampf* (translated by Ralph Manheim [Boston: Houghton Mifflin, 1943], pp. 176–186) wrote of the lessons he had drawn from Allied propaganda during World War I.

motto was "For the Suppressed against the Exploiters," and that "Every German man and every German woman will read 'The Attack' and subscribe to it!"[4]

Even science, particularly psychology, contributed to the understanding of human thought essential to those who sought to shape opinion. The French social psychologist Gustave Le Bon (1841–1931), for example, affected Hitler's political technique. Le Bon's ideas, although doubted today, were highly influential in the early twentieth century. A student of mass psychology, Le Bon claimed that the mind of the crowd was most susceptible to sentiment and emotion, not reason.[5]

The rapid pace of technological development and the equally swift emergence of techniques for molding public opinion meant that, by the 1920s, there existed an incompletely understood, underused, but nonetheless formidable arsenal for the politically ambitious to employ in attaining power. Forces prepared to exploit these technological and methodological developments emerged in the politically unstable environment of much of the post–World War II West.

Rooted in defeat, frustration in World War I, or the economic debacle of the Great Depression beginning in 1929, totalitarian movements emerged in many European countries. None of these movements proved more dangerous to traditional Western values than a German party that began insignificantly in 1919 as one of a multitude of right-wing, nationalist parties founded in response to the German defeat in the Great War. The party came to be known as the National Socialist German Workers' Party (Nazi), and Adolf Hitler quickly emerged not only as its leader but as a master of the new style of politics, including political propaganda.

The successful propagandist must correctly identify the fears and hopes of the people he or she wishes to influence. In Germany after World War I, Nazi propaganda had a great number of fears and hopes to exploit. Most Germans rejected the Treaty of Versailles that ended the war. Humiliated by the treaty's assignment of war guilt to Germany, they were also angered by the huge reparations their country was forced to pay the victorious allies. German nationalists especially rejected the unilateral disarmament the treaty sought to impose on Germany. All Germans hoped for some revision of the Treaty of Versailles.

Some Germans blamed the nation's defeat on internal enemies, not on battlefield disasters. These persons, mostly conservative, identified two chief groups on which to place responsibility for the internal dissent at the war's end that had brought the overthrow of Emperor William II (Kaiser Wilhelm II) and armistice. The first groups condemned for the

4. Described in Ernest K. Bramsted, *Goebbels and National Socialist Propaganda, 1925–1945* (East Lansing, MI: Michigan State University Press, 1965), p. 30.

5. Le Bon's great work was *The Crowd: A Study of the Popular Mind*, originally published in 1897 and available in German.

defeat were the parties of the left, the socialists and communists, who had participated in the Revolution of 1918 that created the Weimar Republic. To many, the communists seemed the greatest threat because that party had attempted to seize power and create a Marxist state by force in the Spartacist Revolt of 1919. The communist threat, moreover, persisted after 1919. The party's voting bloc grew as the economic problems of the Great Depression intensified, and many feared that the communists might gain power through election.

The other group on whom some Germans sought to fix the blame of their defeat was the country's small Jewish minority. Such Germans drew on nineteenth-century nationalist prejudices to allege some Jewish involvement in Germany's defeat. Certain political leaders of the early German republic, the men whose government signed the Versailles Treaty, were Jews. One prominent Jewish official, Walter Rathenau (1867–1922), died at the hands of a nationalist fanatic.

The Great Depression also increased Germans' fears after 1929. The depression hit Germany particularly hard, threatening economic ruin to many. Many parties and movements identified those fears and hopes of postwar Germans and sought to address them by rejecting the Treaty of Versailles, by portraying themselves as anticommunist or anti-Semitic, and by proposing solutions to the depression. But, as we will see, it was the skill of Hitler and the Nazis in the new politics and propaganda that allowed them to exploit

most effectively Germans' fears and hopes to gain power.

It was Hitler who transformed a party that essentially had been little more than a collection of malcontents in the back room of a Munich beer hall into a movement with a considerable following in the 1920s. It was Hitler who gave the party a visual identity by adopting its symbol, the swastika, and by creating its banners. It was also Hitler who exploited the alienation of many war veterans by drawing them into the S.A. (*Sturm Abteilung*), the Storm Troopers or uniformed, paramilitary branch of the party, which was prepared to use violence and intimidation against communists and socialists. And it was Hitler who launched an abortive attempt in 1923 to seize power forcibly for his party.

Hitler's failed revolution resulted in his brief imprisonment, during which he wrote *Mein Kampf* (*My Struggle*), the political statement of his movement. On his release Hitler resolved to seek power within the political system— that is, to win power through the electoral system of the German republic. To his quest for power Hitler brought the Nazi party apparatus and symbols, his excellent oratorical ability, and, most dangerously, a keen understanding of the uses of political propaganda and modern media to mold public opinion. Aiding him in presenting his party to German voters was Joseph Goebbels (1897–1945), a man whose speaking abilities, understanding of propaganda and modern media, and political unscrupulousness rivaled Hitler's own.

In his quest for power after 1923, Hitler led the Nazis through a number of electoral campaigns. The first results of Nazi appeals to German voters disappointed many of Hitler's followers. Indeed, in elections to the Reichstag, Germany's parliament, the party's vote actually declined during the 1920s. In the elections of May 1924, it captured 6.5 percent of the vote; that total declined to 3.0 percent in December 1924 and 2.6 percent in May 1928. The party's electoral breakthrough of 1930, however, reversed this trend as the Nazis increased their share of the Reichstag vote to 18.3 percent. Certainly, in achieving their victory, the Nazis' extreme nationalist message capitalized on the Young Plan of 1929, which had failed to reduce the war reparation payments to the Allies so deeply resented by many Germans. The growing severity of the Great Depression after 1929 also encouraged many Germans to look to the strong leadership that Hitler claimed to offer. As party membership and dues grew, and as Hitler secured some limited financial aid from a few wealthy opponents of the Young Plan such as Alfred Hugenberg,[6] for the first time the Nazis had sufficient funds to exploit the modern media thoroughly.

The Nazi share of the vote increased rapidly after 1930. The party especially demonstrated its media skills in 1932, when Hitler ran for president of Germany against the incumbent, the octogenarian war hero Field Marshal Paul von Hindenburg. Although Hindenburg won the election with 53 percent of the vote to Hitler's 36.8 percent, the campaign built momentum for the Nazis and helped them to perfect their campaign style. In the Reichstag elections held in July 1932, the Nazis won 37.4 percent of the vote to become the largest single party in parliament, a distinction they retained despite a diminished Nazi 33.1 percent of the vote in Reichstag elections in November 1932. On the basis of these victories, which gave the Nazis control of the largest single bloc of seats in the Reichstag, conservative associates of President von Hindenburg finally convinced him to name Hitler chancellor or prime minister on January 30, 1933. The Nazis had gained control of the government, and German democracy was their first victim: by the end of the year the country was a one-party, totalitarian state.

6. **Alfred Hugenberg** (1865–1951): leader of the Nationalist Party and a bigoted conservative ultranationalist with tremendous wealth based in industry and great influence founded on his control of a number of newspapers and Germany's largest film and newsreel firm. His newsreels, shown regularly in German theaters, and his newspapers gave the Nazis considerable coverage. Like other conservatives, Hugenberg made the mistake of classifying Hitler with other politicians. Hitler quickly excluded Hugenberg from the government once the Nazis had gained power.

THE METHOD

This chapter presents a variety of evidence: theoretical writings on Nazi political strategy, visual propaganda used by Nazis to publicize their cause, and observations on the public reception of Hitler's media campaign. Through individual and comparative study of these sources, you should be able to determine the nature of the attraction of the Nazis for German voters.

The evidence opens with two selections by Hitler on the means for gaining power. Sources 1 and 2 are taken from Hitler's *Mein Kampf*, which he wrote during his imprisonment in 1923–1924. In this work, often ignored in his early days, Hitler stated much of his future program, including his rabidly anti-Jewish and anti-Marxist policies and his plans to expand Germany eastward. In the evidence presented in this chapter, you will read Hitler's ideas on the use of propaganda and other tactics for coming to power. How were the ideas for seizing power that he expressed in 1924 to be realized within a decade? How would you assess his understanding of human psychology?

When you finish the Hitler materials, you will find an assortment of evidence selected to further your analysis of how the Nazis sought to win support for their party. You will be examining, in effect, a thoroughly modern public relations effort, complete with slogans. In Source 3, assess the nature of the Nazi propaganda effort as defined by its director, Joseph Goebbels. Why do you think Goebbels so closely controlled the party's propaganda?

Consider next the S.A., remembering, of course, that orders like that in Source 4 are not always rigidly obeyed by subordinates in any organization. Examine the pictorial evidence on the S.A. in Sources 5 and 6. The banners express Nazi slogans; the Regensburg S.A. banner proclaims, "Everything for the Fatherland." Nazi meetings always opened with solemn processions of such banners. What impression did the marching men seek to convey to their audience on the streets of Spandau?

Next read Source 7, the report of the brawl in the Pharus Hall in 1927. You should understand that this brawl was no accident; Goebbels deliberately scheduled the meeting to take place in a hall used by the Nazis' enemies, the communist and socialist political and labor groups. The hall, moreover, was in the heart of a left-wing, working-class district of Berlin. What could Goebbels have hoped to gain from the fight that was bound to ensue from his provocative action in selecting such a meeting site?

The next evidence consists of posters produced by the Nazis. The poster, a traditional political medium, was used extensively by the Nazis. They relied especially on posters in their early days, before they secured the funds necessary to exploit more novel media. The poster in Source 8 was part of the propaganda campaign Nazi leaders organized for the spring 1924 German legislative elections. At the time of the elections, Hitler remained in prison as a result of his failed attempt to seize power in 1923, and his party nominally was outlawed. Thus party leaders entered the campaign as part of a right-wing, nationalist coalition, the "Völkischen Block" identified on the poster. The German word *Volk* is difficult to translate. Superficially, it may be translated as "people" or "nation," but for early-twentieth-century Germans the word had a much more complex meaning conveying the innate superiority of German culture, language, and people over non-German cultures and peoples. Thus its use to identify a right-wing, nationalistic political alliance was not accidental, and was entirely consistent with Nazi ideology. Indeed, the Nazi origins of this poster are evident in the party's insignia, the swastika, in the lower corners of the poster. Analyze the poster to ascertain what sentiments the Nazis appealed to in post–World War I Germany and to which classes they looked for support. What group did the "String-puller" represent (notice his watch chain)? What message did his identity convey to Germans?

The second poster, Source 9, conveys much about Germany in the 1920s. Why might the Nazis address females? Of what problems did this poster, issued in the midst of the depression, remind Germans? What did it promise them? The third poster, Source 10, was the work of a skilled propaganda artist, "Mjolnir" ("Hammer"), who drew cartoons extensively for the Berlin newspaper *Der Angriff,* edited by Goebbels. Analyze the artist's message by examining the faces of the Storm Troopers. What sentiment do you find there? What sort of message does this poster convey about the party and its solutions for Germany?

Another Nazi political device was the public mass meeting, designed to convey the impression of vast support for the party. It was a technique Hitler learned early while observing Social Democratic demonstrations as a youth in Vienna. He wrote in *Mein Kampf*:

> With what changed feeling I now gazed at the endless columns of a mass demonstration of Viennese workers that took place one day as they marched past four abreast! For nearly two hours I stood there watching with bated breath the gigantic human dragon slowly winding by.

As their resources increased, the Nazis perfected the mass meeting. Source 11 shows one such rally in Berlin's Sports Palace, a favored site because it seated a large audience of 12,000 persons. Events like this were always carefully staged: The aisles are lined with the party faithful, ready for the entry of the speakers, accompanied by a uniformed S.A. guard unit and party banners. Why would such an elaborate spectacle have been important to the party cause?

The Nazis also employed music as propaganda to win support. The person whose name the song bears in Source 12, Horst Wessel, was a young Nazi who wrote the words to the song as a poem. The words eventually were set to a traditional stirring tune, but Horst Wessel himself drifted away from the party in pursuit of a female prostitute. He took up residence with her and was fatally shot by her procurer, who coincidentally was a communist, in February 1930. In Goebbels's hands, Horst Wessel's misspent life was transformed into that of a hero martyred in the Nazis' cause by their communist enemies. His song became Germany's second national anthem after *Deutschland über Alles* (*Germany Above All*) in the Nazi era. In reading the song's words, identify the problems it identifies. What benefits does the song claim the party offered Germans?

Also part of Nazi political propaganda was the creation of what Goebbels himself called the "Führer (Leader) Myth." This myth, which Goebbels regarded as one of his great propaganda accomplishments, attempted to convince Germans that a strong, courageous, and brilliant Hitler personified a Germany restored from its defeat. In its more extreme manifestations, the myth almost deified Hitler, appealing to many Germans accustomed to strong rulers during the monarchy and therefore unhappy with what they believed to be the weak government of the republic. Source 13 is drawn from an elementary school textbook published shortly after the Nazis gained power, but it describes Hitler's campaign for power. What qualities did the party's propaganda apparatus wish the young to believe that Hitler possessed?

The Nazis did not come to power solely through conveying a positive image for their party and leader, however. They also used propaganda to exploit fears, employed violence to intimidate voters, and used new technologies to sway the thinking of their fellow Germans. Source 14 is a pamphlet, issued, you must remember, in the midst of the economic collapse of the early 1930s. Recall the events of Germany's past as you read it, and analyze its appeal.

The violence of the Hitler movement can best be viewed on the local level. The graph in Source 15 presents

the rhythm of political life in the German town of Northeim. The number of political meetings, to which the Nazis contributed more than their share, increased sharply at election times. What else increased?

Source 16 presents the political beliefs of Dr. Joseph Goebbels, a fervent Nazi and a master of political propaganda. Convinced of his own historical importance, Goebbels kept a diary from his earliest days in politics to give future generations a record of his thought and activities. He was still making entries in 1945 as the war ended. When Russian armies closed in on Berlin, Goebbels committed suicide. His diary, like any diary, must be used with caution, because most writers tend to put their own behavior and motivations in the best light. Nonetheless, it does offer an important perspective on Goebbels's propaganda work. Assess his command of his job as you read the selection. What new technologies did he employ in winning popular support for the Nazis?

The evidence in this chapter concludes with two observations on the impact of Nazi efforts to win support among Germans. The first is a report by a German Protestant leader noting membership losses from the Protestant youth movement to the Nazis. The second is by the American correspondent William L. Shirer (1904–1993), who covered events in Germany from 1934 to 1941. A perceptive observer of the Hitler movement, Shirer was able to assess the kind of appeal it had been building in Germany during the years before he arrived. What appeal to

Germans do these two very different persons note in the Nazi movement?

Now turn to the evidence. You should read it with the foregoing considerations in mind, seeking to answer the central questions of this chapter: What image did the Nazis convey to German voters? Why did they appeal to German voters? How did the Nazis use media to aid their rise to power?

Sources 1 and 2 from Adolf Hitler, Mein Kampf, translated by Ralph Mannheim (Boston: Houghton Mifflin, 1943), pp. 178–184, 343, 582; pp. 42–44. Copyright 1943 and renewed 1971 by Houghton Mifflin Company. Reprinted by permission of Houghton Mifflin Company. All rights reserved.

THE EVIDENCE

FUNDAMENTAL POLITICAL STRATEGIES OF THE NAZI PARTY

1. Hitler on the Nature and Purpose of Propaganda

The goal of a political reform movement will never be reached by enlightenment work or by influencing ruling circles, but only by the achievement of political power. Every world-moving idea has not only the right, but also the duty, of securing, those means which make possible the execution of its ideas. Success is the one earthly judge concerning the right or wrong of such an effort, and under success we must not understand, as in the year 1918, the achievement of power in itself, but an exercise of that power that will benefit the nation. Thus, a coup d'état must not be regarded as successful if, as senseless state's attorneys in Germany think today, the revolutionaries have succeeded in possessing themselves of the state power, but only if, by the realization of the purposes and aims underlying such a revolutionary action, more benefit accrues to the nation than under the past régime. Something which cannot very well be claimed for the German revolution, as the gangster job of autumn, 1918, calls itself.[7] . . .

---

7. **the gangster job of autumn 1918:** the revolution of October and November 1918 that overthrew Emperor William II and established the Weimar Republic. Hitler, like many of the German right, believed that revolution to have been the work of socialists, communists, and Jews, who, by toppling the old government, had "stabbed in the back" the German army at the front in World War I and made defeat in that conflict inevitable.

The victory of an idea will be possible the sooner, the more comprehensively propaganda has prepared people as a whole and the more exclusive, rigid, and firm the organization which carries out the fight in practice. . . .

To whom should propaganda be addressed? To the scientifically trained intelligentsia or to the less educated masses?

It must be addressed always and exclusively to the masses.

What the intelligentsia—or those who today unfortunately often go by that name—what they need is not propaganda but scientific instruction. The content of propaganda is not science any more than the object represented in a poster is art. The art of the poster lies in the designer's ability to attract the attention of the crowd by form and color. A poster advertising an art exhibit must direct the attention of the public to the art being exhibited; the better it succeeds in this, the greater is the art of the poster itself. The poster should give the masses an idea of the significance of the exhibition, it should not be a substitute for the art on display. Anyone who wants to concern himself with the art itself must do more than study the poster; and it will not be enough for him just to saunter through the exhibition. We may expect him to examine and immerse himself in the individual works, and thus little by little form a fair opinion.

A similar situation prevails with what we today call propaganda.

The function of propaganda does not lie in the scientific training of the individual, but in calling the masses' attention to certain facts, processes, necessities, etc., whose significance is thus for the first time placed within their field of vision.

The whole art consists in doing this so skillfully that everyone will be convinced that the fact is real, the process necessary, the necessity correct, etc. But since propaganda is not and cannot be the necessity in itself, since its function, like the poster, consists in attracting the attention of the crowd, and not in educating those who are already educated or who are striving after education and knowledge, its effect for the most part must be aimed at the emotions and only to a very limited degree at the so-called intellect.

All propaganda must be popular and its intellectual level must be adjusted to the most limited intelligence among those it is addressed to. Consequently, the greater the mass it is intended to reach, the lower its purely intellectual level will have to be. But if, as in propaganda for sticking out a war, the aim is to influence a whole people, we must avoid excessive intellectual demands on our public, and too much caution cannot be exerted in this direction.

The more modest its intellectual ballast, the more exclusively it takes into consideration the emotions of the masses, the more effective it will be. And this is the best proof of the soundness or unsoundness of a propaganda campaign, and not success in pleasing a few scholars or young aesthetes.

The art of propaganda lies in understanding the emotional ideas of the great masses and finding, through a psychologically correct form, the way to the attention and thence to the heart of the broad masses. The fact that our bright boys do not understand this merely shows how mentally lazy and conceited they are.

Once we understand how necessary it is for propaganda to be adjusted to the broad mass, the following rule results:

It is a mistake to make propaganda many-sided, like scientific instruction, for instance.

The receptivity of the great masses is very limited, their intelligence is small, but their power of forgetting is enormous. In consequence of these facts, all effective propaganda must be limited to a very few points and must harp on these in slogans until the last member of the public understands what you want him to understand by your slogan. As soon as you sacrifice this slogan and try to be many-sided, the effect will piddle away, for the crowd can neither digest nor retain the material offered. In this way the result is weakened and in the end entirely cancelled out.

Thus we see that propaganda must follow a simple line and correspondingly the basic tactics must be psychologically sound. . . .

But the most brilliant propagandist techniques will yield no success unless one fundamental principle is borne in mind constantly and with unflagging attention. It must confine itself to a few points and repeat them over and over. Here, as so often in this world, persistence is the first and most important requirement for success.

2. Hitler on Terror in Politics

Like the woman, whose psychic state is determined less by grounds of abstract reason than by an indefinable emotional longing for a force which will complement her nature, and who, consequently, would rather bow to a strong man than dominate a weakling, likewise the masses love a commander more than a petitioner and feel inwardly more satisfied by a doctrine, tolerating no other beside itself, than by the granting of liberalistic freedom with which, as a rule, they can do little, and are prone to feel that they have been abandoned. They are equally unaware of their shameless spiritual terrorization and the hideous abuse of their human freedom, for they absolutely fail to suspect the inner insanity of the whole doctrine. All they see is the ruthless force and brutality of its calculated manifestations, to which they always submit in the end. . . .

I achieved an equal understanding of the importance of physical terror toward the individual and the masses.

Here, too, the psychological effect can be calculated with precision.

Terror at the place of employment, in the factory, in the meeting hall, and on the occasion of mass demonstrations will always be successful unless opposed by equal terror.

NAZI TECHNIQUES FOR
PUBLICIZING THEIR CAUSE

Sources 3 and 4 from Jeremy Noakes and Geoffrey Pridham, editors, Documents on Nazism,
1919–1945 *(New York: Viking, 1975), pp. 103–104; pp. 163–164. Copyright © 1975 by Jeremy
Noakes and Geoffrey Pridham. Reprinted by permission of Sterling Lord Literistic, Inc.*

3. Joseph Goebbels, Directives for the Presidential Campaign of 1932

(1) Reich Propaganda Department to all *Gaue*[8] and all *Gau* Propaganda
Departments.
. . . A striking slogan:
Those who want everything to stay as it is vote for Hindenburg. Those who want
everything changed vote for Hitler. . . .

(2) Reich Propaganda Department to all *Gaue* and all *Gau* Propaganda
Departments.
. . . Hitler Poster. The Hitler poster depicts a fascinating Hitler head on a
completely black background. Subtitle: white on black—"Hitler." In accordance with the Führer's wish this poster is to be put up only during the final
days [of the campaign]. Since experience shows that during the final days
there is a variety of coloured posters, this poster with its completely black
background will contrast with all the others and will produce a tremendous
effect on the masses. . . .

(3) Reich Propaganda Department
Instructions for the National Socialist Press for the election of the Reich President

1. From Easter Tuesday 29 March until Sunday 10 April inclusive, all
National Socialist papers, both daily and weekly, must appear in an enlarged
edition with a tripled circulation. Two-thirds of this tripled circulation must be
made available, without charge, to the *Gau* leadership responsible for its area
of distribution for propaganda purposes. . . .

2. From Easter Tuesday 29 March until Sunday 3 April inclusive, a special
topic must be dealt with every day on the first page of all our papers in a big
spread. Tuesday 29 March: Hitler as a man. Wednesday 30 March: Hitler as a
fighter (gigantic achievement through his willpower, etc.). Friday 1 April:
Hitler as a statesman—plenty of photos. . . .

8. **Gaue:** the administrative divisions of Germany set up by the Nazi party.

3. On Sunday 3 April, at noon (end of an Easter truce), the great propaganda journey of the Führer through Germany will start, through which about a million people are to be reached directly through our Führer's speeches. . . . The press organization is planned so that four press centres will be set up in Germany, which in turn will pass on immediately any telephone calls to the other papers of their area, whose names have been given them.

4. S.A. Order 111 of Adolf Hitler, 1926

1. The SA will appear in public only in closed formation. This is at the same time one of the most powerful forms of propaganda. The sight of a large number of men inwardly and outwardly uniform and disciplined, whose total commitment to fighting is clearly visible or can be sensed, makes the deepest impression on every German and speaks a more convincing and inspiring language to his heart than speech, logic, or the written word is ever capable of doing.

Calm composure and natural behaviour underline the impression of strength—the strength of marching columns and the strength of the cause for which they are marching.

The inner strength of the cause makes the German conclude instinctively that it is right: "for only what is right, honest and good can release real strength." Where whole crowds purposefully risk life and limb and their livelihood for a cause (not in the upsurge of sudden mass suggestion), the cause must be great and true!

Here lies the task of the SA from the point of view of propaganda and recruiting. The SA leaders must gear the details and forms of their appearances to a common line.

2. This instinctive "proof of truth" is not underlined but disturbed and dissipated by the addition of logical arguments and propaganda. The following should be avoided: cheers and heckling, posters about day-to-day controversies, abuse, accompanying speeches, leaflets, festivals, public amusements.

3. It is inappropriate for the SA to work in one way one day and differently the next, according to circumstances. The SA must always and on principle refrain from all actual political propaganda and agitation. This should remain the task of the political leadership alone. However, each SA man is also a member of the Party and as such of course must cooperate as much as he can in the propaganda of the political leadership. But not the SA as such. Not the SA men on duty and in uniform.

The SA man is the holy freedom fighter. The member of the Party is the clever propagandist and skilled agitator. Political propaganda tries to enlighten the opponent, to argue with him, to understand his point of view, to enter into his thoughts, to agree with him to a certain extent. But when the SA arrives on the scene, this stops. It makes no concessions. It goes all out. It only recognizes the motto (metaphorically): Kill or be killed!

4. It is forbidden for an SA to appeal to the public (or its opponents) orally or in writing, either through proclamations, announcements, leaflets, press "corrections," letters, advertisements, invitations to festivals or meetings, or in any other way.

Public consecrations of the colours and sports competitions must take place within the framework of an event organized by a local branch, which alone issues the invitations or announcements for it.

6. S.A. Propaganda Rally in Spandau, 1932

Sources 5 and 6 from Bundesarchiv, Koblenz.

5. Banners of the Regensburg S.A.:
"Everything for the Fatherland, 1923"

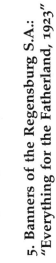

Source 7 from Jeremy Noakes and Geoffrey Pridham, editors, Documents on Nazism, 1919–1945 *(New York: Viking, 1975), pp. 83–84. Copyright © 1975 by Jeremy Noakes and Geoffrey Pridham. Reprinted by permission of Sterling Lord Literistic, Inc.*

7. Report of a Nazi Meeting Held in a Heavily Communist Quarter of Berlin, February 1927

On the 11th of this month the Party held a public mass meeting in the "Pharus [Beer] Halls" in Wedding, the real working-class quarter, with the subject: "The Collapse of the Bourgeois Class State." Comrade Dr Goebbels was the speaker. It was quite clear to us what that meant. It had to be visibly shown that National Socialism is determined to reach the workers. We succeeded once before in getting a foothold in Wedding. There were huge crowds at the meeting. More than 1,000 people filled the hall whose political composition was four-fifths SA to one-fifth KPD.[9] But the latter had gathered their main forces in the street. When the meeting was opened by Comrade Daluege, the SA leader, there were, as was expected, provocative shouts of "On a point of order!" After the KPD members had been told that *we*, not they, decided points of order, and that they would have the right to ask questions after the talk by Comrade Dr Goebbels, the first scuffling broke out. Peace seemed to be restored until there was renewed heckling. When the chairman announced that the hecklers would be sent out if the interruptions continued, the KPD worked themselves into a frenzy. Meanwhile, the SA had gradually surrounded the centre of the disturbance, and the Communists, sensing the danger, suddenly became aggressive. What followed all happened within three or four minutes. Within seconds both sides had picked up chairs, beer mugs, even tables, and a savage fight began. The Communists were gradually pushed under the gallery which we had taken care to occupy and soon chairs and glasses came hurtling down from there also. The fight was quickly decided: the KPD left with 85 wounded, more or less: that is to say, they could not get down the stairs as fast as they had calmly and "innocently" climbed them. On our side we counted 3 badly wounded and about 10–12 slightly. When the police appeared the fight was already over. Marxist terrorism had been bloodily suppressed.

9. **Kommunistische Partei Deutschlands:** the German Communist Party.

Source 8 from Ebenhausen: Langewiesche/Bradt Verlag.

8. Poster: "The String-Puller. White Collar and Manual Laborers: Vote for the Völkischen Block," 1924

9. Poster: "Women! Millions of Men Are Without Work. Millions of Children Are Without a Future. Save the German Family! Vote for Adolf Hitler!," 1932

10. Poster: "National Socialism: The Organized Will of the People," 1932

Source 11 from Bundesarchiv, Koblenz.

11. A National Socialist Rally in the Berlin Sports Palace, September 1930

Source 12 from Liederbuch der Nationalsozialistischen Deutschen Arbeiterpartei *(Munich: Zentralverlag der NSDAP, 1938). Selection translated by Julius R. Ruff.*

12. "The Horst Wessel Song,"
ca 1930

Raise high the banner! Close the serried ranks!
S.A. marches on with calm, firm stride.
Comrades killed by the Red Front and the Reaction[10]
March in spirit in our ranks.

Clear the streets for the brown battalions![11]
Clear the streets for the Storm Troopers!
The swastika gives hope to millions.
The day of freedom and bread is breaking.
The roll call is heard for the last time!

10. **Red Front:** the *Rot Frontkämpfer Bund* or Red Fighters League, the communist opposition to the Storm Troopers. The more traditional right, the Nationalist Party, which sought a restoration of a monarchy and is here called the **Reaction**, had an armed force, too, uniformed in green.

11. The S.A. uniform was brown.

[203]

We all stand ready for the struggle!
Soon Hitler's banner will fly over every street
And Germany's bondage will soon end.

Source 13 from George L. Mosse, editor, Nazi Culture: Intellectual, Cultural, and Social Life in the Third Reich *(New York: Grosset and Dunlap, 1966), pp. 291–293. Selection translated by the editor. Used by permission of the Estate of George L. Mosse.*

13. Otto Dietrich, Description of Hitler's Campaign by Airplane, 1932

On April 8, 1932, a severe storm, beyond all imagining, raged over Germany. Hail rattled down from dark clouds. Flash floods devastated fields and gardens. Muddy foam washed over streets and railroad tracks, and the hurricane uprooted even the oldest and biggest trees.

We are driving to the Mannheim Airport. Today no one would dare expose an airplane to the fury of the elements. The German Lufthansa has suspended all air traffic.

In the teeming rain stands the solid mass of the most undaunted of our followers. They want to be present, they want to see for themselves when the Führer entrusts himself to an airplane in this raging storm.

Without a moment's hesitation the Führer orders that we take off at once. We have an itinerary to keep, for in western Germany hundreds of thousands are waiting.

It is only with the greatest difficulty that the ground crew and the SA troopers, with long poles in their strong fists, manage to hold on to the wings of the plane, so that the gale does not hurl it into the air and wreck it. The giant motors begin to turn over. Impatient with its fetters, the plane begins to buck and shake, eager for the takeoff on the open runway.

One more short rearing up and our wild steed sweeps across the greensward. A few perilous jumps, one last short touch with earth, and presto we are riding through the air straight into the witches' broth.

This is no longer flying, this is a whirling dance which today we remember only as a faraway dream. Now we jump across the aerial downdrafts, now we whip our way through tattered clouds, again a whirlpool threatens to drag us down, and then it seems that a giant catapult hurls us into steep heights.

And yet, what a feeling of security is in us in the face of this fury of the elements! The Führer's absolute serenity transmits itself to all of us. In every hour of danger he is ruled by his granite-like faith in his world-historical mission, the unshakable certainty that Providence will keep him from danger for the accomplishment of his great task.

Even here he remained the pre-eminent man, who masters danger because in his innermost being he has risen far above it. In this ruthless contest between man and machine the Führer attentively follows the heroic battle of our Master Pilot Bauer as he steers straight through the gale, or quickly jumps across a whole storm field, and then again narrowly avoids a threatening cloud wall, while the radio operator on board zealously catches the signals sent by the airfields.

Source 14 from Jeremy Noakes and Geoffrey Pridham, editors, Documents on Nazism, 1919–1945 *(New York: Viking, 1975), p. 106. Copyright © 1975 by Jeremy Noakes and Geoffrey Pridham. Reprinted by permission of Sterling Lord Literistic, Inc.*

14. Nazi Pamphlet, ca 1932

Attention! Gravediggers at work!
Middle-class citizens![12] Retailers! Craftsmen! Tradesmen!
A new blow aimed at your ruin is being prepared and carried out in Hanover!
The present system enables the gigantic concern
WOOLWORTH (America)
supported by finance capital, to build a new vampire business in the centre of the city in the Georgstrasse to expose you to complete ruin. This is the wish and aim of the black-red[13] system as expressed in the following remarks of Marxist leaders.
The Marxist Engels declared in May 1890: "If capital destroys the small artisans and retailers it does a good thing. . . ."
That is the black-red system of today!
Put an end to this system and its abettors! Defend yourself, middle-class citizen! Join the mighty organization that alone is in a position to conquer your arch-enemies. Fight with us in the Section for Craftsmen and Retail Traders within the great freedom movement of Adolf Hitler!
Put an end to the system!
Mittelstand, vote for List 8![14]

12. **Middle-class citizens:** this is a rather imprecise translation of the original German *Mittelstand*. That word, which is difficult to translate, here describes a very specific segment of society to whom the Nazis made special appeal: small shopkeepers and craftsmen whose livelihoods increasingly were threatened by competition from large department stores and big industrial concerns.
13. Prussia was governed by a coalition of the Catholic Center Party and the Social Democrats. Because of its association with the church, the Center was labeled "Black"; the leftist Socialists were labeled "Red."
14. **Mittelstand:** middle-class shopkeepers and craftsmen.

Source 15 adapted from William Sheridan Allen, The Nazi Seizure of Power: The Experience of a Single German Town, 1922–1945, revised ed. (New York: Franklin Watts, 1984), p. 321. Copyright © 1965, 1984 by William Sheridan Allen. Used with permission of the publisher, Scholastic Library Publishing.

15. Political Violence in Northeim, Germany, 1930–1932

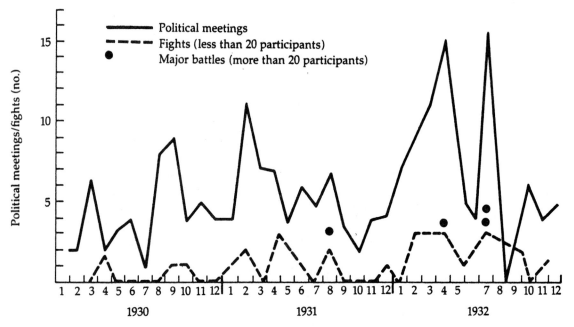

Source 16 from Joseph Goebbels, My Part in Germany's Fight, translated by Kurt Fielder (New York: Howard Fertig, 1979), pp. 44, 47–48, 55, 66, 145–146, 214.

16. Joseph Goebbels, My Part in Germany's Fight, 1934

February 29th, 1932.

Our propaganda is working at high pressure.

The clerical work is finished. Now the technical side of the fight begins. What enormous preparations are necessary to organize such a vast distribution!

Reported to the Leader (Hitler) at noon. I gave him details as to the measures we are taking. The election campaign is chiefly to be fought by means of placards and addresses. We have not much capital, but as the Party is working gratuitously a little money goes a long way.

Fifty thousand gramophone records have been made, which are so small they can be slipped into an ordinary envelope. The supporters of the Government will be astonished when they place these miniature records on the gramophone!

In Berlin everything is going well.

A film (of me) is being made and I speak a few words in it for about ten minutes. It is to be shown in all public gardens and squares of the larger cities. . . .

March 8th, 1932.

Dictate two articles and heaps of handbills. The placard war has reached its climax. Up till now we lead in the race.

Interview with the *Popolo d'Italia.*[15] I describe our methods and means of propaganda. The representative of this influential Italian paper is positively dumbfounded. "The vastest and most up-to-date propaganda of Europe." . . .

March 18th, 1932.

A critical innovation: the Leader will conduct this next campaign by plane. By this means he will be able to speak three or four times a day at various places as opportunity serves, and address about one and a half millions of people in spite of the time being so short.

April 14th, 1932.

The Leader is planning a new plane campaign for the Prussian elections. He intends to start on Sunday. His perseverance is admirable, and it is amazing how he stands the continual strain.

At work again organizing his great 'plane trips. Now we have quite a lot of experience in these matters.

An important problem is how to make use of the Leader's propaganda flights for the Press. Everything has to be minutely prepared and organized beforehand.

October 4th, 1932.

Monday: Berlin. Prepared for the Leader's meeting at Munich. Dashed off designs for seven huge placards. Things knocked off quickly and enthusiastically are always good.

It is difficult to adapt men used to editorial work to the necessities of electioneering. They are too accurate and slow. . . .

January 18th, 1933.

In the evening we go to see the film "Rebel," by Luis Trencker. A first-class production of an artistic film. Thus I could imagine the film of the future, revolutionary in character, with grand mass-scenes, composed with enormous

15. **Popolo d'Italia:** a newspaper founded by the Italian Fascist leader Mussolini in 1914 and edited by him until he gained political control of Italy in 1922, this journal was the official organ of the Fascist dictatorship in Italy by 1932. Indeed, until the newspaper ceased publication in 1943, Mussolini still set its general editorial direction and even contributed articles himself.

vital energy. In one scene, in which a gigantic crucifix is carried out of a small church by the revolutionaries, the audience is deeply moved. Here you really see what can be done with the film as an artistic medium, when it is really understood. We are all much impressed.

February 10th, 1933.

The Sportpalast[16] is already packed by six o'clock in the evening. All the squares in the city swarm with people waiting to hear the Leader's speech. In the whole Reich twenty to thirty millions more are listening in to it.

Drag myself to the Sportpalast, still weak with the illness from which I have not yet fully recovered. On the platform first I address the Press, and then for twenty minutes at the microphone speak to the audience in the Sportpalast. It goes better than I had thought. It is a strange experience suddenly to be faced with an inanimate microphone when one is used to addressing a living crowd, to be uplifted by the atmosphere of it, and to read the effect of one's speech in the expression on the faces of one's hearers.

The Leader is greeted by frantic cheering. He delivers a fine address containing an outspoken declaration of war against Marxism. Towards the end he strikes a wonderful, incredibly solemn note, and closes with the word "Amen"! It is uttered so naturally that all are deeply moved and affected by it. It is filled with so much strength and belief, is so novel and courageous, that it is not to be compared to anything that has gone beforehand.

This address will be received with enthusiasm throughout Germany. The nation will be ours almost without a struggle.

The masses at the Sportpalast are beside themselves with delight. Now the German Revolution has truly begun.

'Phone calls from different parts of the country report on the fine effect the speech has made even over the Radio. As an instrument for propaganda on a large scale the efficacy of the Radio has not yet been sufficiently appreciated. In any case our adversaries did not recognize its value. All the better, we shall have to explore its possibilities.

16. **Sportpalast:** The Sports Palace, a large, indoor sports arena in Berlin.

THE IMPACT OF
NAZI METHODS

Source 17 from Jeremy Noakes and Geoffrey Pridham, editors, Documents on Nazism, 1919–
1945 *(New York: Viking, 1975), p. 108. Copyright © 1975 by Jeremy Noakes and Geoffrey
Pridham. Reprinted by permission of Sterling Lord Literistic, Inc.*

17. Report on the Problem of Stemming the Spread of Nazi Ideas in the Protestant Youth Movement, 1931

The cause which at the moment is most closely associated with the name of
National Socialism and with which, at a moderate estimate, certainly 70 per
cent of our young people, often lacking knowledge of the facts, are in ardent
sympathy, must be regarded, as far as our ranks are concerned, more as an
ethical than a political matter. Our young people show little political interest.
Secondary school students are not really much concerned with the study of
Hitler's thoughts; it is simply something irrational, something infectious that
makes the blood pulse through one's veins and conveys an impression that
something great is under way, the roaring of a stream which one does not wish
to escape: "If you can't feel it you will never grasp it. . . ."

All this must be taken into account when we see the ardour and fire of this
movement reflected in our ranks. A pedantic and nagging approach seems to
me useless, and so do all attempts, however well-intentioned, by the leader to
refute the policy of National Socialism in detail. The majority of the young
fight against this with a strange instinct. We must, in keeping with our
responsibility, though it is difficult in individual cases, try first to influence the
ethos, and in this we must maintain an attitude above parties. We must
educate in such a way that this enthusiasm is duly tempered by deeper
understanding and by disenchantment, that words like "national honour and
dignity" do not become slogans but arouse individual responsibility so that no
brash demagogues grow up among us.

Source 18 from William L. Shirer, Berlin Diary, The Journal of a Foreign Correspondent,
*1934–1941 (New York: Knopf, 1941), pp. 18, 19, 21, 22, 23. Reprinted by permission of Don
Congdon Associates, Inc. Copyright © 1941, renewed 1969 by William L. Shirer.*

18. William L. Shirer,
Reactions to the Nazi Party
Rally at Nuremberg, 1934

NUREMBERG, *September 5*

I'm beginning to comprehend, I think, some of the reasons for Hitler's
astounding success. Borrowing a chapter from the Roman church,[17] he is
restoring pageantry and colour and mysticism to the drab lives of twentieth-
century Germans. This morning's opening meeting in the Luitpold Hall on the
outskirts of Nuremberg was more than a gorgeous show; it also had
something of the mysticism and religious fervour of an Easter or Christmas
Mass in a great Gothic cathedral. The hall was a sea of brightly coloured flags.
Even Hitler's arrival was made dramatic. The band stopped playing. There
was a hush over the thirty thousand people packed in the hall. Then the band
struck up the *Badenweiler March,* a very catchy tune, and used only, I'm told,
when Hitler makes his big entries. Hitler appeared in the back of the
auditorium, and followed by his aides, Göring, Goebbels, Hess, Himmler, and
the others, he strode slowly down the long centre aisle while thirty thousand
hands were raised in salute. It is a ritual, the old-timers say, which is always
followed. Then an immense symphony orchestra played Beethoven's *Egmont*
Overture. Great Klieg lights played on the stage, where Hitler sat surrounded
by a hundred party officials and officers of the army and navy. Behind them
the "blood flag," the one carried down the streets of Munich in the ill-fated
putsch. Behind this, four or five hundred S.A. standards. When the music was
over, Rudolf Hess, Hitler's closest confidant, rose and slowly read the names
of the Nazi "martyrs"—brown-shirts who had been killed in the struggle for
power—a roll-call of the dead, and the thirty thousand seemed very moved.

In such an atmosphere no wonder, then, that every word dropped by Hitler
seemed like an inspired Word from on high. Man's—or at least the
German's—critical faculty is swept away at such moments, and every lie
pronounced is accepted as high truth itself.

NUREMBERG, *September 7*

Another great pageant tonight. Two hundred thousand party officials packed in
the Zeppelin Wiese with their twenty-one thousand flags unfurled in the
searchlights like a forest of weird trees. "We are strong and will get stronger,"
Hitler shouted at them through the microphone, his words echoing across the

---

17. **Roman Church:** the Roman Catholic Church.

hushed field from the loud-speakers. And there, in the floodlit night, jammed together like sardines, in one mass formation, the little men of Germany who have made Nazism possible achieved the highest state of being the Germanic man knows: the shedding of their individual souls and minds—with the personal responsibilities and doubts and problems—until under the mystic lights and at the sound of the magic words of the Austrian they were merged completely in the Germanic herd. Later they recovered enough—fifteen thousand of them—to stage a torchlight parade through Nuremberg's ancient streets, Hitler taking the salute in front of the station across from our hotel.

NUREMBERG, *September* 10

(Later)—After seven days of almost ceaseless goose-stepping, speech-making, and pageantry, the party rally came to an end tonight. And though dead tired and rapidly developing a bad case of crowd-phobia, I'm glad I came. You have to go through one of these to understand Hitler's hold on the people, to feel the dynamic in the movement he's unleashed and the sheer, disciplined strength the Germans possess. And now—as Hitler told the correspondents yesterday in explaining his technique—the half-million men who've been here during the week will go back to their towns and villages and preach the new gospel with new fanaticism. . . .

QUESTIONS TO CONSIDER

This chapter posed three basic questions: What image did the Nazis convey to German voters? Why did they appeal to German voters? How did the Nazis use media to aid their rise to power?

First examine the image the party conveyed to Germans in the 1920s and early 1930s. Start by considering the highly visible uniformed wing of the party, the S.A. Why did the S.A. Order 111 (Source 4) place such emphasis on how the S.A. appeared in public? What was the Storm Trooper supposed to epitomize? How was that visual effect designed to build a certain image for the party? How might columns of marching men and political banners contribute to this image? Reflect, too, on the mass meetings so carefully mounted by the party. What impression might they have conveyed to the average man or woman on the street? How did the Leader myth contribute to a certain image for the party? Remember that Hitler was relatively young, forty-three years of age, when he gained power. How do you think many Germans viewed a young party leader whose use of airplanes made him seem omnipresent?

With your concept of the party's image now clearly in mind, assess the Nazi appeal to voters. You may wish to review the numerous problems facing Germany in the 1920s and early 1930s that we examined in the introduction. What did the Nazis

[211]

propose as solutions to the Versailles Treaty, the threat of communist takeover, and the ills of the depression? Did the Nazis convey an image that would lead Germans to believe the party could solve the country's problems? Consider the S.A. and the Leader myth. How did they reinforce a promise to restore German power?

What groups did the Nazis specifically appeal to in our evidence, and what were their specific problems? What were the alleged conditions of the workers in Source 8, the poster of "The String-Puller"? Who was threatened by the proposed Woolworth's store in Hanover (Source 14)? How did the Nazis win support in these groups?

Beyond its proposed answers to Germany's problems and its specific appeal to certain groups, the Nazi party also had a more general appeal. In what ways do you think participation in mass meetings might combat this feeling? What sorts of positive feelings might it seem to provide? The twentieth century has witnessed for many a weakening of both the ritual and authority of traditional religion. How do the photographs of the banners and rally (Sources 5 and 6) and Shirer's account (Source 18) indicate a conscious attempt by the Nazis to exploit this development? Why would you not be surprised to find German religious youth movements losing members to the Nazis?

Why are you shocked but not surprised at the conclusion of Hitler's speech of February 10, 1933 (Source 16)?

Finally, consider the Nazis' techniques, their use of media and propaganda in achieving their goal of power. In this regard, consider the theoretical bases for Nazi propaganda. What was Hitler's view of the masses? According to Hitler, why would the masses submit to terror? Recall the account of the brawl in the Pharus Hall in Source 7. What effect might this event have had on Hitler's opponents? Reexamine the graph of violence in Northeim. Why did Nazi violence break out when it did? How did it affect the party's image?

Examine the party's use of media technology for propaganda. What was the response of the Italian journalist to Nazi propaganda, according to Goebbels (Source 16)? What new electronic media did the Nazis employ? What do you think the Nazis' level of success would have been without such modern technology as the microphone? What features of Nazi campaign technology have become part of modern campaigning?

As you consider these questions, you should have a better understanding of the Nazi seizure of power in Germany. The Nazis used technology and methods of political manipulation that were new to the modern world.

Nazi media mastery and propaganda worked well enough by January 1933 for the party to secure the chancellorship for Hitler. In free elections, however, the Nazis never secured more than 44 percent of the vote.[18] Once Hitler became chancellor, the task for the party and Goebbels was to use modern media and propaganda either to win the support of the majority of Germans or at least to convince them that opposition to the new political order was futile. As had been the case with the Nazi drive for power, implicit in this effort was the threat that force would be used against the recalcitrant. But Hitler did seem to keep his promises. The communist party was outlawed in 1933; building projects and eventually rearmament stimulated the economy and created jobs; and Germany restored its military power and defied the Treaty of Versailles. Ominously, Hitler's promises also pointed to the terrible tragedy of the Holocaust for European Jews, and to World War II. But Goebbels's propaganda machine never let Germans forget the regime's successes.

The Hitler government centralized control of all information and media in a new Ministry of Public Enlightenment and Propaganda, headed by Goebbels, which closely regulated Germany's press, film, and radio after 1933. Especially significant was Goebbels's understanding of the role of radio as a propaganda device and his use of it once in power. He said, "With the radio we have destroyed the spirit of rebellion,"[19] because the radio could bring the Nazi message into every German home. The regime saw to it that cheap radios were made available to Germans, and the number of receivers increased from 5 million in 1932 to 9.5 million in 1938. A system of government wardens notified citizens to tune in important programs, and the Propaganda Ministry increased their impact still further by setting up loudspeakers in the streets and squares of Germany during key broadcasts.

Goebbels's ministry also sought to sway opinion via the medium of film. After some early crude and unpopular efforts, Goebbels's understanding of film as a propaganda device grew greatly. He wrote in 1942 of the subtle possibilities inherent in the medium:

> Even entertainment can be politically of special value, because the moment a person becomes conscious of propaganda, propaganda becomes ineffective. However, as soon as propaganda as a tendency, as a characteristic, as an attitude remains in the background and becomes apparent through human

18. In the last free Reichstag elections held in March 1933, the Nazis won only 43.9 percent of the vote, despite S.A. intimidation of voters and the great political advantage accruing to the party from Hitler's position as chancellor. The Nazis finally secured a Reichstag majority only when Hitler expelled the communist members from the Chamber.

19. Quoted in Roger Manvell and Heinrich Fraenkel, *Doctor Goebbels: His Life and Death* (London: Heinemann, 1960), pp. 127–128.

beings, then propaganda becomes effective in every respect.[20]

Armed with such methods, the Nazi regime was able to retain power, mobilize its citizens for war, and sustain their morale throughout much of World War II. There was opposition to the dictatorship, including a number of plots against Hitler himself, but the regime managed to contain such active resistance within a minority of the population. Modern media and propaganda techniques and a message that attracted many, combined with the omnipresent threat of state police power, proved to be effective devices that aided the regime in maintaining its ascendancy. Such employment of modern media and propaganda techniques, supported by the police power of the state, would characterize many later twentieth-century totalitarian regimes.

20. Joseph Goebbels, *Tagebuch*, unpublished sections, in Institut für Zeitgeschichte, Munich, entry for March 1, 1942. Quoted in David Welch, *Propaganda and the German Cinema, 1933–1945* (Oxford: Clarendon Press, 1983), p. 45.

CHAPTER EIGHT

CRUCIBLE OF CONFLICT:

THE SUEZ CRISIS (1956)

Looking across the vast sweep of world history, the power and glory of empires and emperors seem fleeting and ephemeral. The poem "Ozymandias," written by Percy Bysshe Shelley, tells of an imposing yet decrepit monument to a dead king:

And on the pedestal these words
  appear:
"My name is Ozymandias, king of
  kings:
Look on my works, ye Mighty, and
  despair!"
Nothing beside remains. Round the
  decay
Of that colossal wreck, boundless and
  bare
The lone and level sands stretch far
  away.

The irony is that when Shelley wrote these lines in the early nineteenth century, his native England was poised to become the greatest empire of modern times. The British would soon be ruling over African and Asian deserts such as those where rulers like Ozymandias had once held sway.

By the late nineteenth century, it could truthfully be said that "the sun never sets on the British empire." By the end of the twentieth century, however, almost nothing was left of that empire except monuments to its now faded glory in cities like Calcutta, Hong Kong, Nairobi, and Alexandria. The reversion of Hong Kong to China in 1997 represented the setting of Britain's imperial sun. As the British flag was lowered and the Chinese flag raised, as "God Save the Queen" gave way to the Chinese national anthem, a process that had begun with the independence of India some fifty years earlier was drawing to a close.

How do we account for imperial decline? One historian, looking at such once impressive empires as those of the Spanish, the Austrians, the French, the Russians, and the

British, has identified a common theme in their fall from power:

> The relative strengths of the leading nations in world affairs never remain constant, principally because of the uneven rate of growth among different societies and of the technological and organizational breakthroughs which bring a greater advantage to one society than to another. . . . [W]ealth is usually necessary to underpin military power, and military power is usually needed to acquire and protect wealth. If, however, too large a proportion of the state's resources is diverted from wealth creation and allocated instead to military purposes, then that is likely to lead to a weakening of national power over the longer term. In the same way, if a state overextends itself strategically—by, say, the conquest of extensive territories or the waging of costly wars—it runs the risk that the potential benefits from external expansion may be outweighed by the expense of it all—a dilemma which becomes acute if the nation concerned has entered a period of relative economic decline.[1]

In this view, military and strategic commitments that are appropriately made by an imperial power during a time of growth can become dysfunctional when they are retained during a period of relative economic decline.

This broad assessment has great relevance to the case of Great Britain in the twentieth century. Through the shocks of two world wars and a great

1. Paul Kennedy, *The Rise and Fall of the Great Powers: Economic Change and Military Conflict from 1500–2000* (New York: Vintage Books, 1987), pp. xv–xvi.

depression, Britain retained control of its vast overseas territories. But the economic power that had allowed Britain to gain that empire was no longer sufficient to sustain it, at least not without severely compromising Britain's economy and international standing. The problem came to a head in a series of events known as the Suez crisis of 1956. After the Egyptian government nationalized the Suez Canal, the British colluded with the French and Israelis to manufacture a war that would give the British a pretext to intervene and reestablish control over that strategic waterway. The Suez crisis was a contest of power between the British and Egyptian leaders, Sir Anthony Eden and Gamal Abdel Nasser, that epitomized a larger crisis for the British Empire. In the end, Eden resigned in disgrace and Nasser became firmly established as an Arab hero.

The Suez crisis offers an important context in which to explore issues of late twentieth-century history broader than this particular Anglo-Egyptian conflict. Two fundamental rifts marked the global community in the 1950s. The first lay across the east/west axis, that is, it followed the lines of the cold war conflict between the United States and the Soviet Union, each with its allies and client states. The second involved conflict between north and south, between long-dominant colonial powers like Britain and the societies of Asia and Africa that were struggling toward national independence and a more nearly equal position in global affairs. These two vectors of conflict have often been confused, but to understand the

Suez crisis and the world in which it took place, we must keep both firmly in mind.

What was at stake in the Suez crisis? What inspired Eden and Nasser to behave as they did before, during, and after the crisis? How were their actions interpreted by various other actors across the east/west and north/south divides? Why did the United States not give stronger backing to its British ally? How did the Soviet Union relate to the crisis? What does this story tell us about issues of anticolonial nationalism and the end of empire during the era of the cold war? These and other questions will emerge from the documents in this chapter.

BACKGROUND

The troubled relationship between Britain and Egypt that culminated in the Suez crisis had its origin in the early nineteenth century. Napoleon's invasion of Egypt in 1798 was part of an ongoing series of conflicts between the British and French empires. While Britain had no territorial claims in North Africa, Napoleon's adventure was a threat to its control of Mediterranean trade and its growing interests in India. Napoleon's decision to attack Britain indirectly through an invasion of Egypt led to a British counterinvasion that successfully chased the French from the Nile.

The British forces then retreated. However, the European invaders had disrupted the political status quo in Egypt by undercutting the power of the local representatives of the Ottoman Empire. Order was soon restored by a dynamic leader named Muhammad Ali (r. 1808–1848), who was successful in building a strong, centralized Egyptian state. He realized that Egyptian autonomy required significant political, military, and economic reorganization. He established new schools, built up a powerful army, and sponsored infrastructural improvements, especially in irrigation, to strengthen the Egyptian economy.

The British were worried about Muhammad Ali's rise to power because he posed a threat to the Ottoman Empire, whose continued existence was considered necessary to maintain the balance of power in the region. They intervened to prevent his rule from spreading beyond Egypt. At the same time, the British began to benefit from an expansion of Egyptian cotton production. By the 1840s, Egyptian cotton was a mainstay of the British textile industry. For the time being, Britain could benefit from its economic relationship with Egypt without having to bear the heavy costs of occupation and colonial rule.

The relationship between Egypt and the Europeans became less equal, however, as time went on. Increasing government debt led Muhammad Ali's successors to support the building of the Suez Canal. Completed in 1869, the canal was designed by a French engineer, financed by European capital, and built with Egyptian labor.

The Egyptian government saw the canal as a means of improving its financial situation, but in fact it only deepened Egypt's dependence on European creditors. By 1875 Egypt had to sell its 44 percent stake in the canal company to the British government in order to help pay off its debt. Western creditors were so concerned about the ability of the Egyptian government to pay its debts that they imposed Anglo-French control over Egyptian finances. Britain now had both a military and a financial stake in the Suez Canal.

The Egyptians' sense that their country was being taken over by Europeans led to a nationalist backlash. In 1882 a revolt within the ranks of the Egyptian army was put down by a British invasion. What was originally intended as a temporary military action to restore order led to the stationing of British forces in Egypt from 1882 to 1954. The British did not feel that it was safe to leave Egypt to its own devices lest it come under the sway of another power. If nothing else, the Suez Canal was now vital to Britain's communication with India, the "jewel in the crown" of the British Empire. Opposition to the British occupation never died away; modern Egyptian nationalism had been born.

Britain was anxious to find a formula that would allow it to control Egyptian affairs without formally adding Egypt to its colonial possessions. Though Egypt was still nominally a part of the Ottoman Empire and was ruled by an Egyptian king (the *Khedive*), British advisers were "temporarily" imposed on the country and became the de facto rulers of the Nile, maintaining "a formidable and ambitious structure of colonial rule" in which "the Egyptian financial system was directed by British financial advisers; Egyptian irrigation schemes were managed by British engineers; judicial advisers devised reforms of the legal system; Egyptian schools were inspected by British inspectors; the Egyptian army was commanded by a British Sirdar."[2] Needless to say, the Suez Canal was guarded by troops under British command.

As impressive as this governmental structure was, British rule in Egypt was never really secure. British governors preferred to deal with Egyptian royalty and the traditional elites, largely ignoring the Western-educated Egyptians, who were beginning to form nationalist political parties and to influence public opinion. Dealing with the forces of Egyptian nationalism became even more difficult during World War I, when the Ottoman Empire, which still claimed Egypt as a province, allied itself with Germany. Many Egyptians sympathized with the Ottoman Turks, and by extension their German allies, on the basis of the old adage "the enemy of my enemy is my friend."

From 1914 to 1918 the Middle East was a theater of war, and issues of military security were paramount. Britain declared a formal protectorate over Egypt, insulting those Egyptians who were seeking to lessen rather than deepen their dependence on Britain. Many sources of friction and

2. P. J. Marshall, ed., *Cambridge Illustrated History of the British Empire* (Cambridge: Cambridge University Press, 1996), p. 74.

confusion in the later history of North Africa and the Middle East can be traced back to the First World War. At the same time as the British were allying themselves with an Arab army to overthrow the Ottoman Turks, they were also promising support to the Zionists, who sought a "national home" for the Jewish people in Palestine. Meanwhile, they were making secret plans with the French to divide former Ottoman provinces (such as Palestine, Syria, Lebanon, and Iraq) between themselves after the war. Intense conflict would result from these incompatible promises.

The effect of World War I on the British Empire as a whole was contradictory. On the one hand, Britain not only successfully defended itself but also accumulated substantial new territories. With the approval of the new League of Nations, former Ottoman provinces like Palestine, Jordan, and Iraq fell under British authority, as did some former German colonies in Africa. At the same time, the cost of the war effort was enormous. The British were forced to sell off many of their global investments. Britain was expanding its empire while at the same time suffering relative economic decline compared to emerging economic powers like the United States. But the two great powers of the twentieth century, the United States and the Soviet Union, largely withdrew from global affairs in the 1920s, giving the British (and the French) a false sense of imperial "normalcy."

One of the promises the British had made during the war was to revisit the question of self-government for Egypt once the emergency was over. But on whose terms would that question be reopened? Egyptian nationalists wanted to put their own case before world leaders at the Paris Peace Conference, but British officials refused to allow them to attend. Public disturbances were the result. In 1922 a new constitution was imposed on Egypt that granted "independence" but kept foreign and military affairs in British hands; the Suez Canal was still guarded by British troops. Tension was rife. Some Egyptian nationalists opposed the British from within the parliament, while those with less patience resorted to violence and terrorism.

The Anglo-Egyptian Treaty of 1936 restored most of Egypt's sovereign rights, but the British were still allowed to keep troops in the canal zone, and the more militant Egyptian nationalists felt that their leaders had once again sold them out to Western powers. The coming of the Second World War revealed the inadequacies of the 1936 treaty. As the war moved into North Africa and Italian forces in Libya threatened Egypt, the British were faced with Egyptian opposition to the deployment of their forces outside the canal zone. They occupied Cairo, and the Egyptian government was forced to acquiesce. The British military effort in North Africa was successful, but the means employed to achieve that success reinforced Arab perceptions of the British as unreformed imperialists.

Once again the victorious British had significant contradictions to deal with after their victory in a world war. On the one hand, Britain remained one of the dominant great powers, had successfully mobilized its empire in the struggle, and was one of five countries with a permanent seat (and veto power) in the new United Nations Security Council. On the other hand, the cost of the war had been catastrophic. The British pound, which had been the principal currency of the world economy for over a century, was weakened by massive debt to the United States. The problem of maintaining strategic and military commitments that were too great for the country's economic strength became difficult to ignore.

It did not take long for the world to learn that Britain could no longer sustain its traditional imperial role. Unable or unwilling to resolve the conflict between Zionists and Arab nationalists, Britain walked away from Palestine. The new nation of Israel came into being, and warfare born of competing Jewish and Arab nationalisms began. India, Britain's most important colony, became independent and joined the family of nations in 1947. While the British were more optimistic about the future of their role in Africa, here too nationalist leaders like Kwame Nkrumah in the Gold Coast were finding audiences receptive to their calls for self-government.

The eastern Mediterranean was another area where the British had long been dominant, but in the late 1940s Britain was unable to hold the balance of power between Greece and Turkey. The United States intervened, and with the Truman Doctrine in 1948 announced that it intended to be the dominant force in the struggle to contain communism. Britain's world role now required compromise with American governments as well as with colonial nationalists.

The cold war gave Britain some room for maneuver. While the United States was anxious to secure access to global markets that had been tilted toward European colonialists, the communist threat was enough to keep it from rocking the boat. The new power of the Soviet Union and the rise of communism in China gave the British an excuse to keep their imperial project alive: It was all too easy to brand anyone in Africa or Asia who opposed them as a "communist." Britain retained its policy of seeking out moderate nationalists who were willing to compromise in a way that protected Britain's economic and strategic interests.

King Farouk of Egypt was one Arab leader who was willing to play by those rules, but in doing so he lost the respect and support of his own people. On July 23, 1952, he was overthrown by a group of Egyptian Army officers led by Colonel Gamal Abdel Nasser. Nasser's ambition was not only to bring true sovereignty to his own country, but to unite the Arab peoples more widely to protect their interests against both Western powers and Israel. At the Bandung Conference in 1955, Nasser joined such other leaders as Jawaharlal Nehru of India and Sukarno of Indonesia in declaring that their newly independent nations would retain their freedom of action in international affairs. As "nonaligned nations," they would not be forced to choose between the power blocs sponsored by the United States and the Soviet Union. Nasser positioned himself as a pan-Arab leader working toward the greater unity of the Arab peoples in an effort to give them a greater voice in world affairs.

None of this was very appealing to the Western powers. For the next four years, Nasser pursued policies that challenged Britain's hegemony in the region. First, he worked to eliminate the single most embarrassing remnant of the old colonial relationship: the presence of British troops in his country. The Evacuation Treaty of 1954 led to the final withdrawal of British troops from the Suez Canal. Second, he refused to consider the entrance of Egypt into a British-sponsored security arrangement known as the Baghdad Pact. Nasser regarded the Baghdad Pact, which was signed in 1955 by Britain, Turkey, Iraq, and Pakistan, as part of Britain's effort to continue its old game of working through compliant Muslim elites to further its own imperial aims. The United States was also reluctant to join the Baghdad Pact, being cautious about taking on more responsibilities in that volatile part of the world.

Having broken his country's military relationship with Britain, and refusing to play by the rules of the Baghdad Pact, Nasser needed a new source of arms for his military. The United States considered negotiating an arms deal with Egypt, but sensitivity over the U.S. relationship with Israel made that politically impossible. Acting on the principle he had affirmed at Bandung, Nasser turned to the Soviet bloc for help.

An arms deal was struck with communist Czechoslovakia in 1955, much to the chagrin of the Western powers.

Another contentious issue was the proposal to build a great dam on the Nile at Aswan. The United States and Britain frustrated Nasser by keeping him waiting and finally refusing his request for financial and technical assistance. By refusing to supply arms or finance the dam, the Western powers lost whatever leverage they had retained in Nasser's Egypt. On July 26, 1956, Nasser surprised the world by announcing the nationalization of the Suez Canal.

The British prime minister, Sir Anthony Eden, saw Nasser's move as an intolerable threat. The British government was now desperate to return its troops to Suez, which they had left just two years earlier, and the removal of Nasser was a subject of conversation at the highest levels of government. But how could Britain justify the introduction of troops into a sovereign state? Publicly, the British government joined the United States and the United Nations in calling for an international conference to defuse the crisis. But while these meetings were being held in London, the British government was pursuing a very different strategy.

In the summer and fall of 1956, Eden, increasingly obsessed with Nasser and the Suez problem, entered into a series of secret talks with representatives from France and Israel. The French were the ones who actually proposed the scheme. Israel would invade Egypt across the Sinai desert. France and Britain would then send troops to the canal to "protect" it. The illusion was to be created that the European powers were disinterested parties who were merely doing their best to separate the Egyptian and Israeli forces while keeping the canal open to international traffic. The United States government was not consulted as this secret plan was devised.

On October 29, 1956, the Israeli army entered the Sinai. Britain and France issued an ultimatum to both Egypt and Israel, demanding that they retreat ten miles from the canal pending an Anglo-French "police action." French and British troops landed in Egypt a few days later under the pretext of separating the two Middle Eastern adversaries. Nasser responded by shutting down the canal to deprive the invasion force of oil and ordering ships to be sunk in order to block canal traffic. He became an instant hero for standing up to the great powers, not only among Egyptians and Arabs, but throughout the colonial and recently colonial world. The Baghdad Pact collapsed, as British allies like Turkey and Iraq, embarrassed by their association with Eden's government, supported the Egyptian cause. Most importantly, the government of the United States reacted with shock and dismay.

Why did the Eisenhower administration not support its old war allies against radical Arab nationalism? After all, the United States had a very recent history of covert action against governments that it saw as falling into the communist camp. In 1953 the Central Intelligence Agency had secretly orchestrated a campaign against the nationalist prime minister of Iran and helped restore the dictatorial powers of the shah. In 1954 the democratically elected government of Guatemala was overthrown by a military dictator backed by the CIA. That did not mean, however, that the American government felt it could safely turn a blind eye to covert actions organized without its input or support. The United States did not want to be too closely associated with a decaying European colonialism. Moreover, the Suez invasion came at a very bad time in cold war relations. The Soviet Union had invaded Hungary in the fall of 1956, and President Eisenhower could not credibly criticize the Russians for invading Hungary and at the same time support the British and French in what might be seen as a similar endeavor. Eisenhower and his secretary of state, John Foster Dulles, supported a Security Council resolution condemning the invasion and began laying the groundwork for United Nations troops to replace the invaders at the canal.

The British were forced to retreat from Suez, having gained nothing and having lost significantly in terms of international prestige. Eden's political career was over. The canal remained in Egyptian hands, and Nasser become a world figure, completing the Aswan Dam with Russian help. The sources of tension between Israel and the Arab world remained unresolved.

THE METHOD

In analyzing the following documents, you will need to keep in mind the perceptions and interests of the various players in the Suez drama as it unfolded in 1956. As always, it is important to consider the origins of the documents and their intended audience. Some of the sources in this chapter were meant to be kept private; others were intended for public audiences. Some were created at the time; others were the product of later reflection. Keep these distinctions in mind as you read.

What led the Egyptian president, Colonel Nasser, to nationalize the canal? What prompted the British prime minister, Sir Anthony Eden, to organize an armed response in collaboration with the French and Israelis? To what extent, and using what arguments, did Eden attempt to bring the United States on board with his plan? What explains the unwillingness of the United States under President Dwight D. Eisenhower to support armed intervention, and its decision to seek a resolution through the United Nations? How did the affair relate to the two basic global conflicts of the time: the cold war and anticolonial nationalism? How did the world respond to the Anglo-French invasion of the canal zone in November 1956? What were the consequences of the Suez crisis for the roles of Egypt, Britain, and the United States in the Middle East?

To help answer these questions, you may find it useful, in your notes, to keep track of the actions of the various players in the drama, and of the motivations that inspired them to act as they did. As you read the sources, you will want to refer back to the following section, which gives additional context for each of the documents.

Source 1 is an evaluation by the British foreign secretary, Sir Anthony Eden (who later became prime minister), of the relationship between his country's economy and its military in the early 1950s, with special reference to relations with the United States. Out of this thinking came the British effort to create the Baghdad Pact—which was weakened by the refusal of the governments of Egypt and the United States to join—and the 1954 agreement to withdraw British forces from the Suez Canal.

On July 23, 1952, King Farouk was forced to abdicate and the rise of Gamal Abdel Nasser began. Source 2 is an extract from Nasser's *The Philosophy of the Revolution*. In this book he attempted to justify and explain the military intervention in Egyptian politics by placing it in the larger context of Egyptian and Arab nationalism.

Source 3 deals with the military balance of power between Egypt and Israel. In 1950, the United States, Britain, and France had agreed not to contribute to an arms race in the Middle East by favoring one country or the other in its arms sales. Frustrated by his inability to secure American arms, and following his policy of "nonalignment," in 1955 Nasser struck a deal to purchase arms from Soviet-allied Czechoslovakia. This document registers the Israeli government's response and gives a general impression of Israeli attitudes toward Egypt at the time.

In the summer of 1956 Nasser received the news that no American support for the Aswan Dam project could be expected. Nasser then stunned the world by announcing the nationalization of the Suez Canal. All of the previous tensions in the region were now focused on Suez. Source 4 is an extract from Nasser's speech of July 26, 1956. Sources 5 and 6 are visual ones, the first a photograph taken a week later, the second a cartoon from an English publication. (The man with the fishing pole is the Soviet foreign minister.) It is useful to compare the similarities and differences in the portrayal of Nasser in these two representations.

Source 7 is part of a record of a British Cabinet discussion of the nationalization issue. As the British considered the consequences of Nasser's action and appropriate lines of response, the United States worked through the United Nations to convene a conference in London to resolve the dispute. Though an agreement was reached, Egypt's lack of participation made it unclear whether such diplomacy would be enough. Knowing that Britain was considering military options, President Eisenhower wrote the telegram reproduced as Source 8 to Prime Minister Eden, and received the reply included as Source 9.

Meanwhile, Israel had its own concerns. Source 10 is an extract from the memoirs of Moshe Dayan, the Israeli minister of defense at the time. In the wake of the Czech arms sales to Egypt, Dayan describes the process by which France, Britain, and Israel came together to develop a common plan. The French perspective is given in Source 11, which is part of the transcript of a television program broadcast in Britain in 1966 entitled "Suez: Ten Years After." It is important to keep in mind that the French were faced with a violent uprising against their colonial rule in another part of the Arab world at the same time as the Suez crisis: An anti-colonial rebellion was taking place in Algeria. Source 12 is a record of the Sèvres Protocol, an agreement reached by the French, British, and Israelis at a secret meeting. Eden was alarmed that a record was kept of this accord, and had the British copy destroyed. This version of the document was reconstructed and translated from the French and Israeli versions.

Less than a week after the Sèvres Protocol was signed, Israeli troops invaded Egypt across the Sinai Peninsula. The next group of sources records world reactions to the Israeli occupation, the Anglo-French ultimatum, and the subsequent invasion of the Suez Canal area by British and French forces. Source 13 is a draft resolution submitted to the United Nations Security Council by the United States. It was vetoed by France and Britain, but the next day in an emergency meeting the General Assembly of the United Nations, where no nation holds a veto, voted overwhelmingly in support of a similar resolution. Source 14 is from a statement by the Indian prime minister, Jawaharlal Nehru, who had cooperated with British authorities to secure Indian independence and retained ties to Great Britain through the Commonwealth. On the other hand, Nehru had cooperated with Nasser in defining the principles of the Non-Aligned Movement at the Bandung Conference just a year earlier. Source 15 records the response of the Soviet government.

Within a week of the Israeli invasion, the British government, isolated in the international community, considered means of extricating itself from the situation. However, it was only when the financial implications of the Suez invasion became clear, as mentioned in Source 16, that Eden and his cabinet moved toward withdrawal of British troops from Egypt. Soon after, the Anglo-French forces were replaced by the United Nations, and the Suez Canal was restored to order. Source 17, an exchange between the American secretary of state and a member of the Senate, deals with the implications of the Suez crisis for American foreign policy. Three days after this statement by Secretary of State Dulles, the "Eisenhower Doctrine" was announced, committing the United States for the first time to significant military and economic responsibilities in the Middle East.

The remaining documents all concern the outcome of the Suez crisis. In Source 18, Eden, soon to resign as head of the British government, in-forms his colleagues of the lessons he had learned. In Source 19, President Nasser of Egypt, in the same British television program quoted in Source 11, reflects back on the events that had occurred a decade earlier, drawing very different conclusions from those reached by Eden. Source 20 is again British in origin. In this document, Harold Macmillan, who replaced Eden as the head of the Conservative Party and as prime minister of Great Britain, addresses the South African parliament in early 1960. Here he speaks of the "winds of change" associated with the rise of nationalism in Africa to members of an all-white government pursuing a policy of apartheid.

Finally, Source 21 is a British cartoon from 1962. By that time the Kennedy administration in the United States was playing a much more proactive role in the politics of the Middle East, Southeast Asia, and Africa, regions where the French and the British had long been dominant. Harold Macmillan is shown as a partially submerged "Britannia," surrounded by sea creatures representing Mao Zedong of China, Charles de Gaulle of France, Fidel Castro of Cuba, and Nikita Khrushchev of the Soviet Union. In the speedboat above is the American secretary of defense, offering precious little help.

THE EVIDENCE

Source 1 from Anthony Gorst and Lewis Johnman, The Suez Crisis (London: Routledge, 1997), pp. 28–30.

1. Sir Anthony Eden, British Foreign Secretary, Discusses British Obligations, June 18, 1952

The essence of a sound foreign policy is to ensure that a country's strength is equal to its obligations. If this is not the case, then either the obligations must be reduced to the level at which resources are available to maintain them, or a greater share of the country's resources must be devoted to their support. It is becoming clear that rigorous maintenance of the presently-accepted policies of Her Majesty's Government at home and abroad is placing a burden on the country's economy which it is beyond the resources of the country to meet. A position has already been reached where there is no reserve and therefore no margin for unforeseen additional obligations.

The first task must be to determine how far the external obligations of the country can be reduced or shared with others, or transferred to other shoulders, without impairing too seriously the world position of the United Kingdom and sacrificing the vital advantages which flow from it. But if, after careful review, it is shown that the total effort required is still beyond the capacity of existing national resources, a choice of the utmost difficulty lies before the British people, for they must either give up, for a time, some of the advantages which a high standard of living confers upon them or, by relaxing their grip in the outside world, see their country sink to the level of a second-class Power, with injury to their essential interests and way of life of which they can have little conception. . . .

If, on a longer view, it must be assumed that the maintenance of the present scale of overseas commitments will permanently overstrain our economy, clearly we ought to recognise that the United Kingdom is over-committed, and reduce the commitment. The only practical way of removing this permanent strain would be for the United Kingdom to shed or share the load of one or two major obligations, e.g., the defence of the Middle East, for which we at present bear the responsibility alone. . . .

The success of this policy will depend on a number of factors, some favourable, some unfavourable. The United States is the only single country in the free world capable of assuming new and world-wide obligations; being heavily committed to the East–West struggle they would not readily leave a power-vacuum in any part of the globe but would be disposed, however reluctantly, to fill it themselves if it was clear that the United Kingdom could no longer hold the position (as they did, for example, in Greece). On the other hand, the history of the Middle East Command negotiations and the unwillingness of the United States Chiefs of Staff to commit forces to it illustrates the American reluctance to enter into new commitments in peacetime. . . . Moreover, distrust of the British and fear of becoming an instrument to prop up a declining British Empire are still strong. . . . As regards the United Kingdom part, a policy of this kind will only be successful with the United States in so far as we are able to demonstrate that we are making the maximum possible effort ourselves, and the more gradually and inconspicuously we can transfer the real burdens from our own to American shoulders, the less damage we shall do to our own position and influence in the world. . . .

[It is] clearly beyond the resources of the United Kingdom to continue to assume the responsibility alone, for the security of the Middle East. Our aim should be to make the whole of this area and in particular the Canal Zone an international responsibility. Hence every step should be taken to speed up the establishment of an Allied Middle East Defence Organisation. It should, however, be recognised that the setting up of such a defence organisation will not result in any immediate alleviation of the burden for the United Kingdom. The United States have refused to enter into any precise commitments in the Middle East or to allocate forces and it should be the constant object of Her Majesty's Government to persuade them to do so. In addition, every possibility should be explored of committing the United States militarily, e.g., to the building of bases, the provision of material, the sharing and reconstruction of airfields. . . . The dilemma is that until we can come to an agreement with Egypt no effective international defence organisation for the Middle East can be established; and so long as there is no settlement with Egypt and no international defence organisation we are obliged to hold the fort alone.

Source 2 from Gamal Abdel Nasser, The Philosophy of the Revolution *(Buffalo, N.Y.: Economica Books, 1959), pp. 43, 49–52, 58–60, 62–66.*

2. From Gamal Abdel Nasser,
The Philosophy of the
Revolution, 1959

What is it we want to do? And which is the way to it?

There is no doubt we all dream of Egypt free and strong. No Egyptian would ever differ with another about that. As for the way to liberation and strength, that is the most intricate problem in our lives. . . .

Fate has so willed that we should be on the crossroads of the world. Often have we been the road which invaders took and a prey to adventurers. . . .

European society passed through the stages of its evolution in an orderly manner. It crossed the bridge between the Renaissance at the end of the Middle Ages and the Nineteenth Century step by step. The stages of this evolution systematically succeeded one another.

In our case everything was sudden. European countries eyed us covetously and regarded us as a crossroad to their colonies in the East and the South.

Torrents of ideas and opinions burst upon us which we were, at that stage of our evolution, incapable of assimilating. Our spirits were still in the Thirteenth Century though the symptoms of the Nineteenth and Twentieth Centuries infiltrated in their various aspects. Our minds were trying to catch up the advancing caravan of humanity. . . .

We live in a society that has not yet crystallized. It is still boiling over and restless. . . .

. . . Any nation, exposed to the same conditions as our country, could be easily lost. It could be swept away by the torrents that fell upon it. But it stood firm in the violent earthquake.

. . . As I consider one normal Egyptian family out of the thousands that live in the capital, I find the following: the father, for example, is a turbanned "fellah" from the heart of the country; the mother a lady descended from Turkish stock; the sons of the family are at a school adopting the English system; the daughters the French. All this lies between the Thirteenth century and the outward appearances of the Twentieth. . . .

Such are, then, the roots from which sprang our conditions of today. Such are the sources from which our crisis flows. If I add to these social origins the circumstances for which we expelled Farouk and for which we wish to liberate our country from every foreign soldier; if we add all these together, we shall discover the wide sphere in which we labour and which is exposed, from every side, to the winds, to the violent storm that raged in its corners, to flashing lightning and roaring thunder. . . .

We should first of all agree upon one thing before we proceed further and that is to define the boundaries of place as far as we are concerned. . . . If I were told that our place is limited by the political boundaries of our country I also do not agree. . . .

We cannot look stupidly at a map of the world not realizing our place therein and the role determined to us by that place. Neither can we ignore that there is an Arab circle surrounding us and that this circle is as much a part of us as we are a part of it, that our history has been mixed with it and that its interests are linked with ours. These are actual facts and not mere words.

Can we ignore that there is a continent of Africa in which fate has placed us and which is destined today to witness a terrible struggle on its future? This struggle will affect us whether we want or not.

Can we ignore that there is a Muslim world with which we are tied by bonds which are not only forged by religious faith but also tightened by the facts of history? . . .

There is no doubt that the Arab circle is the most important and the most closely connected with us. Its history merges with ours. We have suffered the same hardships, lived the same crises and when we fell prostrate under the spikes of the horses of conquerors they lay with us. . . .

. . . As far as I am concerned I remember that the first elements of Arab consciousness began to filter into my mind as a student in secondary schools, wherefrom I went out with my fellow schoolboys on strike on December 2nd of every year as a protest against the Balfour Declaration whereby England gave the Jews a national home usurped unjustly from its legal owners. . . .

And when the Palestine crisis loomed on the horizon I was firmly convinced that the fighting in Palestine was not fighting on foreign territory. Nor was it inspired by sentiment. It was a duty imposed by self-defense.

I do not want now to discuss the details of the Palestine War. This is a subject that needs several many-sided discussions. But one strange lesson of the Palestine War I care to mention: The Arab nations entered the Palestine War with the same degree of enthusiasm. . . . They came out of the war with the same bitterness and frustration. Every one of them was thus exposed, in its own country, to the same factors and was governed by the same forces, that caused their defeat and made them bow their heads low with shame and humiliation. . . .

. . . This was how I felt when, in my wanderings I came upon the children of refugees who were caught in the tentacles of the siege after their homes had been demolished and their property lost. I particularly remember a young girl of the same age as my daughter. I saw her rushing out, amidst danger and stray bullets and, bitten by the pangs of hunger and cold, looking for a crust of bread or a rag of cloth. I always said to myself, "This may happen to my daughter." I believe that what was happening in Palestine could happen, and may still happen today, in any part of this region, as long as it resigns itself to the factors and the forces which dominate now.

After the seige and the battles in Palestine I came home with the whole region in my mind one complete whole. . . . An event may happen in Cairo today; it is repeated in Damascus, Beirut, Amman or any other place tomorrow. This was naturally in conformity with the picture that experience has left within me: One region, the same factors and circumstances, even the same forces opposing them all. It was clear that imperialism was the most prominent of these forces; even Israel itself was but one of the outcomes of imperialism. If it had not fallen under British mandate, Zionism could not have found the necessary support to realize the idea of a national home in Palestine. That idea would have remained a foolish vision, practically hopeless.

Source 3 from Harry Browne, Flashpoints: Suez and Sinai *(London: Longman, 1971), pp. 22–23.*

3. Statement on Foreign Affairs
by Moshe Sharett, Israel
Premier and Foreign Minister,
October 18, 1955

EGYPT–CZECHOSLOVAK ARMS DEAL

And now, honoured members of the Knesset, I come to the very serious event which occurred some three weeks ago and which has cast a deep shadow on the entire scene of the State's foreign and defence affairs. I refer to the agreement between the ruler of Egypt and the Czechoslovak Government—which from a political and military standpoint implies the linking up between Egypt and the entire Soviet Bloc—for the supply of heavy and modern arms to Egypt, by all accounts in very considerable quantities.

This departure is liable to bring about a revolutionary and ominous change in Israel's security situation.

Both parties attempted to describe the arrangement as a purely commercial deal—perfectly simple and legitimate. Both parties went on to explain that the arms were merely intended to satisfy the defence needs of a free and sovereign state. Neither of the parties ignored Israel or pretended that the arms were not destined to be used against her.

Both sought to justify this great addition to Egyptian arms with the argument that they were to enable a handicapped Egypt to attain to Israel's level of armament.

EGYPT'S 'DEDICATION TO PEACE'

Here is his [Nasser's] pledge of dedication to peace as made in a statement to an Egyptian paper:

'It is utterly inconceivable that Egypt should ever consider peace with Israel or even think of recognising it'

And in another statement:

'The problem of Palestine will not be solved and there will be no peace between us and the Jews so long as even the slightest right of the Arabs of that country is controlled by the enemy. A man can forget everything except blood, vengeance and honour' . . .

Yet another clarion call from the same bugle:

'We cannot but be in a state of war with Israel. This impels us to mobilise all Arab resources for its final liquidation. We ask that our production should be military production and meet our war needs. We want all our newspapers and radio stations to proclaim the total mobilisation of forces for the liberation of Palestine.'

WIDENING GAP . . .

The supply of arms by Czechoslovakia to Egypt is dangerous because it flows to an Egypt which is hostile to us. The same applies to the American arms which are at present being supplied to Iraq or to arms of any power which may at any future time be supplied to Syria. These countries are hostile towards us and their arms are liable to be used against us. It is our position that arms must not be given or sold to states which do not seek peace—states whose declared and real policies are war.

Thus it is our stand that there is a duty and an obligation to sell or grant arms to that state which offers peace—but which is compelled to defend itself as against neighbours who deny it peace and conspire aggression against it.

Source 4 from Harry Browne, Flashpoints: Suez and Sinai *(London: Longman, 1971), pp. 34–35.*

4. Gamal Abdel Nasser Announces the Nationalization of the Suez Canal, July 26, 1956

Now, O citizens, . . . now that our rights in the Suez Canal have reverted to us after 100 years, we are building the real foundations of sovereignty and the real edifice of grandeur and dignity. The Suez Canal was a state within a state; it was an Egyptian limited company which depended on foreign plots and on imperialism and the supporters of imperialism. The Suez Canal was built for Egypt and for Egypt's interests but it was a source of exploitation and extortion.

. . . The Suez Canal was one of the facades of oppression, extortion and humiliation. Today, O citizens the Suez Canal has been nationalised and this decree has in fact been published in the Official Gazette and has become law. Today, O citizens we declare that our property has been returned to us. The rights about which we were silent have been restored to us. Today, citizens, with the annual income of the Suez Canal amounting to £35,000,000—that is, 100,000,000 dollars a year, and 500,000,000 dollars in five years—we shall not look for the 70,000,000 dollars of American aid.

Today we greet the fifth year of the revolution and in the same way as Farouk left on 26 July 1952, the old Suez Canal Company also leaves on the same day. . . . We shall march forward as one people who have vowed to work and to proceed on a holy march of industrialising and construction—nay, as one people who are solidly united in opposition to treachery and aggression and to imperialism and the supporters and antics of imperialism.

At this moment as I talk to you some of your Egyptian brethren are proceeding to administer the canal company and to run its affairs. They are taking over the canal company at this very moment—the Egyptian canal company, not the foreign canal company. They have started to take over the canal company and its property and to control shipping in the canal—the canal which is situated in Egyptian territory, which goes through Egyptian territory which is part of Egypt and which is owned by Egypt. They are now carrying out this task so that we can make up for the past and build new edifices of grandeur and dignity. May the Almighty grant you success, and may the peace and blessing of God be upon you.

Source 5: Hulton-Deutsch Collection/Corbis.

5. Gamal Abdel Nasser, Egypt, August 1, 1956

6. English Cartoon, "The Colossus of Suez," 1956

THE COLOSSUS OF SUEZ

Source 7 from Anthony Gorst and Lewis Johnman, The Suez Crisis *(London: Routledge, 1997), pp. 56–60.*

7. The British Cabinet Reacts to the Nationalization of the Suez Canal, July 27, 1956

The Cabinet considered the situation created by the decision of the Egyptian Government to nationalise the Suez Canal Company.

The Prime Minister said that, with some of his senior colleagues, he had seen the French Ambassador and the United States Chargé d'Affaires on the

[233]

previous evening and had informed them of the facts as we knew them. He had told them that Her Majesty's Government would take a most serious view of this situation and that any failure on the part of the Western Powers to take the necessary steps to regain control over the Canal would have disastrous consequences for the economic life of the Western Powers and for their standing and influence in the Middle East. . . . Our first aim must be to reach a common understanding on the matter with the French, as our partners in the Canal enterprise, and with the United States Government. . . . The Cabinet were given the following information of the importance of the Suez Canal to trade and the flow of supplies and of Egypt's financial position:—

1. Oil—Of a total of some 70 million tons of oil which passed annually from the Persian Gulf through the Suez Canal, 60 million tons were destined for Western Europe and represented two-thirds of Western European oil supplies. . . . If the Egyptian Government decided to interfere with the passage of oil through the Canal, it would be necessary for Western Europe to turn to the Western hemisphere for supplies; as much as 10 million tons might be involved, and it would be necessary to ask the Americans to divert to Western Europe the supplies they now receive from the Persian Gulf. We ourselves had supplies sufficient to last for about six weeks. In order to conserve these it would be necessary at an early date to introduce some arrangement for the restriction of deliveries to industry and to garages.

2. Trade—Interference with the traffic passing through the Suez Canal would not seriously affect the flow of imports other than oil into this country, but it would seriously hamper the export trade, particularly to India. Our exports costs would also rise as freight charges would go up. . . .

The Cabinet next considered the legal position and the basis on which we could sustain and justify to international opinion, a refusal to accept the decision of the Egyptian Prime Minister, Colonel Nasser, to nationalise the Canal.

The Cabinet agreed that we should be on weak ground in basing our resistance on the narrow argument that Colonel Nasser had acted illegally. The Suez Canal Company was registered as an Egyptian Company under Egyptian law; and Colonel Nasser had indicated that he intended to compensate the shareholders at ruling market prices. From a narrow legal point of view his action amounted to no more than a decision to buy out the shareholders. Our case must be presented on wider international grounds: our argument must be that the canal was an important international asset and facility and that Egypt could not be allowed to exploit it for a purely internal purpose. The Egyptians had not the technical ability to manage it effectively; and their recent behaviour gave no confidence that they would recognise their international obligations in respect of it. . . .

[234]

The Cabinet agreed that for these reasons every effort must be made to restore effective international control over the Canal. It was evident that the Egyptians would not yield to economic pressures alone. They must be subjected to the maximum political pressure which could be exerted by the maritime and trading nations whose interests were most directly affected. And, in the last resort, this political pressure must be backed by the threat—and, if need be, the use—of force.

The Cabinet then considered the factors to be taken into account in preparing a plan of military operations against Egypt. . . .

The Prime Minister said that against this background the Cabinet must decide what our policy must be. He fully agreed that the question was not a legal issue but must be treated as a matter of the widest international importance. It must now be our aim to place the Suez Canal under the control of the Powers interested in international shipping and trade by means of a new international Commission on which Egypt would be given suitable representation. . . . The fundamental question before the Cabinet . . . was whether they were prepared in the last resort to pursue their objective by the threat or even the use of force, and whether they were ready, in default of assistance from the United States and France, to take military action alone.

The Cabinet agreed that our essential interests in this area must, if necessary, be safeguarded by military action and that the necessary preparations to this end must be made. Failure to hold the Suez Canal would lead inevitably to the loss one by one of all our interests and assets in the Middle East and, even if we had to act alone, we could not stop short of using force to protect our position if all other means of protecting it proved unavailing.

Source 8 from Anthony Gorst and Lewis Johnman, The Suez Crisis *(London: Routledge, 1997), pp. 76–77.*

8. U.S. President Dwight D. Eisenhower Cautions Sir Anthony Eden on the Use of Force, September 3, 1956

As to the use of force or the threat of force at this juncture, I continue to feel as I expressed myself in the letter Foster carried to you some weeks ago. Even now military preparations and civilian evacuation exposed to public view seem to be solidifying support for Nasser which has been shaky in many important quarters. I regard it as indispensable that if we are to proceed solidly together to the solution of this problem, public opinion in our several countries must be overwhelming in its support. I must tell you frankly that American public opinion flatly rejects the thought of using force, particularly when it does not seem that every possible peaceful means of protecting interests has been exhausted without result. Moreover, I gravely doubt we could here secure Congressional authority even for the lesser support measures for which you might have to look to us.

I really do not see how a successful result could be achieved by forcible means. The use of force would, it seems to me, vastly increase the area of jeopardy. I do not see how the economy of Western Europe can long survive the burden of prolonged military operations, as well as the denial of Near East oil. Also the peoples of the Near East and of North Africa and, to some extent of all of Asia and all of Africa, would be consolidated against the West to a degree which, I fear, could not be overcome in a generation and, perhaps, not even in a century particularly having in mind the capacity of the Russians to make mischief. Before such action were undertaken, all our peoples should unitedly understand that there were no other means available to protect our vital rights and interests.

Source 9 from Sir Anthony Eden, Full Circle *(London: Cassell, 1960). Reprinted in Harry Browne,* Flashpoints: Suez and Sinai *(London: Longman, 1971), pp. 42–44.*

9. Sir Anthony Eden, British Prime Minister, Replies to President Dwight D. Eisenhower, September 6, 1956

Thank you for your message and writing thus frankly.

There is no doubt as to where we are agreed and have been agreed from the very beginning, namely that we should do everything we can to get a peaceful settlement. . . .

We are both agreed that we must give the Suez Committee every chance to fulfil their mission. This is our firm resolve. If the committee and subsequent negotiations succeed in getting Nasser's agreement to the London proposals of the eighteen powers, there will be no call for force. But if the committee fails, we must have some immediate alternative which will show that Nasser is not going to get his way. . . .

You suggest that this is where we diverge. If that is so I think that the divergence springs from a difference in our assessment of Nasser's plans and intentions. May I set out our view of the position.

In the nineteen-thirties Hitler established his position by a series of carefully planned movements. These began with the occupation of the Rhineland and were followed by successive acts of aggression against Austria, Czechoslovakia, Poland and the West. His actions were tolerated and excused by the majority of the population of Western Europe. It was argued either that Hitler had committed no act of aggression against anyone, or that he was entitled to do what he liked in his own territory, or that it was impossible to prove that he had any ulterior designs, or that the Covenant of the League of Nations did not entitle us to use force and that it would be wiser to wait until he did commit an act of aggression.

In more recent years Russia has attempted similar tactics. The blockade of Berlin was to have been the opening move in a campaign designed at least to deprive the Western powers of their whole position in Germany. On this occasion we fortunately reacted at once with the result that the Russian design was never unfolded. But I am sure that you would agree that it would be wrong to infer from this circumstance that no Russian design existed.

Similarly the seizure of the Suez Canal is, we are convinced, the opening gambit in a planned campaign designed by Nasser to expel all Western influence and interests from Arab countries. He believes that if he can get away with this, and if he can successfully defy eighteen nations, his prestige in Arabia will be so great that he will be able to mount revolutions of young officers in Saudi Arabia, Jordan, Syria and Iraq. (We know that he is already preparing a revolution in Iraq, which is the most stable and progressive.) These new Governments will in effect be Egyptian satellites if not Russian ones. They will have to place their united oil resources under the control of a united Arabia led by Egypt and under Russian influence. When that moment comes Nasser can deny oil to Western Europe and we here shall all be at his mercy. . . .

In short we are convinced that if Nasser is allowed to defy the eighteen nations it will be a matter of months before revolution breaks out in the oil-bearing countries and the West is wholly deprived of Middle Eastern oil. In this brief we are fortified by the advice of friendly leaders in the Middle East. . . .

. . . I can assure you that we are conscious of the burdens and perils attending military intervention. But if our assessment is correct, and if the only alternative is to allow Nasser's plans quietly to develop until this country and all Western Europe are held to ransom by Egypt acting at Russia's behest it seems to us that our duty is plain. We have many times led Europe in the fight for freedom. It would be an ignoble end to our long history if we accepted to perish by degrees.

Source 10 from Moshe Dayan: Story of My Life *by Moshe Dayan. (New York: William Morrow, 1976), pp. 183–184. Reprinted by permission of Harper Collins Publishers Inc.*

10. From the Memoirs of Moshe Dayan, Israeli Minister of Defense, 1976

Soviet political backing . . . had given Egypt formidable military might and her president, Gamal Abdel Nasser, a tremendous feeling of confidence. On July 26, 1956, he stunned the world with the announcement, made before a cheering crowd of tens of thousands in Cairo's Independence Square, that he had nationalized the Suez Canal. It was undoubtedly the most significant political event of the year, with far-reaching international consequences. One of them was an immediate decision by France and Britain to consult on the steps to be taken, and the French foreign minister arranged to leave for London the next day to meet Prime Minister Anthony Eden. I heard about this move from our representatives in Paris, who informed us that they had been approached by our friends in the French Defense Ministry. They said that Christian Pineau, their foreign minister, would be accompanied by military experts, suggesting that military action against Nasser was not ruled out. What the French wanted from us was up-to-the-minute information on the strength and locations of the Egyptian formations—land, sea and air—so that their delegation to London could be well briefed.

. . . I met with Ben-Gurion and proposed that in the situation created by Nasser's Suez action, and before Egypt attacked us, we should launch one of three operations: capture the Sinai Peninsula up to the Canal and establish international control of the waterway; capture Sharm el-Sheikh and lift the blockade of the Aqaba Gulf; take over the Gaza Strip. . . .

That opportunity was being busily developed in London and Paris in the weeks that followed. After the first meeting of the French delegation with Eden in London, the governments of Britain and France resolved to launch a joint military operation to seize and hold the Suez Canal Zone, cancel the nationalization order, and restore their rights in the Canal Authority. It was also their aim to topple Nasser. The General Staffs of both countries began planning a large-scale operation. Reserves were to be mobilized, forces were to be concentrated in Malta and Cyprus, and ships were to be assembled for a huge amphibious operation, almost on a World War Two scale, to follow up an initial paratroop drop in the Canal area. . . .

France was the driving force behind the policy of action. Britain's Prime Minister Eden also favored military measures, but he faced serious opposition inside his own country. And the United States, even though she had been the object of gross vilification in Nasser's nationalization speech, was firmly opposed to the projected operation by her European allies against Egypt.

There was to be doubt and wavering right up to the last moment—and vestiges of this mood were to linger even after the twelfth hour had struck.

Source 11 from Peter Calvocoressi, Suez: Ten Years After *(London: British Broadcasting Corporation, 1967), pp. 36, 62–65.*

11. Transcript from *Suez: Ten Years After*, Britain, 1966

CALVOCORESSI [NARRATOR]: The comparison between Nasser and Hitler haunted many people of Hitler's generation. Looking back, André Fontaine, Foreign Editor of *Le Monde* at the time of Suez . . . has this to say about what he calls 'the Munich complex.'

ANDRÉ FONTAINE: If we try to make a list of all the reasons why Mollet and Pineau were tempted to do something against Egypt, I think we must put first a feeling of deception about Nasser himself. They very soon began to consider him as another Hitler. . . . I think it was something very silly . . . of course, Egypt is by no means something which could be compared to Hitler's Germany. But that was the feeling at that time. I think the majority of the French people were much in agreement with that view. We all had at that time the Munich complex—just as Anthony Eden had—and when Nasser took the decision to nationalize the Suez Canal, this was taken as a major offence. If we had looked at that in cold blood I think we should have realized at that time that after all many countries in the world had taken such steps without prompting anyone to risk a war. . . .

CALVOCORESSI: I myself went to Paris to find out how it was that Israel was so successful in getting French support. I talked to M. Christian Pineau, who was Foreign Minister in 1956, in his flat in Paris:

CHRISTIAN PINEAU: We decided to give support to Israel because it was for us a possibility to redress the situation in the Middle East. You understand what I mean?

CALVOCORESSI: Yes. When you were thinking of Nasser in these terms as a dangerous politician who was trying to extend his power outside his own country of Egypt, were you thinking primarily of the Middle East as we normally understand it or were you also thinking of the Algerian situation?

PINEAU: No. The situation of Algeria was quite different for us from the situation in the Middle East. But the nationalization of the Canal was for Nasser a great success, and among the Algerian people the success of Nasser was a success of the Arab people in general. For us it was very dangerous if we did nothing.

CALVOCORESSI: How far was there also at the same time in France and especially in left-wing circles in France a definite pro-Israeli feeling, either based on feeling for the Jewish people as a whole, or based on a feeling that these were the people who were conducting a real Socialist experiment in the Middle East?

PINEAU: Yes, it is true that in 1956 it was a Socialist Government—not all Socialist, but part Socialist Government—and the Socialist experience of Israel was very interesting for us. From a spiritual and political point of view the principles of the Government of Israel were for us much more sympathetic than the Nasser principles. But it is not the main reason. If Israel had not some particular reasons to engage in this Sinai campaign, I am sure the French Government would not decide to invade the Suez Canal.

CALVOCORESSI: Your main reason then is that you felt it to be necessary and expedient to build up in Israel a counterbalance to Nasser's power in Egypt. Now does this policy go back some years before 1956, and before the nationalization of the Canal Company?

PINEAU: Yes, maybe one, two years; the aid to Israel was for us a possibility of counter-balance, as you say, between Israel and Egypt. But it is since Nasser was in power in Egypt that we began to aid Israel with a big aid.

CALVOCORESSI: Big aid in terms of arms?

PINEAU: And supplies. Arms and supplies.

CALVOCORESSI: And up to 1956 then, the French policy was to help Israel with arms and supplies against what was regarded as an Egyptian menace, but at some point after 1956, after July 1956, am I right in thinking, the policy developed into something else which one might call a policy of co-belligerency. Is that right?

PINEAU: Yes. Maybe it is not so simple. (I speak personally: it is my point of view, maybe not the point of view of all the French members of Government.) For us, nationalization of [the] Canal was very dangerous. First, because Nasser said we do not want the Israel Navy to pass through the Canal, and we thought at this period if Nasser does not want, it will be the same for the French Navy, for the English Navy. That is very dangerous for us because at this period we had and you had some very big interest in the Far East. . . .

CALVOCORESSI: One of the most skilled and constant observers of these matters is M. André Fontaine. . . . I asked him what other motives France had for re-entering Middle Eastern politics:

ANDRÉ FONTAINE: First of all there was the feeling of solidarity with Israel. I think Israel had a lobbying action in Paris at that time which was very fruitful, very well conducted. Everybody in France was very happy with that. Then there was a feeling among the Radical components of the Government that a victory over Nasser would kill the roots of the rebellion in Algeria, and would bring about a possibility of finding a solution to that irritating problem. That was the reason why the Suez war was conducted and was at that time so popular in this country.

CALVOCORESSI: The reasons: first that Nasser was unreliable and dangerous; secondly that there was a need to settle the Algerian problem and that one way of doing it was to adopt this pro-Israeli policy in the Middle East; and third, this business of Socialist solidarity in Israel?

FONTAINE: Not only Socialist solidarity, although I should say it was the truth for Mollet himself. But for the public in France at large, a feeling of solidarity with Israel was explicit. Maybe we had more or less a feeling of responsibility for what happened to the Jews during the war, you know, and we felt that something was due to them.

Source 12 from "Sèvres Protocol, October 22–24, 1956" from Suez *by Keith Kyle, 2002, pp. 565–566. Reprinted by permission of I. B. Tauris, London.*

12. Sèvres Protocol, October 22–24, 1956

PROTOCOL

The results of the conversations which took place at Sèvres from 22–24 October 1956 between the representatives of the Governments of the United Kingdom, the State of Israel and of France are the following:

1. The Israeli forces launch in the evening of 29 October 1956 a large scale attack on the Egyptian forces with the aim of reaching the Canal zone the following day.

2. On being apprised of these events, the British and French Governments during the day of 30 October 1956 respectively and simultaneously make two appeals to the Egyptian Government and the Israeli Government on the following lines:

   A. *To the Egyptian Government*
      (a) halt all acts of war.
      (b) withdraw all its troops ten miles from the Canal.
      (c) accept temporary occupation of key positions on the Canal by the Anglo-French forces to guarantee freedom of passage through the Canal by vessels of all nations until a final settlement.
   B. *To the Israeli Government*
      (a) halt all acts of war.
      (b) withdraw all its troops ten miles to the east of the Canal.

In addition, the Israeli Government will be notified that the French and British Governments have demanded of the Egyptian Government to accept temporary occupation of key positions along the Canal by Anglo-French forces.

It is agreed that if one of the Governments refused, or did not give its consent, within twelve hours the Anglo-French forces would intervene with the means necessary to ensure that their demands are accepted.

[241]

C. The representatives of the three Governments agree that the Israeli Government will not be required to meet the conditions in the appeal addressed to it, in the event that the Egyptian Government does not accept those in the appeal addressed to it for their part.

3. In the event that the Egyptian Government should fail to agree within the stipulated time to the conditions of the appeal addressed to it, the Anglo-French forces will launch military operations against the Egyptian forces in the early hours of the morning of 31 October.

4. The Israeli Government will send forces to occupy the western shore of the Gulf of Akaba and the group of islands Tirane and Sanafir to ensure freedom of navigation in the Gulf of Akaba.

5. Israel undertakes not to attack Jordan during the period of operations against Egypt.

   But in the event that during the same period Jordan should attack Israel, the British Government undertakes not to come to the aid of Jordan.

6. The arrangements of the present protocol must remain strictly secret.

7. They will enter into force after the agreement of the three Governments.

(signed)

DAVID BEN-GURION   PATRICK DEAN   CHRISTIAN PINEAU

Source 13 from Harry Browne, Flashpoints: Suez and Sinai *(London: Longman, 1971), p. 75.*

13. Draft Resolution from the United States to the U.N. Security Council, October 30, 1956[3]

Noting that the armed forces of Israel have penetrated deeply into Egyptian territory in violation of the General Armistice Agreement between Egypt and Israel.

   Expressing its grave concern at this violation of the Armistice Agreement,

1. Calls upon Israel immediately to withdraw its armed forces behind the established armistice lines:

3. A similar resolution was submitted by the Soviet Union. In both cases it was vetoed by Britain and by France.

2. Calls upon all Members:
    (a) to refrain from the use of force or threat of force in the area in any manner inconsistent with the purposes of the United Nations;
    (b) To assist the United Nations in ensuring the integrity of the armistice agreements;
    (c) To refrain from giving any military, economic or financial assistance to Israel so long as it has not complied with this resolution;

3. Requests the Secretary-General to keep the Security Council informed on compliance with this resolution and to make whatever recommendations he deems appropriate for the maintenance of international peace and security in the area by the implementation of this and prior resolutions.

Source 14 from The Hindu, *2 November 1956. Reprinted in J. Eayrs,* The Commonwealth and Suez *(London: Oxford University Press, 1964), pp. 249–251.*

14. Statement by Jawaharlal Nehru, Indian Prime Minister, November 1, 1956

It has been rather difficult for me during the last day or two even to think of much of the changes in India because my mind was filled with forebodings, with apprehension of what is taking place in what is called the Middle East region. . . . Some extraordinary things have happened in the last two or three days. First was the sudden invasion of Egyptian territory by Israel. Remember, there was no declaration of war. It was a sudden, unheralded invasion of Egyptian territory in large numbers. It was a breach of the Armistice. It was a breach of the rules of the U.N. Charter. It is clear, naked aggression.

Now our sympathies in these disputes have been with Arab countries in the past. We have expressed them so but at the same time we have not been in any sense opposed to Jews or Israelis. We have felt that the Arabs have had a raw deal and that must be ended. . . . But the fact remains that apart from what has happened in the past, in the present case it is clear and naked aggression by Israel on Egypt and every member of the U.N. should try to halt, stop and resist the aggression. What, however, had happened, was that suddenly England and France have issued ultimatums to Egypt to clear off the Canal region—say ten miles away—and agreed to plant their forces to protect the Canal. The Canal has been functioning all this time under Egyptian control. If anything has happened in the Canal, it came from the Israeli invasion. But Egypt is being asked to withdraw. . . .

After fairly considerable experience in foreign affairs, I cannot think of a grosser case of naked aggression than what England and France are attempting to do, backed by the armed forces of the two great powers. I deeply regret to say so, because we have been friendly with both the countries and in particular our relationship with the U.K. has been close and friendly ever since we attained independence. I realize also that the U.K. has made many liberal gestures to other countries and has been a force for peace, I think, for the past few years. Because of this my sorrow and distress are all the greater at this amazing adventure that England and France have entered into. . . .

In the middle of the 20th century we are going back to the predatory method of the 18th and 19th centuries. But there is a difference now. There are self-respecting independent nations in Asia and Africa which are not going to tolerate this kind of incursion by the colonial powers. Therefore I need not say that in this matter our sympathies are entirely with Egypt.

Source 15 from Harry Browne, Flashpoints: Suez and Sinai *(London: Longman, 1971), pp. 68–69.*

15. Soviet Response to the Aggression Against Egypt, October 31, 1956

Egypt has fallen victim to aggression. Her territory has been invaded by Israeli forces and she faces the danger of a landing by British and French forces. . . .

The action of the Israeli government constitutes armed aggression and an open breach of the United Nations Charter. The facts indicate that the invasion by the Israeli forces has clearly been calculated to be used as an excuse for the Western powers, primarily Britain and France, to bring their troops into the territory of the Arab states, notably, into the Suez Canal zone. . . . The government of Israel, operating as a tool of imperialist circles bent on restoring the regime of colonial oppression in the East, has challenged all the Arab peoples, all the peoples of the East fighting against colonialism. The course which the extremist ruling circles of Israel have taken is a criminal one and dangerous, above all to the state of Israel itself and to its future. . . .

The government of the Soviet Union resolutely condemns the act of aggression against Egypt by the governments of Britain, France and Israel. The freedom-loving peoples of the world fervently sympathise with the Egyptian people waging a just struggle in defence of their national independence. . . .

The Soviet government holds that all responsibility for the dangerous consequences of these aggressive actions against Egypt will rest entirely with the governments which have taken the line of disturbing peace and security, the line of aggression.

Source 16 from Anthony Gorst and Lewis Johnman, The Suez Crisis *(London: Routledge, 1997), pp. 142–143.*

16. Discussion by the British Cabinet, November 28, 1956

The Foreign Secretary said that in his judgement the economic considerations were now even more important than the political. We could probably sustain our position in the United Nations for three or four weeks; but, so far from gaining anything by deferring a withdrawal of the Anglo-French force which we could, if we wished, complete within the next fortnight, we should thereby risk losing the good will of public opinion, which in all countries wished the clearance of the Canal to proceed as rapidly as possible. On the other hand if we withdrew the Anglo-French force as rapidly as was practicable, we should regain the sympathy of the United States Government. We should be better placed to ask for their support in any economic measures which we might need to take; . . . it would therefore be possible for the Cabinet, if they agreed, to authorise the withdrawl of the Anglo-French force while emphasising that this action was based on our confident expectation that rapid progress would now be made by the United Nations towards the clearance of the Canal, an agreement about its satisfactory administration thereafter and a comprehensive settlement of the long-term problems of the Middle East.

The Chancellor of the Exchequer said that it would be necessary to announce early in the following week the losses of gold and dollars which we had sustained during November. This statement would reveal a very serious drain on the reserves and would be a considerable shock both to public opinion in this country and to international confidence in sterling. It was therefore important that we should be able to announce at the same time that we were taking action to reinforce the reserves both by recourse to the International Monetary Fund and in other ways. For this purpose the good will of the United States Government was necessary; and it was evident that this good will could not be obtained without an immediate and unconditional undertaking to withdraw the Anglo-French force from Port Said. He therefore favoured a prompt announcement of our intention to withdraw this force, justifying this action on the ground that we had now achieved the purpose for which we had originally launched the Anglo-French military operation against Egypt and that we were content to leave the United Nations, backed by the United States, the responsibility, which the General Assembly could now be deemed to have accepted for settling the problems of the Middle East.

Source 17 from Anthony Gorst and Lewis Johnman, The Suez Crisis *(London: Routledge, 1997), pp. 156–157.*

17. Exchange Between U.S. Secretary of State John Foster Dulles and U.S. Senator Richard Russell, January 2, 1957

SECRETARY DULLES: The fact is that it is more and more developing to be the fact that the British and the French are not going to be able to carry even the share of the so-called free world defense which they had been trying to carry up to the present time.

Their own difficulties are weakening them. The French position is very considerably weakened by the hostilities in North Africa. The British position has been greatly weakened by the effort which they made in the recent attack on Egypt.

Now, partly that created, partly it disclosed, the vulnerability of the British economic and financial position. But it brought the British to a realisation of the fact that they have got to cut their costs more.

They have been cutting these, and this present task of their Secretary of Defense Sandys reflects what they regard as the imperative necessity of getting a sounder economy by cutting out a good many of their military burdens, and particularly their overseas commitments.

SENATOR RUSSELL: Well, I was not dealing with that in this series of questions. But as they do reduce theirs, the total strength of the free world is decreased, unless we fill whatever position they abandon, militarily and economically, is it not?

SECRETARY DULLES: Broadly speaking, that is so, yes.

Source 18 from Anthony Gorst and Lewis Johnman, The Suez Crisis *(London: Routledge, 1997), pp. 151–152.*

18. Letter from British Prime Minister Eden to Senior Cabinet Ministers, December 28, 1956

We have to try and assess the lessons of Suez. The first is that if we are to play an independent part in the world, even on a more modest scale than we have done heretofore, we must ensure our financial and economic independence. Since we have no raw materials but coal, this means that we must excel in technical knowledge. . . .

In the strategic sphere we have to do some re-thinking about our areas of influence and the military bases on which they must rest. Some of the latter seem of doubtful value in the light of our Suez experience. . . .

The conclusion of all this is surely that we must review our world position and our domestic capacity more searchingly in the light of the Suez experience which has not so much changed our fortunes as revealed realities. While the consequences of this examination may be to determine us to work more closely with Europe, carrying with us, we hope our closest friends in the Commonwealth in such development, here too we must be under no illusion. Europe will not welcome us simply because at the moment it may appear to suit us to look to them. The timing and the conviction of our approach may be decisive in their influence on those with whom we plan to work.

Source 19 from Peter Calvocoressi, Suez: Ten Years After *(London: British Broadcasting Corporation, 1967), pp. 55–58.*

19. President Gamal Abdel Nasser of Egypt Discusses Suez, 1966

CALVOCORESSI [NARRATOR]: Here to end the programme are President Nasser's own general conclusions on the impact of Suez:

NASSER: I was accused of many, many things. But all my object was, was to have complete independence in the Arab countries. Some people said Nasser wants to have an empire for himself. It is not a question of a person. As I said before . . . all that we do and all that we work for now is to have independent countries and united Arab countries; but united Arab countries do not mean an empire for somebody; it means to have a strong Arab nation. . . .

CHILDERS: Do you think the Suez could happen again?

NASSER: Yes, yes.

CHILDERS: Do you really think there could be another British or French attack on Egypt?

NASSER: You know, we insist about our independence, but we feel now that they do not like that. I want to add—the United States, they do not like what we say about our independence. They do not like what we feel about the Arab countries. They do not like our insistence to be completely independent. Of course there is also the supplies of arms to Israel. The United States gave Israel two hundred tanks through Germany; then two hundred tanks through the United States; then aeroplanes, helicopters, through Germany. So Israel now is full of arms, and still the policy of Israel is to force a settlement.

CHILDERS: You think that there might again still be an Israeli attack into Sinai?

NASSER: Yes, of course; because there is an Israeli threat continuously not only against Sinai—against Syria, against Jordan, against Lebanon. . . .

CHILDERS: Looking back then overall, what do you think was the outcome of Suez, the effect of Suez, first on Egypt?

NASSER: We were able after Suez to nationalize all the foreign assets in our country and by that Suez regained back the wealth of the Egyptian people to be used for the interests of the Egyptian people. Then, of course, on the other hand it was clear for the Egyptian people that they could defend their country and secure the independence of their country. So we mobilized ourselves for development and raising the standards of living of the people.

CHILDERS: Now, what do you think the effect of Suez was on the Arab nation, the Arab world as a whole?

NASSER: Well, of course, Suez helped the Arab nation, the Arab world, to regain confidence; and it proved to the Arab nation that Arabs are one nation because the reaction was not here in Egypt alone.

CHILDERS: Looking at international history throughout the world, if you were asked by an historian to say what the meaning of Suez was to world history in this mid-twentieth century, what would you say it was?

NASSER: Well, the meaning of Suez is that there is an end to the methods of the nineteenth century: that it was impossible to use the methods of the nineteenth century in the twentieth century. On the other hand, Suez gave confidence to many countries. I think Suez helped many of the African countries to be sure of themselves and insist about their independence.

Source 20 from The Times *(London), February 4, 1960. Reprinted in Anthony Gorst and Lewis Johnman,* The Suez Crisis *(London: Routledge, 1997), pp. 159–160.*

20. Harold Macmillan, British Prime Minister, Addresses the South African Parliament, February 3, 1960

In the twentieth century, and especially since the end of the war, the processes which gave birth to the nation-states of Europe have been repeated all over the world. We have seen the awakening of national consciousness in peoples who have for centuries lived in dependence on some other power.

Fifteen years ago this movement spread through Asia. The most striking of all the impressions I have formed since I left London a month ago is of the strength of this African national consciousness. In different places it may take different forms but it is happening everywhere. The wind of change is blowing through the Continent.

Whether we like it or not, this growth of national consciousness is a political fact. We must all accept it as a fact. Our national policies must take account of it. . . .

. . . As I see it, the great issue in this second half of the twentieth century is whether the uncommitted peoples of Asia and Africa will swing to the east or to the west. Will they be drawn into the Communist camp? Or will the great experiments in self government that are now being made in Asia and Africa, especially within the Commonwealth, prove so successful, and by their example so compelling, that the balance will come down in favour of freedom and order and justice?

21. British Cartoon, 1962

QUESTIONS TO CONSIDER

Now that you have analyzed the documents and placed them in their historical context, it is time to focus on some more specific questions. Many conflicting perspectives are represented in the documents, so it will be important to consider the various ways in which the different participants might have answered these questions at the time.

The most basic questions, perhaps, are these: Why did Britain, France, and Israel decide to launch a military invasion of Egypt? Why did they receive so little support for that action in the wider global community?

In a more general vein, what do the events preceding and following the military action in Egypt in October and November 1956 tell us about the north/south axis of global conflict—that is, about the relationship between colonial powers and their colonies and former colonies? How did Nasser present Egypt's relationship with Britain and Israel? How similar was Nasser's analysis to that of Jawaharlal Nehru of India? How did the British explain or justify their actions in light of their history of colonial empire in the Middle East?

In another context, how do these documents inform our understanding of the east/west axis of conflict—the cold war? The Soviet Union actually played a relatively small role in the crisis, as it was preoccupied with troubles in its own Eastern European sphere of influence at the time. Nevertheless, various actors in this drama invoked the Soviets as having

an actual or potential role. How did the British present the Soviet threat? How did the Americans respond? How did the Soviet Union itself portray its relationships with the Arabs and Israelis? Why did the artist who created Source 6 draw in the Soviet foreign minister as he did? At several points, world leaders wondered if the Suez crisis might lead to World War III. From these documents, can you explain why that did *not* happen?

While the various countries involved had different opinions about Egypt at the time, everyone seemed to agree that Gamal Abdel Nasser was the key figure. In his writings and speeches, what sort of image of himself did Nasser seek to promote? How was he seen by other Arabs? by the Israelis? by the British, French, and Americans? From the understanding you have gained of Nasser's role in Egyptian and Middle Eastern politics, how closely did these varying images correspond to reality? Comparing Sources 5 and 6, what similarities and differences do you find in the representations of Nasser? Which is more sympathetic to him, and why?

The other key figure was the British prime minister, Sir Anthony Eden. What was the source of Eden's personal antipathy toward Nasser? Did he allow his personal obsession with the Egyptian leader to influence his political decisions? How truthful was Eden with the British public and with the American government? Why did he undertake this adventure without firm backing from the United States? Are the "lessons" he says he learned from Suez appropriate or sufficient?

Another set of questions has to do with those issues of imperial decline introduced at the beginning of this chapter. Why did the British reintroduce troops into Egypt in 1956, just two years after they had agreed to remove them permanently? More generally, what factors worked against the British in their drive to maintain a dominant role in the Middle East? Were other policies considered that might have been more successful? Does it seem that the Suez crisis was a symptom or a cause of British imperial decline? What does Source 21 tell us about Britain's self-image six years after Suez?

Finally, we might consider that many of these documents refer to history itself as an explanation or justification for the actions of various participants in the drama. How did Nasser relate Egyptian history to his own actions as president? How did the British and French leaders apply the "lessons of history" to their own actions? What were the American and Israeli perspectives on the ways in which the Suez crisis fit into the history of the Middle East and of the world? Are there aspects of the Suez crisis that still help us to understand the Middle Eastern and world situations today?

EPILOGUE

That final question leads us to ponder the outcomes of the Suez crisis. For Nasser and for Egypt, it represented, at least in the short term, a great victory. Nasser was acclaimed as a hero in the Arab and Muslim worlds, and throughout much of Africa and Asia, for having stood up to the arrogance of an old colonial power. With Soviet help, the Aswan Dam was built, symbolizing Egypt's modernization. But Nasser's dreams of pan-Arabism, of uniting the Arabs in a single political system, came to little. The balance of power between Israel and Egypt turned against Egypt in the Six Day War of 1967. The Sinai was once again invaded by Israel, this time to be occupied for over a decade. In 1979, Nasser's successor, Anwar

Sadat, made peace with Israel in meetings coordinated by the United States. But some Egyptians, nostalgic for Nasser's forthright nationalism, opposed the Camp David accords, and Sadat was subsequently assassinated. Egypt today walks a fine line: As a "moderate" Arab nation, it is willing to work with the United States, but at the same time it retains Nasser's commitment to the liberation of the Palestinian people.

Great Britain has still not entirely resolved the question that the Suez crisis brought so clearly to its attention: how to maintain a role in global affairs. Four possibilities presented themselves. First, Britain could go it alone. That possibility was never a viable one after World War II, as Suez so clearly indicated. Second, Britain could seek influence in global affairs through association with the United

States. The breach in Anglo-American relations caused by the Suez crisis was very brief, and the foundations of the "special relationship" between the two nations still stood. But it could no longer be an association of equals. Even when Ronald Reagan and Margaret Thatcher created a solid personal and political alliance in the 1980s, there was never any question but that American priorities came first. Third, the British could use the Commonwealth as a means of maintaining their power and prestige in former colonies and possessions even after the Union Jack was replaced by the flags of independent states. This policy was pursued with some vigor in the 1960s, but the Commonwealth proved to be more a cultural organization than a body with real political clout. Fourth, the British could seek a closer association with Europe. But as the Germans and the French laid the foundations of what would become the European Union, the British remained aloof. Ambivalence about the European option is still characteristic of Britain today.

None of these options has proved particularly successful. But there are many people in Great Britain who are not all that concerned. Unlike those of Anthony Eden's generation, many British citizens, including some who trace their own families back to Asia, Africa, or the Middle East, take the decline of the British Empire as a simple fact of life.

For the United States, the Suez crisis marked the beginning of its role as the principal power broker in the Middle East. This was just one example of the international commitments that the United States made in the 1950s and 1960s to fill the power vacuum left by the departing Europeans. Vietnam, where the United States succeeded the French as the dominant Western power, is another example. An adequate understanding of the world role of the United States in recent times, including the Persian Gulf War of 1991, also requires close attention to the history of Suez.

CHAPTER NINE

BERLIN: THE CRUX

OF THE COLD WAR (1945–1990)

THE PROBLEM

On April 25, 1945, at Torgau, Germany, American soldiers invading the country from the west met and shook hands with Russian soldiers of the Soviet Union advancing from the east. Their encounter that day, followed within days by the Soviet capture of the German capital of Berlin, seized the attention of much of the world. It marked victory over the Hitler regime after a worldwide conflict that had taken the lives of as many as 60 million persons, and it reflected the hopes of people everywhere for a postwar era of peace and understanding.[1] Few at that

time would have imagined that the World War II allies—the United States, Britain, and France in the west and the Soviet Union in the east—would so fundamentally disagree on their treatment of Germany that the country would remain divided for over four decades, in part along the Elbe River where the armies met in 1945. Even fewer would have imagined that out of those disagreements, and others initially focused on Central and Eastern European matters, would develop a new conflict, a "Cold War" that would occasionally verge on a "hot" war, that is, a third, worldwide conflict in the twentieth century. Indeed, conflict between the Western powers and the Soviet Union dominated much of the second half of the twentieth century, and it is by examining one of the chief sources of that conflict, the postwar treatment of Germany and especially its capital, Berlin, that we may study the Cold War in microcosm.

Berlin brought the Western allies and the Soviet Union perilously close to war twice in less than a decade and a half as part of the enduring conflict known as the Cold War. Your

1. The number of World War II deaths will always be approximate because of loss of records and the massive numbers of civilians who perished with little or no documentation, including some 6 million victims of the Holocaust and large numbers of persons killed by military bombing of civilian populations. However, recent research in Russia and Eastern Europe made possible by the end of the Cold War has forced historians to raise their estimates of military and civilian mortality in World War II. They now estimate deaths in the Soviet Union alone at about 25 million persons, a level of loss that certainly shaped the Soviet Union's response to defeated Germany.

problem in this chapter is to examine the causes of the Cold War and especially the roots of the conflict over Berlin. What were the origins of the Cold War? How did the Berlin crises develop out of wartime agreements? What strategic considerations made Berlin so essential to both the Western allies and the Soviets?

BACKGROUND

Two generations of historians have now examined and debated the origins of the Cold War. The view, once widely held in the West, that it was the result of aggressive Soviet attempts at worldwide domination has been tempered in recent years, especially as historians have been able to examine records that became available after the breakup of the Soviet Union in 1991. The growing scholarly consensus is that each side bore some responsibility for the Cold War. Indeed, the common need to defeat Hitler's Germany in World War II concealed fundamental differences between the Western powers and the Soviet Union. Certainly these differences were ideological: The United States, Britain, and France possessed democratic political institutions and capitalist, free enterprise economic systems while the Soviet Union was a Communist party dictatorship under Joseph Stalin (1879–1953) with a state-dominated economic life. Such ideological differences led the Western powers to intervene militarily against Communist forces in Russia in the civil war of 1918–1920 and to shun the Soviet regime diplomatically until the 1930s. But Cold War differences also were strategic in origin. Stalin and his diplomats sought a post–World War II reorganization of Europe that would shield their country from any repetition of the costly German invasions that it had sustained in the two world wars of the twentieth century. Achievement of this goal all but mandated Soviet domination of the countries of Eastern Europe to create a buffer zone between the Soviet Union and Germany. At the same time, many British and American statesmen envisioned a postwar Europe in which nations like Italy, Greece, and others would fall within a sphere of influence dominated by the Western powers. Germany, in the center of Europe, thus was of vital strategic importance to both the Soviets and the Western powers, and neither side was prepared to see the other dominate this country.

Such considerations contributed to a growing mistrust between the wartime allies even before the defeat of Germany. Stalin, for example, suspected that the Anglo-American negotiations that led to Italy's changing sides in 1943 were a first step toward integrating Germany's former ally into a Western sphere of influence. He also believed that the United States and Britain deliberately delayed their invasion of France until 1944 in order to impose more of the war's burden on the Soviets. American and British statesmen, for their part, grew increasingly uneasy late in the war at unilateral Soviet occupations of

Poland and other Eastern European countries that clearly aimed at post-war communist domination of these lands. Thus, statesmen sought at a number of international conferences during and just after the war in Europe to resolve differences between the Western allies and the Soviets on the war's conduct and the postwar order. A Moscow conference of foreign ministers in October 1943, for example, created a European Advisory Commission (EAC) composed of American, British, and Russian officials to work out the details of Germany's postwar treatment. This group's plan, one whose authors believed would govern defeated Germany only until the Allies worked out a permanent postwar settlement, divided the country into zones of occupation. A line partially following the Elbe River separated a Soviet eastern zone of occupation from British and American zones of occupation in the west. Such a division left the country's capital, Berlin, 110 miles within the Soviet zone of occupation, but, as a symbol of joint victory, the EAC plan divided that city into American, British, and Soviet sectors of occupation.

Successive wartime conferences only slightly modified this basic division of Germany while failing to resolve other fundamental issues about the defeated power. Thus, at Yalta in February 1945, American president Franklin D. Roosevelt (1882–1945), British prime minister Winston Churchill (1874–1965), and Stalin agreed to create a French zone of occupation within the American and British zones in Germany and their sectors of Berlin. They did this at

the behest of the British, who, heeding Roosevelt's view that all American troops would leave Europe within two years of the war's end, wished to involve another Western power in the occupation. The statesmen also agreed on the broad general principle that their occupation policy in Germany would emphasize de-Nazification of the political system, democratization of government, and demilitarization of society. But they failed to agree on the specific policies that would achieve these principles.

At Potsdam in July and August 1945, American president Harry S. Truman (1884–1972) and British prime minister Clement Attlee (1883–1967) did agree with Stalin to set up an Allied Control Council for the administration of occupied Germany that was composed of the powers' military commanders in each zone.[2] But the allied heads of government set down only a general agenda for the council, the ideological disagreements of the Western allies and the Soviets were great, and the French government, which initially favored a permanently divided and weakened Germany, often blocked common policy efforts just after the war. Thus, the four occupation zones evolved from the first without any common policies. This posed great problems, because the Soviets occupied the eastern agricultural lands of Germany while the Western powers occupied

2. President Roosevelt died in April 1945, and Vice President Truman assumed his office. Winston Churchill represented Britain at the opening of the conference, but his Conservative party lost control of the House of Commons in the elections of 1945, and the Labour party leader, Clement Attlee, replaced him as prime minister.

the industrial heartland, which produced only 40 percent of its food needs.

The possibility of common solutions to problems in Germany diminished as relations between the Soviets and the Western powers became increasingly tense. Soviet insecurities mounted with America's abrupt termination of wartime Lend Lease aid in May 1945 after victory in Europe and the successful employment of atomic bombs by the United States to end the war against Japan in August 1945. At the same time, Soviet actions increasingly alarmed Western policymakers. Stalin violated his promises of free elections in Poland, and Soviet officials clearly sought to facilitate communist domination of other governments in Eastern European countries occupied by their Red Army (Czechoslovakia, Hungary, Bulgaria, and Romania). In addition, when a communist insurgency erupted in Greece at the war's end and the Soviet Union began to apply pressure on Turkey to revise the treaty limiting the movement of Soviet warships through the Turkish Straits, American and British statesmen began to fear that Stalin sought a massive expansion of the territory dominated by his country.

The United States government responded to this perceived threat in two important policy initiatives in 1947 that further embittered East-West relations. Militarily, President Truman extended assistance to Greece and Turkey while offering such aid to all other countries resisting communist takeover. This Truman Doctrine created an American policy of "containment" of communist expansion that would be the keystone of post-war United States foreign policy. It meant, too, that American forces remained in Europe not for two years after the end of World War II, as Roosevelt had expected, but for two generations. Economically, American secretary of state George C. Marshall announced a plan of economic assistance to war-torn Europe—the Marshall Plan—to rebuild the Continent and restore its prosperity in order to encourage noncommunist governmental institutions. The United States offered this aid to all European countries, but the Soviets perceived it as a scheme to draw countries into the orbit of the United States. Thus, the Soviets rejected Marshall Plan aid, blocked attempts by Czechoslovakia and Poland to participate in the plan, and forced the removal of noncommunist officials from several Eastern European governments. The Western powers particularly resented a coup in Czechoslovakia, a country with democratic traditions, which replaced a coalition government with a communist one in February 1948.

Developments in Germany reflected such growing tension as the occupation zones increasingly diverged politically. In the eastern zone, the Soviets stripped the area of much of its industrial stock as reparations for their losses in the war and created a one-party state dominated by the Socialist Unity party (SED) led by the Communist Walter Ulbricht. They sought to use this party to win control of Berlin's municipal government, too, in the elections of 1946, but Berliners, recalling the brutality of the Red Army in their city at the end of the war, rejected the party's candidates. One-party government became the lot of Soviet-occupied East Berlin; the Western powers' sectors maintained a free, multiparty political system. Beyond Berlin, in their zones of occupation in western Germany, American, British, and French officials also permitted free elections. Officials chosen in those elections met with SED officials in Munich in June 1947 to discuss the creation of a government for a unified Germany. Disagreement on the nature of a new German government, however, was immediate, and SED representatives walked out of the meeting at its very outset.

If the failure of the Munich conference ruled out immediate unification of the Soviet and western occupation zones, American and British officials evolved an alternative plan. Their plan was the result of serious problems in the western zones of Germany, where they faced the ongoing need to supply large quantities of food for the civilian population because, as we have seen, western Germany was not self-sufficient in food production. The Americans and the British opted to rebuild the western German economy so that their former enemies could exchange manufactured goods in the world market for their own food needs. This decision had important consequences.

The Americans and British began by economically merging their zones on January 1, 1947, to coordinate economic policy on a larger scale. The French zone also eventually joined this entity, and the Western powers' next step in German economic recovery was much-needed

currency reform. At war's end the occupying powers had replaced Hitler-era currency with occupation Reichsmarks, which quickly lost their value as the Soviets printed them in vast quantities to meet their costs of occupation. As merchants increasingly refused to accept this devalued currency, German economic life stagnated and a barter system became widespread in which the most universally accepted currency was American cigarettes. Despite this disastrous situation, the Soviets resisted American-sponsored currency reform because to them it represented a plan to integrate western Germany economically into the sphere of the United States. When the Americans proceeded with currency reform without Soviet approval, they violated the Potsdam agreement, which mandated joint action on this issue, and the Soviets terminated meetings of the Allied Control Council after March 1948 as the Western powers prepared to introduce the new currency, the Deutschmark. Then in June 1948, a meeting of representatives of Western democratic states including the United States, Britain, France, Belgium, the Netherlands, and Luxembourg authorized a meeting of the German states under Western occupation to begin to prepare a constitution for their unification as one nation.

From the Soviet point of view, this progress toward currency reform and the unification of the Western occupation zones put control of western Germany increasingly beyond Soviet grasp, and it seems to have prompted Stalin to take several steps. Many historians view the resulting crisis as the beginning of the Cold War. On April 1, 1948, Soviet officials began to interfere with the Western allies' rail and highway transport into Berlin to make the position of the allied garrisons there more difficult. In addition, they ordered the eastern zone to adopt a new currency, the Ostmark. But when Soviet officials attempted to force the Berlin municipal assembly on June 23, 1948, to adopt their zone's currency instead of the Deutschmark, a clear move to bring the entire city under greater Soviet economic control, they provoked a crisis. The city's assembly rejected the Ostmark, and Soviet officials halted all traffic into Berlin by highway, water, and railroad in what came to be called the Berlin Blockade. Stalin intended either to block the new currency and the unification of the western zones or to starve the city into submission and to force the withdrawal of the Western allies from Berlin. Germany was too important a prize to let the Western powers integrate it more closely into their economic and political system. Indeed, Stalin said as much during the blockade, telling Western diplomats to give up the currency reform and western German unification and "You shall no longer have any difficulties. That may be done even tomorrow . . ."[3]

Clearly the Western allies could not give in to Soviet demands; Germany had great strategic importance for them, too. But the Western response to the blockade had to be a cautious one. Postwar budget cuts had left the United States armed forces in no condition to fight a war in 1948. Thus, the suggestion of the American military governor in Germany, General Lucius D. Clay, that an armed convoy protected by Western soldiers force its way, if necessary, into Berlin had to be rejected. Such an act might well have provoked a war. Instead, on June 26, 1948, the United States Air Force (USAF) and the British Royal Air Force (RAF) began to fly supplies over the Soviet zone of occupation into Berlin along the three air corridors to the city from the west that had been established in wartime agreements. This mission, the Berlin Airlift, required that the USAF and RAF transport all of the food and fuel required by a city of 2.5 million civilians as well as by their own garrisons there. At a minimum, these needs amounted to 3,000 tons of coal and 2,500 tons of food daily. In all, the USAF and the RAF sent 276,926 flights into Berlin before the Soviets ended the blockade on May 12, 1949. At its peak, the airlift landed one transport airplane in Berlin every 63 seconds, twenty-four hours per day, to permit the western sectors of the city to remain free of Soviet control. In the course of the blockade relations between the Western allies and the Soviets only worsened. In April 1949, the United States sponsored the creation of the North Atlantic Treaty Organization (NATO), an alliance whose chief aim was the defense of Western Europe against the Soviets. The following month, the western zones of Germany adopted a constitution and became the Federal

3. Quoted in John Lewis Gaddis, *We Now Know: Rethinking Cold War History* (Oxford: Clarendon Press, 1997), p. 112.

Republic of Germany (often called "West Germany"), a step the Soviet zone echoed when it declared itself the German Democratic Republic (often called "East Germany"). In the years following, the two Germanys went their separate ways. The Federal Republic rapidly rebuilt its economy in what has been called an "economic miracle," and its citizens came to enjoy one of the world's highest standards of living. Moreover, the Western powers increasingly integrated it into their military and economic systems. The Federal Republic also rebuilt its armed forces and assumed a part in NATO, just as it played a role in founding the organization that became the European Union. In the German Democratic Republic, the dictatorial one-party rule of the SED imposed a communist economic system on the country, collectivizing agriculture, nationalizing industry, and launching a drive to transform heavily agricultural East Germany into an industrial power, that consumed much of the nation's resources and made life there austere in the extreme. The East German government sought to enforce it citizens' acquiescence in this situation with an extensive secret police network designed to root out dissent. As a result, large numbers of people fled the Democratic Republic for West Germany, and by the end of the 1950s as many as 4 million persons—20 percent of the area's 1945 population—had left. Such population loss was disastrous for East Germany, especially because the refugees were disproportionately young and well educated, the very people necessary to accomplish communist

goals in the east. Certainly, too, the continuing flight of the most talented citizens of the Democratic Republic was an enduring embarrassment to its regime and to the Soviet Union.

The East German regime sought to stop such emigration by making flight a crime and by better policing its 860-mile-long border with West Germany. But tighter border controls drove increasing numbers of East Germans to Berlin, where the four-power occupation of the city still permitted free movement between the sectors of the Western allies and the Soviet Union. Indeed, departure from the Democratic Republic there could be as simple as boarding a subway in the Soviet zone and detraining in the western sector of Berlin.

While East Germans fled their homes in great numbers in the 1950s, the Cold War continued and became more dangerous when the Soviets acquired atomic weapons. With nuclear warfare between the NATO powers and the Soviets a possibility, Europe settled into a tense equilibrium for a time, despite uprisings in Eastern Europe (East Berlin, 1953; Poland and Hungary, 1956) and many late 1940s and 1950s Cold War confrontations outside of Europe. Thus, a communist insurgency toppled an American-supported regime in China in 1949, and in 1950 through 1953 American-led United Nations forces fought North Korean and communist Chinese forces for control of the Korean peninsula. In addition, a communist-led uprising in Indochina (Cambodia, Laos, and Vietnam) against French rule led to the defeat of the colonial power and increasing American involvement there as part of the containment policy.

Only in 1958 did a major Cold War crisis again confront Europe, but the issue was still Germany. By that time, however, the new leader of the Communist party of the Soviet Union and the country's premier, Nikita S. Khrushchev (1894–1971), was directing policy. For Khrushchev, the continuing flight of refugees from East Germany impeded that state's economic development and demanded resolution. At the same time, he seems to have calculated that the growing nuclear and missile power of the Soviet Union would mean that the United States and its allies would not risk war over Berlin. The result was a second Berlin crisis.

Khrushchev demanded that the wartime Allies sign peace treaties with the two Germanys and that all occupying forces evacuate Berlin, leaving the capital a free city. The United States and the Western allies could not accept this proposal, of course, because it left East Germany in communist hands while raising the possibility of all of Berlin slipping into the Soviet sphere. Nevertheless, negotiations between the two sides opened under Khrushchev's threat to sign a treaty unilaterally with the Democratic Republic. East-West tensions remained high as John F. Kennedy (1917–1963) assumed the American presidency in 1961, and they grew as East Germans, frightened by the prospect of a settlement that would close the Berlin escape route, hastened to flee westward.

Between January 1, 1961, and August 13, 1961, 159,700 persons left behind all that they owned and fled the German Democratic Republic. This was a greater number of refugees than in all of 1959.

When Kennedy and Khrushchev met in Vienna in June 1961, neither side offered any concessions on Berlin, and the Soviet leader adopted a bellicose attitude that even he conceded in his memoirs might have been perceived by the American president as threatening war. Following the meeting both leaders announced large military build-ups. But the Kennedy administration, while preparing to defend the Western sectors of Berlin, clearly signaled that it was not prepared to fight a war if the Soviets and the East Germans confined their actions to stopping the flow of refugees. Thus, before dawn on August 13, 1961, the German Democratic Republic began construction of a wall separating the eastern sector of Berlin from those occupied by the Western powers to stop its citizens' flights to the West. East German police closely guarded the wall and used deadly force against persons attempting to escape. The wall's construction shocked Americans and Western Europeans. But despite a tense face-off between American and Soviet tanks at Checkpoint Charlie (the only point where American and allied officials could cross to East Berlin after the wall's construction) on October 27, 1961, the great powers avoided war over Berlin a second time.

THE METHOD

Modern government produces a vast written record that is of great value to the student of history in understanding a country's foreign policy, and much material is readily available. Treaties, for example, are widely disseminated in the press and in government publications because many democratic governments, like that of the United States, require that legislative bodies ratify the commitments that they contain. Less well known is the record of what went into the making of foreign policy, since policymakers often draw on top-secret analyses of strategic matters drawn up by military, diplomatic, and security officials. National law in most countries governs the release of such documents for study, and in most cases scholars and the public can see such records only after a considerable lapse of time, in some cases fifty years or more, or when the contents of the records no longer compromise national security. Because the Cold War is now over, records of the latter sort are becoming available to historians, and the present chapter combines such records with those more traditionally made available to researchers for examination of the Berlin crises.

Source 1 is a record of the Potsdam Conference (technically called the "Berlin Conference"; Potsdam is a suburb of Berlin) concluded on August 2, 1945. Nations maintain extensive written records of such international meetings because they often result in treaties that have the effect of inter-

national law. The United States, for example, published a written record of the conference more than 2,700 pages in length.[4] Source 1 is the Potsdam protocol that Clement Attlee, Harry Truman, and Joseph Stalin signed on behalf of their respective nations on August 2, 1945. A protocol is an official diplomatic document summarizing the agreements reached at an international meeting, and that at Potsdam dealt with the very broad range of issues that arose with the end of World War II in Europe. But the statesmen were especially concerned with Germany, and the excerpts from the Potsdam protocol in Source 1 offer you a synopsis of the arrangements made to govern Germany as well as the legal background for much of the cold war confrontation over Berlin. Why do you conclude that the signatories to the Potsdam agreement viewed their arrangements for Germany as temporary in nature? The signatory powers concluded treaties with Italy, Romania, Bulgaria, Hungary, and Finland, Germany's wartime allies, in the course of 1947. Why do you think the statesmen at Potsdam might have expected that a treaty with Germany shortly would have followed these agreements? What sort of postwar policies did the Allies seek to impose on Germany? Given the very different governmental systems of the signatory powers, why do you think

4. *Foreign Relations of the United States. Diplomatic Papers: The Conference of Berlin (The Potsdam Conference), 1945*, 2 vols. (Washington, D.C.: United States Government Printing Office, 1960).

that they might have interpreted differently such words as *democracy*? What was the clear message of the Potsdam agreement in regard to such postwar developments in Germany as separate currency systems and, indeed, separate governments for East and West Germany?

Source 2 is a map of Europe after World War II showing the division of Germany and Berlin into occupation zones, the territorial changes resulting from World War II, and the demarcation point between Soviet and Western spheres in Europe, a line Churchill called "the Iron Curtain." Policymakers frequently consult maps drawn up by their security services to better understand the strategic implication of their decisions. What strategic difficulties does the map reveal in a joint American, British, French, and Soviet occupation of Berlin? How did the war permit the Soviet Union to add territory to protect itself better from future attacks from Germany? How did Communist party domination of the Eastern European countries make these nations part of the buffer zone that the Soviets wished to create on their western border? According to the map, what was the strategic importance of Germany to both sides in the Cold War?

Source 3 is an example of the kind of government record that is seldom published. It is a top-secret report from the Soviet Union's ambassador to the United States, Nikolai Novikov, to the foreign minister, Viacheslav Molotov, sent in 1946. Ambassadors for centuries have provided their governments with such secret information on the countries in which they represent their nations; indeed, intelligence gathering was one of the original functions of such diplomatic representatives. The intent of Novikov's communication was to provide the foreign minister with the latest intelligence on American foreign policy goals. Molotov apparently paid close attention to the report; he annotated it (the underlining in the text is his), and he kept it handy in his personal files. Soviet authorities believed that it played a key role in shaping their government's strategic thinking about the United States in the 1950s, and they thus released it to Western scholars in 1990 at a conference in the last days of the Soviet Union. What sort of wartime calculations did Novikov impute to Americans? What sort of policy outlook did he identify in America after the death of President Roosevelt? What specifically did Novikov see the United States doing in Germany? What did he see as America's postwar goal in the world? How did Germany fit into this plan? Why would this increase the strategic importance of Germany to the Soviets? How did the Soviet definition of *democracy* differ from that which the Americans would have assigned to it? To which country did this report assign all of the blame for the emerging Cold War? How might its message have affected the Cold War's early days, especially since Novikov predicted a war?

If ambassadors long have provided their governments with strategic information, modern states also have created specialized intelligence agencies to gather data on foreign nations, if necessary through spying. Such agencies also analyze the data they collect and make policy recommendations to their governments. The United States developed such an agency during World War II, the Office of Strategic Services (OSS), and after the war President Truman decided to centralize the government's intelligence activities in the Central Intelligence Group (CIG) that he created in January 1946. In 1947, the National Security Act replaced the CIG with the Central Intelligence Agency (CIA), which still provides intelligence data to American policymakers. The analyses of security data collected by the CIG/CIA almost always are classified "Secret" or "Top Secret" and are meant for the use of the president and his closest advisers in making national policy. During the early Cold War years, the intelligence agencies sent daily, weekly, and monthly summaries and analyses of events to the president and his advisers. The intelligence analyses received by these statesmen played a considerable role in shaping American policy in the Cold War and in the Berlin Blockade, and Source 4 offers three brief excerpts from such reports that were declassified by the government after the end of the Cold War in the late 1990s.

Source 4A is a general statement of the Soviet threat to the United States by American intelligence analysts written in 1948. How did American experts characterize the general relationship between the United States and the Soviet Union? What did they

see as the long-term goals of the Soviet Union? Did these experts perceive a worldwide threat to the United States? How did the Americans' vision of the Soviet Union compare with Novikov's vision of the United States in Source 3? Under what circumstances might the Cold War CIA analysts envisioned erupt into a "hot" war? Did such circumstances exist in 1948? Source 4B is from a weekly summary of events written in the first days of the Berlin Blockade. What did CIA analysts see as the Soviet Union's primary goal in cutting off Berlin? Why did they see gaining control of the city itself as almost a secondary goal? How do you think such an analysis stiffened American determination to maintain the Western allies' position in Berlin? How is this analysis consistent with that of the agency in 1946? How did CIA analysts describe the attitude of Berliners in the western sectors of the city toward Soviet domination? How might this have affected American policy? Source 4C is from a weekly summary of events written as the Berlin Blockade came to an end in 1949. What consistent Soviet goal for Germany did CIA analysts identify? How did analysts envision the Soviets achieving this goal? Why would Germany remain a preoccupation of American Cold War policy even as the roads and railroads to Berlin were reopened? How did the CIA attempt to guide American statesmen with predictions of the Soviet attitude in upcoming negotiations?

Sources 5 and 6 provide us a much closer vantage point for observing matters in Germany than that of CIA analysts in Washington. These sources are from the papers of General Lucius D. Clay (1897–1978), who served first as American military governor in Germany from the war's end to 1947 and then as commander of all United States forces in Europe until 1949. It was General Clay who coordinated American policy in Germany and who had to deal directly with the Berlin crisis in 1948–1949. Source 5 is Clay's response to the impact of the American War Department's decision to reduce food shipments to the American zone in Germany in 1946. Knowing that a daily human food intake equal to 2,400 calories is necessary to sustain moderate labor, what do you conclude about the food situation in the American zone of Germany? What sort of German responses to these food shortages did Clay foresee? How might such American difficulties in provisioning their occupation zone have encouraged the economic reforms that contributed to the Berlin Blockade crisis of 1948 and 1949?

Source 6 is a radio communication from General Clay to Assistant Secretary of War William H. Draper, Jr., during the Berlin Blockade. Clay's position made him extremely influential in Washington policymaking circles, and this communication is revealing about the thinking of American policymakers early in the crisis. Given the options posed in the communication, did the United States seem firmly determined, at first, to resisting the blockade? What did Clay see at stake in the Berlin Blockade?

Why did he believe retreat from Berlin was not possible? What does this tell you about his view of the Soviet threat? How did Clay propose to show American force in the Berlin Blockade?

Source 7 presents excerpts from the text of the treaty establishing the North Atlantic Treaty Organization (NATO) in 1949. The treaty came as a direct response to events of 1948, including the Berlin Blockade and a coup in Czechoslovakia that brought that country under complete communist control. What sort of an alliance is NATO? Its original members were the United States, Belgium, Britain, Canada, Denmark, France, Iceland, Italy, Luxembourg, the Netherlands, Norway, and Portugal. Assessing this list of nations, against whom was their alliance clearly directed? What impact do you think such an alliance had on East-West relations in Europe? What impact do you think the creation in 1955 of an opposing alliance system, the Warsaw Pact (the Soviet Union, Albania, Bulgaria, Czechoslovakia, the German Democratic Republic, and Romania), had on those relations?

With Source 8 we turn our attention to the second Berlin crisis, that of 1961. Source 8 is an *aide-mémoire*, a diplomatic document that summarizes a proposal. Nikita Khrushchev handed it to John F. Kennedy at the Vienna meeting as his first step in reopening with a new American administration his proposal of 1958 for a treaty with Germany. The great powers conducted post–World War II international relations in an age of electronic media that focused public attention as never before on the national policy of countries like the United States and the Soviet Union. Reading Source 8, why might you conclude that part of its purpose was propaganda in the Cold War? How did it portray both East and West Germany and the motives of the Soviet Union? Why do you think that the United States failed to accept Khrushchev's invitation to draft a treaty with Germany? What role would a post-treaty West Germany have had in NATO? What sort of Berlin did the Soviets envision? From the American standpoint, would this new status for the city have provided an opportunity for communist control of the former Western sectors of the city? What sort of consistency do you find in American policy regarding Berlin in the postwar era?

Source 9 is a radio and television report to the Soviet people by Khrushchev on his Vienna meeting with Kennedy. Certainly propaganda is part of the purpose of this speech, but it also is a fundamental statement of Soviet policy and as such is an important part of the documentary evidence on the Berlin situation. In the course of his speech, Khrushchev restated his proposal for a treaty with Germany. But he added much that alarmed statesmen in the West. Of what does he accuse the United States and other Western powers? What do you make of Khrushchev's references to military force, especially when he asserts "times are different now," apparently referring to the Soviets' possession of nuclear weapons? Remember that he made this statement

as the Soviet Union began a build-up of its military forces. What effect do you think Khrushchev's statement that East Germany would control access to a post-treaty Berlin had on Western statesmen?

Source 10 is President Kennedy's response to Khrushchev on July 25, 1961. Again, it is a statement in the form of a radio and television address. The president sought to build support at home for his policies by addressing the Berlin issue in this fashion, but he also sent several messages to the Soviets. What was the most obvious message? What effect could the president's announcement of an American military build-up, a partial mobilization of the nation's reserve forces, and the preparation of civilian bomb shelters have had on the Soviets? But there was a less obvious message in the speech, too. To whose defense did the president commit American arms? You will note that Kennedy emphasized American commitment to West Berlin, not to all of Berlin. If you had been a Soviet diplomat skilled in analyzing language, you would immediately have noted the distinction. What conclusions would you have drawn? At the same time, prominent figures in Washington, like the chairman of the Senate Foreign Relations Committee, J. William Fulbright, suggested in interviews that while the United States would fight to remain in West Berlin, it would not resist measures to terminate the immediate problem for the Soviets, the flood of refugees. How would Soviet observation of signals such as this have shaped their actions? Why might you conclude that the president was forcing Khrushchev to back down from his threats while giving him a way out of the crisis short of war?

As you now read the evidence for this chapter, keep this background information and the questions it raised in mind. It will aid you in answering the central questions of this chapter. What were the origins of the Cold War? How did the Berlin crises develop out of wartime agreements? What strategic considerations made Berlin so essential to both the Western allies and the Soviets?

THE EVIDENCE

Source 1 from Germany, 1947-1949: The Story in Documents *(Washington, D.C.: U.S. Government Printing Office for the Department of State Division of Publications, 1950), pp. 47–57.*

1. Protocol of the Proceedings of the Berlin Conference

There is attached hereto the agreed protocol of the Berlin Conference.

JOSEPH V. STALIN
HARRY TRUMAN
C. R. ATTLEE

PROTOCOL OF THE PROCEEDINGS OF THE BERLIN CONFERENCE

The Berlin Conference of the Three Heads of Government of the U.S.S.R., U.S.A., and U.K., which took place from July 17 to August 2, 1945, came to the following conclusions:

I. *Establishment of a Council of Foreign Ministers*
A. The Conference reached the following agreement for the establishment of a Council of Foreign Ministers to do the necessary preparatory work for the peace settlements:

"(1) There shall be established a Council composed of the Foreign Ministers of the United Kingdom, the Union of Soviet Socialist Republics, China, France, and the United States . . .

"(3) (i) As its immediate important task, the Council shall be authorized to draw up, with a view to their submission to the United Nations, treaties of peace with Italy, Rumania, Bulgaria, Hungary and Finland, and to propose settlements of territorial questions outstanding on the termination of the war in Europe. The Council shall be utilized for the preparation of a peace settlement for Germany to be accepted by the Government of Germany when a government adequate for the purpose is established."

II. *The Principles To Govern the Treatment of Germany in the Initial Control Period*

A. Political Principles

1. In accordance with the Agreement on Control Machinery in Germany, supreme authority in Germany is exercised, on instructions from their respective Governments, by the Commanders-in-Chief of the armed forces of the United States of America, the United Kingdom, the Union of Soviet Socialist Republics, and the French Republic, each in his own zone of occupation, and also jointly, in matters affecting Germany as a whole, in their capacity as members of the Control Council.

2. So far as is practicable, there shall be uniformity of treatment of the German population throughout Germany.

3. The purposes of the occupation of Germany by which the Control Council shall be guided are:

(i) The complete disarmament and demilitarization of Germany and the elimination or control of all German industry that could be used for military production . . .

(ii) To convince the German people that they have suffered a total military defeat and that they cannot escape responsibility for what they have brought upon themselves, since their own ruthless warfare and the fanatical Nazi resistance have destroyed German economy and made chaos and suffering inevitable.

(iii) To destroy the National Socialist Party and its affiliated and supervised organizations, to dissolve all Nazi institutions, to ensure that they are not revived in any form, and to prevent all Nazi and militarist activity or propaganda.

(iv) To prepare for the eventual reconstruction of German political life on a democratic basis and for eventual peaceful cooperation in international life by Germany . . .

9. The administration in Germany should be directed towards the decentralization of the political structure and the development of local responsibility. To this end:

(i) local self-government shall be restored throughout Germany on democratic principles and in particular through elective councils as rapidly as is consistent with military security and the purposes of military occupation;

(ii) all democratic political parties with rights of assembly and of public discussion shall be allowed and encouraged throughout Germany;

(iii) representative and elective principles shall be introduced into regional, provincial and state (Land) administration as rapidly as may be justified by the successful application of these principles in local self-government;

(iv) for the time being, no central German Government shall be established. Notwithstanding this, however, certain essential central German administrative departments, headed by State Secretaries, shall be established, particularly in the fields of finance, transport, communications, foreign trade and industry. Such departments will act under the direction of the Control Council.

10. Subject to the necessity for maintaining military security, freedom of speech, press and religion shall be permitted, and religious institutions shall be respected. Subject likewise to the maintenance of military security, the formation of free trade unions shall be permitted.

B. Economic Principles

11. In order to eliminate Germany's war potential, the production of arms, ammunition and implements of war as well as all types of aircraft and sea-going ships shall be prohibited and prevented. Production of metals, chemicals, machinery and other items that are directly necessary to a war economy shall be rigidly controlled and restricted to Germany's approved post-war peacetime needs. . . . Productive capacity not needed for permitted production shall be removed in accordance with the reparations plan recommended by the Allied Commission on Reparations and approved by the Governments concerned or if not removed shall be destroyed. . . .

14. During the period of occupation Germany shall be treated as a single economic unit. To this end common policies shall be established in regard to:

(a) mining and industrial production and. its allocation;

(b) agriculture, forestry and fishing;

(c) wages, prices and rationing;

(d) import and export programs for Germany as a whole;

(e) currency and banking, central taxation and customs;

(f) reparation and removal of industrial war potential;

(g) transportation and communications.

In applying these policies account shall be taken, where appropriate, of varying local conditions.

2. Map of Europe after World War II

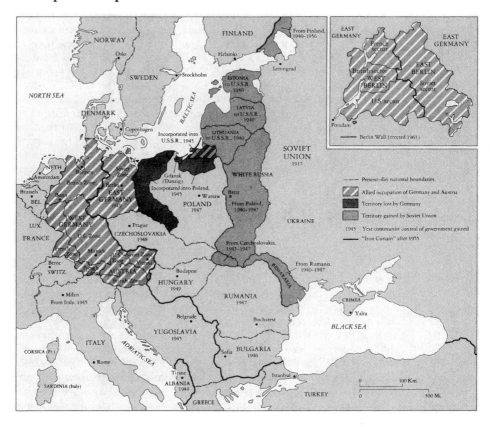

3. The Novikov Telegram, Washington, September 27, 1946

U.S. Foreign Policy in the Postwar Period

[*All underlining replicates that of Foreign Minister Viacheslav Molotov.*]

The foreign policy of the United States, which reflects the imperialist tendencies of American monopolistic capital, is characterized in the postwar period by a striving <u>for world supremacy.</u>[5] This is the real meaning of the many statements by President Truman and other representatives of American ruling circles: that the United States has the right to lead the world. All the forces of American diplomacy—the army, the air force, the navy, industry, and science—are enlisted in the service of this foreign policy. For this purpose broad plans for expansion have been developed and are being implemented through diplomacy and the establishment of a system of naval and air bases stretching far beyond the boundaries of the United States, through the arms race, and through the creation of ever newer types of weapons.

The foreign policy of the United States is conducted now <u>in a situation that differs greatly</u> from the one that existed in the prewar period. This situation does not fully conform to the calculations of those reactionary circles which hoped that during the Second World War they would succeed in avoiding, at least for a long time, the main battles in Europe and Asia. They calculated that the United States of America, if it was unsuccessful in completely avoiding direct participation in the war, would enter it only at the last minute, when it could easily affect the outcome of the war, completely ensuring its interests.

In this regard, it was thought that the main competitors of the United States would be crushed or greatly weakened in the war, and the United States by virtue of this circumstance would assume <u>the role of the most powerful factor</u> in resolving the fundamental questions of the postwar world. These calculations were also based on the assumption, which was very widespread in the United States in the initial stages of the war, that the Soviet Union, which had been subjected to the attack of German Fascism in June 1941, would also be exhausted or even completely destroyed as a result of the war. . . .

Europe has come out of the war with a completely dislocated economy, and the economic devastation that occurred in the course of the war cannot be

---

5. Molotov's marginal notation to this sentence was: "A difference from [the] prewar [period]?"

overcome in a short time. All of the countries of Europe and Asia are experiencing a colossal need for consumer goods, industrial and transportation equipment, etc. Such a situation provides American monopolistic capital with prospects for enormous shipments of goods and the importation of capital into these countries—a circumstance that would permit it to infiltrate their national economies.

Such a development would mean a serious strengthening of the economic position of the United States in the whole world and would be a stage on the road to world domination by the United States. . . .

At the same time the USSR's international position is currently stronger than it was in the prewar period.[6] Thanks to the historical victories of Soviet weapons, the Soviet armed forces are located on the territory of Germany and other formerly hostile countries, thus guaranteeing that these countries will not be used again for an attack on the USSR. In formerly hostile countries, such as Bulgaria, Finland, Hungary, and Romania, democratic reconstruction has established regimes that have undertaken to strengthen and maintain friendly relations with the Soviet Union. In the Slavic countries that were liberated by the Red Army or with its assistance—Poland, Czechoslovakia, and Yugoslavia—democratic regimes have also been established that maintain relations with the Soviet Union on the basis of agreements on friendship and mutual assistance.

The enormous relative weight of the USSR in international affairs in general and in the European countries in particular, the independence of its foreign policy, and the economic and political assistance that it provides to neighboring countries, both allies and former enemies, has led to the growth of the political influence of the Soviet Union in these countries and to the further strengthening of democratic tendencies in them.

Such a situation in Eastern and Southeastern Europe cannot help but be regarded by the American imperialists as an obstacle in the path of the expansionist policy of the United States. . . .

Obvious indications of the U.S. effort to establish world dominance are also to be found in the increase in military potential in peacetime and in the establishment of a large number of naval and air bases both in the United States and beyond its borders.

In the summer of 1946, for the first time in the history of the country, Congress passed a law on the establishment of a peacetime army, not on a volunteer basis but on the basis of universal military service . The size of the army, which is supposed to amount to about one million persons as of July 1, 1947, was also increased significantly. The size of the navy at the conclusion of the war decreased quite insignificantly in comparison with wartime. At the present time, the American navy occupies first place in the world, leaving England's navy far behind, to say nothing of those of other countries. . . .

6. **USSR:** the Union of Soviet Socialist Republics, the formal name of the Soviet Union.

Along with maintaining a large army, navy, and air force, the budget provides that these enormous amounts also will be spent on establishing a very extensive system of naval and air bases in the Atlantic and Pacific oceans. . . .

The establishment of American bases on islands that are often 10,000 to 12,000 kilometers from the territory of the United States and are on the other side of the Atlantic and Pacific oceans clearly <u>indicates the offensive nature of the strategic concepts</u> of the commands of the U.S. army and navy. . . .

All of these facts show clearly that a decisive role in the realization of plans for world dominance by the United States is played by its armed forces. . . .

The <u>"hard-line" policy with regard to the USSR</u> announced by Bynes[7] after the rapprochement of the reactionary Democrats with the Republicans is at present the main obstacle on the road to cooperation of the Great Powers.[8] It consists mainly of the fact that in the postwar period the United States no longer follows a policy of strengthening cooperation among the Big Three (or Four) but rather has striven to undermine the unity of these countries.[9] The <u>objective</u> has been to <u>impose</u> the will of other countries on the Soviet Union. . . .

The present policy of the American government with regard to the USSR is also directed at limiting or dislodging the influence of the Soviet Union from neighboring countries. In implementing this policy in former enemy or Allied countries adjacent to the USSR, the United States attempts, at various international conferences or directly in these countries themselves, to support reactionary forces with <u>the purpose of creating obstacles to the process of democratization of these countries. In so doing, it also attempts to secure positions for the penetration of American capital into their economies</u>. Such a policy is intended to weaken and overthrow the democratic governments in power there, which are friendly toward the USSR, and replace them in the future with new governments that would obediently carry out a policy dictated from the United States. In this policy, the United States receives full support from English diplomacy.

One of the most important elements in the general policy of the United States, which is directed toward limiting the international role of the USSR in the postwar world, is the <u>policy with regard to Germany</u>. In Germany, the United States is taking measures to strengthen reactionary forces for the purpose of opposing democratic reconstruction. Furthermore, it displays special insistence on accompanying this policy with completely inadequate measures for the demilitarization of Germany.

The American occupation policy does not have the objective of eliminating the remnants of <u>German Fascism</u> and rebuilding German political life <u>on a</u>

---

7. **Byrnes:** United States Secretary of State James F. Byrnes. Byrnes took office in 1945, and Novikov imputed to him and President Truman an anti-Soviet foreign policy.

8. Molotov also marked the underlined phrase with a check for added emphasis.

9. **Big Three, Big Four:** the "Big Three" refers to Britain, the Soviet Union, and the United States, the great powers whose leaders shaped the postwar world at Yalta and Potsdam. With the addition of France, this group was the "Big Four."

democratic basis, so that Germany might cease to exist as an aggressive force. The United States is not taking measures to eliminate the monopolistic associations of German industrialists on which German Fascism depended in preparing aggression and waging war. Neither is any agrarian reform being conducted to eliminate large landholders, who were also a reliable support for the Hitlerites. Instead, the United States is considering the possibility of terminating the Allied occupation of German territory before the main tasks of the occupation—the demilitarization and democratization of Germany—have been implemented. This would create the prerequisites for the revival of an imperialist Germany, which the United States plans to use in a future war on its side.

The numerous and extremely hostile statements by American government, political, and military figures with regard to the Soviet Union and its foreign policy are very characteristic of the current relationship between the ruling circles of the United States and the USSR. . . .

The basic goal of this anti-Soviet campaign of American "public opinion" is to exert political pressure on the Soviet Union and compel it to make concessions. Another, no less important goal of the campaign is the attempt to create an atmosphere of war psychosis among the masses, who are weary of war, thus making it. easier for the U.S. government to carry out measures for the maintenance of high military potential. . . .

Of course, all of these measures for maintaining a high military potential are not goals in themselves. They are only intended to prepare the conditions for winning world supremacy in a new war, the date for which, to be sure, cannot be determined now by anyone, but which is contemplated by the most bellicose circles of American imperialism.

Careful note should be taken of the fact that the preparation by the United States for a future war is being conducted with the prospect of war against the Soviet Union, which in the eyes of American imperialists is the main obstacle in the path of the United States to world domination.

[signed]
N. Novikov

Source 4 from Woodrow J. Kuhns, ed.. Assessing the Soviet Threat: The Early Cold War Years (Washington, D.C.: Center for the Study of Intelligence of the Central Intelligence Agency, 1997), pp. 61, 220–21, 243, 311–312.

4A. Central Intelligence Agency, Office of Reports and Estimates Report 60–48:

THREATS TO THE SECURITY OF THE UNITED STATES SUMMARY

[*As in Source 3, underlining replicates that in the original document.*]

1. For the foreseeable future the USSR will be the only power capable of threatening the security of the United States. The Soviet regime, moreover, is essentially and implacably inimical toward the United States.

2. The power of the USSR to endanger the security of the United States is a consequence not only of Soviet strength, but also of the weakness and instability prevalent in Europe and Asia and of weaknesses in the military posture of the United States. The principal restraint on hostile Soviet action is the greater potential strength of the United States. . . .

4. In general, the probable basic intentions of the Kremlin for the next decade are:
a. To avoid war with the United States, but to exploit to the utmost, within that limitation, the coercive power inherent in the preponderance of Soviet military strength in Eurasia, relying on the disinclination of the United States to resort to war.
b. To build up as rapidly as possible the war potential of the Soviet orbit, in an effort to equal and surpass, eventually, the war potential of the United States.
c. To wage political, economic, and psychological warfare against the United States and its allies, with a view to undermining their potential strength and increasing the relative strength of the USSR: in particular, to prevent or retard the recovery and coalition of Western Europe and the stabilization of the situation in the Near East and Far East.
d. To exploit every opportunity presented by the weakness and instability of neighboring states to expand the area of Soviet domination by political and subversive means.

5. Although the Kremlin is unlikely to resort deliberately to war to gain its ends within the next decade, it would do so if ever it came to consider such a course expedient, particularly if convinced that time was on the side of the United States. In this respect the situation will remain critical pending the

successful accomplishment of US efforts to redress the balance of power. Moreover, there is constant danger of war through accident or miscalculation.

6. In any case, the fundamental hostility of the Soviet Government toward the United States and its formidable military power require, in common prudence, that the United States be prepared for the eventuality of war with the USSR.

4B. Central Intelligence Agency Weekly Summary, July 2, 1948

Western Europe

GERMANY

[*Underlining replicates that in the original document.*]

<u>The Soviet Union has further threatened the position</u> of the western powers in Berlin by increasing existing restrictions on communications between the city and the western zones. The recent Soviet action in cutting off all rail communications and road and barge traffic represents the near-maximum curtailment of ground facilities within Soviet capabilities. On 23 June when the new embargoes were put into effect, the western sectors had food stocks adequate for a six-week minimum German ration and fuel stocks to supply light, power, and water for three weeks. The Soviet action, ostensibly taken to retaliation against the western decision to introduce the new west German currency in Berlin, has two possible objectives: either to force the western powers to negotiate on Soviet terms regarding Germany, or failing that, to force a western power withdrawal from Berlin.

The USSR does not seem ready to force a definite showdown but for the present appears more inclined to compel the western powers to negotiate locally regarding Berlin in the hope that such negotiations could be broadened to include Soviet demands on major issues such as the Ruhr. . . .

4C. Central Intelligence Agency Weekly Summary, May 6, 1949

Eastern Europe

SOVIET UNION

German Objectives

Soviet agreement to lift the Berlin blockade and enter into four-power discussions on Germany does not represent any change in the Soviet objective to establish a Germany which will eventually fall under Soviet domination. It is still too early, however, to predict the sincerity of the Soviet desire to achieve an understanding with the West on Germany or the extent of the concessions the USSR would make in order to reach an agreement. . . . Progress of the CFM alone, therefore, will demonstrate whether the USSR: (1) has agreed to enter into four-power discussions to sound out the western position and retrieve itself from the unfavorable situation created by the Berlin blockade; or (2) now considers it a sounder strategy to seek a "neutral" Germany in order to delay the final consolidation of the West German state and give the USSR some voice in all Germany.[10]

CFM Proposals

Initial Soviet proposals at the forthcoming CFM will be designed to appeal strongly to an increasingly articulate German nationalism. After attempting to secure a commitment on postponing the West German state, the USSR will probably propose a general settlement for all Germany based on a return to four-power cooperation and the Yalta and Potsdam agreements. The Soviet terms will include . . . : (1) establishment of a centralized government for all Germany; (2) conclusion of a peace treaty and withdrawal of occupation troops within one year; and (3) control over Ruhr production and distribution by the US, the USSR, the UK, and France. Depending primarily upon the intensity of the Soviet desire to obtain the withdrawal of US troops from Europe, the USSR may later in the negotiations seek a "compromise" agreement. Such a compromise might involve the acceptance of a federal government composed of the East and West German zonal organizations. The USSR would insist, however, that such a federation be established in a manner which, in addition to not threatening Soviet political and economic control in East Germany, would provide for sufficient Soviet influence in West Germany to offer reasonable prospects for subsequently establishing a centralized Germany not wholly western-oriented and susceptible to eventual Soviet domination.

10. **CFM:** Council of Foreign Ministers, that is, a high-level meeting of the diplomats who headed their countries' respective foreign policy offices.

Sources 5 and 6 from Jean Edward Smith, ed., The Papers of Lucius D. Clay: Germany, *1945–1949 (2 vols.; Indiana University Press, 1974), 1: 180–181; 2: 743–746. Reprinted by permission of Indiana University Press.*

5. Food Situation in U.S. Zone

18 March 1946
From CLAY for McNARNEY[11]

Recommend the dispatch of the following Eyes Only cable from you to General Eisenhower:[12]

"Clay advises me that War Department requires an immediate reduction in the present German ration from 1550 calories to 1313 calories with no shipments of food prior to 1 July except to replace French loan.[13] No assurance is provided for supplies after 1 July which would permit any increase in the reduced ration. The present ration is inadequate to sustain a working population. Health authorities have indicated time and time again that it is insufficient to maintain health over any long period of time. The reduced ration is insufficient to maintain a living standard even for a short period. Sickness and malnutrition are certain to result. Even more important, the population will be incapable of the work necessary in reviving even a minimum economy with a consequent increased financial burden to the United States. While the difficulties in maintaining a higher ration in the U.S. zone than in the adjacent French and British zones are recognized, I believe the reduced ration to be less than the ration allowed in the Russian zone. . . ."

Our reduction in occupational forces has been based on a stabilized U.S. zone in which reasonable food supplies were available for the German people. I do not believe that the reduced ration is sufficient to prevent disease and unrest. Therefore I shall have to reconsider the size of the occupational forces required to maintain order and security.

6. The Berlin Blockade

19 July 1948   TOP SECRET—EYES ONLY

From CLAY for DRAPER

Have received copy of cablegram from Douglas[14] to [Under Secretary of State] Lovett of 17 July which suggests that we are now faced with three

11. **McNarney:** General Joseph T. McNarney, who succeeded General Dwight D. Eisenhower as commander of American forces in Europe in November 1945. Eisenhower had returned to the United States to serve as army chief of staff. Clay was seeking more impact for the message by asking McNarney to send it out under his signature.

12. **Eyes Only:** a security notation indicating that the message was secret and was to be read only by the person to whom it was addressed.

13. **French loan:** refers to food supplies dispatched to the American zone from that of the French to meet the food needs of German citizens there.

14. **Douglas:** Lewis Douglas was American ambassador to Britain at this time.

alternatives: (A) to abandon Berlin at the risk of losing Europe; (B) to abandon Berlin but under strong commitments to western European nations which would serve to salvage some prestige; and (C) to attempt through the employment of all devices at our command to remain in Berlin.

We might avoid or defer being faced with these alternatives if we now agree to a quadripartite discussion of the entire German problem at governmental level and concurrently suspend our program in western Germany pending such discussion.

Certainly, last November when the Council of Foreign Ministers broke up and again this spring in meetings with the French and British in the London Conference, we recognized fully the probabilities of Soviet counter-measures, and certainly we must have made the decision then that we had to go ahead if democracy was to take the initiative in Europe. This we did, and also added an even greater deterrent to the Soviet expansion policy which was the adoption of the European Recovery Program.[15] The very violence of Soviet reaction now is proof of the success or our several programs to restore and build up democracy in Europe. Having committed ourselves to a course of action to this end and having backed it with large sums of money, can we afford now to throw it away as we encounter our first major evidence of Soviet resistance?

Of course it would be difficult if not impossible for the three western nations to refuse to discuss the German problem with Russia. However, we should refuse to discuss the problem if it means abandonment or suspension of our program in western Germany. No solution of the German problem can be found which does not give USSR a voice in the Ruhr. A failure on our part to establish a German government now could only be interpreted as weakness and apprehension on our part. Even if it were now possible with Soviet participation to establish a unified Germany, could we afford to include it in the ERP, and if we could afford it would not Soviet participation in such a government prevent it from attaining any success? Increased production from a western Germany oriented toward western European recovery must be conceded by all as essential to a successful program for European recovery. If we give up that opportunity, can we hope to carry the ERP to a successful conclusion? No final solution of the German problem is possible until ERP has invigorated western Europe so that it may develop a military strength which makes Soviet domination of Europe impossible. I doubt if such a military strength would be developed with Germany under quadripartite control. We have gone too far with western Europe to have any hope of establishing a quadripartite control of Germany which would not retard the development of western Europe and a unified Germany can come now with safety only when the balance of power in Europe is restored.

Soviet measures now being taken must be based on one of two premises: (A) the first premise is that the Soviet Government, recognizing the rising tide of anti-communistic forces under European recovery, are determined to exert

---

15. **European Recovery Program (ERP):** the Marshall Plan.

[279]

pressures to retard such recovery to the point of, but short of, war. In other words, they are still bluffing but will continue to do so until it is absolutely evident that their bluff is being called. In such case they will recede. To support this premise there is their evident lack of real readiness for war and their lack of preparation for immediate and major war in Europe.

(B) The second premise is that the Soviet Government has now made up its mind that European recovery can be stopped only by war. Having advised their population for three years now that America is getting ready to attack the USSR, it would be their intent to force us to the first overt act so that they could charge us with being the aggressor. If this premise is correct, war will come now because the USSR has determined it to be inevitable and that time is against the USSR. If war has been determined, it will not be fought to gain possession of Berlin, and the pressures now being exerted in Berlin if we withdraw will be applied elsewhere next, probably in Vienna, and will continue until we are provoked into an act of war. The Soviet Government may well believe that with passing time our position will become relatively stronger than at present, and hence if the USSR does want war it is to their advantage for it to come sooner rather than later. There are no reports of military movements to support this premise except the very large expenditure programs of the Soviet Government during the past three years to maintain its military establishment.

While I fully appreciate the importance of diplomatic procedures to include the further exchange of notes, the placing of the issue before the United Nations, the imposing of sanctions elsewhere, and any other measures which seem feasible, we must recognize that all of these measures take time under which our own situation may well deteriorate. Moreover, unless we and the western nations take far more vigorous measures for preparedness than we are taking now, we can only hope that the passage of time will make us really prepared for war. Certainly the Soviet Government during this same period of time, with its absolute control of the Soviet economy, can be increasing its own efforts to prepare for war at an accelerated rate. Thus, a delay, if war is inevitable, does not necessarily find the West better prepared. . . .

It is only by a showing of force which is in the nature of an armed reconnaissance that we can determine the real intent of the Soviet Government.

Our right to move an armed force for garrison purposes into and out of Berlin, as far as I know, has not been questioned, The movement of such a force could be stopped only by attack.[16] This attack would not occur unless the Soviet Government is determined upon a war course. If it has so determined, a retreat now will merely be followed by pressure elsewhere within a matter of

16. Clay alludes here to the plan he put forward early in the crisis for "calling the bluff" of the Soviets. Because they alleged that they had closed land routes to Berlin because of "technical problems," that is, destroyed bridges and other obstacles, Clay proposed sending a force of American, British, and French troops, equipped with artillery as well as bridging equipment, from the west across the Soviet zone to Berlin. Of course, such an armed incursion into the Soviet zone risked war.

weeks or months. If war is inevitable, the time that we can gain by retreat now is so relatively short that it has little value.

The choice before us is a hard choice. However, if we do decide to retreat now, this retreat will not save us from again and again having to choose between retreat and war. With each retreat we will find ourselves confronted with the same problem but with fewer and fewer allies on our side.

I am sending this radio to you personally rather than officially to the Department as I realize that my views and comments go beyond my responsibilities as theater commander. Thus I leave to you entirely the decision as to how you use these views, if at all. I shall keep no copy here. However, I cannot but feel that the world today is facing the most critical issue that has arisen since Hitler placed his policy of aggression in motion. In fact, the Soviet Government has more force immediately at its disposal than did Hitler to accomplish his purpose. Only America can exert the world leadership, and only America can provide the strength to stop this policy of aggression here and now. The next time may be too late. I believe determined action will stop it short of war. It cannot be stopped without the serious risk of war.

Source 7 is from Lawrence Friedman, ed., Europe Transformed: Documents on the End of the Cold War *(New York: St. Martin's Press, 1990), pp. 14–15.*

7. The North Atlantic Treaty, April 4, 1949

The Parties to this Treaty *reaffirm* their faith in the purposes and principles of the Charter of the United Nations and their desire to live in peace with all peoples and all governments.

They *are determined* to safeguard the freedom, common heritage and civilization of their peoples, founded on the principles of democracy, individual liberty and the rule of law.

They *seek to promote* stability and well-being in the North Atlantic area.

They are *resolved* to unite their efforts for collective defence and for the preservation of peace and security.

They therefore agree to this North Atlantic Treaty:

Article 1

The Parties undertake, as set forth in the Charter of the United Nations, to settle any international dispute in which they may be involved by peaceful means in such a manner that international peace and security and justice are not endangered, and to refrain in their international relations from the threat or use of force in any manner inconsistent with the purposes of the United Nations.

Article 2

The Parties will contribute toward the further development of peaceful and friendly international relations by strengthening their free institutions, by bringing about a better understanding of the principles upon which these institutions are founded, and by promoting coalitions of stability and well-being. They will seek to eliminate conflict in their international economic policies and will encourage economic collaboration between any or all of them.

Article 3

In order more effectively to achieve the objectives of this Treaty, the Parties, separately and jointly, by means of continuous and effective self-help and mutual aid, will maintain and develop their individual and collective capacity to resist armed attack.

Article 4

The Parties will consult together whenever, in the opinion of any of them, the territorial integrity, political/independence or security of any of the Parties is threatened.

Article 5

The Parties agree that an armed attack against one or more of them in Europe or North America shall be considered an attack against them all and consequently they agree that, if such an armed attack occurs, each of them, in exercise of the right of individual or collective self-defence recognized by Article 51 of the Charter of the United Nations, will assist the Party or Parties so attacked by taking forthwith, individually and in concert with the other Parties, such action as it deems necessary, including the use of armed force, to restore and maintain the security of the North Atlantic area. . . .

Source 8 from Department of State Bulletin 45 *(1961): 231–233.*

8. Soviet Aide-Mémoire of June 4, 1961

Official Translation

1. The years-long delay in arriving at a peace settlement with Germany has largely predetermined the dangerous course of events in Europe in the post-war period. The major decisions of the Allies on the eradication of militarism

in Germany, which once were considered by the Governments of the United States and the U.S.S.R. as the guarantee of stable peace, have been implemented only partially and now are actually not being observed in the greater part of German territory. Of the Governments of the two German States that were formed after the war, it is only the Government of the German Democratic Republic that recognizes and adheres to those agreements. The Government of the Federal Republic of Germany openly proclaims its negative attitude to those agreements, cultivates sabre-rattling militarism and advocates the review of the German frontiers and the results of the Second World War. It tries to establish a powerful military base for its aggressive plans, to kindle a dangerous hotbed of conflicts on German soil, and to set the former Allies in the anti-Hitler coalition against each other.

The Western Powers have allowed the Federal Republic of Germany to start accumulating armaments and setting up an army, which are clearly in excess of defense needs. . . .

2. The Soviet Government is earnestly striving towards removing the sources of tension between the United States and the U.S.S.R. and to proceed to constructive, friendly cooperation. The conclusion of a German peace treaty would allow the two countries to come much closer to the attainment of this goal. The U.S.S.R. and the United States fought together against Hitlerite Germany. Their common duty is to conclude a German peace treaty and thereby create a reliable guarantee that German soil will never again give birth to forces that could plunge the world into a new and even more devastating war. It the desire of the Soviet Union to consolidate peace and to prevent the unleashing of a new world war in Europe does not run counter to the intentions of the United States Government, then it will not be difficult to reach agreement. . . .

4. The Soviet Government is not pursuing the goal of harming the interests of the United States or other Western Powers in Europe. It does not propose to change anything either in Germany or in West Berlin in favor of any one State or group of States. The U.S.S.R. deems it necessary in the interests of consolidating peace formally to recognize the situation which has developed in Europe after the war, to legalize and to consolidate the inviolability of the existing German borders, to normalize the situation in West Berlin on the basis of reasonable consideration for the interests of all the parties concerned.

In the interests of achieving agreement on a peace treaty the Soviet Union does not insist on the immediate withdrawal of the Federal Republic of Germany from NATO. Both German States could for a certain period, even after the conclusion of a peace treaty, remain in the military alliances to which they now belong. . . .

5. The conclusion of a German peace treaty would also solve the problem of normalizing the situation in West Berlin. Deprived of a stable international

status, West Berlin at present is a place where the Bonn revanchist[17] circles continually maintain extreme tension and organize all kinds of provocations very dangerous to the cause of peace. We are duty-bound to prevent a development where intensification of West German militarism could lead to irreparable consequences due to the unsettled situation in West Berlin.

At present, the Soviet Government does not see a better way to solve the West Berlin problem than by transforming it into a demilitarized free city. The implementation of the proposal to turn West Berlin into a free city, with the interests of all parties duly taken into consideration, would normalize the situation in West Berlin. The occupation regime now being maintained has already outlived itself and has lost all connection with the purposes for which it was established, as well as with the Allied agreements concerning Germany that established the basis for its existence. The occupation rights will naturally be terminated upon the conclusion of a German peace treaty, whether it is signed with both German States or only with the German Democratic Republic, within whose territory West Berlin is located.

The position of the Soviet Government is that the free city of West Berlin should have unobstructed contacts with the outside world and that its internal regulations should be determined by the freely expressed will of its population. The United States as well as other countries would naturally have every possibility to maintain and develop their relations with the free city. In short. West Berlin, as the Soviet Government sees it, should be strictly neutral. Of course, the use of Berlin as a base for provocative activities, hostile to the U.S.S.R., the G.D.R. or any other State, cannot be permitted in the future, nor can Berlin be allowed to remain a dangerous hotbed of tension and international conflicts. . . .

Source 9 from The Soviet Stand on Germany: Nine Key Documents Including Diplomatic Papers and Major Speeches by N.S. Khrushchev *(New York: Crosscurrents Press, a division of International Book Company, Moscow, 1961), pp. 22, 30, 34–36, 38.*

9. Radio and Television Address to the Soviet Union by Nikita S. Khrushchev, July 15, 1961

DEAR COMRADES, FRIENDS:

As you know, I recently returned from Vienna where for two days I met and had comprehensive talks with John F. Kennedy, the President of the United States of America.

---

17. **Bonn revanchist:** Bonn was the West German capital; revanchists seek revenge, a desire that Soviet cold war officials consistently imputed to the government of Chancellor Konrad Adenauer.

Many materials were published in our press, just as in the entire world press, on this score. Many of you have already read the memoranda which were handed to President Kennedy. The first memorandum dealt with the question of ending nuclear weapons tests; and the other, with the conclusion of a peace treaty with Germany and a solution of the West Berlin problem on this basis.[18] Obviously many of you also read President Kennedy's radio and television speech, which was published in full in our newspapers. Thus Soviet public opinion is well informed about the views which the United States President set forth and his appraisal of our meeting. . . .

Permit me now to turn to the German question, which occupied an important place in our talks with President Kennedy.

The Soviet Government has repeatedly stated its position on this question. And the Western powers cannot complain that they do not know our proposals sufficiently well. We have done and are doing everything to convince the Governments of Britain, the United States of America, France, and the other nations which took part with us in the war against Hitler Germany that the absence of a peace treaty with Germany has created a deeply abnormal and dangerous situation in Europe.

It has always been recognized that peace treaties should be concluded after wars between states have ended. This has already become a custom and, if you wish, a standard of international law. Instances of this can also be found in international practice after the end of World War II. Peace treaties with Italy and the other states that fought on the side of Hitler Germany were signed more than fourteen years ago. The United States of America, Britain and the other countries concluded a peace treaty with Japan in 1951. But the governments of these selfsame countries will not countenance the conclusion of a peace treaty with Germany.

Every person, if not deprived of common sense, understands that the signing of a peace treaty is the road toward improving relations between states. The refusal to sign a peace treaty and the perpetuation of the occupational regime in West Berlin are directed at continuing the cold war, and who can say where lies the borderline between a cold war and a war in the full sense of the word? Surely it is clear that a cold war is a period of preparation, of accumulating forces for war.

I speak of all this so that everyone may understand the gravity of the danger incurred by any further delay in the conclusion of a German peace treaty.

When we suggest signing a peace treaty with Germany and turning West Berlin into a free city, we are accused of wanting, allegedly, to deprive the Western powers of access to this city. But that is a wrong and an unworthy argument. The granting to West Berlin of the status of a free city would mean that all countries of the world wishing to maintain economic and cultural ties with this city would have the right and opportunity freely to maintain these

---

18. This is the *aide-mémoire* in Source 8.

ties. Of course, agreement would have to be reached with the country across whose territory pass the communications that link West Berlin with the outside world. That is normal. Otherwise the sovereignty of the state in which West Berlin is situated would be jeopardized. . . .

When the Soviet Government suggests concluding a peace treaty and normalizing on this basis the situation in West Berlin, it wants only peace, it wants to remove from relations between states everything that causes friction and could cause a dangerous conflict. It is not the socialist countries but the Western powers that are throwing out a challenge to the world, when despite common sense they declare that they will not recognize the conclusion of a peace treaty and will seek to preserve the occupation regime in West Berlin, which they—if you please—conquered. That is not a policy of peace; that is trampling on the most elementary norms in relation between states. It is a desire to preserve a state of extreme tension in international relations and, moreover, it is a threat of war.

The Soviet Union and our friends do not want war, and we will not start it. But we will defend our sovereignty, will fulfill our sacred duty to defend our freedom and independence. If any country violates peace and crosses the borders—land, air or water—of another, it will assume full responsibility for the consequences of the aggression and will receive a proper rebuff.

The world press has published many comments on our meetings and talks with President Kennedy. Among these comments there are many sensible statements made in the United States, in Britain, in France and in West Germany, not to mention the German Democratic Republic and the other socialist countries. But there are hate-ridden persons, deprived of common sense, who oppose negotiations with the Soviet Union and call for a crusade against communism. . . .

The governments of some countries have announced in advance that they will not take part in a peace conference. The Soviet Union will, of course, regret it if some countries evade the signing of a German peace treaty; we have always wanted and still want all countries of the anti-Hitler coalition to take part in the peaceful settlement of the German question.

But even should certain countries refuse to take part in the negotiations on the conclusion of a peace treaty, that will not stop us; together with other countries which do desire it, we shall sign a peace treaty with the two German states. Should Federal Germany not agree to sign a peace treaty, we shall sign it with the German Democratic Republic alone, which has long declared her desire to conclude a peace treaty and has agreed to the formation on her territory of a free city of West Berlin.

There are some in the West who threaten us, saying that if we sign a peace treaty it will not be recognized, and that even arms will be brought into play to prevent its implementation.

Evidently they forget that times are different now. If even in the past the "position of strength" policy was useless against the Soviet Union, then now it is more than ever doomed to failure. The Soviet Union is against the use of force in relations between states. We stand for a peaceful settlement of controversial questions between states. However, we are capable of giving a proper rebuff to any use of force, and we have what is needed to defend our interests. . . .

Source 10 from Public Papers of the Presidents of the United States: John F. Kennedy, Containing the Public Messages, Speeches and Statements of the President, January 20 to December 31, 1961 *(Washington, D.C.: U.S. Government Printing Office, 1962), pp. 533–536.*

10. Radio and Television Report to the American People on the Berlin Crisis, July 25, 1961

Good evening:

Seven weeks ago tonight I returned from Europe to report on my meeting with Premier Khrushchev and the others. His grim warnings about the future of the world, his aide memoire on Berlin, his subsequent speeches and threats which he and his agents have launched, and the increase in the Soviet military budget that he has announced, have all prompted a series of decisions by the Administration and a series of consultations with the members of the NATO organization. In Berlin, as you recall, he intends to bring to an end, through a stroke of the pen, *first* our legal rights to be in West Berlin—and *secondly* our ability to make good on our commitment to the two million free people of that city. That we cannot permit. . . .

We are there as a result of our victory over Nazi Germany—and our basic rights to be there, deriving from that victory, include both our presence in West Berlin and the enjoyment of access across East Germany. . . .

Thus, our presence in West Berlin, and our access thereto, cannot be ended by any act of the Soviet government. The NATO shield was long ago extended to cover West Berlin—and we have given our word that an attack upon that city will be regarded as an attack upon us all. . . .

We do not want to fight—but we have fought before. . . .

We cannot and will not permit the Communists to drive us out of Berlin, either gradually or by force. For the fulfillment of our pledge to that city is essential to the morale and security of Western Germany, to the unity of Western Europe, and to the faith of the entire Free World. . . .

The new preparations that we shall make to defend the peace are part of the long-term build-up in our strength which has been underway since January. They are based on our needs to meet a world-wide threat, on a basis which stretches far beyond the present Berlin crisis. Our primary purpose is neither propaganda nor provocation—but preparation.

A first need is to hasten progress toward the military goals which the North Atlantic allies have set for themselves. In Europe today nothing less will suffice. We will put even greater resources into fulfilling those goals, and we look to our allies to do the same.

The supplementary defense build-ups that I asked from the Congress in March and May have already started moving us toward these and our other defense goals. They included an increase in the size of the Marine Corps, improved readiness of our reserves, expansion of our air and sea lift, and stepped-up procurement of needed weapons, ammunition, and other items. . . .

But even more importantly, we need the capability of placing in any critical area at the appropriate time a force which, combined with those of our allies, is large enough to make clear our determination and our ability to defend our rights at all costs—and to meet all levels of aggressor pressure with whatever levels of force are required. We intend to have a wider choice than humiliation or all-out nuclear action. While it is unwise at this time either to call up or send abroad excessive numbers of these troops before they are needed, let me make it clear that I intend to take, as time goes on, whatever steps are necessary to make certain that such forces can be deployed at the appropriate time without lessening our ability to meet our commitments elsewhere. . . .

Accordingly, I am now taking the following steps:

(1) I am tomorrow requesting the Congress for the current fiscal year an additional $3,247,000,000 of appropriations for the Armed Forces.

(2) To fill out our present Army Divisions, and to make more men available for prompt deployment, I am requesting an increase in the Army's total authorized strength from 875,000 to approximately 1 million men.

(3) I am requesting an increase of 29,000 and 63,000 men respectively in the active duty strength of the Navy and the Air Force.

(4) To fulfill these manpower needs, I am ordering that our draft calls be doubled and tripled in the coming months; I am asking the Congress for authority to order to active duty certain ready reserve units and individual reservists, and to extend tours of duty. . . .

We have another sober responsibility. To recognize the possibilities of nuclear war in the missile age, without our citizens knowing what they should do and where they should go if bombs begin to fall, would be a failure of responsibility. In May, I pledged a new start on Civil Defense. . . . Tomorrow, I am requesting of the Congress new funds for the following immediate objectives: to identify and mark space in existing structures—public and private—that could be used for fall-out shelters in case of attack; to stock those shelters with food, water, first-aid kits and other minimum essentials for survival; to increase their capacity; to improve our air-raid warning and fall-out detection systems, including a new household warning system which is now under development; and to take other measures that will be effective at an early date to save millions of lives if needed. . . .

QUESTIONS TO CONSIDER

A fundamental cause of the Cold War may be found in each of the great powers' understanding, or misunderstanding, of the other. Begin your analysis of the Cold War's origins by considering the Soviet view of the United States. What view was Novikov expressing when he wrote of the "imperialist tendencies of American capital"? What American actions during World War II did Novikov allege were part of the American policy? How did he see postwar American business as a tool of this policy? Where did the military establishment fit into American plans for Novikov? What was his vision of his own country's motives as it pursued "democratic reconstruction" in Eastern Europe? Why did he conclude that the ultimate American goal was war against the Soviet Union? Fifteen years after Novikov wrote, Nikita Khrushchev made his radio and television address. What views of the United States and its allies did this Soviet leader express? Do you think that his assertion that there were some in the West who wished to perpetuate Cold War tensions as well as "hate-ridden persons, deprived of common sense" was simply propaganda, or might he have believed what he said? After all, American students of Soviet policy in the 1940s and 1950s consistently reported that

Soviet leaders were not well informed about foreign countries.

Next, consider the American vision of the Soviets. What objectives did CIA analysts ascribe to the Soviet Union? Why did they envision the Soviet Union as the worldwide enemy of the United States and its European allies? What chances for war between the Soviet Union and the United States existed according to the CIA? What did General Clay believe were the goals of the Soviet Union? Why does he compare its threat to that of Hitler? Why was he prepared to risk war against the Soviets?

Finally, consider the specific issue of Germany and its capital. What does the map suggest about the strategic viability of the American-British-French position in Berlin after World War II? How do you think the Western allies maintained their position in Berlin for almost two generations, given the numerical superiority of Soviet forces in the region? Was it perhaps because they convinced Soviet authorities that they were prepared to fight a general war over the German capital? What sort of machinery had the Potsdam agreement set up for administering occupied Germany? In retrospect, what sort of differences between the Western allies and the Soviets might have been foreseen in establishing this machinery? What did Soviet observers like Novikov believe that the Americans were doing in Germany?

For their part, how did American policymakers understand Soviet actions in Germany? How, for example, did General Clay characterize the Soviet threat in the first Berlin crisis, even as he noted that he had no evidence of Soviet troop movements to give tangible form to that threat?

Once you have analyzed the perspectives of both sides in the Cold War, you should be ready to address this chapter's central questions. What were the origins of the Cold War? How did the Berlin crises develop out of wartime agreements? What strategic considerations made Berlin so essential to both the Western allies and the Soviet Union?

EPILOGUE

The construction of the Berlin Wall in 1961 dramatically decreased the number of East Germans fleeing to the West by surrounding the western sectors of the German capital with a wall twenty-nine miles in length that was guarded by heavily armed policemen. Nonetheless, East Germans continued to attempt to escape; some tunneled under the wall, others attempted to smash through the barriers with trucks, and a few tried to climb over it. Many failed in such attempts, as did Peter Fechter, an eighteen-year-old who tried to scale the wall in August 1962. Shot in the back and stomach by East German border guards as he climbed the wall, Fechter fell back into the eastern sector, where East German guards left him unattended for an hour, despite his calls for help, as he bled to death. Fechter's tragic fate sparked anti-Soviet riots in West Berlin, and it, and other incidents like it, dramatized the human price of a wall that divided a city as well as families.

Beyond Germany the Cold War continued for another generation. Discovery of Soviet missiles in Cuba, ninety miles off the American coast, provoked the last great direct confrontation between the United States and the Soviet Union in 1962. Although the Kennedy administration forced the removal of the missiles, a costly arms race between the Americans and the Soviets ensued. The United States also fought a long war in Vietnam against communist forces there. But by the early 1970s, an era of *détente*—improvement in East-West relations—developed. Improved relations between West Germany and the Soviets were essential in this process, and in 1970 Chancellor Willy Brandt did something no earlier West German leader had done by officially recognizing Germany's World War II territorial losses in the east (see Source 2) to the Soviet Union and Poland. His government was able to build on this first step in improving relations with Eastern block countries by negotiating rights for West Germans to visit relatives in East Germany. The Western allies also concluded an important agreement with the Soviets in the Quadripartite Agreement of 1972, which fully recognized the Western powers' rights of access to Berlin. The German capital then faded from the world's attention until events of the 1980s propelled it back into the news.

In 1985 the Soviet Union got new leadership in Mikhail Gorbachev. Recognizing that the restrictive economic and intellectual life of the Soviet Union made competition with the West increasingly difficult, Gorbachev announce a policy of *perestroika* (restructuring of government to achieve more democracy) and *glasnost* (greater freedom of expression). He also sought better relations with the United States and other Western powers. Most importantly, however, Gorbachev was unwilling, or unable, to maintain Soviet domination of the nations of Eastern Europe, and beginning in the late 1980s these states increasingly asserted their rights to be free political systems. In East Germany, the SED dictatorship faced growing dissatisfaction among its citizens, and in 1989 opposition groups began to protest for the first time in years. East Germans also expressed their dissatisfaction once again by leaving their country when the opportunity arose. Thus, when neighboring Hungary opened its western border to the free movement of people, 25,000 East Germans with travel permits for vacations in that country simply left for the West by way of Hungary in just three days in September 1989.

Indeed, throughout 1989 the SED regime had growing difficulties maintaining its accustomed control in East Germany. The number of protests demanding fundamental political and economic changes grew in size and number throughout the year and forced changes in a party leadership that ultimately proved incapable of controlling events. Finally, on November 9, 1989, the authorities ceased to enforce their control of the Berlin Wall, and free movement between the eastern and western sectors of Berlin resumed. In the first four days of such freedom, 4.3 million East Germans crossed into West Berlin. Most returned home, but many stayed in the western zone. As the East German regime grew increasingly weak, it joined with West Germany to take the first steps toward German reunification. The wall at last came down, and on July 1, 1990, East Germany adopted the currency and free economic system of West Germany. The final obstacle to German reunification fell when the Soviets dropped their long-standing objection to a reunified Germany belonging to NATO. Thus, in the so-called Two (East and West Germany) Plus Four (Britain, France, the Soviet Union, and the United States) Treaty of 1990, the World War II Allies finally signed a treaty ending occupation and paving the way for German unification. A unified German state, holding membership in NATO, became a reality at midnight on October 3, 1990, and the Cold War issue of Berlin ceased to threaten the world's peace.

CHAPTER TEN

FEMINISM AND THE PEACE

MOVEMENT (1910–1990)

Beginning in the 1820s, women throughout the world formed organizations that worked for demilitarization, pacifism, and, following the invention of the atomic bomb, an end to nuclear weapons. These organizations were particularly active in two periods: the pre– and post–World War I years, when they protested the military buildup that led to that war and then worked with other groups after Versailles to prevent future military conflicts; and the decades of the 1960s–1980s, when they protested the mushrooming nuclear arsenals that chilled the Cold War between the United States and the Soviet Union. Women's peace organizations, because they were often international or had international connections, promoted dialogue among women from diverse cultures, as well as working toward change in the policies of specific governments. Women who were peace activists varied widely in age, level of educa-

tion, and social background. Some of them were also involved in groups pressing for womens' rights; others joined groups that included both female and male members and worked in other areas of social concern, such as civil rights or labor organizing.

Many of the women who belonged to women's peace groups were also active in peace organizations for both women and men that were forming at the same time. Those involved in women's groups, however, had to confront an issue that did not face those involved in mixed-sex groups— why was it important that there be separate groups for women working for peace? This was a tricky issue for many, for they were often also advocates of women's equality or greater political rights, and to stress the ways in which men and women *differed* might be counterproductive. Many women activists have left a record of the way in which they addressed this issue, both in the formal position papers of the groups they founded or were involved in, and in oral interviews conducted later. In this chapter you will be using both position papers and interviews, along with posters and drawings made by women peace activists, to answer the following questions: How did twentieth-century women involved in women's peace groups view the relationship between their being women and their advocacy of peace? How did they translate their ideas into actions, and how did their ideas shape the types of actions they regarded as appropriate to achieving their aims?

BACKGROUND

Though the peace movement was probably most visible during the 1960s and 1970s in protests against the Vietnam War, calls for peace and disarmament have a long history. In 1793, Dr. Benjamin Rush, a signer of the Declaration of Independence, and Benjamin Bannecker, an African American mathematician and architect, called for the establishment of a department of peace to go along with the recently established War Department. (In 1949, this branch of the government was reorganized and given the title Department of Defense; it is the largest federal department and, since its inception, has received the major portion of the federal budget.) After the Napoleonic Wars in 1816, English Quakers formed the London Peace Society, which quickly established branches in many other English towns. Women participated in these societies, and in the 1820s a few of them set up Female Auxiliary Peace Societies, the first organized women's peace groups. Swedish author Fredrika Bremer continued these efforts in continental Europe, forming the Women's Peace Union in 1854 and writing against war during the Crimean War (1854–1856).

In the United States, the Civil War acted as a catalyst for peace groups in the way that the Napoleonic and Crimean Wars had sparked them in Europe. The American Civil War is often regarded as the first modern "total war," fought not only against a government or armed forces but against an opponent's economic means of existence and civilian population. It was clear to many people that future wars would bring similar devastation, and in the mid-nineteenth century a series of international peace congresses was held in Europe; these conferences called for the establishment of a congress of nations and international court of arbitration, the end of military education, and the control of arms sales. In the Western Hemisphere, the first Pan-American Congress met in 1889–90, and in 1899 one of the aims of these congresses became a reality with the establishment of the Permanent Court of Arbitration at The Hague in the Netherlands. (With the founding of the League of Nations after World War I this body became the World Court, and, with the founding of the United Nations after World War II, the International Court of Justice; its permanent seat is still in The Hague.)

[293]

The peace movement of the nineteenth century was one of many movements of social reform whose agendas and aims were linked, and in which women played major roles. Individuals and groups advocating the abolition of slavery or the restriction of alcohol often linked their goals with those of the peace movement; the largest U.S. temperance group, for example, the Women's Christian Temperance Union, believing that the violence at home caused by alcohol was connected to the international violence of war, had a department of peace. The connections between the women's rights movement and the peace movement were even stronger. The major women's suffrage organizations, the International Council of Women and the International Woman Suffrage Alliance (later renamed the International Alliance of Women), had platforms that supported peace and arbitration, viewing their own international cooperation as a model that nations could follow. Not all peace organizations allowed women to be full members, inspiring some women to step up their call for equal rights in the same way that the abolition movement's exclusion of women had led female abolitionists to become stronger advocates of women's suffrage.

Despite all efforts for the peaceful arbitration of international disputes, the late nineteenth and early twentieth century saw a military buildup throughout Europe that, combined with intense nationalism and imperialistic rivalries, led to the outbreak of World War I in 1914. Though the war caused a break in the workings of the Permanent Court of Arbitration and other international bodies, it served as a spur for women's peace activities. In 1915 Aletta Jacobs, a physician from the Netherlands, and Chrystal Macmillan, a lawyer from Scotland, organized an international women's peace conference. This was held at The Hague, with over one thousand delegates from twelve nations, though the British, French, and Russian delegates were forbidden by their governments to attend. The U.S. delegation of forty-seven women included many involved with the newly formed Women's Peace Party (WPP), including its chair, the social reformer Jane Addams. The meeting sent delegations to the leaders of many countries to lobby for an end to the war, and linked peace and women's rights explicitly in its closing statement:

> The International Congress of Women is convinced that one of the strongest forces for the prevention of war will be the combined influence of the women of all countries. . . . But as women can only make their influence effective if they have equal political rights with men, this Congress declares that it is the duty of the women of all countries to work with all their force for their political enfranchisement.[1]

In the United States, the two aims of the International Congress for Women—world peace and political

---

1. "Program from the International Women's Congress, April 28, 29, 30, 1915," quoted in Harriet Hyman Alonso, *Peace as a Women's Issue: A History of the U.S. Movement for World Peace and Women's Rights* (Syracuse: Syracuse University Press, 1993), p. 68.

rights for women—came into conflict. Carrie Chapman Catt, one of the founders of the Women's Peace Party and the president of the National American Woman Suffrage Association, decided to offer President Wilson the assistance of suffragists as the United States entered the war, in 1917, in return for his support of women's suffrage. This move angered Addams and other leaders of the WPP (such as Crystal Eastman), who felt that the group's pacifism should never be compromised. The split, combined with government surveillance of antiwar groups and legal restrictions on their publication or dissemination of materials, meant that the WPP was not very active during the rest of the war. Immediately afterward, both sides gained victories: Women were granted the vote in 1920, and the WPP, still alive, reorganized as the U.S. branch of the Women's International League for Peace and Freedom (WILPF).

Government harassment of peace activists did not end when the war ended, for the WILPF offices in Chicago were frequently raided, and Emily Green Balch, the group's secretary-treasurer, lost her position on the faculty of Wellesley College because of her peace work. Women were often charged with being Communists because of their international interests and connections; the most notorious example was the "Spider Web" conspiracy chart, which from the early 1920s linked peace groups and Communist organizations. This chart was distributed by the War Department and often included the poem: "Miss Bolshevicki has come to town/With a Russian cap and German Gown/

In Women's clubs she's sure to be found/For she's come to disarm AMERICA."[2] Balch's reputation was somewhat redeemed when she received the Nobel Peace Prize in 1946; Jane Addams received it in 1931, making them the only two U.S. women ever so honored.

During the 1920s and 1930s the major international peace efforts centered around establishing legislative or negotiated alternatives to war. The League of Nations was established by the peace treaties that ended World War I and was successful in preventing a number of conflicts during the 1920s. In 1928 many nations signed the Kellogg-Briand Pact calling for the use of peaceful means of resolving conflicts and condemning war as an instrument of national policy, though the lack of any measures of enforcement meant that the pact would not have much actual effect.

In their efforts to achieve world peace, all of the women's groups used tactics they had developed in the suffrage campaign—parades, letter-writing campaigns, conferences, petitions, direct lobbying—and in some cases they also used tactics of nonviolent resistance developed by Gandhi in the campaign for Indian independence from the British. During this period they often worked on Latin American issues, calling, for example, for the removal of U.S. troops from Haiti, where they were stationed from 1915 to 1937.

The rise of Nazism in Germany brought an end to the League of Nations, a renewal of war, and a crisis

2. Quoted in Nancy Cott, *The Grounding of Modern Feminism* (New Haven: Yale University Press, 1987), p. 94.

of conscience for peace groups. Most groups and individuals eventually gave up their absolute pacifist stance and opposed fascism, while continuing to oppose government policies that restricted freedom at home. For example, WILPF members in the United States supported conscientious objectors and opposed the internment of Japanese Americans in camps, while those in Denmark and Norway were active in the resistance against the Nazis. After the war, WILPF was made an official nongovernmental organization affiliated with the United Nations, and it pushed for the establishment of UNICEF and the UN High Commission for Refugees.

The atomic bombs that ended World War II created a new issue for peace groups—nuclear disarmament. WILPF combined with mixed-sex groups such as the National Committee for a Sane Nuclear Policy (SANE) to protest nuclear testing. In 1961, five women in Washington who were members of SANE formed Women Strike for Peace (WSP) to organize one-day actions protesting American and Soviet nuclear policies. They galvanized thousands of women who had not been active before, particularly around the issue of the contamination of milk by strontium 90, a radioactive isotope that is the chief immediate hazard in the fallout from above-ground nuclear tests. WSP was intentionally nonhierarchical, with no dues or official membership; most of the women who took part in its one-day strikes across the country were white, middle-class mothers who wore white gloves and brought photographs of their children along on demonstrations. Their

ladylike demeanor and middle-class status did not protect them from government investigations in this virulently anticommunist period, and in 1962 members of WSP testified before the House Un-American Activities Committee. Their testimony made the committee look ridiculous, a point captured in a Herblock cartoon in the *Washington Post* in which one congressman is shown asking another: "I came in late; which was it that was un-American—women or peace?"[3] WSP actions influenced the passage of the 1963 Test-Ban Treaty, which banned testing of atomic weapons in the atmosphere, outer space, and below water.

From 1962 to 1975, the overriding issue for U.S. peace groups was the Vietnam War, and women's groups combined with many other peace groups in actions ranging from literature distribution to nonviolent protests to mass demonstrations such as the 1969 Vietnam Moratorium. Protests against the war took place not only in the United States but throughout the world, often organized by student groups as part of the international student movement. At the same time, the civil rights movement in the United States used similar tactics and often involved the same people as the antiwar movement, in the same way that the abolitionist and peace movements of the nineteenth century had been linked. Like those in the nineteenth century, these twentieth-century movements for social change also led to a reinvigoration of the women's rights movement. Though they had the right

3. *Washington Post*, December 11, 1962.

to vote and were working for social justice, women activists discovered that they were still excluded from leadership positions and that their opinions were not taken seriously. This twentieth-century women's rights movement is usually termed the *women's liberation movement*, and it eventually led to sweeping changes in women's legal rights, employment opportunities, and political power.

For women's peace organizations, this renewal of feminism often led to their making explicit connections again between the violence of war and violence against women. This became a more prominent part of women's peace activities after the end of the Vietnam War, when the attention of peace organizations in many parts of the world was focused on the buildup of nuclear arsenals and an increase in military spending that was accompanied by cuts in social programs. New groups were formed, such as Women's Action for Nuclear Disarmament (WAND), Babies Against the Bomb, Women Opposed to the Nuclear Threat (WONT), and Women Against Military Madness (WAMM). New types of strategies were adopted, such as the establishment of permanent peace camps at missile and military production sites in Europe, the United States, Canada, Japan, and Australia, and the theatrical action of thousands of women encircling the Pentagon in the Women's Pentagon Actions of 1980 and 1981. Older strategies, such as marches, petition campaigns, and civil disobedience, continued as women pressured their governments to begin nuclear disarmament. In 1985 an international group of women

formed Women for a Meaningful Summit and visited the diplomats involved in the disarmament talks between the United States and the Soviet Union. (There were, however, no women present as negotiators.)

The decade 1975–1985 was designated by the United Nations as the Decade for Women, bringing worldwide organizing around issues involving women's economic, political, and social roles. The decade was highlighted by three international conferences: Mexico City in 1975, Copenhagen in 1980, and Nairobi in 1985. WILPF members tried to get disarmament language into the official statements at the Mexico City conference, but they were not successful; UN organizers regarded disarmament and peace issues as "too political" and not truly "women's issues." By the Copenhagen conference, however, this attitude had changed, and by 1985 the whole conference in Nairobi was titled "Equality, Development, and Peace." Alongside the official UN conference, nongovernmental organizations had their own much larger conference that brought together over 14,000 women from around the world. Statements emerging from this conference clearly defined peace as a primary women's issue, and also pointed to the environmental and economic costs of the arms race. In the years since Nairobi, and at the UN World Conference of Women in Beijing in 1995, women's peace groups have addressed issues of racism and uneven worldwide development more directly, as their idea of "peace" has broadened from a focus on disarmament to include many issues of social justice.

THE METHOD

Traditionally, political history was thought of as the history of politics, with governmental and military leaders as the main actors, and laws, decrees, parliamentary debates, and other official documents as its primary records. These are still important, but today political history is being seen in a broader sense as the history not only of politics but of all relations involving power, and a wider range of sources is now being used to understand the power relationships in past societies and the ways in which individuals and groups who are not officially part of the government have shaped political decisions. This has meant relying on the documents produced by such individuals and groups, as well as interviews and discussions with a wide range of people. Political historians now use techniques of *oral history* first developed by anthropologists and social historians, which combine interviews with the exploration of written sources to arrive at a fuller picture of political changes and events.

Historians interested in women's lives in the recent past have also found oral history to be a valuable tool. Women's experiences and opinions are much less likely to make it into official records, both because women have been excluded from positions of political power until very recently and because groups that did include women often assumed that their views would be the same as those of the men in the group and so did not record them. Women's groups were much less likely than

men's to keep formal records of their discussions, and their actions and roles have often been downplayed in newspaper and other published accounts. Thus interviews with participants are one of the few ways we can reconstruct women's involvement in groups that worked for political and social change and get some idea of their motivations and goals.

Because it allows you to come into direct contact with the history makers you wish to study, oral history is a very appealing research method, but it is most useful when written records are available for verification. Memories are not always accurate, and people may have reasons to vary their stories from what actually happened. For example, Margaret Hope Bacon discovered while writing a biography of Mildred Scott Olmsted, who held various national offices with WILPF from 1922 to 1966, that Olmsted "had forgotten the very existence of men and women who opposed her. Even when I would show her in writing the evidence of such opposition, she continued not to remember it."[4]

Your sources for this chapter include selections from the written documents and speeches of women involved in the peace movement, position papers and posters of several peace groups, and selections from oral interviews with several women activists. They have generally been arranged in chronological order because it is important to keep the historical context in mind as you are reading and evaluating them. The

4. Margaret Hope Bacon, *One Woman's Passion for Peace and Freedom: The Life of Mildred Scott Olmsted* (Syracuse: Syracuse University Press, 1993), p. xvii.

documents come from the two key periods of the women's peace movement: the World War I era and the 1960s to the 1980s. These two periods were chosen because (1) women's peace groups were most active during these periods, and (2) these were periods of strong women's rights movements. Thus, women who were active in the peace movement during these times often felt compelled to address our first question directly, to comment about how they viewed the relationship between their being women and their advocating peace.

As you use the sources to answer the first question, you will be addressing an issue not only in political and women's history, but also in a quite new area of historical investigation: *gender.* Only very recently have historians begun to study how past societies fashioned their notions of what it means to be male or female. They stress the fact that gender is not simply biological, but socially constructed and historically variable, for norms of feminine and masculine behavior change. Women peace activists were one of the few groups forced to confront the social construction of gender directly in what they were doing and thinking, as they addressed such questions as whether men were naturally more warlike than women or whether being mothers or prospective mothers made women more inclined to peace. As you read and look at the sources in this chapter, note whether they view women as somehow more peaceful than men. If they do, to what do the authors ascribe these differences: biology? education? social pressures?

Do they think this inclination can or should be changed? Do they view women's peacefulness in a completely positive manner, or do they also see it as reflecting passivity? How do sources that do *not* view women as more peaceful than men explain why they feel there should be separate women's peace groups and why wars have traditionally been fought by male combatants?

Whatever their opinions about gender differences with regard to war and peace, women's peace groups carried out various actions to attempt to change government policies. Your sources discuss some of these actions. The second question in this chapter asks you to examine how these groups turned their ideas into actions, and how their ideas about gender differences shaped the types of actions they regarded as appropriate. As you read and look at the sources, note the types of actions that are discussed. Which of these appear to be shaped, either implicitly or explicitly, by the fact that these are *women's* peace groups? What special problems and opportunities do the women involved in these groups see as arising from their being women or from their training about acceptable female norms of behavior? Do they see any tensions between their ideas and actions, and how do they resolve these?

Along with thinking about the content of your sources for this chapter, you also need to keep in mind differences between the types of sources that you are using, as would anyone using oral interviews. How might ideas expressed in the official position papers and speeches differ from those conveyed in interviews conducted later? All of the interviews published here were conducted by women sympathetic to the peace movement. How might this have shaped their content? As you answer the questions in this chapter, you should also think about the appropriateness of each type of source. What do the oral interviews add that could not be gained from other sources? What does the information gained from all these sources add to our picture of political developments in the twentieth century?

THE EVIDENCE

Source 1 from Olive Schreiner, Woman and Labor *(New York: Frederick A. Stokes, 1911), pp. 175, 176, 178–179, 180, 185.*

1. From Olive Schreiner, *Woman and Labor*, 1911

[*Olive Schreiner (1855–1920) was a South African writer and women's rights advocate.*]

There is, perhaps, no woman, whether she have borne children, or be merely potentially a child-bearer, who could look down upon a battlefield covered with slain, but the thought would rise in her, "So many mothers' sons! So many young bodies brought into the world to lie there! So many months of weariness and pain while bones and muscles were shaped within! So many hours of anguish and struggle that breath might be! So many baby mouths drawing life at women's breasts;—all this, that men might lie with glazed eyeballs, and swollen faces, and fixed, blue, unclosed mouths, and great limbs tossed. . . ."

On that day when the woman takes her place beside the man in the governance and arrangement of external affairs of her race will also be that day that heralds the death of war as a means of arranging human differences. . . .

It is not because of woman's cowardice, incapacity, nor, above all, because of her general superior virtue, that she will end war when her voice is fully and clearly heard in the governance of states—it is because, on this one point, and on this point almost alone, the knowledge of woman, simply as woman, is superior to that of man; she knows the history of human flesh; she knows its cost; he does not. . . .

Men's bodies are our woman's works of art. Given to us power to control, we will never carelessly throw them in to fill up the gaps in human relationships made by international ambitions and greeds. The thought would never come to us as women, "Cast in men's bodies; settle the thing so!" . . .

War will pass when intellectual culture and activity have made possible to the female an equal share in the control and governance of modern national life; it will probably not pass away much sooner; its extinction will not be delayed much longer.

It is especially in the domain of war that we, the bearers of men's bodies, who supply its most valuable munition, who, not amid the clamor and ardor of battle, but singly, and alone, with a three-in-the-morning courage, shed our blood and face death that the battlefield might have its food, a food more precious to us than our heart's blood; it is we especially who, in the domain of war, have our word to say, a word no man can say for us. It is our intention to enter into the domain of war and to labor there till in the course of generations we have extinguished it.

Source 2 from Maude Royden, "War and the Women's Movement," in C. R. Buxton and G. L. Dickinson, Towards a Lasting Settlement *(London: Allen and Unwin, 1915), p. 106.*

2. Maude Royden on Women and War, 1915

[*A. Maude Royden (1876–1956) was a British writer and strong supporter of women's suffrage. She edited a suffragist newspaper and became the first woman to hold a regular preaching position in the Anglican Church.*]

The belief that women are innately more pacific than men has been severely shaken, if not altogether destroyed. It is now very evident that they can be as virulently militarist, as blindly partisan, not as the soldier, for in him such qualities are generally absent, but as the male non-combatant, for whom the same cannot always be said. Among women, as among men, there are extremists for war and for peace; pacifists and militarists; women who are as passionately convinced as Bernhardi[5] that war is a good thing, women who accept it as a terrible necessity, women who repudiate it altogether. All these views they share with men. There appears to be no cleavage of opinion along sex lines.

---

5. Friedrich von Bernhardi (1849–1930) was a German general and military writer known for his strong expression of German ambitions.

[301]

Source 3 from Jane Addams, "Account of Her Interview with the Foreign Ministers of Europe," speech published in The Survey, *New York, July 17, 1915. Quoted in Cambridge Women's Peace Collective,* My Country Is the Whole World: An Anthology of Women's Work on Peace and War *(London: Pandora Press, 1984), pp. 86–87.*

3. Jane Addams on Women and War, Carnegie Hall, New York, 1915

[*Jane Addams (1860–1935), the American social reformer and founder of Hull House (a settlement house for immigrants in Chicago), was the first president of WILPF and, in 1931, was awarded the Nobel Peace Prize.*]

Let me say just a word about the women in the various countries. The belief that a woman is against war simply and only because she is a woman and not a man, does not, of course, hold. In every country there are many, many women who believe that the War is inevitable and righteous, and that the highest possible service is being performed by their sons who go into the Army; just as there are thousands of men believing that in every country; the majority of women and men doubtless believe that.

But the women do have a sort of pang about it. Let us take the case of an artist, an artist who is in an artillery corps, let us say, and is commanded to fire upon a wonderful thing, say St Mark's at Venice, or the Duomo at Florence, or any other great architectural and beautiful thing. I am sure he would have just a little more compunction than the man who had never given himself to creating beauty and did not know the cost of it. There is certainly that deterrent on the part of the women, who have nurtured these soldiers from the time they were little things, who brought them into the world and brought them up to the age of fighting, and now see them destroyed. That curious revolt comes out again and again, even in the women who are most patriotic and who say: "I have five sons and a son-in-law in the trenches. I wish I had more sons to give." Even those women, when they are taken off their guard, give a certain protest, a certain plaint against the whole situation which very few men I think are able to formulate.

Now, what is it that these women do in the hospitals? They nurse the men back to health and send them to the trenches, and the soldiers say to them: "You are so good to us when we are wounded, you do everything in the world to make life possible and to restore us; why do you not have a little pity for us when we are in the trenches? Why do you not put forth a little of this same effort and this same tenderness to see what might be done to pull us out of those miserable places?"

That testimony came to us, not from the nurses of one country, and not from the nurses who were taking care of the soldiers on one side, but from those who were taking care of them upon every side.

And it seems to make it quite clear that whether we are able to recognize it or not, there has grown up a generation in Europe, as there has doubtless grown up a generation in America, who have revolted against war. It is a god they know not of, that they are not willing to serve; because all of their sensibilities and their training upon which their highest ideals depend, revolt against the whole situation.

Source 4 from Crystal Eastman, "A Program for Voting Women," pamphlet of Women's Peace Party of New York, March 1918, quoted in Blanche Wiesen Cook, Crystal Eastman on Women and Revolution (New York: Oxford University Press, 1978), pp. 266–267.

4. Crystal Eastman on the Women's Peace Movement, 1919

[Crystal Eastman (1881–1928) was an American feminist, socialist, and labor lawyer. She was one of the founders of the Woman's Peace Party and the American Civil Liberties Union, which was originally set up to defend conscientious objectors.]

Why a *Woman's* Peace Party?, I am often asked. Is peace any more a concern of women than of men? Is it not of universal human concern? For a feminist— one who believes in breaking down sex barriers so that women and men can work and play and build the world together—it is not an easy question to answer. Yet the answer, when I finally worked it out in my own mind, convinced me that we should be proud and glad, even as feminists, to work for the Woman's Peace Party.

To begin with, there is a great and unique tradition behind our movement which would be lost if we merged our Woman's Peace Party in the general revolutionary international movement of the time. Do not forget that it was women who gathered at The Hague, a thousand strong, in the early months of the war, women from all the great belligerent and neutral countries, who conferred there together in friendship and sorrow and sanity while the mad war raged around them. Their great conference, despite its soundness and constructive statesmanship, failed of its purpose, failed of its hope. But from the beginning of the war down to the Russo–German armistice there was no world step of such daring and directness, nor of such honest, unfaltering international spirit and purpose, as the organization of the International Committee of Women for Permanent Peace at The Hague in April, 1915. This Committee has branches in twenty-two countries. The Woman's Peace Party is the American section of the Committee, and our party, organized February 1 and 2, is the New York State Branch.

When the great peace conference comes, a Congress of Women made up of groups from these twenty-two countries will meet in the same city to demand that the deliberate intelligent organization of the world for lasting peace shall be the outcome of that conference.

These established international connections make it important to keep this a woman's movement.

But there is an added reason. We women of New York State, politically speaking, have just been born. We have been born into a world at war and this fact cannot fail to color greatly the whole field of our political thinking and to determine largely the emphasis of our political action. What we hope, then, to accomplish by keeping our movement distinct is to bring thousands upon thousands of women—women of the international mind—to dedicate their new political power, not to local reforms or personal ambitions, not to discovering the difference between the Democratic and Republican parties, but to *ridding the world of war.*

Source 5 from the International Alliance for Women papers, Sophia Smith Collection, Smith College. Original in French; English translation by Charlotte Weber and Jeffrey Merrick.

5. Huda Sha'rawi, Speech to the Congress of the International Alliance of Women, Istanbul, Turkey, 1935

[*Huda Sha'rawi was the founder of the Egyptian Feminist Union and a representative to the Congress.*]

Madame President, Ladies, and Gentlemen:

I have a double mission to fulfill today in speaking to you of the cooperation between the East and the West; first, as a member of the Board of the International Alliance of Women, then as a representative of one of the oldest countries of the East, famous since antiquity for its feminism and its pacifism. . . . On these magnificent premises and in this propitious atmosphere, the women of forty nations vowed yesterday to form a united front against all threats of war. Four new associations, representing the Arab women of Damascus, Beirut, Palestine, as well as those of Iran and of the All-India Conference, have come to reinforce our ranks with the addition of their youthful energy and ardent faith.

The enthusiastic ovations with which the Congress welcomed their admission into the bosom of the Alliance were the most striking manifestation of this desire for cooperation between East and West. Fervent admirers of the western women's movement for peace and the equality of rights, these women of the East have wanted to join with you for a long time to place their good will in the service of this noble cause. Indeed, like you, ladies, they desire peace ardently, but they want it based on justice and respect for the law of nations. . . .

This is why, ladies and gentlemen, you see present at this Congress—which will inscribe a fine page in the annals of international feminism and pacifism—representatives of almost all of the countries of the East. They have come, confident in the ideal of justice that you are pursuing, convinced that if the ambition of men has created wars, the feeling of equity, innate in women, will help [the triumph] of peace.

"Make the causes of war disappear, and the wounds of war will heal," said the Savior of Turkey [Kemal Ataturk] wisely. We beg you therefore, eminent women of the Eastern and Western countries—who sincerely desire universal understanding—to remember the words spoken yesterday by our dear president, Mrs. Corbett Ashby, "that women are responsible, like men, for the good or bad policies of their governments, and that instead of demanding peace in tears they must, in all the free countries, criticize the policies of parties, choose their representatives, influence the press and the courts, and monitor the radio and cinema."

My sisters in the West your mission is doubly sacred—because if you have been somewhat responsible before the world for the faults committed by your governments, you are even more so vis-a-vis women who still do not have the right to vote and to whom you serve as examples.

Source 6 from Käthe Kollwitz, The Sacrifice (Das Opfer), Rosenwald Collection, © 2003 Board of Trustees, National Gallery of Art, Washington, #1922/23. Woodcut in black, reworked with white gouache, on japan paper. Plate 1 from "War" (Klipstein 1955 177.ii/vii (trial proof). Image: .372 × .402 cm. (14 5/8" × 15 13/16"); sheet: .415 × 437 cm. (16 5/16" × 17 3/16").

6. Käthe Kollwitz, *The Sacrifice*, 1922

[Käthe Kollwitz (1867–1945) was a German artist and sculptor whose works were ordered removed from public view by Adolf Hitler in the 1930s because of their political and social content.]

Source 7 from Miyako Shinohara, "Branded" in Women Against War, *compiled by the Women's Division of Soko Gakkai, trans. Richard L. Gage (Tokyo: Kodansha International Ltd., 1986), pp. 138–142. Copyright © Soka Gakkai 1986. Reprinted by permission of Soka Gakkai.*

7. Miyako Shinohara, "In the Name of Peace," 1986

[*Miyako Shinohara is a Japanese woman involved in Soko Gakkai, a movement within Buddhism that stresses community and peace.*]

It is difficult to say how much pain, anguish, and frustration I have suffered owing to the fact that I was permanently branded with the words *prenatal atomic-radiation victim.*

When the atomic bomb was dropped on Hiroshima, my mother was in Kusunoki-machi, one and a half kilometers from the explosion center. She was pregnant with me at the time. She and my grandmother fled to Yaguchi, in the outskirts of the city, and then to Tokyo. On October 2, 1945, I was born in Itabashi Ward, Tokyo.

As a small child I always felt sympathic, but no direct involvement, when my grandmother told me stories of the atomic bombing. Both Mother and Grandmother were in good health, and it never occurred to me that I might one day suffer from the effects of the bomb.

In 1947 my family moved back to Hiroshima. One day, when I was in middle school and we were rehearsing a play for the culture festival, a classmate suddenly said, "You've got blood on your teeth." A look in the mirror showed that my gums were covered with liver-colored clots of blood. Several times I wiped the blood away with my handkerchief, but each time it returned. Later I noticed red spots all over my arms and legs. No amount of rubbing would make them go away. . . .

To my persistent questions, Mother finally told me that the name of my sickness was purpura. I had no idea what that was, but suspected it might be a fatal atomic-radiation sickness. Unable to understand why I had to go through such suffering, I began to blame Mother for having given birth to me when I was doomed to be afflicted with such a disease. Often when Mother came into my room, I would turn away and refuse to speak to her. Obviously, I was trying to escape my own torment by striking out at Mother. Now I can imagine the grief this must have caused her.

Praying that my purpura could be cured, I started making a thousand cranes out of *origami* paper, which is a Japanese custom when making an important wish. Just as I finished the thousandth, the blotches on my body faded away and the blood clots stopped forming on my gums. I was discharged after a month in the hospital and allowed to return home. But the medication I was under caused my face to swell to twice its normal size and made me allergic to penicillin and aspirin. . . .

For some years, Grandmother had been a member of Soka Gakkai, the lay religious organization affiliated with Nichiren Shōshū Buddhism. At about this time, on Grandmother's recommendation, I joined too. Together she and I chanted the Daimoku (*Nam-myōhō-renge-kyō*) and prayed for my recovery.

Amazingly, as we continued the chant, I began to get better. The blotches began to fade away, and I came to see how strong religious faith is. Filling my handbag with tissue paper and cotton in case something should happen, I attended many different Soka Gakkai meetings and functions. By now a full-fledged member of society, in my own way I lived a full life as a young adult, and sometimes even managed to forget the atomic bombing and my own illness.

But before long I was shown that my fate extended to areas of life I had never thought it would touch. Like all other normal women, I dreamed of getting married and having children. I was shocked one day when the young man I was seeing asked me whether I was certain my children would be healthy and normal. I immediately answered yes, but gradually began to have doubts myself. Little by little, this young man stopped seeing me and finally broke off all relations. . . .

From that time, I turned my back on marriage and devoted myself quietly to my work and religious activities. It was while engaged in religious work that I met the man who is now my husband. When he proposed to me, I told him frankly of my two attacks of purpura. He only said, "It's not your fault. And if you ever get sick again, we'll fight it together." I wept with joy that my dream of getting married—a dream I had once abandoned—was about to come true. In 1974, in spite of the violent opposition he encountered from others, we were married. . . .

In February 1976, I gave birth to a son, and the doctor assured me that he was the perfect picture of health. Before I could believe it, however, I examined my baby over and over. Finally satisfied that he was as healthy as could be, I wept for happiness. As for myself, I had hemorrhaged abnormally and was kept immobile on the delivery table for eight hours. Thereafter, however, mother and son grew strong and before long left the hospital. Today I am the mother of three healthy children.

In my youth, I had been unwilling to see or hear anything about the atomic bombing. As a mother, however, I realized that we must not turn away from the facts. One day, though it required courage, I took my children to the Peace Memorial Museum in Hiroshima. Seeing the displays there strengthened my conviction that we must never allow war to happen again. To this end, mothers must take the firmest possible stand in the name of peace and the protection of their children.

Sources 8 and 9 from Judith Porter Adams, Peacework: Oral Histories of Women Peace Activists *(Boston: Twayne Publishers, 1991), pp. 194–198. © 1990, Twayne Publishers. Reprinted by permission of The Gale Group.*

8. An Oral Interview with Dagmar Wilson, 1991

[*Dagmar Wilson (b. 1916) is a graphic designer and children's book illustrator who was one of the founders of Women Strike for Peace.*]

Thirty years ago I was responsible for an action that resulted in a national peace movement which is still going strong, Women Strike for Peace. I'm not really a "political" person, although I was brought up as a pacifist. As a child growing up in the years following the "war to end wars"—World War I—I believed that nations would work out their conflicts rather than fight. Other wonderful things were happening too. Women had been liberated—my mother was a voter. I went to a progressive school for boys and girls, which in Europe, where I grew up, was not common. Socialism seemed like a wonderful experiment. I really believed that the world was moving forward in many areas, all favorable to mankind.

However, after World War II, I realized that there was something happening that was beyond politics and that affected all human beings. I felt that the question of survival on earth was not a matter of politics, nor a matter of power between governments, but was a matter of deeper concerns common to all humanity.

Many things moved me to become active step by step. . . . This was . . . the time of the Berlin Wall. The media had said it might mean war, and of course, war would mean nuclear war. Our administration was telling us to build fallout shelters to protect our families. I felt indignant, more than indignant. I felt insulted as a human being that responsible people, governments, were asking us to do anything so stupid, as ineffectual as this, instead of coming to grips with the problems that were causing the tensions we were facing. My husband, who knew me well enough to realize that I was getting quite tense, said, "Well, women are very good at getting their way when they make up their minds to do something."

That phrase stayed with me. . . .

. . . I said to myself, "Well, what about a women's movement?" I picked up the telephone and started calling all my women friends from my phone book and Christmas card list. I wanted to see what they thought. I have always been very telephone-shy, so this was an unusual thing for me to do. It turned out that everybody that I spoke with had been worrying about this problem. We women thought that the fallout shelter idea was an inane, insane, and an unsuitable response to the world situation and spelled disaster. The response I got was really quite enlightening. Each woman had it in the front of her mind, including a lot of women who were really not politically active.

I soon gathered together in my own living room a small group of women out of those whom I had called. Three days later we met at my house. Six days later, at a big meeting planned by SANE, we announced an "action." This marked the formation of Women Strike for Peace.

What we planned was a one-day event. The women would go on strike and leave the men "holding the baby." We said: "Now what do you think would happen if all the women went on strike?" The whole country would stand still. We thought it was a good way to demonstrate our own power and show that women were an essential part of our social structure and had a right to be heard. Six weeks from that day, there were demonstrations in sixty cities in the United States.

We were not part of the women's liberation movement. Ours was a peace movement activated by women. And there is a difference. We were women working for the good of humanity. One woman in our early group who was a very good writer wrote a statement of purpose that was powerful. One of the strengths of the movement was that it was cliché free. We were not political activitists who were used to the old phrases. We were speaking much more out of our everyday experiences, but we were educated and literate. This was our statement:

> We represent a resolute stand of women in the United States against the unprecedented threat to life from nuclear holocaust. We're women of all races, creeds, and political persuasions who are dedicated to the achievement of general and complete disarmament under effective international control. We cherish the right and accept the responsibility of the individual in democratic society to act and influence the course of government. We demand of governments that nuclear weapons tests be banned forever, that the arms race end, and that the world abolish all weapons of destruction under United Nations safeguards. We urge immediate planning at local, state and national levels for a peacetime economy with freedom and justice for all. We urge our government to anticipate world tensions and conflicts through constructive nonmilitary actions and through the United Nations. We join with women throughout the world to challenge the right of any nation or group of nations to hold the power of life or death over the world.

That really sums up my personal beliefs; I couldn't have stated it as well.

We saw women as a vehicle for a new peace action. There were already many peace groups and individuals, but the situation was still grave. These groups had become part of the peace establishment, and we didn't think they were as effective as they once were. We were able to do things that couldn't have happened in an already existing organization. I hoped that WSP would go on as long as it was effective, but I believed that in time it would be replaced by something else.

We had learned that nuclear testing was having hazardous effects on our environment, specifically on the open fields on which cows were grazing. This was contaminating the milk supply with strontium 90. This touched us very closely. We found out that strontium 90 was replacing calcium in children's bones. When we heard voices from Capitol Hill saying, "Well, well, it's too bad; this is just one of the hazards of the nuclear age," we really began to wonder about the sanity of our nation's leaders. Women Strike for Peace was an idea whose time had come. I was the lightning conductor; it just happened to be me. The time had come when either the people of the Earth would live together or die together.

In January of WSP's second year the New York women decided to come to the White House to stage a demonstration. They filled the longest train that had ever left Pennsylvania Station in the history of the railway, all with women. That day President Kennedy was scheduled for a press conference, and we thought no one would pay any attention to our demonstration. There was an enormous rain storm that soaked all the women who were coming off the train, ruining their hats—we always made a "respectable" appearance with hats and gloves. They walked through the rain to the White House and became soaked to the skin. At the president's press conference a well-known journalist representing the *New York Post* asked, "Do you think that demonstrations at this time have any influence on you and on the public and on the direction which we take in policy?" The president replied by saying that he had seen the large numbers of women out there in the rain and that we could understand that he agreed with our message and that our message had been received. We got wonderful publicity out of that, since the press conference was televised and broadcast nationally. . . .

WSP played a critical role in the 1963 Partial Test Ban Treaty's passage, but our greatest triumph was our confrontation with the House Un-American Activities Committee. They pounced on us in 1962 by subpoenaing nine WSP women. We were advised by others who had a go-around with the Committee that we "should not make a big fuss." But one of our women said, "No, this is not the way we're going to do it. If they're subpoenaing Dagmar Wilson, we should all volunteer to testify." Now that was an absolutely brilliant idea. We sent telegrams through our network saying, "Volunteer to testify. Come if you can. Hospitality offered. Bring your baby." Hundreds of women volunteered to testify. This was a new twist—most people were tempted to run a mile when the Committee pointed its magic wand at them. . . .

Our WSP meetings were very informal, with no protocol; we ran them like we ran our carpools. Well, that was extremely baffling to these political gentlemen. And at one point one said, "I don't understand how you get anything done at all." I answered, "Well, it puzzles us sometimes too."

The Committee was trying to find out if there was Communist influence in the peace movement. WSP was concerned about war and peace; we didn't think the world was worth blowing up over political differences. We could see ourselves marching arm in arm with Soviet mothers for the sake of our children, so we were not intimidated by the Committee's strategies. I was asked at the end of my testimony whether we would examine our books to see if we had Communist women in our midst, and I said, "Certainly not"—we would not do anything of the kind. "In fact," I said, "unless the whole human race joins us in our quest for peace, God help us."

One of the funny things about our "inquisition" before the Committee was that we were asked, in a sinister tone, if we had a mimeograph machine. It's true that we were mimeographing materials to distribute among ourselves. You know, someone's baby was always around, and we kidded ourselves that the print might appear on a child's diaper. Anybody turning a baby over might find a description of where our next meeting was going to be. So much for the sinister implication of a mimeograph machine.

We got very good press. I think that everybody was thoroughly fed up with the Committee. Congress was embarrassed by it, and the press was bored with it.

9. An Oral Interview with Madeline Duckles, 1991

[*Madeline Duckles (b. 1916) joined WILPF in the 1940s and was an organizer for Women Strike for Peace. During the Vietnam War, she helped organize a program to fly napalm-burned children to the United States for treatment.*]

We've made progress in civil rights, environmental issues; we've progressed on every level except for peace. Here we are, armed to the teeth when Women Strike for Peace began protesting nuclear testing when strontium 90 was appearing in children's teeth. We wanted to do something quickly. So women all over the country called a "strike" and left their work and families to protest. At that time, we had exploded two bombs and now the world has about fifty thousand nuclear weapons. So we haven't made any progress at all! And WILPF was working hard right after women's suffrage trying to get women more involved in the political process, trying to stop war toys and get the U.S. out of Central America in 1917 and we're still there now. The problems persist.

My political education began when I went to the University of California here at Berkeley. At that time the YWCA was where the action was. There were a few remarkable women in charge of it. There were discussions of race relations, the Spanish Civil War, and labor issues. I began at the University in 1933, and this was the year of the great longshoremen's strike in San Francisco. I had never been to a union meeting before. We were gathering canned goods for the strikers. It was for me a very exciting time. All kinds of political issues were discussed.

I don't remember rejecting the values of my family, which I suppose you would call redneck, but working for peace and justice issues seemed to me natural and right and proper. When people say to me, "How do you happen to be in the peace movement?" it always seems to me the most ridiculous question because we've reached the point where this *should* be the normal thing for people to do. But still, war and preparation for war is normal, and to be in the peace movement is abnormal.

Women bring to the peace movement the best feminist qualities, which are patience, tolerance, compassion, and a hell of a lot of intelligence. We're much more loath to make judgments. We have the courage to change our minds. We're not nearly so reticent about admitting mistakes and changing course when we do wrong. Of course, there are aggressive women, but they are not the "norm" for women.

The women's movement activated a great many women, and it activated them on the issues of equality for women in jobs and the Equal Rights Amendment more than it did on the peace issues. For a long time we were trying to get to NOW to set up a peace platform. I have a speech I give on any occasion that peace is a woman's issue. My current speech, in case you would like to hear it, is that foreign policy must become a community issue, when in an administration, foreign policy is military policy. Military policy means a loss of our community services and ultimately a loss of our lives. We're in double jeopardy: if the weapons they're making are used, we'll all be dead, and meanwhile, the arms race is killing us economically. I'll stop my speech there.

Source 10 from a leaflet distributed at the Women's Pentagon Action in 1980 and published by the Women's Pentagon Action Group, Washington, D.C.

10. Unity Statement, Women's Pentagon Action, 1980

These are the frightening facts, and the hopeful ideas and feelings that are bringing women together. We invite you to read them.

We are gathering at the Pentagon on November 16 because we fear for our lives. We fear for the life of this planet, our Earth, and the life of the children who are our human future.

We are women who come in most part from the northeastern region of our United States. We are city women who know the wreckage and fear of city streets, we are country women who grieve the loss of the small farm and have lived on the poisoned earth. We are young and older, we are married, single, lesbian. We live in different kinds of households, in groups, families, alone; some are single parents.

We work at a variety of jobs. We are students-teachers-factory workers-office workers-lawyers-farmers-doctors-builders-waitresses-weavers-poets-engineers-homeworkers-electricians-artists-blacksmiths. We are all daughters and sisters.

We have come here to mourn and rage and defy the Pentagon because it is the workplace of the imperial power which threatens us all. Every day while we work, study, love, the colonels and generals who are planning our annihilation walk calmly in and out the doors of its five sides. They have accumulated over 30,000 nuclear bombs at the rate of three to six bombs every day.

They are determined to produce the billion-dollar MX missile. They are creating a technology called Stealth—the invisible, unperceivable arsenal. They have revived the cruel old killer, nerve gas. They have proclaimed Directive 59 which asks for 'small nuclear wars, prolonged but limited.' The Soviet Union works hard to keep up with United States initiatives. We can destroy each other's cities, towns, schools, children many times over. The United States has sent 'advisors,' money and arms to El Salvador and Guatemala to enable those juntas to massacre their own people.

The very same men, the same legislative committees that offer trillions of dollars to the Pentagon have brutally cut day care, children's lunches, battered women's shelters. . . .

The President has just decided to produce the neutron bomb, which kills people but leaves property intact.

There is fear among the people, and that fear, created by the industrial militarists is used as an excuse to accelerate the arms race. "We will protect you . . ." they say, but we have never been so endangered, so close to the end of human time.

We women are gathering because life on the precipice is intolerable.

We want to know what anger in these men, what fear which can only be satisfied by destruction, what coldness of heart and ambition drives their days.

We want to know because we do not want that dominance which is exploitative and murderous in international relations, and so dangerous to women and children at home—we do not want that sickness transferred by the violent society through the fathers to the sons. . . .

We want an end to the arms race. No more bombs. No more amazing inventions for death.

Source 11 from Coretta Scott King, "The Judgement of History Will Show," speech given at the International Women's Conference for Peace and Nuclear Disarmament (1984), and published in the Newsletter of the Center for Defence Information, vol. 13, no. 8. CDI is located at 1779 Massachusetts Avenue, NW, Washington, DC 20036, <www.cdi.org>

11. Coretta Scott King on Women and the Nuclear Arms Race, 1984

[*Coretta Scott King (b. 1927), the widow of Dr. Martin Luther King, Jr., is a civil rights activist and has been an active member of WILPF since 1960. She is president of the Martin Luther King, Jr., Center for Non-Violent Social Change.*]

You can't fight poverty and discrimination, you can't provide health, security and decent housing, and you can't have a clean environment in the lengthening shadow of nuclear arsenals. The nuclear arms race creates far-reaching social problems in a number of ways. The judgement of history will show that the massive economic insecurity and the psychological numbing and alienation caused by militarization of commerce and society have had a profound effect upon our lives. The proliferation of nuclear weapons is not only the major threat to the survival of humanity; it is also the primary cause of poverty and economic stagnation around the world. The arms race is a shameful theft of funds from programs that would enrich our planet. Here in America, the cost of one bomber could pay for two fully equipped hospitals. With a serious arms control program (not just shallow treaties for show which allow weapons to continue to proliferate less noticed by the public than before), the nations of the world could apply countless billions of dollars saved to advancing social and economic progress.

The supporters of the nuclear arms race claim that peace can only be achieved through strength. Apparently, they mean an ability to destroy the world an infinite number of times. We must ask just what it is that makes the nation safe and secure. If we ruin our economy to engage in an accelerated arms race, are we really any stronger? When we demoralize and polarize millions of jobless, homeless and impoverished Americans, it seems to me that we are dangerously weak at the very fabric of our society. In this sense, the nuclear arms race breeds insecurity, not strength.

Sources 12 and 13 from Lynne Jones, ed., Keeping the Peace: A Women's Peace Handbook *(London: The Women's Press, 1983), pp. 23, 24, 25–26; pp. 64–67. Reprinted by permission of Lynne Jones.*

12. Nottingham Women Oppose the Nuclear Threat (WONT) on Working as a Group, 1981

Nottingham WONT started as a women's group against nuclear power. . . .

As our group has evolved, another motive for meeting as women on the nuclear issue has become important—that is, the need to develop a specifically feminist analysis of nuclear threat, and to show the links between women's oppression and nuclear technology. We feel that feminism has a particular analysis of the structures and causes of all violence (not just the "women's issues" of sexual and domestic violence), and of the changes necessary to remove it. We identify the primary source of violence as gender structure in the individual, in families, in societies, and believe that while society remains deeply sexist, no peace movement can win long-term substantial victories.

We don't think that women have a special role in the peace movement because we are "naturally" more peaceful, more protective, or more vulnerable than men. Nor do we look to women as the "Earth Mothers" who will save the planet from male aggression. Rather, we believe that it is this very role division that makes the horrors of war possible. The so-called masculine, manly qualities of toughness, dominance, not showing emotion or admitting dependence, can be seen as the driving force behind war; but they depend on women playing the opposite (but not equal) role, in which the caring qualities are associated with inferiority and powerlessness. So women's role in peacemaking should not be conciliatory but assertive, breaking out of our role, forcing men to accept women's ideas and organisation, forcing them to do their own caring. Women have for too long provided the mirrors in which men see their aggression as an heroic quality, and themselves magnified larger than life. Nuclear technology is built on the arrogance and confidence of mastery (over nature as over women) which this has fed. . . .

WONT groups are specifically feminist, so they could not by themselves constitute a broad-based mass women's anti-nuclear movement. Most of the women involved in WONT are also involved in the women's movement, and many have an "alternative life-style," living in shared households, not having a 'straight' job, etc. However, we want to reach all kinds of women, and to do this, we have tried giving talks to women's groups, running workshops, doing street theatre, etc. Our aim is to help create a broad-based women's peace movement of which WONT would be an autonomous part. . . . Our approach to actions is close to that of the nonviolent direction action wing of the national movement, and we use street theatre, striking symbolic actions, and music, rather than mass demonstrations and rallies.

WONT is a decentralised organisation. Local groups are autonomous and very varied. WONT exists nationally through national gatherings once or twice a year, regional meetings, personal contacts and an occasional newsletter. There is a national contact address, and groups take turns at answering mail. We have a telephone tree for urgent messages. Nottingham WONT meets weekly, and we often see each other during the week as many of us live or work close to each other. (This creates problems for new women joining the group who are not in that particular community.) There are no "officers" but we take turns to facilitate. This means preparing an agenda, seeing that we stick to the point in discussions, are working reasonably efficiently, and that everyone gets a chance to contribute. It's an easy job in our group, for everyone is aware of these things; so the facilitator just had to be a bit more aware, to notice the time, to sense we are nearing a decision. We reach decisions by consensus. If we cannot reach a decision, it is usually because we are all unsure, rather than because different women hold irreconcilable views. We usually approach decisions by a general discussion, and then let each woman say what she thinks to see if there is general agreement. If one woman disagrees with a generally held view, then we try to see if any accommodation can be made to satisfy her as well. We will postpone a decision to another meeting if the discussion goes on a long time without getting anywhere

.

13. Tamar Swade on Nuclear
Weapons, 1983

[*Tamar Swade was an English antinuclear activist and the founder of Babies Against the Bomb.*]

Being pregnant and in the anti-nuclear movement happened at the same time for me. I joined a study group with five other women and we gave talks on nuclear power. This led to our writing the booklet, *Nuclear Resisters*.

By then my baby had been born and the effort of demand-feeding it at the same time as researching and writing my share of the booklet was enormous. The group was wonderfully supportive, but I felt that the pressures of coping with a newborn baby—the lack of sleep, exhaustion and lack of time—clashed with the needs of an ordinary group. I wasn't free to run off and collect things or proofread as the others were, and I could no longer get out easily in the evenings when the usual anti-nuclear/peace meetings take place.

I'd suddenly become a different kind of social being and I realised I needed to start a group where everybody understood my position because they were in it too, where it was fine to go "brrm-brrm" or "whoopsy!" to a child in the middle of a sentence if necessary, or change a nappy.

I found that I had joined a separate species of two-legged, four-wheeled creatures who carry their young in push-chair pouches, who emerge from their homes during the day to swarm the parks, forage in the super-markets and disappear without trace at nightfall. Occasionally some converged for a "coffee morning" or a mother-and-baby group run by the National Childbirth Trust. Here there was much discussion about nappy rash, (not) sleeping and other problems pertaining to the day-to-day survival of mother and infant.

If only these thousands of women could inform and organise themselves, what an untapped force for peace! Why not start a mother-and-baby group whose discussions included *long-term* survival?

At first, therefore, we were called "Mother and baby anti-nuclear group." As this was rather a mouthful, we were somehow gradually shortened to "Babies against the Bomb," which stayed with us. We meet during the day, with our babies or young children. Meetings are friendly and informal and we campaign wherever and however we feel we can be most effective.

Several women who have enquired about the group have never been involved in any campaigning at all, but the fact of having a child has made them think differently about the future. Those of us who had been involved before often feel an added urgency to our desire for peace after having a child.

There are some feminists who frown upon this attitude and I would like to answer them.

There is something utterly vulnerable and loveable about a newborn baby, something wholly fascinating about this creature whose every impulse is towards survival but who is so dependent for it upon others. Its cries wrench the heart and it is agonising to think of someone so little and blameless being hurt.

[317]

I am responsible for its existence—and no amount of word-juggling can get away from this. It is my responsibility and my urgent desire to ensure its survival, to speak for its rights since it can't do so for itself.

And it's not only for my child I feel this. The same feeling now extends to all children. Through my child the immorality of this world where people needlessly starve to death, has become intolerable. With pain I could not have known before, I grieve for those women in the Third World who hear their children crying for food but who can't feed them or themselves.

I know hundreds of women who feel this. Each of them in turn probably knows hundreds of others who feel the same. Some are feminists through and through, others don't know what "feminism" means. One woman told me that the mention of nuclear war conjures up the waking nightmare of her children burning. Another pictures kissing her children goodbye for the last time. A third said her particular nightmare was that the four-minute warning would come while she was at work and she wouldn't be able to cross town in time to get to them. . . .

In fact, it seems that millions of women in numerous cultures throughout history have had similar experiences in relation to their children. Should we all feel ashamed of this deep gut-feeling? For me, feminism is about choice, about every woman's freedom to feel and act and be valued. Does it make me any less of a person if my immediate, instinctive reaction to nuclear war is in my capacity as a mother? Judging by my friends in the campaign who are mothers, certainly not! Does it mean that I suddenly care less about living myself? Rubbish! It's more that another dimension had been added to my caring.

Our priority is peace. What does it matter how we come to want it? Let's be tolerant, supportive, sisterly. This will make us stronger and more effective; we are less likely to succeed if we are divided. If *we* can't do it, what hope is there for the rest of the world?

Sources 14 and 15 from Lynne Jones, ed., Keeping the Peace: A Women's Peace Handbook
(London: The Women's Press, 1983), p. 125; p. 19.

14. Poster for Families Against the Bomb Rally, 1982

15. Poster for a Multigroup Demonstration in Amsterdam Against the Installation of Cruise Missiles, 1981[6]

6. The main text reads "Against new atomic weapons in Europe."

Source 16 from Ann Snitow, "Holding the Line at Greenham Common: Being Joyously Political in Dangerous Times," Mother Jones, February/March 1985. © 1985, Foundation for National Progress.

16. Ann Snitow on Women Against Military Buildups, 1985

[*Ann Snitow (b. 1943) is an American writer who also teaches literature and women's studies.*]

Back in 1981 when I first heard about the women's peace camp at Greenham Common, I was impressed but a little worried, too. Here was a stubborn little band of squatters obstructing business as usual at a huge military base. But the early media reports celebrated these women as orderly housewives and mothers who would never make this vulgar noise just for themselves but were naturally concerned about their children, innocent animals, and growing plants.

My feminist reaction was: not *again*. I had joined the women's liberation movement in 1970 to escape this very myth of the special altruism of women, our innate peacefulness, our handy patience for repetitive tasks, our peculiar endurance—no doubt perfect for sitting numbly in the Greenham mud, babies and arms outstretched, begging men to keep our children safe from nuclear war.

We feminists had argued back then that women's work had to be done by men, too: no more "women only" when it came to emotional generosity or trips to the launderette. We did form women-only groups—an autonomous women's movement—but this was to forge a necessary solidarity for resistance, not to cordon off a magic femaleness as distorted in its way as the old reverence for motherhood. Women have a long history of allowing their own goals to be eclipsed by others, and even feminist groups have often been subsumed by other movements. Given this suspiciously unselfish past, I was uneasy with women-only groups that did not concentrate on overcoming the specific oppression of women.

And why should demilitarization be women's special task? If there's one thing in this world that *won't* discriminate in men's favor, it's a nuclear explosion. Since the army is a dense locale of male symbols, actions, and forms of association, let men sit in the drizzle, I thought; let *them* worry about the children for a change.

But even before going to Greenham I should have known better than to have trusted its media image. If the women were such nice little home birds, what were they doing out in the wild, balking at male authority, refusing to shut up or go back home? I've been to Greenham twice now in the effort to understand why many thousands of women have passed through the camps, why thousands are organized in support groups all over Britain and beyond, why thousands more can be roused to help in emergencies or show up for big actions.

What I discovered has stirred my political imagination more than any activism since that first, intense feminist surge 15 years ago. Though I still have many critical questions about Greenham, I see it as a rich source of fresh

[321]

thinking about how to be joyously, effectively political in a conservative, dangerous time. . . .

The Greenham women I talked to take great pains to point out that the purpose of Greenham is not to exclude men but to include women—at last. Though a few women there might still tell you women are biologically more peaceful than men, this view has been mostly replaced by a far more complex analysis of why women need to break with our old, private complicity with public male violence. No one at Greenham seems to be arguing that the always evolving Greenham value system is inevitably female. The women recognize their continuity with the Quakers, with Gandhi, with the entire pacifist tradition, and with the anarchist critique of the state. At the same time, women, the Greenham campers believe, may have a separate statement to make about violence because we have our own specific history in relation to it. . . .

. . . A woman's body lying down in a road in front of a missile launcher has a very different symbolic resonance for everyone from that of a male body in the same position. Greenham's radical feminist critics wonder just what kind of peace a female lying down can bring. Won't men simply allow women to lie in the mud forever because the demonstrators themselves only underline men's concept of what is female (passivity, protest, peace) and what is male (aggression, action, war)?

Before I came to Greenham, I shared these worries. But at Greenham at its best, women's nonviolent direct action becomes not another face of female passivity but a difficult political practice with its own unique discipline. The trick—a hard one—is to skew the dynamics of the old male-female relationships toward new meanings, to interrupt the old conversation between overconfident kings and hysterical, powerless jesters. This will surely include an acknowledgment of our past complicity with men and war making and a dramatization of our new refusal to aid and assist. (I think of a delicious young woman I heard singing out to a group of also very young soldiers: "We don't find you sexy anymore, you know, with your little musket, fife, and drum.")

Perhaps some of the new meanings we need will be found buried in the old ones. If women feel powerless, we can try to share this feeling, to make individual men see that they, too, are relatively powerless in the face of a wildly escalating arms race. Naturally, this is a message men resist, but the women at Greenham are endlessly clever at dramatizing how the army shares their impotence: The army cannot prevent them from getting inside the fence or shaking it down. It cannot prevent them from blockading the gates. It cannot prevent them from returning after each eviction.

Or, rather, it could prevent all this, but only by becoming a visibly brutal force, and this would be another kind of defeat, since the British armed services and police want to maintain their image of patriarchal protectors; they do not want to appear to be batterers of nonviolent women. Greenham women expose the contradictions of gender: by being women they dramatize powerlessness but they also disarm the powerful. . . .

[322]

Source 17 from Lynne Jones, ed., Keeping the Peace: A Women's Peace Handbook *(London: The Women's Press, 1983), pp. 98–101, 103–107.*

17. Leonie Caldecott, "The Shibokusa Women of Kita Fuji," 1983

[*Leonie Caldecott is an English writer, feminist, and peace activist; she is currently the associate director of the Centre for Faith and Culture in Oxford, England.*]

It was in winter—the sixth of December 1981—that I first met the Shibokusa women. It was also in an environment to which neither of us belonged: the teeming megalopolis of Tokyo. I had come to Japan, for the first time in my life, to address a Japanese women's peace rally about the European peace movement and women's initiatives within it. It also happened that this was the first major rally at which I had ever spoken. That it had been organised by women was very exciting to me. After the rally 2,500 of us marched through the towering, modern blocks of Tokyo's commercial district, behind a banner declaring: "We will not allow the way towards war!" As I marched in their midst, I felt like Gulliver in Lilliput—the only European and at least a head taller than most of them. Yet these proud, jubilant women chanting "No more Hiroshima! No more Nagasaki! No more Bikini!" and *Onnanatadé Héva!* ("Women for Peace!") more than made up for their lack of physical stature with their infectious sense of determination. At that point the Japanese peace movement had not yet reached its new peak (which resulted in nearly half a million people demonstrating in Tokyo six months later). I got the distinct impression that women had played a large part in keeping the movement alive during its bleak period.

This is hardly surprising when you look at the Shibokusa women. When they got up at the women's rally, dressed in traditional peasant cotton trousers and jacket and wide straw hat—four of them holding their banner and one of them delivering an impassioned, angry speech against the military—I almost jumped out of my seat. Next to their heart-felt and evident emotion, the rest of the speeches paled into insignificance. Excitedly, I asked Yumiko Jansson, who had translated my own speech into Japanese and was acting as my interpreter, who these women were. She explained that their land, which was at the north foot of Mount Fuji, was being used by the Japanese self-defence force (Japan is not supposed to have an army as such) for military exercises, and that some of the women in the area had established a resistance movement to protest against this. My mind's eye leapt out of the city to the foot of the mountain. I had to get up there and talk to those women. . . .

A taxi took us outside the town and down a dirt track through some woods, the mountain lying ahead of us. We soon came to the perimeter of the military base; right next to the gate leading into it, there was a cottage enclosed in a small compound. It is from here, said Mrs. Shimizu, that the Shibokusa women coordinate their resistance activities. . . .

As we walked into the compound where the cottage stood, I saw that the thatch on the roof had been covered with shiny sheets of corrugated metal. Mie Amano, noticing our inquiring glances, told us that right-wing groups had started harassing the women, gathering outside the cottage with taunts and cries of "go home you old witches!" throwing stones and burning brands. The women, afraid that the thatch would catch fire, had been forced to cover it. . . .

During the conversation that followed, I began to piece together the story of the Shibokusa women. The land which lay between the cottage and the mountain had been used by the local people since the Edo period—around the seventeenth century. This was called *Iriaiken,* the right of common people to cultivate and earn a living from a certain place—in this case the Shibokusa area. It was in fact rather poor land, but years of work had enabled them to grow beans and radish there, and even create a silkwork industry. Then in 1936, the militarisation of Japan came to disrupt the fragile prosperity of the community: the army began to execute drills on the Shibokusa land. After the war, the US army stationed troops on the site, which, say the Shibokusa women, led to a startling increase in prostitution in the area. "We women were treated like the dust on the ground," says Mie Amano. Even after the 1952 San Francisco Peace Treaty was signed between Japan and the US, the land was not released by the military. Finally on 20 June 1955, seventy farmers staged a protest on the Shibokusa land. "We were arrested as rioters," says Mie Amano, "but as they were taking us by jeep to Fuji Yoshida, the jeep crashed and the chief of police was killed. . . . It was an accident, but it drew attention to what we had been doing. Officials from Tokyo came and promised us another 50 hectares of land in compensation for some people who had lost their livelihood, and these people planted pine trees on it. Now that the trees are fully grown, the government claims it is state land again. Really, we are treated little better than slaves."

Because of the poverty of the land, men in the area have tended to go away to find work, leaving the subsistence-level cultivation to the women—all the more so since the loss of the Shibokusa area to the military. And so the women took over the struggle, building a series of cottages on or around the military base and occupying them, small bastions of ordinary life amid the soldiers' incessant preparations for death. The cottage I was sitting in, listening to their story with the hens pecking the ground outside and the steaming pot of green tea on the table, was the fifteenth one they had built.

In 1970, 1000 riot police turned up to evict a small group of women from one of these cottages. "We were determined to die rather than move," recalls Mie Amano. "We had dressed ourselves in the appropriate way to face death—all in white. Lots of people turned up, expecting to see bloodshed: we'd threatened to blow ourselves and the police up with some unexploded grenades we found on the base. But at the last minute Kimie Watanabe said

[324]

that in fact our dying would serve no purpose, and that if we remained alive we could go on resisting, building new cottages, not letting anyone forget about us. So we surrendered."

This was a crucial turning point. Once you have faced death and accepted it, but decided to go on living, many fears and anxieties lose their power over you. The Shibokusa women have, in a sense, nothing to lose, and this is what makes them strong. "Many people in the town have been bought off by the authorities," says Mie Amano. "They are comfortable and can't see anything wrong with the way this land is being used. They despise us and treat us with contempt. So we are not only struggling against the government and the military, but against attitudes which we have to confront every day. If there were not people in the outside world who supported us"—and here she bowed to Mrs Shimizu—"we should not be able to continue this fight. We also try to combat local corruption—making sure that people don't get bribed to vote a certain way in local elections, for instance."

The Shibokusa women make it their business to disrupt military exercises. In groups of up to ten, they make their way into the exercise area (there are a host of routes, they say, the secret of which they keep to themselves), crawling around the undergrowth and popping up in the middle of the firing. They plant scarecrows to decoy the troops. Sometimes they'll build a fire and sit round it singing and clapping their hands, totally ignoring officials who try to move them on. They are frequently arrested and taken to the police station. "They are quite gentle, because they are afraid of provoking us—they hate it when we start screaming, and the police have realised that though we are physically easier to arrest than men, we're more trouble afterwards! Men put up a fight, but once it's over they just give everything away. We never give our name, age or anything. We just say we're so old, we can't remember when we were born or who we are. . . ."

Indeed most of them are in their late fifties and sixties, or older. They say that by taking on the struggle themselves, they free younger women for child-rearing or other work. "If anything happens to us, it's not a disaster. The younger ones could soon take our place."

I asked Mie Amano what they hoped to achieve in the long run. She answered that it now went much deeper than the desire to get their land back. "As we carried on with our campaign, we realised that the whole phenomenon of militarism is violence against the land, wherever it takes place. So we are really a part of the wider anti-war movement. You see, Mount Fuji is the symbol of Japan. If they are preparing war on her flanks, how can they say Japan desires peace?"

Before leaving, I went outside the compound to take photographs and to gaze through the fence at the mountain. I felt as though I could never have my fill of that sight, and understood at last why Japanese artists have never tired of drawing it. One of the Shibokusa women tugged at my sleeve and pointed into the tall grass a little way from where we were standing. A Japanese soldier crouched there, taking photographs of us with a telescopic lens. I recalled the women in Tokyo pointing out two men taking photographs during the demonstration the week before, telling me they were not from the press. I had pointed my own camera at them, and the men had turned away, embarrassed. Now it didn't seem to matter. Let them know who we are, I thought, let us stand up and be counted. The women were laughing at the soldier. I noticed that Mie Amano's plump, tanned face was criss-crossed with laughter lines. She had a distinctly mischievous look about her.

"Don't imagine our lives are miserable," she said, nodding emphatically as Yumiko translated. "It's fun to make a nuisance of ourselves and embarrass those men. This work is our whole life—we enjoy every minute, but we're not lazy about it. This kind of long-term resistance is the first of its kind in Japan. We will continue it to the end. I have seen time and time again how Japanese men will not endure the worst: they have no patience, they give up or get violent, rather than sitting it out."

She folded her arms in her sleeves and faced the mountain. "This land used to be green, but they have destroyed so much vegetation with their explosions. . . . A lot of grass and bushes were also removed to prevent us having cover for our activities!"

I asked her whether there were ever moments when they felt it was hopeless. She thought for a minute and then replied.

"We are not clever, most of us have hardly been educated at all. But we are strong because we are close to the earth and we know what matters. Our conviction that the military is wrong is unshakeable." She waved her arm at the others, blinking their eyes in the winter sun, and laughed. "We are the strongest women in Japan! And we want other women to be like us."

I too laughed, and we bowed to one another, Japanese style. It was much more than a polite formality. I salute your spirit, sister, mother, warrior against war.

QUESTIONS TO CONSIDER

As you read and look at the sources, you need to keep in mind the historical context in which the women were writing, and think how this influenced their ideas and plans for action. Source 1 was written in 1911, before women in most U.S. states or any European country (except Finland) had the vote and before the outbreak of World War I. How might these factors have affected Olive Schreiner's views of what would happen when women gained a political voice? To what does she attribute gender differences in attitudes toward war?

Sources 2 and 3 both date from 1915. The outbreak of World War I was accompanied by intense nationalistic and anti-German rhetoric and demonstrations, first in England and later in the United States. How might this have shaped Maude Royden's and Jane Addams's views about whether women were "naturally" more peaceful?

Both Schreiner and Addams comment on a woman's role as a mother to explain the source of women's dislike of war; what differences do you see in the two authors on this point?

Sources 4 and 5 date from 1919 and 1935, after the end of World War I and as women in some countries were being given the right to vote. In Source 4, what does Crystal Eastman hope will be the focus of women's political activities? Why does she feel the Women's Peace conference at The Hague was important? What makes the women's peace movement distinctive, in her opinion? How does this differ from the ideas of Schreiner and Addams about why women are particularly interested in peace? In Source 5, what does Huda Sha'rawi view as the cause of war? In the quotation she cites from Mrs. Ashby, what actions does she suggest women should do for peace? Why does she view Western women as particularly responsible in terms of these issues?

Source 6 is the first visual source for this chapter, a woodcut created by the German artist Käthe Kollwitz shortly after World War I. Kollwitz lost her son in that war, and though she had been a supporter of German aims at the beginning of the war, by its end she was joining antiwar demonstrations and promoting pacifism. She produced numerous images in the 1920s and 1930s that were later used by various peace groups on posters and pamphlets, including this one, entitled *The Sacrifice*. How does this fit with the ideas expressed in the written sources about mothers' response to war?

With Source 7, we jump ahead to the antinuclear movement. Source 7 is an interview with Miyako Shinohara, a Japanese woman involved with Soko Gakkai, a Buddhist movement that emphasizes community, understanding, and peace. Sources 8 and 9 come from oral interviews with two of the women who started Women Strike for Peace, Dagmar Wilson and Madeline Duckles. Unlike Sources 1 through 5, which are speeches and position papers, Sources 7, 8, and 9 are oral histories produced long after the events they describe. What drew these women into working for peace? What do they see as distinctive about women's involvement in peace groups? Sources 8 and 9 refer explicitly to the types of actions WSP was involved in; how were these shaped by the fact that this was a women's peace group? How was the response these actions generated on the part of political officials shaped by the gender of those who took part? By their status as middle-class women and mothers? How do the organizational structures and methods of making decisions in WSP make it different from other political groups? How is this—at least in Wilson's eyes—related to the fact that this is a women's group?

Sources 10 through 13 are again statements of individuals or groups, written in the early 1980s to describe their motivations, aims, and methods of action. Source 10 is the "Unity Statement" for the Women's Pentagon Action, written in 1980 by Grace Paley in consultation with many others. What does it say has motivated women to action? Source 11

[327]

comes from a speech given by Coretta Scott King at an International Women's Conference for Peace and Nuclear Disarmament. These two sources are implicit rather than explicit in their connection between the arms race and what have traditionally been considered "women's concerns." How do they link these? The audiences for these statements were predominantly women; how might their arguments have been shaped by this?

Source 12 is the official statement of Women Opposed to the Nuclear Threat in Nottingham, England. What does it view as the reason for women's special role in the peace movement? What other issues does it link with a control of the arms race? What actions does Nottingham WONT undertake, and how does it view these as shaped by the gender of its members? How does its organizational structure and decision-making process compare to that of WSP? To other organizations with which you are familiar?

Source 13 is a statement from Tamar Swade, the founder of Babies Against the Bomb. How would you compare her motivation and the way this group was founded with that of Dagmar Wilson and WSP? How would you compare her views about motherhood as a motivation for peace work with those of Olive Schreiner in Source 1? Why do you feel these views led to her being criticized, and what is her answer to this criticism?

Sources 14 and 15 are posters from two demonstrations organized by women's peace groups against the installation of the Cruise and Pershing II missiles in Europe, scheduled

for 1983. How do the images in the posters differ in their depiction of women responding to the nuclear threat? How do they fit with the ideas you have read of the various individuals and groups?

Sources 16 and 17 are in some ways oral history in the making; that is, they are discussions by women interested in peace issues about their encounters with other women involved in actions protesting military buildups. They can thus be the raw material for an oral history of the *author's* development as a peace activist, or for a history of the women's encampments at Greenham Common in England and Shibokusa in Japan based on oral interviews. Therefore, you will need to pay attention to a variety of things at once as you read these: the actions that the women activists undertake; the reasons they give for these actions; the way in which they see these actions as shaped by the fact that they are women; the way in which the author explains the women's motivations; the interplay between the author and the women she is speaking with. As you would when evaluating any oral history (or actually any history at all), you need to think about how the author's preconceptions might have shaped her analysis. In these selections, the authors are fairly explicit about their opinions, making this issue perhaps easier to address here than it is in many studies in which the authors do not reveal their preconceptions and point of view.

You have now read and looked at a great many sources stretched out over seventy-five years, and can return to the central questions: How did twentieth-century women involved in women's peace groups view the relationship between their being women and their advocating peace? How did they translate their ideas into actions, and how did their ideas shape the types of actions they regarded as appropriate to achieving their aims?

EPILOGUE

The collapse of the Soviet Union and the end of the Cold War arms race marked another shift in focus for women's peace groups. Some of them ceased to be active, while others turned their attention to military spending worldwide and broader economic, social, and political concerns. WILPF, for example, at an international congress in 1986 adopted as its new program, "Toward a Nuclear-Weapon and Hunger-Free Twenty-first Century." This was not a completely new direction, of course, for we have seen the connection between military expenditures and economic hardship made in the writings of peace activists from earlier decades. Noting the continuing use of rape as a means of military coercion throughout the world, WILPF started an international campaign in 1990 to confront the issue of violence against women, not limiting this to rape but working against all forms of physical, economic, and political coercion. At the moment women's peace groups are not often the chief organizers of mass demonstrations or theatrical actions, but they are part of many such actions, such as those that opposed the Persian Gulf War in 1991 and those for victims of AIDS.

Other women involved in peace work have turned their attention to education, for example developing programs for kindergartners about how to resolve conflicts nonviolently and establishing peace studies programs at colleges and universities. More than two hundred campuses across the United States now have peace studies programs of some sort, and Syracuse University offers a Ph.D. in peace studies. A long-time peace activist with many groups, Rose Marciano Lucey, was one of the key forces in a citizens' lobby to establish a U.S. Peace Academy, approved by Congress in 1986. Should you wish to use this chapter as a springboard for further investigation, perhaps doing some oral history yourself, the peace studies program at your own or a nearby college or university would be a good place to start.

Just as women's peace groups are changing but still thriving, exploring gender differences in terms of peace and war remains a thriving industry. Public opinion polls have discovered what they have labeled the "gender gap" in terms of support for military involvement; with respect to every engagement or contemplated engagement, women are consistently more opposed to war than men. Particularly during national elections, this

[329]

translates into votes for the candidate perceived to be less militarily aggressive, and, because more women than men vote, the gap in votes may be even wider than the gap in public opinion. This gap has not been wide enough, as Olive Schreiner hoped, to "herald the death of war as a means of arranging human differences," but it is something contemporary women peace activists note they will be looking to in the future. At the same time, some feminist groups and many individual women favor an increased role for women in combat, supporting Maude Royden's words that "the belief that women are innately more pacific than men has been severely shaken." The connection between feminism and pacifism continues to be a complex and debated issue.

CHAPTER ELEVEN

THE PERILS OF PROSPERITY: THE UNREST OF

YOUTH IN THE 1960s

Commuters just emerging from subway exits in the university district of Paris on the evening of Friday, May 3, 1968, must have been bewildered. They stepped out into a neighborhood transformed since morning into a war zone in which police and students battled over the future of France's governmental and economic systems. These commuters witnessed a conflict in which French students, like students in many other countries in 1968, called into question a material prosperity purchased, in their view, with a loss of individual liberty in the face of the power of the modern state and giant industrial concerns.

The postwar Western world indeed was experiencing unprecedented prosperity by the late 1960s. The United States enjoyed the world's highest living standard. In Western Europe, the European Economic Community (or EEC), also called the Common Market, served as a key

instrument for economic recovery and growth for war-ravaged France, West Germany, Italy, Belgium, the Netherlands, and Luxembourg. Non-EEC countries, including Great Britain and the Scandinavian nations, also shared in this economic success. Even in communist Eastern Europe, war damage was repaired and the socialist economies of the region produced standards of living for their peoples substantially improved over those of the early postwar years.

Behind the façade of material success, however, were a number of problems that led to widespread unrest, especially among the young, in the 1960s. Workers were uncertain about the security of their jobs in an economy undergoing rapid change, and students were dissatisfied with the structure and content of higher education. In both western and eastern Europe, workers' and students' groups advocated radical change, and sought to sway public opinion to their side. These campaigns were most dramatic in France and Czechoslovakia, and these two countries will be the focus of our research in this chapter. In both countries, government controls of the media made gaining support for change more difficult. In France, the radio and television systems were state-controlled; in Czechoslovakia, the regime controlled not only electronic media but the press as well. Your problem in this chapter is to analyze events in France and Czechoslovakia in 1968 by examining the materials issued by those who sought to rally support for change. Deprived of media controlled by the political establishment, proponents of change issued leaflets, posters, and cartoons designed to win support. What aspects of the modern state and economy provoked the events of 1968? What vision of the future did the leaders of the French and Czechoslovakian movements embrace? How did they propose to achieve it?

BACKGROUND

Part of the basis for discontent and demand for change may be found in the very economic success of the postwar period. Several Western countries, including France and Great Britain, encouraged growth by government intervention in the economy or national ownership of industries. The economic life of Communist Eastern Europe, of course, was entirely under government control. The result was a growing state economic bureaucracy in which the individual had little voice. The nature of the economic growth was unsettling, too. The West was entering a new phase of industrialization. New and sophisticated industries, such as computers and electronics, flourished; the service sector of the economy grew while older heavy industries declined in importance. The result was deep concern among many workers, who found little demand for their traditional skills and who felt powerless to avoid unemployment or underemployment. Worker dissatisfaction with the existing system only increased with economic recessions like that of 1968 in France, which added to unemployment and reduced the buying power of those who retained their jobs. Economic growth, for many, was not an unqualified success.

Many European students were dissatisfied with the system of higher education. A partial reason may be found in the West's great population growth after World War II. The postwar baby boom of 1946–1964, which affected both Europe and America, coincided with a prosperity that permitted Western democracies to provide their youth with greater educational opportunity than had been offered any earlier generation. In two decades student populations vastly increased. From 1950 to 1970, university enrollments increased from 123,000 to 651,000 in France; from 190,000 to 561,000 in Italy; from 117,000 to 410,000 in West Germany; and from 67,200 to 250,000 in Great Britain.[1] But often the quality of the educational experience declined as the system strained to cope with un-

1. B. R. Mitchell, ed., *European Historical Statistics*, abridged ed. (New York: Columbia University Press, 1978), pp. 396–400.

precedented enrollments. University faculty and facilities failed to grow as fast as their student bodies, resulting in crowded lecture halls and student-faculty ratios that went as high as 105 to 1 in Italy and rendered professors inaccessible to students.

Other problems also affected the student population. University curricula often provided a traditional education that did little to prepare a student to succeed in the new service-oriented economy. When European governments decreed half-hearted curriculum reforms to respond to economic change, they often, as in France, extended a student's course of study. The university also seemed divorced from the real problems of society, such as poverty and crime, a fact reflected in the rarity of sociology courses dealing with those problems.

These curricular problems and the impersonal nature of the modern university led to student demands for sweeping change in the educational establishment. The students wished a voice in the decisions that affected them. They increasingly demanded a say in what was taught, who taught, and how the universities were administered. As we will see, such demands also reflected the feelings of many nonstudents who bitterly felt their inability to affect the modern institutions that controlled their lives.

Students of the 1960s were disappointed and angered by educational shortcomings, but they were even more frustrated by their inability to effect political change. The student generation of the 1960s was physically more mature than any previous generation, thanks to improved nu-trition. Their sense of adulthood was heightened by the spread of techniques of birth control that freed women from the fear of pregnancy outside of marriage and fostered a youthful revolt against traditional sexual mores. That revolt could have political ramifications; a slogan frequently heard among French students in 1968 was: "Every time I make love I want to make the revolution; every time I make the revolution I want to make love." But these self-consciously mature young people could change little around them. Everywhere, those under twenty-one were eligible for military service but had no right to vote. Nor had students even a voice in their universities' governance. Typically, European governments controlled universities through centralized bureaucracies. In France, for example, such minor events as student dances had to be approved by the Ministry of Education.

Yet for all the dissatisfaction among students and workers, traditional twentieth-century political ideologies offered scant appeal. The cold war had polarized Europe for twenty years, and neither of the opposing doctrines—Russian communism or the democratic capitalism of the United States—offered real answers to student demands. Indeed, in a political sense both doctrines increasingly lost credibility for students. For some, the democratic ideals of the United States no longer seemed attractive because of that nation's increasingly unpopular war in Vietnam. Many saw that Southeast Asian conflict, which engaged about 500,000 American servicemen by 1968, as a war to uphold a favored minority in South Vietnam through military involvement. Those who looked toward a communist vision of a better world similarly were disappointed. The Soviet Union, with its regimented society, inefficient economy, and forceful crushing of dissent in its East German, Polish, and Hungarian satellites in the 1950s, was hardly the best advertisement for Marxian socialism.

Ideological disillusionment led a minority of students to radical doctrines rejecting orthodox Marxism as well as liberal democracy. The ideas of Leon Trotsky, a Marxist who rejected the need for a bureaucracy in a socialist state, attracted some. The example of Mao Zedong, the Chinese revolutionary, stirred other students to reject all authority and to attempt to rally working people to the cause of revolutionary change. Still others were attracted by nineteenth-century anarchist thought that rejected any hierarchy of control over the individual. Some also found inspiration in the revolutionary activism of Cuba's Fidel Castro and Che Guevara. Common to all was the belief that the institutions of society favored the rich, manipulated the poor, and substituted materialism bred of postwar economic growth for individual liberty and any high-minded questioning of the established order. Everywhere student demands could be summed up as calls for participation by individuals in all the decisions that shaped their lives, a concept that French students labeled *autogestion.*

Whatever their ideology, student radicals sought confrontation with established governmental and educational authority in the hope of garner-

ing a mass following for change among the nonrevolutionary majority of students, workers, and others. The radicals increasingly found student followers in many countries. Unrest due to the Vietnam War was widespread on campuses in the United States from the mid-1960s. In Europe, riots began in Italy in 1965 at the universities of Milan and Trento as students demanded a voice in academic policy. Italian unrest continued into the late 1960s, when student radicals combined ideas for a complete overthrow of traditional society with their demands for educational change. Incidents rooted in the desire for political change were common to German and British universities, too. In most of these countries, however, youthful radicals generated little support beyond their campuses. France was the only Western European country in which youthful unrest spread beyond students and thus threatened the existence of the government.

In 1968 France had been led for ten years by President Charles de Gaulle, the seventy-eight-year-old hero of World War II whose imperial style of government only increased the extreme state centralization traditional in that country. Significantly, too, France was suffering an economic recession that heightened the discontent of many workers. Problems began at the new Nanterre campus of the University of Paris. Placed amid slums housing immigrant workers, this modern university center seemed to radicals a dramatic illustration of the failings of modern consumer society. Led by the anarchist Daniel Cohn-Bendit in a protest of university regulations, Nanterre students forced the closing of their campus in the spring of 1968.

Nanterre radicals next focused their attention on the main campus of the University of Paris, at the Sorbonne, after university authorities had begun disciplinary action against Cohn-Bendit and others on May 3, 1968. As police removed protesting student radicals from the Sorbonne, antipolice violence erupted among crowds of students around the university. The very appearance of the police on university grounds provoked student anger. University confines were normally beyond the jurisdiction of the police, who had last entered the Sorbonne in 1791. The crowd threw rocks and, more dangerously, the heavy cobblestones of Paris streets. Police beat students brutally, and the broadcast of such scenes on the evening television news generated widespread support for the radicals, who now demanded a change in France's government.

For the next two weeks, the university district of Paris was the scene of street fighting between police and students that drew on the traditions of a Paris that had often defied government in the past.[2] Ominously for the government, the student unrest spread to other parts of society. On May 13, 1968, unions scheduled a twenty-four-hour general strike to protest police brutality, despite the opposition of the large French Communist party, which feared the unorthodoxy of the spreading revolt. On May 14 workers began to occupy factories and to refuse to work, the young among them demanding, like the students, a voice in decisions affecting them. For other workers, improved wages were a demand. Within a week, perhaps as many as 10 million workers nationwide had seized their factories and were on strike. Even professionals in broadcasting, sports, and other fields joined the strike. The country was paralyzed, and the government seemed on the brink of collapse as opposition leaders began to discuss alternative regimes.

As the government faltered, both sides in the confrontation clearly saw the significance of the growing revolt. Cohn-Bendit characterized it as "a whole generation rising against a certain sort of society—bourgeois society." A leader of the establishment, France's Prime Minister Georges Pompidou, defined the revolt as one against modern society itself. Even the authoritarian de Gaulle heard the message, conceding on May 19, "Reform yes, anarchy no."[3]

Prime Mister Pompidou began to defuse the crisis by offering wage increases to the striking unions. Faced with destroying the consumer society or enjoying more of its benefits, many striking workers quickly chose the

---

2. Students fought much as Parisians had in the eighteenth and nineteenth centuries, tearing up paving stones and piling them with overturned vehicles and fallen trees to create street barricades from behind which they fought police. When the student revolt ended, the government paved cobblestone streets with asphalt.

3. In the present context, *anarchy* is probably the best English word to convey briefly what de Gaulle meant. De Gaulle probably sought a certain effect by using an army colloquialism, *chien lit*, which even the French press had difficulty expressing adequately. It means making "a mess in one's own bed"; in other words, "fouling one's own nest."

latter option. Then, on May 29, de Gaulle flew to West Germany, assured himself of the support of French army units stationed there in case of the need of force, and returned to Paris to end the crisis. Addressing the nation on radio the next day, the president refused to resign as the protesters demanded and instead dissolved the National Assembly, calling for new elections to that body. The maneuver saved the government's cause. The protesters could not call repressive a government that was willing to risk its control of the legislature in elections called ahead of schedule. Although student radicals tried to continue the revolt, most workers accepted proffered pay increases and new elections and returned to work. De Gaulle's supporters won a majority of the seats in the National Assembly on June 23, 1968, and the president retained the power to govern.

As students and workers battled police in France, equally dramatic events were moving to a climax across Europe in Czechoslovakia. Although unrest in democratic France and one-party Czechoslovakia displayed differences, the revolts in both countries had common roots in a rejection of highly centralized and unresponsive authority.

Czechoslovakia, an industrialized country with Western democratic traditions, experienced a coup in 1948 that established a communist government. The leaders of that regime, party First Secretaries Klement Gottwald (1948–1953) and Antonín Novotný (1953–1968) were steadfast followers of authoritarian Stalinist

communism, even though the Soviet Union itself began a process of "de-Stalinization" after 1956. But by 1967 Novotný's style of communism was becoming increasingly unacceptable to Czechoslovakians in two chief regards. The most basic problem concerned the nation's two largest ethnic groups: the Czechs and the Slovaks. For a long time the Slovaks had been unhappy with Czech domination of both the Communist party and the state apparatus. The Novotný regime perpetuated this Czech domination as the Slovaks clamored for a stronger voice in national affairs.

Even more fundamental than the regime's ethnic difficulties, however, was its rigid and authoritarian Stalinist communism. Economically, this meant a managed economy, oriented toward heavy industrial goods rather than consumer items, that was hampered by centralized control, no profit motive, and low productivity. The nation had experienced serious economic problems since 1962. Politically, Novotný's government gave the country rigid control by a small party inner circle sustained by a secret police, press censorship, and extreme curbs on intellectual freedom.

A series of events led to change in Czechoslovakia through the efforts of the younger generation of party officials, intellectuals, and students. As in France, loss of support for the regime began among those who were being groomed in the educational system as future leaders, not with the materially deprived. Pressure for change in the country's highest leadership mounted as Novotný's authoritarian style of government resisted reform and economic problems persisted.

In 1963 the Slovak branch of the Communist party named a new First Secretary, the reform-minded Alexander Dubcek. In a country where literature long had been politicized, writers began to desert the regime; at the Congress of Czechoslovak Writers in June 1967, they demanded an end to censorship and freedom for their craft. Other intellectuals also grew restive with the regime. But, as in France, it was young people who brought matters to a crisis point. Cries of "We want freedom, we want democracy" and "A good communist is a dead communist" punctuated traditional student May Day observances in 1966 and resulted in arrests by policemen whom the students called "Gestapo," after the Nazi security police. The government responded forcefully, expelling from the universities and drafting into the army leaders of student organizations who had called for more freedom. Nonetheless, opposition to the Novotný regime not only continued but increased, especially after the events of October 31, 1967. On that night, as on numerous previous occasions, an electrical failure left the large complex of student dormitories in Prague, the capital, without light. Students took up candles and began a procession chanting "We want light," a phrase that could indicate far more than their need for electric power. The brutal acts of the police in confronting the students outraged public opinion, thus strengthening reform elements in the party's Central Committee sufficiently for them to gain a majority in that body. On January 5, 1968, the reformers replaced Novotný with the Slovak Alexander Dubcek as first secretary of the national Communist party. On March 22, 1968, war hero Ludvik Svoboda replaced Novotný as president of the nation. A bloodless revolution had occurred in Prague.

The spring of 1968 was an exhilarating one for the people of Czechoslovakia. Dubcek announced his intention to create "socialism with a human face," a socialism that would allow "a fuller assertion of the personality than any bourgeois democracy," a socialism that would be "profoundly democratic." Rigid press censorship ended, as did other controls on the individual. But Dubcek soon found himself in a difficult position. Permitted freedom of expression for the first time in twenty years, Czechoslovaks demanded far more, including even a free political system with a role for noncommunist parties. Such developments, however, threatened neighboring communist dictatorships in East Germany and Poland and risked depriving the Soviet Union of strategically located Czechoslovakia in its Warsaw Pact alliance system.

On August 21, after having watched developments in Prague for months with growing alarm, the Soviet Union acted. Troops from the Soviet Union, East Germany, Hungary, Poland, and Bulgaria entered Czechoslovakia. In the largest movement of troops in Europe since 1945, they forcibly ended the "Prague Spring" experiment.

[337]

The Soviets were met with widespread passive nationalist resistance. The majority of the population seemed to wish continuation of reform, but earlier unrest in Eastern Europe, as in the failed Hungarian revolt of 1956, had demonstrated the futility of civilians' active opposition to Soviet arms. Students again took part in resistance, however, and two, Jan Palach and Jan Zajíc, burned themselves alive in early 1969 in protest. Force prevailed, however, and Soviet pressure assured the gradual replacement of Dubček and his reform leadership with men more subservient to Moscow's wishes. Soviet party First Secretary Leonid Brezhnev announced that events in Czechoslovakia represented an expression of what came to be called the "Brezhnev Doctrine"—that is, the Soviet Union's policy to act against any threat to the stability of an East European communist regime.

THE METHOD

Modern political causes seek to mobilize support in various ways. Because posters, pamphlets, and other publications as well as simple slogans scrawled on walls all aim to energize support for a movement by publicizing its ideas, analyzing such materials provides a broad understanding of the goals and methods of any cause. In this chapter we have assembled two groups of evidence, one relating to the French disorders and the other to the Czechoslovakian reform movement of 1968.

Let us consider the French evidence first. Source 1 is a pamphlet distributed to striking workers by the March 22 Movement, a student group whose name commemorated the student upheaval at the Nanterre campus. It appeared on May 21, 1968. What were the students' goals for the future society and economy of France? What were the aims of workers in their strike? How did student leaders try to unify student and worker causes in this pamphlet? Source 2, a leaflet that appeared on May 22, 1968, was issued by a number of student and worker groups. Consider the views expressed here about President de Gaulle, the government, and the economy. Would the authors have been satisfied only with the departure of de Gaulle from the political scene? What do you deduce from their refusal of "summit negotiations" with government and management? To whom does the leaflet appeal? What vision of the future does it advocate?

You must analyze the language of Source 3 to understand the message it seeks to convey. This is a list of slogans that the student Sorbonne Occupation Committee suggested to its followers on May 16, 1968. Note the locations proposed for such slogans. The one advocating the end of bureaucrats was painted across a large mural in the Sorbonne administration building. How did this and some of the other suggested locations reflect student attitudes toward authority? Now turn to the words themselves. Slogans are important in politics; the simpler they are, the more easily they can be spread to influence large numbers of people. Each side of the 1968 confrontations sought to dismiss the validity of the other's ideas by extreme and often inaccurate name calling. In France as well as in the United States and other countries, students referred to policemen as "pigs" or "fascists." French students' chants of "CRS—SS!" likened the riot police, the CRS (*Compagnies Républicaines de Securité*), to the Nazi SS (*Schutz Staffeln* or security echelon, whose insignia resembled a sharp double S). The students' opponents responded in kind, often calling them "commies." What views of their opponents do the students convey in these slogans? What sort of society do they advocate? What methods do they advocate for their cause?

With the French Sources 4 through 12, you must analyze pictorial attempts to mobilize opinion. The artists conveyed these messages graphically in pictures, with a minimum of words. Here you must ascertain the nature of the message and the goals of the students and workers.

The visual evidence is of several types. In 1968 posters appeared all over the university district of Paris in defiance of long-standing laws against posters on public buildings. Often they were fairly sophisticated in execution because many advanced art students put their skills in the service of the May revolt. The political cartoon also flourished in a number of new radical publications in Paris. The cartoons presented here originated in *L'enragé* ("The Mad-

man"), a publication that consisted entirely of cartoons critical of established authority in France.

Cartoons and posters often magnify the physical characteristics of public figures, sometimes to ridicule but also to make perfectly clear the subject of the message. Thus you will find the prominent nose of President de Gaulle quite exaggerated, as well as certain poses. De Gaulle often embellished his speeches by raising both arms, the same gesture he used when leading the singing of the national anthem, *La Marseillaise*, a frequent occurrence after a public address. This pose is duplicated in the cartoons and posters along with his uniform of a French general, complete with the cylindrical cap known as a *kepi*, making him instantly recognizable. Artists further identified de Gaulle by including in their pictures the Cross of Lorraine, the symbol of his World War II resistance movement, with its two transverse bars.

In analyzing the material, remember that political posters and cartoons, though based on real events, are not intended to report those occurrences accurately. They are meant instead to affect public opinion. By carefully examining the posters and cartoons, you can discover the artists' views of events and how they wished to sway public opinion. What action does each picture represent? What message is the artist trying to convey? What reaction does he or she wish to evoke in viewers? What do the pictures tell you about the participants, methods, and aspirations of the French movement?

Now let us examine the Czechoslovakian sources. The Czechoslovakian writings should be examined with the same methods you applied to the French. Source 13 is a tract that circulated illegally in Czechoslovakian literary circles as early as April 1967 and was republished in a Prague student publication in March 1968. Notice first the use of language. What effect do the authors seek in condemning their opponents as "knaves"? What view does the statement as a whole express toward established ideologies, both Soviet Marxist and U.S. capitalist? What methods for change are advocated? Did young Czechoslovakians follow the course of action recommended in the tenth commandment? Why should the intellectuals, students, and professors be the leaders in change?

Source 14 is an extract from a statement that appeared in an influential publication, *Literární Listy* (*Literary Papers*), the journal of the Czechoslovakian Writers' Union. *Literární Listy* was the chief forum in 1968 in which intellectuals expressed their views on reform. It had a large circulation (300,000 copies in June 1968), and it published the manifesto for change, "Two Thousand Words." Source 14 appeared on March 5, 1968, as one of a number of replies to the question of the nation's political future posed by the editors: "Wherefrom, with Whom, and Whither?" The answer reprinted here was made by Ivan Sviták, a philosophy professor and reform leader. Notice his choice of language. Who, in his view, was the enemy of change? How does he characterize these people? What sort of social and political system did Czechoslovakian intellectuals seek?

Sources 15 through 20 are cartoons drawn from *Literární Listy* and its successor, *Listy*. Use the same methods of analysis here as you employed with the French posters and cartoons. You again will note exaggeration of certain physical features to clarify the cartoon's message. Alexander Dubček had a large nose, as de Gaulle did, and it was exaggerated by Czechoslovak cartoonists, just as French artists exaggerated de Gaulle's nose.

The Czechoslovakian cartoonists represented here also used symbols to illuminate their messages. The Phrygian cap worn by the woman in Source 15, for example, represents revolution and liberty. Dubček is depicted in Source 16 as Jánašík, a legendary Slovak "Robin Hood." Source 19 shows the Soviet president Leonid Brezhnev as Saint Florian. Old statues of this saint stand in many Czechoslovakian villages because he was thought to offer protection from fire.

Using the analytical methods described here, you should be able to answer the central questions of this chapter: What aspects of the modern state and economy provoked the events of 1968? What vision of the future did leaders of the French and Czechoslovakian movements embrace? How did they propose to achieve it?

FRANCE

Sources 1 through 3 from Vladimir Fišera, editor, Writing on the Wall, May 1968: A Documentary Anthology *(London: Allison & Busby, 1978), pp. 133–134; p. 137; pp. 125–126.*

1. The March 22 Movement, "Your Struggle Is Our Struggle," May 21, 1968

We are occupying the faculties, you are occupying the factories. Aren't we fighting for the same thing? Higher education only contains 10 percent workers' children. Are we fighting so that there will be more of them, for a democratic university reform? That would be a good thing, but it's not the most important. These workers' children would just become like other students. We are not aiming for a worker's son to be a manager. We want to wipe out segregation between workers and management.

There are students who are unable to find jobs on leaving university. Are we fighting so that they'll find jobs, for a decent graduate employment policy? It would be a good thing, but it is not vital. Psychology or sociology graduates will become the selectors, the planners and psychotechnicians who will try to organise your working conditions; mathematics graduates will become engineers, perfecting maximum-productivity machines to make your life even more unbearable. Why are we, students who are products of a middle-class life, criticising capitalist society? The son of a worker who becomes a student leaves his own class. For the son of a middle-class family, it could be his opportunity to see his class in its true light, to question the role he is destined for in society and the organisation of our society. We refuse to become scholars who are out of touch with real life. We refuse to be used for the benefit of the ruling class. We want to destroy the separation that exists between those who organise and think and those who execute their decisions. We want to form a classless society; your cause is the same as ours.

You are asking for a minimum wage of 1,000 francs in the Paris area, retirement at sixty, a 40-hour week for 48 hours' pay.

These are long-standing and just demands: nevertheless, they seem to be out of context with our aims. Yet you have gone on to occupy factories, take your managers as hostages, strike without warning. These forms of struggle have been made possible by perseverance and lengthy action in various enterprises, and because of the recent student battles.

[341]

These struggles are even more radical than our official aims, because they go further than simply seeking improvements for the worker within the capitalist system, they imply the destruction of the system. They are political in the true sense of the word: you are fighting not to change the Prime Minister, but so that your boss no longer retains his power in business or society. The form that your struggle has taken offers us students the model for true socialist activity: the appropriation of the means of production and of the decision-making power by the workers.

Our struggles converge. We must destroy everything that seeks to alienate us (everyday habits, the press, etc.). We must combine our occupations in the faculties and factories.

Long live the unification of our struggles!

2. "Producers, Let Us Save Ourselves," May 22, 1968

To ten million strikers, to all workers:

No to parliamentary solutions, with de Gaulle going and the bosses staying.

No to summit negotiations which give only a new lease of life to a moribund capitalism.

No more referenda. No more spectacles.

Don't let anybody speak for us. Maintain the occupation of all workplaces.

To continue the struggle, let us put all the sectors of the economy which are hit by the strike at the service of the fighting workers.

Let us prepare today our power of tomorrow (direct food-supplies, the organisation of public services: transport, information, housing, etc.).

In the streets, in the local committees, wherever we are, workers, peasants, wage-earners, students, teachers, school students, let us organise and coordinate our struggles.

FOR THE ABOLITION OF THE EMPLOYERS, FOR WORKERS' POWER.

3. Sorbonne Occupation Committee, Slogans to Be Circulated by Any Means, May 16, 1968

(leaflets—announcements over microphones—comics—songs—painting on walls—texts daubed over the paintings in the Sorbonne—announcements in the cinema during the film, or stopping it in the middle—texts written on the posters in the underground—whenever you empty your glass in the bistro—before making love—after making love—in the lift)

Occupy the factories.

Power to the workers' councils.

Abolish class society.

Down with a society based on commodity production and the spectacle

Abolish alienation.

An end to the university.

Mankind will not be happy until the last bureaucrat has been strung up by the guts of the last capitalist.

Death to the pigs.

Free the four people arrested for looting on 6 May.

THE ENEMY

Sources 4 through 8 from Bibliothèque Nationale de Paris, France, Les Affiches de Mai 68 ou
l'imagination graphique *(Paris: Bibliothèque Nationale, 1982), p. 64; p. 15; p. 9; p. 63; p. 47.*

4. Poster, May 1968

6. Poster: "Light Salaries, Heavy Tanks," May 1968

5. Poster: "Let Us Smash the Old Gears!," May 1968

7. Poster: "Beauty Is in the Street!" May 1968

LA BEAUTÉ

EST DANS LARUE

8. Poster: "Less than 21 Years of Age: Here Is Your Ballot!" May 1968

MOINS DE 21 ANS

voici votre bulletin de VOTE

Source 9 from Jean-Jacques Pauvert, editor, L'enragé: collection complète des 12 numéros introuvables, mai–novembre 1968 *(Paris: Jean-Jacques Pauvert, 1978).*

9. Cartoon, June 10, 1968

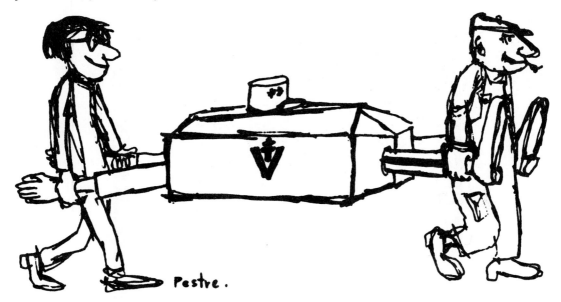

THE STUDENTS' VISION

Sources 10 and 11 from Bibliothèque Nationale de Paris, France, Les Affiches de Mai 68 ou
l'imagination graphique, *p. 10; p. 24.*

10. Cartoon: "Each One of Us Is the State," May 1968

L'ETAT C'EST CHACUN DE NOUS

11. Cartoon: "Popular Power," May 1968

THE STUDENTS IN DEFEAT

Source 12 from Jean-Jacques Pauvert, L'enragé: collection complète des 12 numéros introuvables, mai–novembre 1968 (Paris: Jean-Jacques Pauvert, 1978).

12. Cartoon, June 17, 1968

CZECHOSLOVAKIA

Sources 13 and 14 from Ivan Sviták, The Czechoslovak Experiment, 1968-1969 *(New York: Columbia University Press, 1971), pp. 17-18; p. 16.*

13. "Ten Commandments for a Young Czechoslovak Intellectual," March 1968

There are no more knaves than before; it is only that their field of activity is larger. . . . And so all of us are living in close collaboration with a few knaves.

LUDVÍK VACULÍK, in *Orientation*, 1967[4]

1. Do not collaborate with knaves. If you do, you inevitably become one of them. Engage yourself against the knaves.

2. Do not accept the responsibility forced upon you by the knaves for their own deeds. Do not believe such arguments as "we are all responsible," or the social problems touch "all of us," or "everyone has his share of guilt." Openly and clearly dissociate yourself from the deeds of the knaves and from arguments that you are responsible for them.

3. Do not believe any ideology that consists of systems of slogans and words which only speculate about your feelings. Judge people, political parties, and social systems concretely, according to the measure of freedom they give, and according to how tolerable the living conditions are. Judge them according to results, not words.

4. Do not solve only the narrow generational problems of youth; understand that the decisive problems are common to all human beings. You cannot solve them by postulating the demands of young men, but by vigorously defending the problems of all people. Do not complain about the privileges of one generation, but fight for human rights.

5. Do not consider the given social relations as constant. They are changing in your favor. Look forward. If you do not want to be wrong today, you must think from the point of view of the year 2000.

6. Do not think only as a Czech or a Slovak, but consider yourself a *European.* The world will sooner adapt to Europe (where Eastern Europe belongs) than to fourteen million Czechs and Slovaks. You live neither in America nor in the Soviet Union; you live in Europe.

---

4. **Ludvik Vaculik:** a novelist and one of the leaders of the Czechoslovakian reform movement; he also drafted the manifesto "Two Thousand Words."

7. Do not succumb to utopias or illusions; be dissatisfied and critical. Have the sceptical confidence of a negotiator, but have confidence in the purpose of your negotiations. The activity has its own value.

8. Do not be afraid of your task in history and be courageous in intervening in history. The social changes and transformations of man take place, no doubt, without regard to you, but to understand these changes and to influence them with the limited possibilities of an individual is far better than to accept the fatal inevitability of events.

9. Do not negotiate out of good motives alone; negotiate with sound arguments and with consideration of what you can achieve. A good deed can rise from a bad motive and vice versa. The motives are forgotten, but deeds remain.

10. Do not let yourself be *shot* in the fight between the interests of the power blocs. *Shoot* when in danger. Are you not in danger right now when you collaborate with the few knaves? Are you a knave?

14. Ivan Sviták, "Wherefrom, with Whom, and Whither?," March 5, 1968

From totalitarian dictatorship toward an open society, toward the liquidation of the power monopoly and toward the effective control of the power elite by a free press and by public opinion. From the bureaucratic management of society and culture by the "hard-line thugs" (C. Wright Mills)[5] toward the observance of fundamental human and civil rights, at least to the same extent as in the Czechoslovakia of bourgeois democracy. With the labor movement, without its *apparatchiks*;[6] with the middle classes, without their groups of willing collaborators; and with the intelligentsia in the lead. The intellectuals of this country must assert their claim to lead an open socialist society toward democracy and humanism.

---

5. **C. Wright Mills** (1916-1962): a Columbia University sociologist, the author of influential books including *White Collar* and *The Power Elite* and a severe critic of modern institutions.

6. **apparatchik:** a Russian word describing an individual who is part of the existing power structure.

THE PEOPLE'S VISION

Sources 15 and 16 from Literární Listy, *in Sviták,* The Czechoslovak Experiment, 1968–1969, *p. 2; p. 51. (New York: Columbia University Press).*

15. Cartoon: "If There Are No Complications the Child Should Be Born in the Ninth Month," 1968

16. Cartoon, 1968

THE ENEMY

Source 17 from Robin Alison Remington, editor, Prague in Winter: Documents on Czechoslovak Communism in Crisis *(Cambridge, Mass.: M.I.T. Press, 1969), p. 289.*

17. Cartoon, "Workers of All Countries Unite—Or I'll Shoot!," August 28, 1968

Sources 18 and 19 from Literární Listy, *in Sviták,* The Czechoslovak Experiment, 1968–1969, p. 196; p. 155. *(New York: Columbia University Press).*

18. Cartoon: "Liberté, Egalité, Freundschaft!" ("Liberty, Equality, Friendship!"), 1968

IN DEFEAT

19. Cartoon: "But There Is No Fire!," 1969

Source 20 from Robin Alison Remington, Prague in Winter: Documents on Czechoslovak Communism in Crisis *(Cambridge: MIT Press, 1969), p. 373.*

20. Cartoon: "It Is Only a Matter of a Few Tactical Steps Back," January 30, 1969

JDE JENOM O NĚKOLIK
TAKTICKÝCH ÚSTUPKŮ...

Vladimír Jiránek

QUESTIONS TO CONSIDER

France and Czechoslovakia are two very different countries at opposite ends of Europe. Let us compare the events of 1968 as they unfolded in these two locations. Do they illustrate a common response to problems basic to modern life in the noncommunist and communist West?

Consider first the demands of French and Czechoslovakian protest leaders. Examine again the written and visual evidence, and consider the protesters' views on working conditions in France. What problems do they identify in Sources 1, 2, and 3? How are these problems defined graphically? Why do you think that the artist in Source 4 portrayed modern capitalism as a puppeteer? What is the significance of the puppeteer's appearance? Why did the artist show de Gaulle as part of the industrial gears of France in Source 5? Turn next to the Czechoslovakian statements on working conditions.

Notice particularly Source 14, with its references to management by "hard-line thugs" and "apparatchiks." What great lie about communism (whose slogan is, "Workers of the World Unite!") do the Czechoslovakians discern in Source 17? What common theme do you find in French and Czechoslovakian protesters' ideas on the conditions of labor in the modern economy?

Next consider the political vision of the 1968 activists. Take the French first. What sort of government did the formulators of Source 3 envision? How is that idea amplified in Sources 9, 10, and 11? These cartoons spell their messages in words, but their art contains a message, too. Look closely at Source 10. How does the artist see the individual faring against big government, industrial giants, and powerful unions? What solution does the artist propose in the caption? Which groups did the creator of Source 11 hope would seize political power? Does the same message appear in Source 9? Who is being buried? What does his body represent? Notice the clothing and grooming of the pall-bearers. Can you identify the occupational groups that the artist hopes will seize power after the burial?

The Czechoslovakians also had a political vision. Review Sources 13 and 14. What political outlook do these statements express? What groups did Czechoslovakian reformers expect to lead change? Combine this message with Source 15. How do the reformers regard their chances for success? How were the political visions of the French and Czechoslovakian reformers similar?

Both movements also expressed images of their opponents and the methods to be employed in their struggles. What sort of action does the artist of Source 7 recommend to the French? What secondary message do you think underlies the portrayal of the fighter as a woman? Source 8 shows a close-up view of a Parisian paving stone. What message do you find in its accompanying statement? In Sources 6 and 12, we find some statements of the reformers' view of the opposition and its power. Why do you think the artist pictured a silhouette of a tank in Source 6? The final French selection, Source 12, is a cartoon that appeared on the cover of *L'enragé* after the defeat of the students and workers. What significance do you find in the portrayal of de Gaulle? What has crippled him? What supports him? What view of the government does the shape of his crutches convey?

The Czechoslovakian sources also characterize the reformers' opposition and their chances of success. In Source 15 what does the woman's obvious pregnancy represent? When does Dubcek predict the birth? How long did the Czechoslovakian experiment in greater democracy actually last? What does Dubcek's strange activity in Source 16 convey about the artist's view of the future? Sources 18 and 19 are cartoons that appeared as the Soviet Union and its Warsaw Pact allies invaded Czechoslovakia. The inspiration for Source 18 is the painting by Eugène Delacroix, *Liberty Leading the People,* in which a bare-breasted female Liberty (in a Phrygian cap) leads revolutionaries to freedom. In our cartoon, however, the artist portrays Liberty as Walter Ulbricht, the head of the East German Communist party. What is the artist's view of the friendship of this Liberty? The cartoon also employs a modified version of the motto of the French Revolution of 1789, *"Liberté, Egalité, Fraternité"* ("Liberty, Equality, Brotherhood"), rendered as *"Liberté, Egalité, Freundschaft"* (German for "friendship"). Considering the preceding twenty-five years of European history, why might the artist have used French for "Liberty" and "Equality" while using German for the last word? Why is Brezhnev/ Florian in Source 19 pouring water on a house representing Czechoslovakia (CSSR: Czechoslovak Socialist Republic)? Why does Dubcek object? What significance do you ascribe to the difference in the two figures' sizes?

The last cartoon, Source 20, reflects Czechoslovakia in defeat. Many alleged that making peace with the country's Russian conquerors would be simple: "It is only a matter of a few tactical steps back!" Where do the steps backward lead in this case? What does this tell us about the fate of the reform movement? What common sentiment do you detect in the French and Czechoslovakian evidence regarding the reformers' chances for meaningful success in the face of the modern state?

Answering these questions should prepare you to formulate your replies to the central questions of this chapter: What aspects of the modern state and economy provoked the events of 1968? What vision of the future did leaders of the French and Czechoslovakian movements embrace? How did they propose to achieve it?

EPILOGUE

As you continue your reading on subsequent events, it will become clear that the student unrest in France and other parts of Western Europe as well as events in Czechoslovakia is of enduring importance.

Perhaps in partial response to this agitation, significant political changes occurred in much of the West in the 1970s and 1980s. In most Western democracies, eighteen-year-olds won the vote. In many countries, too, at least a partial reversal of political centralization began, perhaps in some measure stemming from youthful demands for more "power to the peo-

ple." This impulse to diminish state authority defied ideological labels: In France and Sweden it was begun by socialist governments, whereas in the United States it has been the work of conservative administrations. No country, however, has yet approached the French students' vision of autogestion.

In France, where student movements amassed the broadest nonstudent support, other changes occurred. His power tarnished by the events of 1968, de Gaulle resigned within a year of the student strikes over a minor issue of government reform. Universities and their curricula were radically restructured in an attempt to meet some student demands, and working conditions in the factories were improved. Even in France, however, fundamental educational and industrial policy remained firmly in the hands of government officials and corporate managers. Student political activism and bitter labor disputes, many originating in issues raised in 1968, persist.

Elsewhere, the student revolt garnered less support, produced fewer changes, and led some frustrated student radicals to turn their energies from protest to brutal political violence in the 1970s. In West Germany, some student radicals formed terrorist groups like the Baader-Meinhof gang, which lashed out violently at West German symbols of the conservative consumer society and American military installations. The Red Brigades terrorist groups in Italy had the same roots and objectives.

In the 1980s youthful discontent in Western Europe partially manifested itself in the Green movement. Especially strong in West Germany, this movement represents the continued alienation of many from the West's industrial economy and modern society. The Green movement attacks the effects of modern industry on our environment and particularly the failure of traditional governing parties to address environmental issues. The Greens in West Germany also advocated an end to their country's participation in the North Atlantic Treaty Organization (NATO). While not always well organized, Greens entered the political life of a number of countries and by 1992 had elected members to parliaments in Germany and Switzerland as well as to the European Parliament. Indeed, in 1998,

the Greens became part of the governing coalition (with the Social Democratic party) in Germany, and the party's leader became foreign minister. Such a governing role led the Greens to accept NATO membership for Germany.

Eastern Europe felt the effects of Soviet actions in Czechoslovakia in 1968 for two decades, as those seeking political, economic, and social change in that region consciously confined reform within the boundaries established by the Brezhnev Doctrine. Discontent with communist rule and Soviet domination, however, grew in the 1980s, led by the rise in Poland of an independent, noncommunist labor movement, Solidarity. By the late 1980s, events in the Soviet Union also actually fostered change in Eastern Europe. Soviet President Mikhail Gorbachev (1985–1991) proclaimed a policy of *glasnost* (openness) and *perestroika* (restructuring) and abandoned the Brezhnev Doctrine, allowing Eastern European nations to determine their own destinies. The result was a largely peaceful revolution in 1989, when one-party communist political systems collapsed in Poland, Hungary, East Germany, Romania, and Czechoslovakia. Indeed, by the end of 1991, the ultimate result of Gorbachev's new path was the dissolution of the Soviet Union and its one-party communist political system, replaced by the Commonwealth of Independent States. Events in Czechoslovakia provide an example of the rapidity of Eastern European change in 1989 and remind us of the enduring importance of the events of 1968 in promoting that change.

In Czechoslovakia the rigid, one-party communist rule reimposed by Soviet arms in 1968 proved particularly resistant to change. The government dealt harshly with those favoring change: 500,000 dissidents lost their party memberships, hundreds of thousands of others linked with reform endured exclusion from professional employment for which they were qualified, and Dubcek found himself demoted to work as a mechanic. Nevertheless, opposition continued. In January 1977, a number of dissidents established Charter 77 to pressure the government to respect human rights. Its leaders included the playwright Václav Havel and the philosopher Jan Patocka. Havel spent five years in prison for his reform efforts, and Patocka died after police questioning, but by the mid-1980s the success of Solidarity in Poland and the reforms of Gorbachev in the Soviet Union inspired new hope for change.

In 1988 widespread demonstrations against the communist regime began, despite the authorities' consistently forceful responses to this dissent. The year 1989 opened with a massive demonstration commemorating the twentieth anniversary of the death of the student Jan Palach protesting the loss of the Prague Spring reforms. Indeed, a demonstration by students was key in bringing down the communist government. On November 17, 1989, the authorities permitted a seemingly harmless student observance in Prague of the fiftieth anniversary of an act of student resistance to Czechoslovakia's occupation by Germany in World War II. The commemorative event quickly turned into a demonstration for greater democracy that drew 100,000 participants. Armed riot police brutally dispersed the unarmed crowd, seriously injuring 291 and arresting over 100 persons. But the brutality revolted the country, especially as unfounded rumors of a student death circulated, and opposition to the government dramatically rose. Students seized university buildings. Reformers, led by Havel, who had recently been released from prison, founded Civic Forum in the Czech lands and Public Against Violence in Slovakia to coordinate resistance. A general strike on November 27 brought the country to a virtual halt, and additional demonstrations for democracy were widespread in late November and in December. Faced with great opposition, Communist party leaders finally relinquished power in late December. The country's legislature selected a new presiding officer for its deliberations, Alexander Dubcek, the reformer of 1968, and a new president for the country, the playwright Václav Havel. In what has been called the "Velvet Revolution" because so little bloodshed occurred, Czechoslovakia reestablished the democratic system it had lost in the coup of 1948. The newly democratic Czechoslovakia was not safe, however, from some of the problems that had undone its former communist regime. By 1992 long-standing nationalist tensions between the country's two chief language groups, the Czechs and the Slovaks, broke the country into two separate nation-states, the Czech Republic and Slovakia. Thus, many of the issues of 1968, here, as elsewhere, still affect Europe and the rest of the world.

CHAPTER TWELVE

THE NEW EUROPEANS: LABOR,

MIGRATION, AND THE PROBLEMS

OF ASSIMILATION

THE PROBLEM

The French newsmagazine *Le Nouvel Observateur* was almost beside itself: "This evening France is crazy," it exulted, "crazy and beautiful." It was the evening of July 12, 1998, and the French men's national soccer team had just upset the heavily favored team from Brazil 3–0 to win the World Cup, the most coveted sports trophy on the planet. France was delirious with joy, inflated with national pride.[1]

Of particular interest was the composition of the French national team. Only two of the starting players (Christophe Dugarry and Laurent Blanc) were traditional ethnic Frenchmen. The remainder were Algerian, New Caledonian, Guadeloupian, West Indian, Armenian, Ghanian, Congolese, Argentinian, Portuguese, Basque, and Breton. "The France of the three colors [traditionally the blue-white-red of the French flag,

the tricolor]," commented *Le Nouvel Observateur*, "is France black-white-brown.[2] Has soccer allowed the French to realize their oldest dream, brotherhood?"

But later in the newsmagazine, the editors struck a more somber note. In the voice of a non-Frenchperson living in France, *Le Nouvel Observateur* thanked the team for

> facilitating our integration in this country where, even if we carry French passports, we are still uncomfortable, not really at home. Never would we have dreamed that one day the integrative power of the army, the Church, and even the school would be replaced by that of sports competition.

The French triumph in the 1998 World Cup and France's reaction to that victory shows in microcosm two important trends in Western nations

1. Le Nouvel Observateur, July 16-22, 1998.

2. We have translated the French word *beur* here as "brown" to maintain the color analogy. *Beur* designates a North African person living in France.

Chapter 12

The New

Europeans: Labor,

Migration, and

the Problems

of Assimilation

since approximately the end of World War II: (1) the dramatic increase in the influx of non-Western workers and their families into the West, and (2) Western people's varied reactions to the new immigrants. As the West faces new challenges and opportunities in European union and global economic, natural resource, and environmental problems, it must at the same time deal with the effects of non-Western immigration on the economic, political, and cultural life of the West and its people. In short, just as Western Europe can no longer insulate itself from trends and events occurring elsewhere, so also Western Europe is no longer a "European island" inhabited only by Europeans.

As you near the end of this book, perhaps you would like to reflect on what you have learned. For one thing, you have learned to examine and analyze evidence to answer historical

questions and solve historical problems. Moreover, you have learned that these skills can be employed in other academic disciplines and in the careers that lie ahead of you (health sciences, law, business, teaching, engineering, journalism, etc.).

So in this chapter, it is appropriate for you to put what you have learned to the test. Using the information in the Background section and the Evidence, answer the following questions: What effects has non-European immigration had on Western Europe? What opinions have Europeans expressed concerning non-European immigration? Are opinions in France, Germany, and Great Britain similar or different? Using the evidence, your reading, and your historical imagination, what alternatives do you believe are available to Europeans with regard to non-European immigration and assimilation?

BACKGROUND

The migration of non-Westerners to the West is but the most recent chapter in the history of Western demography,[3] an often-ignored but critically important part of the study of the past. From 1840 to 1930, the general trend of European population movement was outward, principally to the nations of North and South America and to European colonies in Africa, Asia, and the Pacific. More than 40 million people left Europe in

3. **demography**: the study of human population, encompassing birth, death, marriage, migration, growth, density, distribution, etc.

those years, either to escape hard times or persecution or in search of opportunities elsewhere. By 1920, the foreign-born population in the United States alone numbered roughly 7.78 million (approximately 7.34 percent of the total population). At the same time, the Industrial Revolution and rural-to-urban migration resulted in declining birth rates in the West. In France, for example, the excess of births over deaths between 1821 and 1830 was 5.8, whereas by 1891–1900 it had slipped to 0.7. In France in 1770, the average number of children per marriage was 4.5, but by 1911–1913 it had dropped to 2.4. This combination of outmigration and declining birth rates resulted in severe labor shortages, especially among rural agricultural workers and in the least desirable industrial jobs. As early as 1912, Gaeton Piou noted in the *Revue socialiste* that "foreign workers specialize in the tasks that are the most repugnant, the most difficult, and the least skilled."[4] Migrants from Belgium, Italy, Spain, and Eastern Europe were preferred, but non-Europeans were imported in modest numbers when the need arose. By 1912, there were 4,000 to 5,000 Algerians working in France, and Germany, Switzerland, and the United Kingdom all had sizable numbers of foreign workers (in Switzerland by 1910 they approached 15 percent of the total population).

The staggering losses of life during World War I made the labor shortages even more acute. In each of the European Great Powers (not including Italy), between 1 and 2 million were killed and twice that number were wounded. In France, for example, the 1920 census recorded a total of 6,216,000 women between the ages of 20 and 39 and only 5,178,000 men. In addition, the influenza epidemic of 1918 resulted in over 20 million deaths worldwide. These deaths, with the concomitant declining birth rates and aging population, obliged Western European nations to import increasingly large numbers of foreign workers, a trend that actually began before and during the war but increased in volume after the conflict.

As one example, France signed recruiting agreements with Poland, Czechoslovakia, Italy, and other nations in the 1920s, thus opening its doors to almost 2 million foreign workers. Germany employed Eastern European immigrants, and the British imported both Irish and West Indian workers. Racial violence against blacks erupted in London, Liverpool, Cardiff, and Glasgow. In addition to Europeans, France accepted workers from Algeria, Morocco, French Indochina, China, and Madagascar. In France, as many as 400,000 foreign workers were employed to fill in the trenches and level the bomb-scarred terrain left by World War I.

The worldwide economic depression of the 1930s resulted in massive unemployment throughout the West. By 1932, for instance, unemployment in Germany had reached 30.1 percent of the civilian labor force (Great Britain's was 17.6 percent and the United States' was 23.6 percent). A rise in xenophobia[5] was almost predictable, with unemployed Westerners calling for the forced repatriation or deportation of foreign laborers. In France, common cries were "France First for Frenchmen" and "Discharge immigrants first." Thus, in spite of the fact that many employers hoped to retain foreign workers (who were willing to work for lower wages), many immigrants, faced with unemployment and threatened with xenophobic violence, drifted back to their respective homelands. In addition, the rise of Nazism and the threat of

---

4. *Revue socialiste*, May 15, 1912, quoted in Gary S. Cross, *Immigrant Workers in Industrial France: The Making of a New Laboring Class* (Philadelphia: Temple University Press, 1983), pp. 9–10.

5. **xenophobia:** fear of or contempt for foreigners or strangers.

Chapter 12

The New

Europeans: Labor,

Migration, and

the Problems

of Assimilation

another bloody war spurred between 1 and 2 million people to leave Europe.

The post–World War II era was much like the period after World War I, except that the economic upturn was sharper and of longer duration, and thus the need for foreign labor was even greater. In France, demographer Alfred Sauvy called for a minimum of 5.29 million immigrants to provide workers for the postwar recovery and also repopulate a demographically depleted nation. This call for permanent immigrants was echoed by Charles de Gaulle, and the French government even went so far as to encourage German prisoners of war to remain in France. But the economic recovery rapidly exhausted the traditional labor reservoirs, and in 1946 only 30,171 foreign workers entered France. Hence, desperate for workers, France recruited massive numbers from Algeria, Morocco, Mali, Tunisia, Senegal, and Mauritania.[6] By the outbreak of Algeria's anticolonial rebellion against France (the War of National Liberation to Algerians) in 1954, there were approximately 300,000 Algerian Muslims living in France. By the mid-1970s, the number of Algerians in France (both French who had lived there for generations but who left after the war and Algerian Muslims, mostly

Berbers) numbered over 800,000. Many immigrants lived in *bidonvilles* (shantytowns) in "the most reprehensible social conditions of any group of workers in Europe."[7] In 1973, French Prime Minister Pierre Messmer exclaimed sardonically, "This is a trap set by history. We in France and Europe have been accustomed to colonizing the world. Now the foreigners are coming here to us."[8]

Great Britain preferred to use Irish immigrants to provide the muscle for its economic recovery but also received immigrants from India, Pakistan, and the West Indies, in part recruited by the British Hotels and Restaurants Association and by London Transport. From the mid-1950s until 1962, when the government tried to curb immigration from the Commonwealth, approximately 30,000 black workers arrived annually. For its part, West Germany avoided recruiting workers until the 1960s, as it was able to use the 12 million Germans who had lived in East Prussia, Silesia, the Baltic states, Danzig, the Sudetenland, Hungary, Yugoslavia, Russia, and Romania and after the war were "expelled" into West Germany, and also the 3 million escapees from East Berlin and East Germany before the Berlin Wall was built in 1961. But continued labor shortages forced West Germany to recruit workers in Turkey, Morocco, Portu-

6. Non-Western governments were willing to sign recruiting agreements because Western nations would draw off the unemployed, discontented population and because wage earners in the West would send a portion of their wages home. For example, in 1964 the money Algerian migrants sent home amounted to 23 percent of Algeria's total imports. See Rosemarie Rogers, ed., *Guests Come to Stay: The Effects of European Labor Migration on Sending and Receiving Countries* (Boulder, Colo.: Westview Press, 1985), p, 281.

7. Gary P. Freeman, *Immigrant Labor and Racial Conflict in Industrial Societies: The French and British Experience, 1945–1975* (Princeton, N.J.: Princeton University Press, 1979), p. 78. Ethnic French who had lived in Algeria for generations were referred to as *pieds noirs*.

8. Quoted in Freeman, p. 20.

gal, Tunisia, and elsewhere. By 1970 there were almost 3 million foreign workers (*Gastarbeiter* or "guest workers") in the Federal Republic of Germany. Immigrants from Turkey alone numbered almost 470,000 (by 1982 that figure would be almost 1.6 million).

Within two decades after the end of World War II, non-European workers had become a necessity in Western Europe. Not only did they fill large labor gaps caused by outmigration, war, and dislocations and also take jobs that Western Europeans increasingly found unpleasant, but they also increased postwar corporate profits (in the textile, automobile, construction, and food products industries especially), dampened any threat of inflation due to sharp wage increases, and actually raised the living standards of the host populations by providing cheap services (public transportation, tourism, etc.). Between 1950 and 1975, approximately 30 million people (laborers and their families) immigrated to Western Europe. No longer were they seasonal or temporary workers who intended to earn some money and return to their native lands. Now, in the words of one study of Western Europe's ethnic minorities, they were "here for good."[9]

Instead of returning home, foreign workers sought to bring their families to their adopted homelands. Between 1974 and 1981, the number of foreign *workers* in Germany declined by around 330,000, and yet at the same time the total foreign *population* rose by approximately 503,000. In

France, in 1968 there were 786 foreign women for every 1,000 foreign men. By 1981, the ratio was more even, at 856:1,000. And, of course, there were children and elderly where before there had been almost exclusively able-bodied workers. This increased the immigrants' need for social services. Moreover, these families were less vulnerable to cultural assimilation, and they steadfastly refused to abandon their traditional language, culture, religion, and folkways. In France, Algerians who clung to their traditional culture were supported by the Amicale des Algériens en Europe (Friends of Algerians in Europe, the AAE), which operated cultural centers, published newspapers and magazines, conducted regular radio and television shows, and encouraged the construction of beautiful and permanent mosques. By 1980, next to Roman Catholicism, France's largest religion was Islam.

The realization that non-European immigrants intended to be permanent residents and refuse cultural assimilation combined with an economic recession and stagnation to produce a severe wave of xenophobic violence beginning in the late 1960s and early 1970s. In France, more than twenty Algerians were murdered between 1967 and 1973, and off-duty police officers often engaged in what they called *ratonnades* ("rat hunts") in the Algerian *bidonvilles*. In the summer of 1973, the stabbing to death of a Marseilles bus driver by a mentally disturbed Arab touched off a wave of violence in which the police made no arrests. And although Prime Minister Pierre Messmer said that racism

9. Stephen Castles et al., *Here for Good: Western Europe's New Ethnic Minorities* (London: Pluto Press, 1984).

Chapter 12

The New

Europeans: Labor,

Migration, and

the Problems

of Assimilation

"horrifies me" and compared what was going on in France to Nazi Germany under Hitler, anti-immigrant violence continued, with bombings of AAE headquarters in Paris, Lyons, and Roubaix. Bowing to public pressure, including the rise of a far right-wing political movement under Jean-Marie LePen,[10] the government stopped issuing foreign work permits, tried to deport unemployed foreigners, and even offered to pay foreigners 10,000 francs to return home (only 45,000 of a foreign population of approximately 3.5 million did so). Even so, a 1973 survey of French people reported that 92 percent thought that there were "too many foreigners in France," and 53 percent said that they could not be assimilated.

In West Germany, violence erupted when it became clear that the government's efforts to keep the foreign population mobile, rotating, and temporary were not working. Unlike the case in France, where the government in 1972 passed a law prohibiting racial discrimination and violence and the prime minister had spoken out against antiforeigner rioting, in the Federal Republic of Germany, Christian Democratic Union (CDU) leader Helmut Kohl (chancellor of West Germany and unified Germany from 1982 to 1998) used anti-immigrant

sentiment as a campaign device in 1982 when he said there were "too many foreigners in the Federal Republic," a sentiment that was later seconded by CDU leader Klaus Landowski when he exclaimed, "We cannot allow foreigners to . . . shout 'asylum' and live at the taxpayers' expense." These statements appeared to give the green light to a wave of xenophobia, and shouts of "*Ausländer raus*" ("foreigners out"), "*Deutschland den Deutschen*" ("Germany for Germans"), and even "*Sieg Heil*" could be heard on the streets. As one observer noted, "Violence against foreigners, Jews, political opponents, homeless people, homosexuals, handicapped people has escalated into an ugly feature of daily life in Germany."[11] In 1991, a week-long pogrom in the Saxon town of Hoyerswerda terrorized and forced out all 230 foreigners living there; the police did nothing to intervene, and Kohl did not condemn the violence. In 1992 alone, there were 2,506 reported violent attacks on non-Europeans, including 712 bombings and cases of arson. Of the suspected perpetrators, 90 percent were younger than 26 years old.

For its part, Great Britain has not been immune from racial violence. In the late 1960s, some working-class youth calling themselves "skinheads," fired up by class-based and racist rock-and-roll bands and lyrics, began to engage in what they called

10. For a good biographical sketch of LePen, see Harvey G. Simmons, *The French National Front: The Extremist Challenge to Democracy* (Boulder, Colo.: Westview Press, 1996). In October 1998 the European Parliament voted to strip LePen of his political immunity so that he could stand trial in a German court on a charge of "belittling the Holocaust." See *New York Times*, October 7, 1998.

11. Tore Björgo and Rob Witte, eds., *Racist Violence in Europe* (New York: St. Martin's Press, 1993), p. 162. In September 1998 Kohl, in a public campaign address, said that "Germany is not a land of immigrants and never will be." That same month he lost to Social Democrat Gerhard Schröder.

"paki bashing" (violence against non-whites). In the 1960s and 1970s thirty blacks were murdered, and foreigners were convinced that the police had sided with the skinheads and other perpetrators of violence. On April 10–12, 1981, a particularly nasty riot took place when a group of 300 to 400 young people, mostly blacks, attacked policemen with stones, bottles, bricks, and gasoline bombs, injuring 279 police officers. General destruction and looting followed until order eventually was restored. And yet this was only the most serious of approximately 7,000 incidents that took place that year in England and Wales. As in France and Germany, nonwhites felt especially victimized.

THE METHOD

In previous chapters of this book, you have learned to use a wide variety of evidence in order to solve selected historical problems. In this chapter, many of the types of evidence that you have used earlier (statistical charts and graphs, fiction, oral interviews, public opinion polls, cartoons, government reports, news stories and editorials, photographs) will be combined to give you a more complete picture of the problem under consideration. Almost no historians work with just one or two types of evidence. Instead, they try to find and employ all the available evidence to answer the questions they have asked of the past.

Sources 1 through 5 are statistical charts that will help you to understand immigration to Western Europe. Source 1, for example, compares various socioeconomic factors in the host countries and selected emigrating nations. Does this chart help you see why people might want to move to Western Europe (what historians of migration call the "push" and "pull" factors—those factors that compel people to leave their native lands and those factors that attract them to Western Europe)? By looking at the statistics concerning literacy, natural increase, infant mortality, etc., identify some problems that non-European immigrants might pose for their host nations.

Sources 2 through 5 are charts that show the changes in the amount and sources of immigration to selected Western European nations. How has the total amount of foreign immigration changed? How have the nations of origin (where immigrants are coming from) changed for France? for Germany? for Great Britain? Who are the primary immigrants into each of these nations?

Sources 6 through 9 have to do with foreign immigration to France and the reactions of some French people to the influx of non-European workers and their families. Source 6 is an excerpt from a 1993 interview with Jean Raispail, author of the novel *The Camp of the Saints,* which was published in French in 1973 and in English in 1975. *The Camp of the Saints* is a fictional account of over 100 ships that embark from Calcutta carrying almost 1 million people

Chapter 12

The New

Europeans: Labor,

Migration, and

the Problems

of Assimilation

seeking an escape from starvation, poverty, and disease. The armada gradually makes its way to the southern coast of France. Thousands have died during the fifty-day voyage, but over 800,000 remain, determined to come ashore. In the meantime, in the slums of Europe and the United States, the underclasses plan their uprisings. Should the oncoming starving horde be allowed to land and perhaps overwhelm France and the rest of Europe, or should it be stopped, if necessary with troops, planes, and warships? As Raispail said in his 1985 introduction to a new French edition of the novel, *The Camp of the Saints* "is only a parable, but in the end the result will not be any different. . . . Christian charity will prove itself powerless. The times will be cruel." In the novel, Western Europeans, who have lost the belief in the superiority of their culture and, indeed, themselves, allow the immigrants to land and are immediately swallowed up and destroyed by them. Since its initial publication, the novel has been attacked as fiercely racist and as fueling the fires of anti-immigrant hostility. In what ways does the interview help you to understand Raispail's thinking? Also, can the 1974 public opinion poll and the 1985 cartoon from *Le Monde* (Sources 7 and 8) help you to assess the climate of public opinion in which the novel *The Camp of the Saints* was received?

Source 9, a sketch of French film star Isabelle Adjani, on the surface is quite different in tone, since Ms. Adjani had won the César Award (comparable to the Oscars in the United States) in 1989 and was one of the most popular French film actresses of her time. And yet, below the surface, is there a much darker picture portrayed? How can you account for this rather schizophrenic reaction to Isabelle Adjani?

Sources 10 and 11 deal with anti-immigrant sentiment in Great Britain in general, and specifically with the 1981 riot in Brixton, a working-class, poor, immigrant section of London. On the weekend of April 10–12, 1981, in a working-class area of South London known as Brixton, police intervened in what appeared to be a knife fight, but were in turn attacked by "a few hundred young people—most, but not all of them black." Police were attacked with stones, bricks, iron bars, and "petrol bombs" (Molotov cocktails). Rioting and looting went on throughout the weekend until order finally was restored on Sunday. On Saturday evening alone (April 11), 279 police officers were injured, 45 civilians were hurt, and 28 buildings were damaged or destroyed. On April 14, Parliament appointed Lord Scarman to investigate and issue a report of his findings, which he did on October 31, 1981. According to the government-commissioned Scarman Report, what were the underlying causes of the Brixton riot? What role, if any, did the police themselves play? In the view of the Scarman Report, how can future conflicts be avoided? What is Devon Thomas's opinion (Source 11) of the Scarman Report? What would he add to that document?

Sources 12 through 17 are concerned with foreign immigrants in the Federal Republic of Germany. The Heidelberg Manifesto (Source 12) was written in 1982 by eleven German university professors. What do these academicians have to say about foreign immigration? Do they propose any solutions? The September 9, 1991, issue of *Der Spiegel* also was devoted to the issue of foreign immigration. The article reproduced here (Source 14) appears to be a rather sympathetic look at the reasons why immigrants seek to come to Germany, even if that entrance is an illegal one. And yet, how does the cover of the magazine (Source 13) suggest a different opinion of that immigration?

Sources 15 through 17 examine an anti-immigrant riot that took place in September 1991 in Hoyerswerda, in northern Saxony. Before the reunification of Germany in 1990, the vast majority of immigrants had come into West Germany. And yet what had formerly been East Germany was the scene of the troubling Hoyerswerda riot. Do the sources suggest any explanation for this seemingly curious phenomenon? How can you account for the rise of the "skinheads"? In the view of *Stern Magazin*, who must share the blame for Hoyerswerda?

Chapter 12

The New

Europeans: Labor,

Migration, and

the Problems

of Assimilation

THE EVIDENCE

1. Statistics from Host Nations and Selected Emigrating Nations

	Per Capita Gross Domestic Product	Natural Increase (%)	Life Expectancy, Female (yrs)	Life Expectancy, Male (yrs)	Infant Mortality per 1000 Live Births	Physicians/Person	Literacy (%)
Host Nations							
United Kingdom	$22,800	0.1	80.8	75.3	5.5	1/610	100
France	24,400	0.3	83.1	75.2	4.4	1/330	99
Germany	23,400	-0.14	81.1	74.6	4.7	1/286	100
Switzerland	28,600	0.1	82.9	77.0	4.4	1/309	100
Emigrating Nations							
Algeria	$5,500	1.7	71.1	68.9	39.1	1/1,182	62
Morocco	3,500	1.8	72.1	67.5	46.5	1/2,174	44
Mozambique	1,000	1.1	34.6	36.2	138.6	NA	40
Mali	850	3.0	48.6	46.2	119.6	NA	31
Pakistan	2,000	2.1	62.1	61.0	78.5	1/1,754	38
India	2,200	1.5	63.9	62.5	61.5	1/2,083	52
Mauritania	2,000	2.9	53.7	49.4	75.2	1/7,246	38
Jamaica	3,700	1.2	77.7	73.7	13.7	1/714	85
Turkey	6,800	1.2	74.0	69.2	45.8	1/826	82
Vietnam	1,950	1.5	72.5	67.4	29.3	1/2,083	94

Chapter 12

The New

Europeans: Labor,

Migration, and

the Problems

of Assimilation

Source 2 from Rosemarie Rogers, editor, Guests Come to Stay: The Effects of European Labor Migration on Sending and Receiving Countries *(Boulder, Colo.: Westview Press, 1985), p. 11; and Stephen Castles et al.,* Here for Good: Western Europe's New Ethnic Minorities *(London: Pluto Press, 1984), p. 43.*

2. Foreign Immigrants in Selected European Host Countries, Early 1960s, Early 1970s, 1981

FOREIGN IMMIGRANTS IN EUROPEAN HOST COUNTRIES

Dates	Host Countries/All Migrants (in 1000s)			
	France	Germany	Switzerland	Great Britain
Early 1960s	2,169.7	686.2	584.7	2,205
Early 1970s	3,873.1	4,127.4	1,181.2	2,983
1981	4,223.9	4,629.8	909.9	3,360

Sources 3 and 4 from Rosemarie Rogers, editor, Guests Come to Stay: The Effects of European Labor Migration on Sending and Receiving Countries *(Boulder, Colo.: Westview Press, 1985), pp. 5–11. Copyright © 1985. Reprinted by permission of The Estate of Rosemarie Rogers.*

3. Foreign Immigrants in France, by Country of Origin, 1961–1981

Country of Origin	Number of Immigrants (000s) and Dates		
	1961	1971	1981
Italy	629.0	572.8	452.0
Portugal	50.0	812.0	859.4
Spain	441.7	570.6	412.5
Algeria	350.5	845.7	816.9
Morocco	33.0	269.7	444.5
Tunisia	26.6	148.8	193.2

4. Foreign Immigrants in Germany, by Country of Origin, 1961–1981

	Number of Immigrants (000s) and Dates		
Country of Origin	1961	1971	1981
Greece	42.1	406.4	299.3
Italy	196.7	629.6	624.5
Portugal	0.8	121.5	109.4
Spain	44.2	272.7	177.0
Turkey	6.7	1,027.8	1,546.3
Yugoslavia	16.4	707.8	637.3

Source 5 from Stephen Castles et al., Here for Good: Western Europe's New Ethic Minorities *(London, Pluto Press, 1984), pp. 43, 105. Copyright © 1984. Used by permission of Pluto Press.*

5. Foreign-Born Residents in Great Britain, by Regions of Origin, 1951–1981

FOREIGN RESIDENTS OF GREAT BRITAIN (000S), 1951–1981				
Birthplace	1951	1961	1971	1981
Other European nations	724	845	980	1,086
Irish Republic	532	709	709	607
Old Commonwealth[12]	99	110	143	153
New Commonwealth[13]	218	541	1,151	1,513

12. Old Commonwealth includes Australia, Canada, New Zealand.
13. New Commonwealth includes India, Pakistan, West Indies.

Chapter 12

The New

Europeans: Labor,

Migration, and

the Problems

of Assimilation

Source 6 from Katharine Betts, "An Interview with Jean Raspail," The Social Contract, vol. 5 (Winter 1994–95), pp. 85–87. © 1995. Reprinted with permission.

6. Interview with Jean Raspail

Our first question is the obvious one: Do you think that the vision portrayed in your book is coming true? The answer: Haven't you seen the preface to the third (1985) French edition of the book? No, indeed we hadn't.

We should read it. This preface explains that the book is symbolic, a parable. History is speeded up to happen over the course of days rather than a couple of decades or a generation. In real life things don't come about so quickly, but the principle remains the same. The Third World invasion of the West is unavoidable. If we don't see it, our children will.

How did people react when the book first came out? M. Raspail said that the response was very different in the United States compared to France. He wasn't very well known in France in 1973 and the immediate reaction to the book was silence. It only began to sell six or eight months after it first appeared. It sold by word of mouth. Some people bought large numbers of copies—100 to 150 at a time. In contrast, in the U.S. there was a strong reaction in the press immediately, some against, many for. He still receives many letters from the States. . . .

We knew of Shapiro's English translation but we asked him about others. It has now been translated into every major European language, Spanish, Portuguese, German, Italian, Dutch, and so on. In France, it is constantly in print. . . .

It had struck me that the book was every bit as much about his disgust with French society as it was about the Third World population explosion. So we asked him if the events of May 1968 in France, the student uprising, the wave of strikes, had had much influence on him. Yes, they had. When he was writing the book he had been full of a sense of the degeneration of his society and of its lack of intelligence.

We asked him about his vision of the West, this West that had lost all confidence in itself as a worthwhile civilization. Where did he think this mentality ("the beast") had come from? He said this was a difficult question. It was a collection of things; one couldn't really say. In one sense the West is more than ever triumphant, but it has a conception of the rights of man. In its original form this was an excellent idea, but it has now been misapplied and it is being used against France, the very country that had first conceived it.

We also asked him about his opinion of recent actions that the French government had taken to try to tighten the rules governing entry for family reunion and for people seeking political asylum. Did he think that these measures would amount to anything? No. It is impossible to do anything. It's too late. There have been mass movements of people already and there are now too many to send back. "These steps that Balladur (the Prime Minister) and Pasqua (Minister for the Interior) are taking are just to appease the electorate. They won't make any difference."

How did he see the future of the West? *"Je n'en sais rien."* (Literally, "I know nothing about it," but "I have no idea" is probably a better translation.)

Source 7 from Gary P. Freeman, Immigrant Labor and Racial Conflict in Industrial Societies: The French and British Experience, 1945–1975 *(Princeton, N.J.: Princeton University Press, 1979), p. 268. Copyright © 1979 by Princeton University Press. Reprinted by permission of Princeton University Press.*

7. Public Opinion Poll of French Attitudes Toward Particular Nationality Groups, 1974

Q: What is your opinion of each of the following nationalities?

Nationality	Good	Rather Good	Rather Bad	Bad	No Answer	Total
Italian	53%	30%	16%	2%	9%	100%
Spanish	55	30	4	1	10	100
Portuguese	43	33	10	3	11	100
Yugoslav	30	21	8	2	39	100
Turkish	15	13	9	6	57	100
Black African	28	29	15	8	20	100
North African	17	16	34	21	12	100

Chapter 12

The New

Europeans: Labor,

Migration, and

the Problems

of Assimilation

Source 8 from Gunther Glebe and John O'Loughlin, eds., Foreign Minorities in Continental European Cities *(Stuttgart: Franz Steiner Verlag Wiesbaden GMBH, 1987), p. 183. Reprinted from* Le Monde, *October 16, 1985, by permission of Plantu.*

8. Cartoon from Le Monde, October 16, 1985

MARIANNE (the national symbol of France): "I have a headache!"
PURITAN-LIKE MAN at her bedside: "The foreigners!"
MARIANNE: "I am dizzy!"
PURITAN: "The foreigners, I tell you!"

Source 9 from Meggan Dissly, "Isabelle Adjani: The Wounded Bird," France Magazine, *vol. 20 (Fall 1991), pp. 20–21. Copyright © 1991. Reprinted by permission of the author.*

9. Article on French Film Star
Isabelle Adjani, 1991

When Isabelle Adjani accepted the 1989 French César for best actress in her role as Camille Claudel, she read a poem. At first, the meaning of the lofty, obscure verses totally escaped the audience, who wondered what the French actress was talking about. The other award winners had gushed the usual trivialities ("I owe it all to Mother . . . !"), but Adjani was unsmiling, grave. She finished reading and said, "From the *Satanic Verses*, by Salman Rushdie." There was a heavy moment of silence. Eyes glistened. Then the crowd burst into applause. Once again, Adjani had brought the house down.

Isabelle Adjani likes to give her audience a jolt. That is her job, after all. But few actresses are as unpredictable, provocative and utterly beguiling as the 35-year-old Adjani. A "Beur," as the French call second-generation immigrants in France, Adjani knows what it is to be both an integral part of French society and the eternal outsider. Born of an Algerian father and a German mother, Adjani was painfully aware of the humiliation and shame her parents felt at being immigrants. Perhaps this is what made the actress more rebellious—and vulnerable—than most.

Adjani grew up in Gennevilliers, a northern suburb of Paris, in low-rent housing. As a child, she was completely cut off from her North African roots. Only later did she learn that her father, Mohammed Charif Adjani, had given her a middle name, Yasmina. Her mother discouraged any reference to the family's origins. Adjani's parents were both acutely conscious of being "different" and kept to themselves. When they fought, they slung racist insults at each other.

As a teenage actress who found herself suddenly plunged into the limelight, Adjani dissimulated her Arab background. Her early biographies mention her distant Turkish ancestry but omit her Algerian ties. She never discussed her family with reporters. But later, she was angry at having been robbed of her heritage. Her father spoke little about his country and his people before he died. She felt fiercely loyal to him and even refused roles as Jewish girls out of "a kind of solidarity" with the Arab cause. At the same time, she has never understood why he was not more courageous in asserting his identity in the face of a condescending wife and scornful French society.

As an adult, the blue-eyed, dark-haired woman has struggled to come to terms with her mixed heritage. It hasn't been easy. One of her former directors once described her as victim of an "inner North-South" conflict. Some call her the "wounded bird." Adjani admits herself that her behavior sometimes borders on the schizophrenic. "I always felt like a Beur," she once said in an interview. "But I was very unhappy because I felt that my father was against it."

Ambiguities remain despite Adjani's seemingly wholehearted espousal of the anti-racist cause in France. Like her father, Isabelle Adjani gave her son a French first name, Barnabé, and Saïd, after her father's father, as a middle name. Adjani once posed in ELLE magazine wearing the famous SOS-Racisme badge, a hand raised in friendship. Yet she has never belonged to SOS-Racisme or participated in a street rally. "I am too narcissistic to be part of a movement," she has said. "For me to demonstrate, you'd have to drag me there."

Once she does make up her mind to throw herself into a cause, Adjani is a fount of energy, although procrastination often tends to get the better of her.

Chapter 12

The New

Europeans: Labor,

Migration, and

the Problems

of Assimilation

She is wary of blindly going along with the crowd, or falling for something that may turn out to be a momentary fad. Adjani greatly admires Benazir Bhutto, who, she points out, took up her country's cause after her father's death even though she was quite detached before. Adjani would like to do the same. "But first I would have to examine the consequences of such a commitment. I would have to see how it would be possible—how it could happen and be carried out—before I could take the slightest step." To be or not to be . . .

Beneath the china-doll complexion lies a flinty will. Adjani was deeply moved during the 1986 Algerian anti-government demonstrations when the population rioted against price increases and for more democracy. On an impulse, Adjani flew to Algeria, first as an observer. But she couldn't hold her tongue for long, and, in a gesture of solidarity, she addressed students at the Bab-Ezzouar campus. "I come not as an Algerian, but as a French person," she told them. Adjani was furious with the French Government for not taking a stand against torture and human rights abuses. She was later accused of overstepping her role and substituting herself for the Government. "I hope I shocked them," she said. "I certainly shocked myself."

The experience was both exhilarating and frustrating. "It was strange. Here (in France) everyone emphasized my Algerian side, and there I was someone who had tossed off her origins and become French. I found myself a foreigner everywhere, yet without a country anywhere," she later admitted.

Some say stardom came to Adjani when she was too young and too tender to deal with it. Adjani began her acting career when she was only 14 with the movie *Le Petit Bougnat.* Two years later, she was invited to join the prestigious theatrical company La Comédie-Française, despite her lack of formal training. Her best-known theater performances were in Molière's *L'Ecole des femmes* and Jean Giraudoux's *Ondine.* When she was 19, Adjani deserted the theater for motion pictures. First *La Gifle* (*The Slap*), directed by Claude Pinoteau; then *The Story of Adèle H.* by François Truffaut. Her star status was secured. Adjani had become a phenomenon whose every move was scrutinized and reported to the public.

Adjani's image shifted with her move from the stage to the screen. In her early movies, she played the role of victim. People associated her with the beleaguered young girls—marginalized, brutalized and slightly weird—that she played. Not surprisingly, Adjani's mother fretted that her daughter had chosen a bedeviled profession. But Isabelle Adjani insists that acting enables her to exorcise the devil in her. As a star under close scrutiny, she has to respect certain limits. As an actress, she can be as rebellious and nonconformist as she likes through characters like Adèle H., Victor Hugo's wayward daughter, or Camille Claudel, Auguste Rodin's mistress.

Adjani personally identified strongly with both characters. Each in her own way lived without regard for the dictates of society. It is tempting to draw parallels between the proud, spirited Adjani and the talented but eccentric

Camille Claudel, committed by her family to an insane asylum for 30 years. A French critic suggested that it could as well have been Camille Claudel playing the role of Isabelle Adjani. Indeed, Adjani likens Claudel's martyrdom to her own: "After actualizing her talents, [Camille Claudel] is eaten up by trials. It reminds me of the itinerary of an actress."

Her own trials have turned Adjani into something of a recluse. She admits to being introverted and solitary: "I am an impure subject. I do not have a good relationship with the outside world," she says. Adjani walked off the set of Jean-Luc Goddard's *Prénom Carmen* because the director "brutalized her intimacy." She is adamant about keeping her private life private. The actress's legendary high-handedness with photographers led them to boycott her one year at a Cannes film festival. Aloof, provocative, Adjani either charms or annoys. Some see her as France's greatest actress; others, as a spoiled brat. The two are not incompatible. Her long absences from public view, interrupted by some impetuous act or provocative statement, have made her vulnerable to vicious rumors.

In 1986, a rumor that Isabelle Adjani was dying of AIDS spread like a brush fire. Adjani took this to be a racist act: "They can't call me a dirty Arab," she explained later, "so they find other ways of getting at me. Rumors are very destructive." Adjani at first ignored the rumors. Then she counteracted by making herself more visible. She appeared in a magazine, dined with Paris Mayor Jacques Chiroc, and even cut a record. But the rumors persisted. At one point she was reported dying in three different hospitals in Marseille and Paris at the same time. Photographers burst into the emergency rooms of several hospitals on the basis of hot tips. After nine months, Adjani broke down. Angry, but at the same time deeply affected, she appeared on French television news. "It is incredible to have to come here to say I am not sick, the way one would say I am not guilty," she said and hastily left the studio.

Isabelle Adjani has not appeared on the movie screen since her interpretation of Camille Claudel. She appears to be waiting for the right role, perhaps that of an Arab woman she has always wanted to play. With Adjani, you never know. She can disappear from public view for months at a time, then lunge back into the limelight with another stunning performance—or another provocation. "I am an actress, and anything can happen. Anything does happen." Trust her to know how to make things happen.

Chapter 12

The New

Europeans: Labor,

Migration, and

the Problems

of Assimilation

Source 10 from The Brixton Disorders, 10–12 April 1981. Report of an Inquiry by the Rt. Hon. the Lord Scarman, O.B.E. *(London: Her Majesty's Stationery Office, 1981), pp. 1–2, 73, 135–136. Crown copyright is reproduced with permission of the Controller of Her Majesty's Stationery Office.*

10. The Scarman Report, 1981

Two views have been forcefully expressed in the course of the Inquiry as to the causation of the disorders. The first is:—oppressive policing over a period of years, and in particular the harassment of young blacks on the streets of Brixton. On this view, it is said to be unnecessary to look more deeply for an explanation of the disorders. They were "anti police." The second is that the disorders, like so many riots in British history, were a protest against society by people, deeply frustrated and deprived, who saw in a violent attack upon the forces of law and order their one opportunity of compelling public attention to their grievances. I have no doubt that each view, even if correct, would be an over-simplification of a complex situation. If either view should be true, it would not be the whole truth. . . .

Nothing that I have heard or seen can excuse the unlawful behaviour of the rioters. But the police must carry some responsibility for the outbreak of disorder. First, they were partly to blame for the breakdown in community relations. Secondly, there were instances of harassment, and racial prejudice among junior officers on the streets of Brixton which gave credibility and substance to the arguments of the police's critics. Thirdly, there was the failure to adjust policies and methods to meet the needs of policing a multi-racial society. The failures of the police, however, were only part of the story and arose in difficult circumstances. The community and community leaders in particular must take their share of the blame for the atmosphere of distrust and mutual suspicion between the police and the community which developed in Lambeth during the 1970s and reached its apogee in the weeks prior to the disorders. I hold it as a hopeful sign that in the closing stages of the Inquiry there was evidence of an apparent willingness on both sides to acknowledge past errors and to try to make a new start. And I repeat—the failures of the police and of the community leaders neither justify nor excuse the disorders or the terrifying lawlessness of the crowds. . . .

A—CONCLUSION

The evidence which I have received, the effect of which I have outlined in Part II, leaves no doubt in my mind that racial disadvantage is a fact of current British life. It was, I am equally sure, a significant factor in the causation of the Brixton disorders. Urgent action is needed if it is not to become an endemic, ineradicable disease threatening the very survival of our society. It would be unfair to criticise Government for lack of effort. The real question is whether the effort, which is undoubted, has been properly directed. . . .

The role of the police has to be considered against this background. As I have said in Part VI, the police do not create social deprivation or racial disadvantage: they are not responsible for the disadvantages of the ethnic minorities. Yet their role is critical. If their policing is such that it can be seen to be the application to our new society of the traditional principles of British policing, the risk of unrest will diminish and the prospect of approval by all responsible elements in our ethnically diverse society will be the greater. If they neglect consultation and co-operation with the local community, unrest is certain and riot becomes probable.

A new approach is required. I am satisfied, as Mr Hazan QC submitted in his final speech on behalf of the Metropolitan Police, that it has already begun. But determination and persistence in the formulation and application of the necessary policies will be required. I would add that an equal persistence in striving to the same end is also required of all sections of the responsibly minded public.

On the social front, I find myself broadly in agreement with the House of Commons Select Committee. The attack on racial disadvantage must be more direct than it has been. It must be co-ordinated by central government, who with local authorities must ensure that the funds made available are directed to specific areas of racial disadvantage. I have in mind particularly education and employment. A policy of direct co-ordinated attack on racial disadvantage inevitably means that the ethnic minorities will enjoy for a time a positive discrimination in their favour. But it is a price worth paying if it accelerates the elimination of the unsettling factor of racial disadvantage from the social fabric of the United Kingdom. . . .

I end with the quotation from President Johnson's address to the nation, which appears at the very beginning of the US Report of the National Advisory Commission on Civil Disorders (1968):–

". . . The only genuine, long-range solution for what has happened lies in an attack—mounted at every level—upon the conditions that breed despair and violence. All of us know what those conditions are: ignorance, discrimination, slums, poverty, disease, not enough jobs. We should attack these conditions—not because we are frightened by conflict, but because we are fired by conscience. We should attack them because there is simply no other way to achieve a decent and orderly society in America . . ."

These words are as true of Britain today as they have been proved by subsequent events to be true of America.

Chapter 12

The New

Europeans: Labor,

Migration, and

the Problems

of Assimilation

Source 11 from John Benyon, editor, Scarman and After: Essays Reflecting on Lord Scarman's Report, the Riots and Their Aftermath *(Oxford: Pergamon Press, 1984), pp. 184–185, 189–190. Reprinted by permission of Lord Benyon.*

11. Devon Thomas, "Black Initiatives in Brixton"

I am a black person, of Afro-Caribbean origin. I have spent the major part of my life in this society, so I feel I know it well. While having spent my early formative years in Jamaica, most of my education both formal and informal took place in England. My parents came to this country in the early 1950s when they themselves were relatively young people. They did not come because they saw Britain as the promised land, or because they thought the streets of London were paved with gold. In fact they had quite a lot of information about the reality of life for blacks in this society. Members of my family and community in Jamaica had served in the armed forces during the war and had reported what it was like to those back home. In their letters they talked of meeting some nice people and seeing some interesting sights, but they also talked about cold weather, fog, and racism. . . .

The social scientists and researchers who have examined the black community mercilessly over the past few years are fond of saying that the first generation of immigrants who came after the war were unskilled. From my personal experience I know this to be a fallacy. Many members of my family had formal qualifications in academic and vocational areas on their arrival, but were told—in spite of the fact that our home territories were the responsibility of this country at the time—that these qualifications were "colonial" ones, and no good. Other members of the community who did not have formal qualifications had long years of experience in many different areas, including agriculture, construction, dock work and other fields, but the role this society had for them was unskilled labour at the bottom of the pile, so any experience or qualifications were irrelevant.

The other qualities and skills that these people had were ones of resilience, fortitude and determination to see things through in spite of difficult circumstances. These are the qualities that had brought us through three hundred years of grinding colonial existence, and it is the same experience that we have had to draw on to survive the last thirty years inside this society. . . .

The central issue is therefore one of power and how we are to organise and mobilise ourselves for the acquisition of more power. The leaders of this society are putting heavier pressure on black people and trying to take away the little gains that we have made over the years. They are promulgating more racist and restrictive nationality and immigration laws, instigating heavier and more oppressive policing in our communities, and moving in similar ways in a whole host of areas. 1981 signalled the intention of black people, young people, poor people and many others living in the inner city to resist this trend by force if necessary. Many other levels of response are now emerging.

I have resisted the temptation to discuss the issues outlined above within the context of Lord Scarman and his work. I have done so because I believe that Scarman has been the most successful diversionary mechanism that the state could have constructed. It created a false sense of hope for many who thought that the Inquiry would investigate the *real* causes of the 1981 uprisings and make recommendations accordingly. It fooled many into thinking that the Government would then take substantive action. In reality the way the Scarman Inquiry was constituted made it highly unlikely that it could get at the facts of the events of spring and summer.

Lord Scarman himself had to admit that the crucial people who should have given evidence came nowhere near his deliberations. The description of events therefore lacks that vital perspective. In addition, Lord Scarman had insufficient resources and inclination to research the background to the events adequately, and so his recommendations are also inadequate. Where he has made progressive suggestions, whether by design or accident, these have largely been ignored and the law and order aspects have been accentuated and implemented. It would be foolhardy, therefore, for black people in particular to be sucked into the trap of discussing their needs in terms of Scarman.

In the period since summer 1981 nothing fundamentally has changed. Using Brixton as an example, unemployment has risen and most social and economic indicators have worsened. The response by central and local government has been superficial at best. Anything that does not move gets painted, and every available vacant space gets landscaped and tree-planted. While not decrying these efforts, they do not go to the *heart* of the matter. When resources are directed to the area, they do not reach those that most need them. Increasing numbers of people are engaged in making cases for grants, administering grants, writing reports and the like, but much of this activity does not address itself to the people it is supposed to. The people with the needs have to start determining the programmes that meet their needs, and the achievement of this is the task in hand.

Source 12 from Info-Zentrum für Rassimusforschung, *dir@maile.uni-marburg.de. Copyright D. I. R. Translated by Sam Ali Mustafa.*

12. The Heidelberg Manifesto, 1982

With great concern we observe a series of developments in which roughly five million foreign workers and their families have come to live in our country— the result of a euphorically optimistic economic policy. Obviously, efforts to

Chapter 12

The New

Europeans: Labor,

Migration, and

the Problems

of Assimilation

limit this influx have not been successful. In the year 1980 alone the number of incoming foreigners reached 309,000, of whom 194,000 were Turks.

The situation has been made more difficult because only a little more than half the number of children have been born, that would be necessary even for zero population growth of the German population in the Federal Republic. The renewal of the generative function of the German family is absolutely crucial.

Many Germans are already foreigners in their own neighborhoods, and in their own homeland, even though the foreign workers are aliens in these surroundings.

The influx of foreigners was supported by the Federal government, for the questionable purpose of furthering uninhibited economic growth. The German people never had the meaning and implications of it explained to them. Thus we call for the founding of a non-partisan and ideologically neutral league for the purpose of finding a fair possible solution to the problem—in a dialogue with politicians—of determining the fate not only of the foreign workers but of our country. What makes it so difficult to find a solution to this problem is the fact that we can no longer have public discussion without people who raise these issues being called "Nazis." We plead, therefore, for a calm discussion and to find a solution, on the basis of the Basic Law—against ideological nationalism, racism and extremism of both Left and Right.

It is not possible to integrate huge masses of non-German foreigners into our people, without endangering our language, culture, and religion. Every people, including the German people, has a natural right to preserve its identity and individuality in its living-area. The preservation of societies is served best by caution, not by their *Einschmelzung*.[14] We understand that Europe is an organism of distinct peoples and nations, with a common basis in history. As Solzhenitsyn said, "Each nation is a single facet of God's plan." . . .

Although we all know about the misuse of the word "*Volk*," we must in all earnestness remember that the Basic Law's idea of "*Volk*" clearly means the German people, and that the Federal President and the members of the Federal government must take the oath: "I swear that I will devote all my powers to the well-being of the German people, to serve their needs, and to turn from all that would hurt them."

We also don't shy away from remembering that the Basic Law is committed to protect and preserve the German people. The preamble of the Basic Law is committed to the goal of re-unification.

How can reunification remain possible, when the regions [of Germany] become ethnically foreign? What hopes for the future remain to the hundreds of thousands of foreign children who are trying to learn their alphabets in both German and their mother-tongue? What hopes for the future do our own children have, who are being educated in classrooms with a majority of

14. **Einschmelzung**: intermingling, or melting together.

foreigners? Will they still be willing to pay the billions required for the defense of our country, after such a development? Only intact German families can lead our people into the future.

Technological developments offer new possibilities, and raise the levels [of education], in order to keep us ahead of foreign businesses. This must be an objective: to keep control of our sciences, not so we can turn people into machines, but rather so we can bring machines to our people. The evil at the root of it all is this: we devote so much to developing and helping [the education of] the foreign workers in our homeland, and do none of this for ourselves. The re-uniting of foreign workers with their families in their native lands (obviously without force) will benefit our country, which is being overindustrialized, and our environment, which is being destroyed.

Virtually none of the representatives and functionaries of the major corporations has been willing to confront this problem, or to offer politically realistic suggestions. We thus consider it necessary to build a non-partisan union, which would represent all factions, unions, etc., who want to preserve our people, language, culture, religion, and way of life, but will also empower individuals.

Thus, we educators, undersigned here, must consider the consequences of making it possible for foreigners (especially those from the so-called Third World) to enter our country for an education. We must make people aware, and advise them of these developments.

Chapter 12

The New

Europeans: Labor,

Migration, and

the Problems

of Assimilation

Sources 13 and 14 from Der Spiegel, *Sept. 9, 1991. Cover reprinted with permission. Article translated by Arthur Haas. © 1991 by Der Spiegel. Reprinted by permission of* The New York Times Syndicate, *Paris.*

13. Cover: "The Onslaught of the Poor," 1991

14. "Soldiers to the Borders,"
1991

The influx of asylum applicants and illegal immigrants is reaching new records, massive hatred for foreigners develops in Germany. Authorities for foreigners, Border Protection, and the justice system are hardly equal to the onrush. Can the asylum procedures, which often take many years, be speeded up without changing the constitution?

A man wants to come to Germany. Mihai Ciobanu, 22, by trade working with milling machines (a Fräser[15]), has sold whatever little he owns and travelled from Romania via Warsaw to Zgorcelec, the Polish twin city of Görlitz. There the "Schlepper",[16] in exchange for DM 200, showed him the way across the green border. "Everything OK" they promised him.

They could not keep their promise. Ciobanu was caught as he illegally crossed the border and now he sits at the BGS[17] and is interrogated together with 12 compatriots.

Eagerly the man follows all directions. "I am sorry" he says again and again. "He has to wash his hands" a "Grenzer"[18] says. He takes Ciobanu's hand and presses each finger on a stamp pad and then on a form.

The finger prints are added to a new folder, together with the interrogation protocol, the deportation protocol, and the charge of illegal border crossing. Only gradually does it dawn on the refugees that they are to be deported— they did not know the magic word asylum which would have opened them the way to the country of their dreams. Now they are poorer than before— after the useless expenditures for bus- and train fare, for the visa to Poland, and the "Schlepper" to Germany.

Just one of them tries to talk courage to himself: "We have to try again" says Ciobanu the Fräser from the little town of Roman to which he never wants to return. . . .

It is not political persecution, but fear of the economic future that makes millions of people from the new democracies of the East think of Emigration to Germany. Ten million Russians will travel to the West if now the crumbling Soviet Union too opens its borders, according to estimates by the Vienna Interior Minister Frank Löschnak. According to a poll in the USSR by the Munich Sinus Institute it is even every fourth grown-up who would rather live in Germany than in the homeland.

One can also expect a mass-immigration from the South. The European Community (EC) expects that within ten years there will be no foundation for

---

15. **Fräser**: A person working with milling machines.
16. **Schlepper**: a person who smuggles people across the border for money.
17. **LBGS**: Budesgrenzschutz, Federal Border Protection.
18. **Grenzer**: A member of the BGS.

Chapter 12

The New

Europeans: Labor,

Migration, and

the Problems

of Assimilation

the existence (no livelihood) for 100 million people in the southern mediterranean countries. 2.3 million young Turks alone would right now leave their homeland in the direction of the EC if only they were allowed to.

Source 15 from Knud Pries, "East Germans Have Yet to Learn Tolerance," Süddeutsche *Zeitung, Munich, Sept. 24, 1991, republished in English in* The German Tribune, *Oct. 6, 1991, pp. 3–5.*

15. Report of Antiforeign Violence in Germany

The police headquarters in Dresden, the capital of Saxony, announced that "a political situation" had developed in the town of Hoyerswerda. Political leaders and the police needed to examine the problem and corresponding measures should be taken: "In the near future the residents of the asylum hostel will be moved."

The people of Hoyerswerda prefer to be more direct, referring to the problem of *Neger* (niggers) und *Fidschis* (a general term for Asian foreigners). The loudmouths of the neo-fascist gangs make the message clear: "Niggers Go Home!"

It looks as if some Germans have had enough of bureaucratic officialese. What is more, they will soon make sure that no more foreign voices are heard in Hoyerswerda.

The municipality in northern Saxony has a population of just under 70,000, including 70 people from Mozambique and Vietnam who live in a hostel for foreigners and about 240 asylum-seekers in a hostel at the other end of town.

The "political situation" was triggered by an attack by a neo-Nazi gang on Vietnamese traders selling their goods on the market square on 17 September. After being dispersed by the police the *Faschos* carried out their first attack on the hostel for foreigners.

The attacks then turned into a regular evening "hunt" by a growing group of right-wing radicals, some of them minors, who presented their idea of a clean Germany by roaming the streets armed with truncheons, stones, steel balls, bottles and Molotov cocktails. Seventeen people were injured, some seriously.

After the police stepped in on a larger scale the extremists moved across the town to the asylum hostel. To begin with, only the gang itself and onlookers were outside the building, but on the evening of 22 September members of the "Human Rights League" and about 100 members of "autonomous" groups turned up to help the foreigners who had sought refuge in the already heavily damaged block of flats.

A large police contingent, reinforced by men from Dresden and the Border Guard, prevented the situation from becoming even more critical. Two people were seriously injured. The mob was disbanded with the help of dogs, tear gas and water-cannons.

Thirty-two people were arrested, and blank cartridge guns, knives, slings and clubs were seized. On 23 September, a police spokesman announced that the situation was under control. It seems doubtful whether things will stay this way, since the pogroms have become an evening ritual. Politicians and officials are racking their brains about how to grapple with the current crisis and the basic problem. One thing is clear: without a massive intervention by the police the problem cannot even be contained. But what then?

Saxony's Interior Minister, Rudolf Krause, initially recommended that the hostels concerned should be "fenced in," but then admitted that this was "not the final solution." Providing the Defence Ministry approves, the "provisional solution" will be to move the foreigners to a barracks in Kamenz.

Even if this operation is completed without violence it would represent a shameful success for the right-wing radicals. Although the Africans and Asians still living in Hoyerswerda will have to leave at the end of November anyway once the employment contracts drawn up in the former GDR expire, they are unwilling to endure the terror that long. "Even if we're going anyway—they want all foreigners to go now," says 29-year-old Martinho from Mozambique.

His impression is that the gangs of thugs are doing something for which others are grateful: "The neighbours are glad when the skinheads arrive."

Interior Minister Krause feels that the abuse of asylum laws, the social problems in East Germany and an historically rooted deficit explain this situation: "The problem is that we were unable in the past to practise the tolerance needed to accept alien cultures."

In the opinion of extremism expert Eberhard Seidel-Pielen, however, such explanations fail to state "how high the standard of living and per capita income must be to prevent a descent into social neo-fascism." The chairman of the police trade union, Hermann Lutz, stresses that politicians must do more to foster tolerance.

Chapter 12

The New

Europeans: Labor,

Migration, and

the Problems

of Assimilation

Sources 16 and 17 from Stern Magazin, *Hamburg, Germany, Oct. 2, 1991. "On Niggers and People," 1991. Editorial translated by Sam Ali Mustafa. Rolf Schmidt-Holtz/Stern/PicturePress. Reprinted with permission.*

16. Cover: "The German Shame: The Hunt for Foreigners," 1991

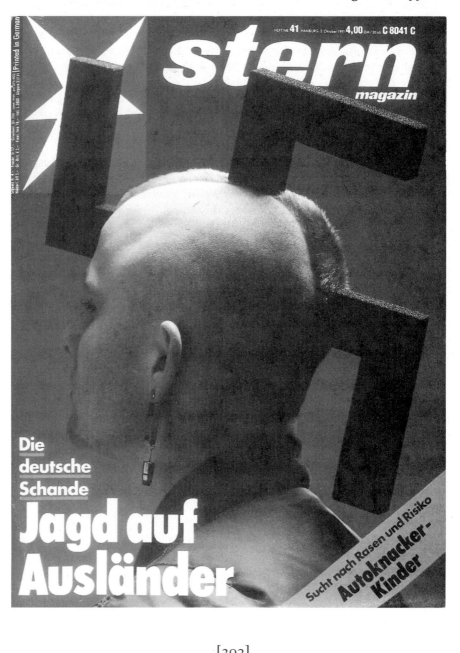

17. Editorial: "On Niggers and People," 1991

The dignity of humanity is indisputable. To give it attention and protection is the obligation of all state authorities. The German people commit themselves to unshakable and irreplaceable human rights as the basis to every human society, and of peace and justice in the world.

Article I, Basic Law [Constitution] of the Bundesrepublik Deutschland.

With these first sentences, the fathers of the Constitution wanted to draw a final curtain on the years of persecution, degradation, and murder of people in the name of National Socialism; in the name of a criminal popular racism. Thus the new, democratically legitimate state administration of the Federal Republic should have been solemnly obligated—above all else—to protect the dignity of humanity. In Hoyerswerda, Saxony, the government broke the Constitution. In the days and nights of the hunt for foreigners by neo-Nazi hordes, our state capitulated to the mob. Romanian, Vietnamese, and Mozambicans fled in terror before German boots, Hitler-salutes, and xenophobia. And all it took to ruin our valiant justice system: a pair of public buses.

Our justice system can be powerful when it wants to be. When it cares about something like protecting the comical hoarding of a piece of sand and forest in Wackersdorf, an atomic-limitation agreement can result. Then they're on the job like greased lightning: the legions of all Germany for protecting justice. . . .

In Hoyerswerda the foreign children screamed and cried all through the night in fear of Molotov cocktails and paving stones and German hate. They were afraid of being struck down or killed. And the hateful Germans howled in delight at every blow.

There is no excuse for this; there is only shame. Naturally, many factors are involved: forty years of living isolated [in the communist East], insufficient practice in social intercourse with foreigners, the psychological disturbances of the German unification process, the despair of those who settle in the ghettoes, and the unemployment of many East Germans. But these things can be no excuses. The xenophobia of Hoyerswerda is, in frightening ways, typically German. And the applauding Germans are accomplices to the mob.

Why didn't the Federal helicopters land in Hoyerswerda with Interior Minister Wolfang Schäuble, or with Chancellor Helmut Kohl? Where was Saxony's Minister-President Kurt Biedenkopf? They all—sworn to the Constitution—did not defend the dignity of humanity in Hoyerswerda.

In this issue of *Stern*, you can read how many attacks against foreigners and asylum-seekers were committed in the last fourteen days. And by no means only in the East. Xenophobia is a broadly German thing.

[393]

Chapter 12

The New

Europeans: Labor,

Migration, and

the Problems

of Assimilation

The politicians are all guilty. Their cynical and partisan discussion about the asylum problem makes common citizens less safe, and emboldens the perpetrators. In addition, the inactivity in the fight against asylum abuses destroys the sympathy for asylum in the [German] population. And if CDU General Secretary [Volker Rühe] has his way, and the SPD refuses a reform of the Constitution, then this issue is shifted onto the backs of the poorest [in society].

Indeed, Bishop Dyba, Bishop Wetter . . . where was the Church in Hoyerswerda? You unswervingly protect with all your might the fetuses against the "Holocaust of the unborn lives." Why do you protect so few of the born?

QUESTIONS TO CONSIDER

It is clear from the evidence in Sources 1 through 5 that there will continue to be a steady influx of workers and their families from non-Western nations into Western Europe. Sources 2 through 5 make it clear *who* is coming, and Source 1 offers partial evidence as to *why* they are coming. In what ways are these immigrants valuable to their host nations? What alternatives are available to those host nations that might wish to limit or even cut off this immigration? Looking again at Source 1, the United States has worked to build up the economies of Mexico, Haiti, and other nations in hopes of decreasing immigration from those countries. Is this an alternative?

Jean Raispail's novel is an undisguised attack on what he views as the West's retreat from its belief (a correct one, in his opinion) in the superiority of Western society, Western culture, and the Western economic and political systems. Thus the West, according to Raispail, lacks the courage to protect itself against an onslaught of non-Europeans. Without having read the book (it is still in print), can you imagine what effect this novel might have had? Does the interview with the author provide clues as to how he himself feels about these issues? With whom might he ally himself or side? What, if any, is the relationship (causal or otherwise) between the popularity of the novel *The Camp of the Saints* and the public opinion poll and cartoon (Sources 7 and 8)? In what ways does Source 9 offer a different view of French public opinion—if indeed it does? In what ways could *all* these documents (Sources 6 through 9) be genuine expressions of French public opinion? What is the opinion of the cartoonist (Source 8)? What is the point of the cartoon?

Sources 10 and 11 are concerned with the Brixton riot of April 1981, in which police attempting to assist the victim of a knife fight were attacked by working-class young people, most of whom were black, who then expanded their activities to building destruction and general looting. In the views of Sources 10 and 11, what were the underlying causes of that riot? How do these sources help you in identifying and assessing the alternatives available to leaders of Western Europe with regard to immigration, multiculturalism, and xenophobia? What is your opinion of the actions recommended by Devon Thomas (Source 11)?

Sources 12 through 17 involve the Federal Republic of Germany. As the academicians who wrote and signed the Heidelberg Manifesto (Source 12) viewed it, what is the nature of the immigration problem? By inference, what would be their recommended solution? What problems would that alternative pose for German industry? Might the Heidelberg Manifesto be used by other people to advocate solutions that the German academicians would have opposed? In what ways do the cover and the article in the September 9, 1991, issue of *Der Spiegel* (*The Mirror*) support the Hei-

delberg Manifesto of 1982? Are alternatives offered or implied?

Sources 15 through 17 deal with the 1991 Hoyerswerda antiforeign riot. Source 15 assesses a number of possible alternatives for eradicating the problem of anti-immigrant violence. Which alternative is implied to be the best one? How did the article excerpted in Source 15 define the word "best"?

By titling its article "The German Shame," *Stern Magazin* left no doubt as to what it considered was the nature of the problem. Whom does *Stern* charge with aiding and abetting the rioters? What, by implication, is *Stern*'s preferred alternative?

EPILOGUE

Like the United States, Western Europe has become considerably more ethnically diverse since World War II. Immigrants from former colonies in Africa, Asia, and the Caribbean settled in Belgium, France, Great Britain, and the Netherlands. "Guest workers" from the Middle East, North Africa, and Southeast Asia sought employment in Germany and other countries. The majority of these immigrants found jobs in lower-paid positions, in what some scholars have characterized as "unpleasant" work. They also encountered prejudice and even violence as it became increasingly clear that these once-temporary workers had no intention of returning to their native lands, that they were sending for their families and estab-

lishing permanent residences in their adopted countries, and that they actively resisted cultural assimilation but instead were determined to retain their traditional ways.

How have Western Europeans reacted? In France, after some conflict, Muslim schoolgirls were permitted to wear headscarves, and there were no incidents. In Lyons in 1994, Interior Minister Charles Pasqua helped dedicate a mosque for the Rhone-Alpes region's 200,000 Muslims, and Pasqua was joined by representatives of Lyons's Christian and Jewish communities. And yet Jean-Marie LePen and his National Front, France's foremost advocates of "France for the French," won some significant local government victories in the 1995 elections.

In the Federal Republic of Germany, some hopeful signs followed

Chapter 12

The New

Europeans: Labor,

Migration, and

the Problems

of Assimilation

the terrible events at Hoyerswerda. Thousands of Germans marched in opposition to skinheads and anti-ethnic violence. Moreover, in 1998, the Social Democrats and the environmentalist Green Party promised that their coalition government would push for liberalization of Germany's "nationality based on blood" citizenship laws, which were first enacted in 1913.[19] In addition, Turkish families were beginning to appear "more German" demographically, as the average family size declined by over one-half. Yet, at the same time, disturbing racial incidents continued. In the words of an immigrant from Kazakstan, "Sometimes, it makes you weep."[20]

And so the question remains: Was the celebration of the French soccer team's 1998 World Cup victory a hopeful sign of an increasingly more tolerant West or a temporary aberration that disguises the fact that so little has changed? Are there better alternatives than those that are being tried?

Historians cannot—and should not—predict the future, what is going to happen. Indeed, the more conservative historians do not believe that a historian should study any event that has occurred since he or she was born. Why do you think those historians believe this?

And yet, although historians should not offer predictions or analyze contemporary events, they still have an important role to play in today's policymaking and public arena. As political leaders attempt to formulate and carry out policies, they often need the rudder of a sound historical perspective. Historians can be valuable because of their ability to examine and analyze all the evidence at their disposal, both traditional types of evidence and less orthodox sources, and offer a sound historical perspective to our future leaders. Moreover, whatever your own particular career goals may be, you too will need to be able to examine and analyze the mountain of evidence that stands before you.

19. *New York Times,* Oct. 16, 1998.
20. *New York Times,* March 24, 1996.

CHAPTER THIRTEEN

McDOMINATION:[1] THE AMERICANIZATION

OF GLOBAL POPULAR CULTURE

(1950s TO THE PRESENT)

In his utopian novel *Looking Backward* (1888), author and journalist Edward Bellamy (1850–1898) predicted that by the year 2000, the world would be linked together in a "single planetary consumer market." As Bellamy saw it, such a global economy would eradicate poverty and want worldwide by making everyone a participant—both as a producer and as a consumer—in government-planned and government-directed industrialization and distribution of goods. To Julian West, the novel's hero, who had fallen asleep in 1887 and had not reawakened until September 10, 2000, it was a world that had eliminated not only poverty but also national conflicts and class warfare.

Although Bellamy's socialist vision never materialized, his dreams of a global economy and a worldwide consumer market seemed prophetic to people actually living in the year 2000. Brand names and products such as Nike footwear, Nokia cellular telephones, and Pokemón trading cards and films are perhaps better known to men, women, and children worldwide than the names of the most important global political leaders. As Zygmunt Bauman commented in his book *Globalization: The Human Consequences* (1998), global commerce and consumption creates "a strange circle whose center is everywhere."[2]

While many nations and cultures contribute products, services, and advertising images to the global marketplace, none has been more successful in doing this than the

1. We first encountered this term in an un-published lecture by University of Tennessee historian Vejas Liulevicius: "Europe's Fear of McDomination."

2. Zygmunt Bauman, *Globalization: The Human Consequences* (New York: Columbia University Press, 1998), pp. 77–78.

Chapter 13

McDomination:

The

Americanization

of Global Popular

Culture

(1950s to the

Present)

United States. The near–tidal wave of U.S. exports has raised serious questions about the power of multinational corporations and the efforts of other nations to withstand the American economic onslaught and to protect their own manufacturers—something that Bellamy clearly did not anticipate. The central issue in this chapter, however, is less economic than *cultural*: the possible effects of economic globalization on those cultures that consume American products. For as Benjamin R. Barber has explained in his thoughtful book *Jihad vs. McWorld*, "selling American products means selling America: its popular culture, its putative prosperity, its ubiquitous imagery . . . and thus its very soul."[3]

No American corporation has been as successful in its efforts to capture the global marketplace as McDonald's, the fast-food giant that by 1999 boasted more than 25,500 restaurants in over 120 nations and served an average of 30 million customers *each day*. So pervasive are the company's trademarked golden arches that one eight-year-old youngster from South Korea saw a McDonald's restaurant while visiting Boston, Massachusetts, and exclaimed, "Look! They have our kind of food here."[4] The world's largest McDonald's (with 700 seats, 29 cash registers, and 605 employees) opened in 1990 in Mos-

cow, while in 1992 the first McDonald's opened in Beijing, with 40,000 customers being served on its very first day. Somewhere in the world, three new McDonald's restaurants open for business every day.[5]

This global spread of American products and popular culture, however, has not been without opposition. Often many people in the West and non-West alike, labeling this phenomenon cultural imperialism, accuse the United States of undermining and even destroying other cultures that allow American products and popular culture to gain footholds on their native soils by eroding their traditions, cultures, languages, and even identities. This resistance thus far has been most prominent in France, where farmer Jose Bové touched off a wave of assaults on McDonald's restaurants in 1999 and in doing so became a national and even international hero.[6] Although opposition to American cultural intrusion in general and McDonald's restaurants in particular has been less dramatic elsewhere, there is little doubt that deep opposition to American cultural ubiquity[7] is widespread.

By examining and analyzing the material in the Evidence section of this chapter, answer the following questions:

3. Benjamin R. Barber, *Jihad vs. McWorld* (New York: Times Books, 1995), p. 60.

4. James L. Watson, "China's Big Mac Attack," *Foreign Affairs*, vol. 79 (May/June 2000), p. 131. In Source 8, Thomas L. Friedman claims the child was Japanese and that she saw the McDonald's in Los Angeles.

5. For the Moscow opening, see *New York Times*, Feb. 1, 1990. For the Beijing opening, see James L. Watson, ed., *Golden Arches East: McDonald's in East Asia* (Stanford, Calif: Stanford University Press, 1997), p. 39.

6. *The Times* (London), Aug. 21, 1999.

7. **ubiquity:** presence everywhere.

1. How does McDonald's give us insight into the globalization of popular culture?

2. What are the *benefits* of the globalization of popular (largely American) culture? What are the *liabilities*?

3. Do you agree or disagree with those who accuse the United States in general and American commercial enterprises in particular of a different form of imperialism (*cultural imperialism*)?

BACKGROUND

The economic dominance of the United States could easily have been predicted as early as the mid-nineteenth century—or even earlier. It boasted a burgeoning population that, as a result of natural increase and immigration, doubled every twenty-five years (providing ample numbers of laborers and consumers), a huge market within the nation and its territories, abundant raw materials, easy access to rich energy sources (water power, wood, coal), and modern technology (often "borrowed" from other nations). By the eve of the American Civil War in 1860 the United States ranked third among all nations in manufacturing output. And the Civil War (1861–1865) itself further accelerated industrialization by encouraging the growth of factories to produce war materiel, concentrating investment capital in the hands of a few large bankers and heads of investment firms, and maintaining in Washington a government friendly to business. Finally, after the Civil War, the United States dramatically reduced its military expenditures, thereby allowing it to pour even more resources into economic growth and development (by 1880 the nation ranked only eighth in the number of military and naval personnel).[8]

During the early twentieth century, these trends continued. By 1900 the United States led the world in manufacturing output, with 23.6 percent of the world's total. And by 1929 that gap had widened even more significantly: The nation's share of world manufacturing stood at an incredible 43.3 percent. Indeed, it seemed as if the United States would become the world's manufacturer.

The worldwide economic depression in the 1930s severely reduced the United States' share of world manufacturing (to 28.7 percent by 1938). But by 1953 the United States' share had rebounded to 44.7 percent, due in large part to wartime devastation in Europe and Asia. After that, however, the rise of manufacturing in developing nations (which increased to 9.9 percent of the world's share by 1973), the resurgence of industrialization in Germany and Japan (with new factories), the surprisingly rapid obsolescence of U.S. establishments, and foreign competition from nations with significantly lower labor costs

8. Paul Kennedy, *The Rise and Fall of the Great Powers: Economic Change and Military Conflict from 1500 to 2000* (New York: Random House, 1987), p. 203.

[399]

Chapter 13

McDomination:

The

Americanization

of Global Popular

Culture

(1950s to the

Present)

combined to decrease the nation's share of world manufacturing. The United States' trade deficits with other industrial nations grew to disturbing proportions.

At the same time that the United States' share of world manufacturing was decreasing, however, other American exports were burgeoning. United States occupation troops and American films, television, and recorded music introduced people throughout the world to American *popular culture*. Young people especially became avid consumers of Hollywood-produced films,[9] American popular music and clothing, and American products came to represent the "good life" or what was up-to-date or "cool." Michael Jordan became as well known in the People's Republic of China as he was in the United States; American baseball became a world sport; and Elvis Presley was famous nearly everywhere. Even American words or phrases found their way into other languages: chewing gum, cheeseburgers, prime time, talk shows, software. When American citizens finally were allowed to visit the People's Republic of China, they often were inundated by young people seeking to practice their English and their use of "cool" American speech. And as young people throughout the world gradually became more affluent, their appetites for American popular culture increased all the more.

McDonald's was not the first United States company to take advantage of the Americanization of global popular culture. The ubiquity of the soft drink Coca-Cola led one British sociologist to grumble about "Coca-colonization."[10] But in many ways it was McDonald's that most successfully fused American popular culture with a product and a particular style of delivering that product. Indeed, by 1982 McDonald's was the largest owner of retail real estate in the *world*.[11]

Although brothers Maurice and Richard McDonald opened the first McDonald's window-service-only hamburger stand in San Bernardino, California, pioneered the golden arches as a trademark, and began selling McDonald's franchises (six in California by 1955), it was salesman-promoter Ray Kroc (1902–1984) who can be credited with making McDonald's a giant fast-food operation and worldwide cultural icon. Kroc, who at various times had worked as a piano player in a band, an announcer at a Chicago radio station, and a salesman of Florida real estate, was selling milk shake makers when he first met the McDonald brothers in 1954. The McDonalds ordered eight of them, and Kroc immediately set out for San Bernadino to visit a place that needed to make forty milk shakes at one time (each machine had five spindles). Kroc was stunned

9. In 1991, *Terminator 2* and *Dances with Wolves* were the two most popular films in the world. Of the twenty-two nations surveyed by *Variety International Film Guide*, only two nations (Finland and Holland) had domestic films that topped all others. Barber, *Jihad vs. McWorld*, pp. 299–301.

10. On "Coca-colonization," see Barry Smart, ed., *Resisting McDonaldization* (London: Sage, 1999), p. 1.

11. John F. Love, *McDonald's: Behind the Arches* (New York: Bantam Books, rev. ed. 1995), p. 4.

when, upon arrival, he found a modest walk-up hamburger stand that sold "the best hamburger you ever ate" for fifteen cents and a bag of french fried potatoes for a dime. People were lined up at all the windows.

Kroc ultimately won permission from the McDonald brothers to be the franchise agent to sell and set up new McDonald's stands (the first franchise fee was $950). By 1958, Kroc had opened 80 new stores (the first store was in Des Plaines, Illinois, outside of Chicago); by 1959 he had opened 100, by 1960 there were over 200. Kroc later claimed that the keys to McDonald's success were good food at a low price (the french fries were the most profitable item), courteous and well-groomed employees (who were schooled to say "thank you" and "have a nice day"), and clean, well-lighted stores and spotless restrooms (Kroc once claimed that "I *couldn't* hire a guy from Harvard because the son of a bitch wouldn't get down and wash the toilets").[12] The McDonald brothers were bought out for $2.7 million and McDonald's Systems, Inc., was on its way. By 1965 there were 710 McDonald's stores with over 20,000 employees serving the traditional fare plus double burgers (1963), Filet-O-Fish (1964), Big Macs (1968), Quarter Pounders (1971), and Egg McMuffins (1971). By 1971, about 1 percent of all

beef wholesaled in the United States was purchased by McDonald's (300,000 cattle per year), and the company was the nation's top purchaser of processed potatoes and fish, exceeding the U.S. Army in the volume of food served. It was the nation's leading employer of young people (1 in 15 of all people who work began their working careers at a McDonald's).[13]

Kroc's claim that McDonald's success could be attributed to good food at low prices, courteous employees, and clean stores and restrooms was only partly correct. The growth of McDonald's paralleled and was affected by important shifts in America's demography, economy, and culture. Chief among these changes was the postwar mass exodus of comparatively affluent young married couples to the new suburbs, where they created and participated in a suburban culture that centered much of its attention on its children (the "baby boomers"). In order to support the new, credit-based lifestyles of these young families, women increasingly began to enter the workforce. For these dual-income young couples with children, McDonald's was almost made to order. Families could pick up quick meals at the stores' drive-through windows, thus relieving working wives of having to prepare meals after full workdays. Also, these busy parents could offer their children meals at McDonald's as "rewards." And they could depend

12. See Max Boas and Steve Chain, *Big Mac: The Unauthorized Story of McDonald's* (New York: Dutton, 1976), p. 24. See also Ray Kroc with Robert Anderson, *Grinding It Out: The Making of McDonald's* (Chicago: H. Regnery, 1977), p. 131.

13. The first female crew workers were not hired until 1969.

Chapter 13

McDomination:

The

Americanization

of Global Popular

Culture

(1950s to the

Present)

on McDonald's for predictable food and clean restrooms as they took to the road in their automobiles as a new generation of tourists. Indeed, McDonald's was only the most successful of the many new franchises that were founded in the midst of these important demographic, economic, and cultural changes in American life.

Although by 1971 the company was selling approximately one billion burgers every four months (to say nothing of over 300 million pounds of french fries and well over 800 billion slices of pickles), the real profit for the company was in real estate. McDonald's would locate promising restaurant[14] sites, lease them from the landowners, and then sublease them to the person who bought the McDonald's franchise (the franchisee).[15] When McDonald's was able to purchase the land outright and then lease it to the franchisee, the profits were even greater.

It was almost inevitable that Kroc would take the McDonald's concept abroad. But questions abounded. Would the food be accepted in other lands? What accommodations would McDonald's have to make to other cultures? Would the behavior of American customers (standing in lines, cleaning up their own tables, etc.) be adopted by others? Would the demeanor of McDonald's employees be understood or appreciated? Would

people see McDonald's as another example of American intrusion into their diets, their businesses, and their customs?

For the most part, these fears were unfounded. Opening first, perhaps timidly, in Canada in 1967, McDonald's spread rapidly in the early 1970s in Japan, Australia, Germany, France, Sweden, England, Hong Kong, and New Zealand. By the mid-1990s, almost half of the McDonald's corporation's gross sales came from restaurants outside the United States.[16] To be sure, some alterations had to be made. For example, when the McDonald's on Leningradskoe shosse in Moscow opened a drive-through window in 1996, tray liners had to be printed instructing people how to use the store's drive-through service. In Japan, to "accommodate the Japanese tongue," *Ronald* McDonald became *Donald* McDonald. In Israel no cheese was served on Big Macs; in India Big Macs were made of mutton; no pork was served in Muslim countries; McSpagetti was a favorite in the Philippines; frankfurters and beer were on the McDonald's menus in Germany; in Norway customers could order a grilled salmon sandwich; in the Netherlands vegetarian burgers were available. And yet in most cases the basic menu of burgers, fries, and soft drinks remained the same.[17]

At the same time, McDonald's customers in other cultures adapted to the "McDonald's concept." In Mos-

14. The first McDonald's with indoor seating (hence, a more traditional restaurant) opened in July 1966 in Huntsville, Alabama.

15. In real estate parlance, such a deal is called a "sandwich position."

16. Watson, *Golden Arches East*, p. 3.

17. *Ibid.*, pp. 23–24.

cow, a woman employee had to stand outside the restaurant with a bullhorn, explaining, "The employees inside will smile at you. This does not mean that they are laughing at you. We smile because we are happy to serve you." In Japan, McDonald's had to overcome traditional table manners, which hold that one does not actually touch food with the hands while eating. Yet at the same time, comfortable seating made the McDonald's in Beijing a favorite courtship site for young people (one area of the mammoth restaurant was nicknamed the "lovers' corner"). In Hong Kong, McDonald's became the catalyst for changes in restaurant and public restroom standards of sanitation.[18]

And yet the Americanization of global popular culture has not been without opposition. Concerned about the purity of its native tongue, the French Ministry of National Culture convinced the legislature to outlaw certain modern English/American words and phrases (chewing gum, for example, reverted to *gomme a*

macher). In 1994 Mexicans ransacked a McDonald's in Mexico City and scrawled "Yankee Go Home" on the windows.[19] Cultures as disparate as those in Great Britain, Italy, Turkey, and Korea have witnessed opposition to American popular culture that focused on McDonald's. It is as if they fear that the liabilities of global cultural homogenization might outweigh the benefits.

As you examine and analyze the evidence, remember the questions posed in the Problem section:

1. How does McDonald's give us insight into the globalization of popular culture?

2. What are the *benefits* of living in a global (largely American) culture? What are the *liabilities*?

3. Do you agree or disagree with those who accuse the United States in general and American commercial enterprises in particular of a different form of imperialism (*cultural* imperialism)?

THE METHOD

Near-fascination with American popular culture by peoples outside the United States is not a terribly new phenomenon. Although Americans from colonial times to the twentieth century have exhibited a kind of

18. *Ibid.*, pp. 28, 34, 51, 89. In Cantonese, the restaurant is named *mak dong lou.*

19. Barber, *Jihad vs. McWorld,* p. 171; *New York Times,* November 9, 1994.

cultural inferiority complex when it came to "high" culture (painting, sculpture, architecture, symphonic and classical music, etc.), at the same time non-Americans have often embraced aspects of American popular (or "low") culture such as jazz, rock 'n' roll, "pop" art, and so forth. This accelerated dramatically after World War II because of exposure to American servicemen and -women abroad, films, televisions, and recorded music; by the late 1990s,

Chapter 13

McDomination:

The

Americanization

of Global Popular

Culture

(1950s to the

Present)

British sociologist Barry Smart was hardly exaggerating when he remarked that "most of the globally ubiquitous commodities have their roots in America; they are the products of the first mass consumer society."[20]

By now you have been asked to familiarize yourself with and analyze many different types of historical evidence. Moreover, you have come to appreciate the fact that *everything* created by men, women, and children in the past can be used as evidence, if only we can learn how to properly examine it. This chapter, therefore, contains a mixture of types of evidence for you to employ in answering the chapter's central questions. As you examine and analyze the evidence, keep those central questions in mind.

As you read each piece of evidence, you will find it helpful to determine which of the central questions that piece of evidence would help to answer. In this way you can divide the evidence into more manageable groups. Remember that certain pieces of evidence may help to answer more than one question.

Source 1 is a tray liner that McDonald's uses to cover the plastic trays before food is placed on them, proof of the above statement that everything can be used as historical evidence. What clues are contained in the tray liner from Norway (Source 1)? What does this tray liner tell you?

Sources 2 through 6 are newspaper accounts involving McDonald's outlets in various countries, four from the *London Times* and one from the *Washington Post*. Which question(s) can each newspaper report help to answer?

Source 7 is an editorial cartoon by John Deering that originally appeared in the *Arkansas Democrat-Gazette* and was reprinted in the May 26, 2000, issue of *USA Today*. Deering clearly was dealing with the spread of McDonald's in the People's Republic of China. And yet, what does Deering juxtapose against the golden arches? What question does this cartoon help you to answer?

Source 8 is an editorial piece from the *New York Times* by foreign affairs writer Thomas L. Friedman, author of the important book on globalization *The Lexus and the Olive Tree*. In Friedman's opinion, what are the benefits of cultural globalization? What are the liabilities?

The final source, Source 9, is an excerpt from an essay written by Harvard professor of Chinese studies and anthropology Thomas L. Watson that appeared in the May/June 2000 issue of the influential journal *Foreign Affairs* (influential because many U.S. government officials subscribe to and carefully read the quarterly journal). Which question does Watson's essay intend to answer? What are his conclusions?

Now put all the evidence from each group together. Having done so, how would you answer the chapter's central questions?

---

20. Smart, *Resisting McDonaldization*, p. 1. For one example of the exporting of American popular culture see John Haag, "*Gone with the Wind* in Nazi Germany," *Georgia Historical Quarterly*, vol. 73 (Summer 1989), pp. 278–304.

THE EVIDENCE

Source 1 from McDonald's restaurant, Oslo, Norway. Used by permission from McDonald's Corporation.

1. McDonald's Tray Liner, Norway

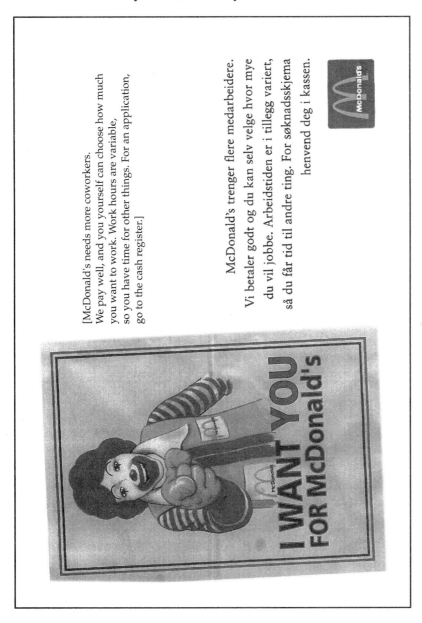

[McDonald's needs more coworkers. We pay well, and you yourself can choose how much you want to work. Work hours are variable, so you have time for other things. For an application, go to the cash register.]

McDonald's trenger flere medarbeidere. Vi betaler godt og du kan selv velge hvor mye du vil jobbe. Arbeidstiden er i tillegg variert, så du får tid til andre ting. For søknadsskjema henvend deg i kassen.

Chapter 13

McDomination:

The

Americanization

of Global Popular

Culture

(1950s to the

Present)

Source 2 from The Times *(London), June 24, 1998 by James Pringle.* © NI Syndication, *London, 1998, 1999. Reprinted by permission.*

2. McDonald's in China, 1998

MCDONALD'S OUSTS STALIN AS CHINA SHOWS CHANGING FACE TO US LEADER

As Richard Nixon's limousine sped across Tiananmen Square on his ground-breaking visit to China in February 1972, he could hardly have missed a 30ft high portrait of Stalin.

If President Clinton glances in the same direction when his motorcade crosses the square on its way to the same state guest house on Friday, he will see the McDonald's arches. Stalin is long gone. . . .

Culturally in China, things seem very different. When Nixon was here, the roly-poly female attendants at the state guest house seemed sexless in pigtails and khaki Mao suits. The female attendants that Mr Clinton will see, chosen for their beauty, are tall, slim and beguiling with fashionable hairstyles and *cheongsams* cut to the thigh.

Nixon was taken to see *Red Detachment of Women,* a revolutionary ballet about people's militias struggling with Chinese nationalist reactionaries. Mao's sour-faced wife, the late Jiang Quing, hosted Nixon at a rather grubby theatre for the performance, and he smiled as she told him that the face on a target that the people's heroes were firing at was that of Chiang Kai-shek, the Taiwanese leader and America's friend.

Nowadays, the movie *Titanic* has been seen by millions of Chinese and it is impossible to escape its theme tune anywhere in China—even in the Foreign Ministry's briefing room. In Nixon's time, *The East is Red* and *Chairman Mao is the Bright Red Sun in our Hearts* were still top of the pops.

International youth culture—in effect American culture—has taken over China. Michael Jordan is a youth icon. Tight T-shirts, jeans, baseball caps and trainers are de rigueur for the young. Discos, bars and nightclubs abound, and young ladies of the night are now almost as common as Red Guards once were.

Political slogans like "Serve The People" and "Down with American Imperialism and all its running dogs" have given way to poster boards and jingles for consumer goods.

"You let us rule you and we will let you get rich," is the pact the Communist Party has made with the people, though this is fraying at the edges as the economy falters in this authoritarian, but not now totalitarian, state.

Source 3 from The Times *(London), August 1, 1998 by Alan Hamilton.* © *NI Syndication, London, 1998, 1999. Reprinted by permission.*

3. Queen Elizabeth Visits McDonald's, 1998

THE PEOPLE LONGED FOR A LESS REMOTE MONARCH: YESTERDAY THEY MET HER

Those determined to portray the monarch as a people's Queen could hardly have designed a more populist day out for her yesterday: she spent the morning in Ellesmere Port, shopping for kitchenware and a pair of trainers, sustaining herself with a visit to a drive-in McDonald's.

Being the Queen, she bought neither canvas shoes nor plastic washing-up bowl, and no Big Mac passed the royal lips. But as an exercise in carefully stage-managed window-shopping, it opened the eyes of both Sovereign and subjects.

Her visit to the Cheshire Oaks Designer Outlet Village fitted the new pattern that has emerged to counter criticisms of remoteness that surfaced after the death of Diana, Princess of Wales. Typically on an awayday, the Queen now meets far more ordinary people in everyday situations and far fewer flunkeys.

As the royal limousine drew up outside the burger bar, there seemed a momentary danger that the Queen might have to go inside to learn the mysteries of Quarter-Pounders and Chicken McNuggets, but she was spared, and her visit was restricted to meeting the staff on the pavement outside. She looked a mite glum.

Pausing briefly to talk to members of a shopping motability group, and to be told that it would cost her £3 to hire a battery wheelchair, the Queen decided to walk, first to Whittard's Coffee and Kitchenware store to browse among the utensils. "She was fascinated by the plastic bowls; she couldn't make out what they were made of," the manageress Katie Bellis said later. The shop presented her with a green glass bowl and some barbecue tools, which may yet find employment at Balmoral.

The royal shopping entourage moved on to the Reebok store, where she engaged the manager Darryl Peacock in conversation on the latest in sports shoes. "I asked if she would like to buy a pair, but she just smiled. She did take an interest in one sweater which she said Prince Philip might like," Mr. Peacock reported.

Chapter 13

McDomination:

The

Americanization

of Global Popular

Culture

(1950s to the

Present)

Source 4 from **The Washington Post, October 11, 1998.**

4. A McDonald's Promotion in Hong Kong, 1998

SNOOPY FAD TAKES HONG KONG BY STORM:
THOUSANDS LINE UP OUTSIDE MCDONALD'S

HONG KONG—They began lining up at dawn, outside every branch in the city. Soon the lines grew to hundreds of people, stretching around city blocks. On a few occasions, police were called to keep order.

What was the cause of this city-wide pandemonium? A run on a failing bank? A mad rush for visas, perhaps?

No, it was Snoopy. Not Snoop Dogg, the rapper, but Snoopy, the world's most famous beagle, Charlie Brown's pooch from the Peanuts cartoon strip.

Every day for four weeks McDonald's offered three-inch Snoopy figurines for a mere 6 Hong Kong dollars—equivalent to about 75 cents—with the purchase of a McDonald's meal. Each day brought a Snoopy dressed in a different national costume—a Chinese Snoopy, a Mexican Snoopy, a Mongolian Snoopy, an American Snoopy in an Uncle Sam hat, as well as one in a cowboy hat with a pair of six-shooters around his waist.

What McDonald's probably never anticipated was that in collector-crazed Hong Kong, the Snoopies became the hottest item in town. For the duration of the offer, which ended last week, thousands of people lined up outside McDonald's outlets each day, beginning as early as 6 a.m. Some people sent their maids or their elderly grandparents. Some came equipped with cell phones, to take Snoopy orders from friends and co-workers.

One businesswoman reportedly sent employees to McDonald's outlets in Malaysia and Singapore to grab excess Snoopies. And a Snoopy black market opened in Wan Chai and Mongkok, selling bootleg versions of the most popular Snoopies for 50 times the going rate.

A 72-year-old retiree said he got up every morning at 4 a.m. to do his exercises, then headed straight to the neighborhood McDonald's in Sheung Wan. "I used to go have dim sum every day," he said. "Now I have no dim sum—I just go to McDonald's." His goal was to collect all 28 Snoopies for his grandson, 8, who would face ostracism at school and serious social humiliation should a single Snoopy be missing from his set.

"I just get a lot of satisfaction when I get a new one of the 28 Snoopies," said housewife Kitty Poon, 38. She has spent more than 4,000 Hong Kong dollars, or more than $500, buying the meals to get the Snoopies, including 20 of the Uncle Sam Snoopy alone. "It's just like buying property!" she exclaimed.

Of course, very few people actually ate the food, especially after four weeks of daily visits. Some simply bought the meals to get the Snoopies, and then threw the food away or gave it to strangers. The homeless and poor of Hong Kong began gathering near McDonald's to take the unwanted food.

What lay behind the craze? Some psychiatrists say that in this climate of economic recession, collecting something seen as a bargain alleviates the stress of hard times. And Hong Kong residents are known as collectors of virtually anything that might have value one day, as witnessed by lines outside post offices for a chance to buy the last postage stamp with Queen Elizabeth's image last year before Britain handed the territory back to China and the imperial emblem was replaced with a flower.

With the success of the "Snoopy World Tour," the irreverent local weekly newspaper HK Magazine questioned why McDonald's would continue making hamburgers. "Why not close up shop and open Snoopy stores instead?" it asked.

Source 5 from The Times *(London), July 23, 1999 by Danian Whitworth. © NI Syndication, London, 1998, 1999. Reprinted by permission.*

5. Bermuda Resists McDonald's, 1999

BERMUDA BURGHERS KEEP "BIG MAC" BAN

Bermuda, one of the last remaining outposts of the British Empire, has struck a blow against American cultural imperialism. A drive to allow McDonald's to open a restaurant on the island has been firmly rebuffed.

The Privy Council in Britain, the highest court in the land for the most populous remaining colony, upheld a special Act of the Bermuda Parliament which bars McDonald's—and similar fast-food franchises—from setting up there. The Act has been the source of a long-running legal battle.

Those who had vigorously opposed the famous golden arches were celebrating yesterday. "It was clear that we were carrying out the wishes of the majority of the people and tourists," said Trevor Moniz, a lawyer who had led the action. "McDonald's is against Bermuda's image."

Six hundred miles off the coast of North Carolina, Bermuda has retained a colonial way of life. People wear Bermuda shorts and blazers to work, break for tea at 4pm and drive no faster than a sedate 20mph. The population, which includes David Bowie, the rock star, and the American billionaire Ross Perot, is 60,000—but ten times that number of tourists, the vast majority Americans, arrive each year.

The tranquillity of paradise was disrupted when Sir John Swan, the former Prime Minister, thought that visitors and natives alike might like the occasional Big Mac. He and a government backbencher, Maxwell Burgess, were given permission in 1996 by the then finance minister to set up a franchise.

[409]

Chapter 13

McDomination:

The

Americanization

of Global Popular

Culture

(1950s to the

Present)

The move further divided the ruling United Bermuda Party (UBP), then facing dissent in its ranks over a 1995 referendum on independence from Britain. The referendum was initiated by Sir John, who resigned when it failed.

The franchise approval led to five UBP MPs; including Mr Moniz, speaking out against the party in what the local press dubbed the "burger wars." The five initiated the Prohibited Restaurants Act.

Sir John's company, Grape Bay Ltd, sued the Bermudian Government, winning their case in the Supreme Court, losing in the Court of Appeal and winding up in front of the Privy Council.

Meanwhile the divided UBP, which had dominated government since party politics emerged in the late 1960s, lost its first general election last year as the Labour party swept into power. Mr Moniz, who retained his seat in the upset, said the grant of the franchise in 1996 helped to undermine the party's credibility.

Bermuda, home to countless millionaires and a port of call for the world's swankiest yachts, is believed to be unique in specifically legislating to stop Ronald McDonald setting foot on its soil. The ban is an unusual experience for the food outlet which now peddles its burgers in 24,500 restaurants worldwide.

Source 6 from The Times *(London), September 1, 1999 by Charles Bremmer. © NI Syndication, London, 1998, 1999. Reprinted by permission.*

6. The French Protest McDonald's, 1999

FRENCH FARMERS FIGHT US 'IMPERIALISM'

McDonald's fast-food restaurants bore the brunt of demonstrations across France yesterday by farmers protesting against what they see as an American-led threat to their livelihoods and the French way of life.

About 100 farmers gathered in central Paris to support protests by hundreds more at about 20 McDonald's restaurants from Lille in the north to Lyons and rural towns across the south of the country. Their immediate aim was to win the release of Jose Bové, a southern farm activist who has become something of a hero with his campaign against American trade sanctions on Rocquefort cheese and other traditional French fare.

M Bové was arrested last month after leading a squad of farmers that ransacked a McDonald's site at Millau, in the Aveyron département. The region has been hit by Washington's punitive duty on ewe's cheese, imposed as part of the retaliation for Europe's ban on hormone-fed American beef.

With 750 restaurants, McDonald's is a convenient target for the latest rebellion by France's ever-angry farmers. Coca-Cola is also a target in a protest aimed as much at global economic pressures as at American "imperialism."

"I am a hostage to global commercialisation," M Bové said at the Montpellier courthouse yesterday, as judges considered whether to release him on bail. Guy Kastler, a farmer, said: "We are here to defend the right of people to feed themselves with their own food in their own way and against the determination of the United States to impose their way of eating on the whole planet."

McDonald's says that it wants to drop charges against M Bové and claims that 90 per cent of its products are French-produced. Worried about local mayors' threats to impose "Coca-Cola taxes," the soft-drink firm said yesterday that it was "working closely with the national farming organisations in France to make sure they understand our contributions to the French economy."

However, the struggle shows signs of broadening into national resistance, backed by the Communist Party, the Greens and much of the public, against industrialised food production and the supposed ills of the globalised economy. "Jose Bové has fulfilled every ecologist's dream: dismantling a McDonald's," said Denis Baupin, spokesman for the Green Party, which is a partner in the Government of Lionel Jospin.

Farmers are protesting against low prices, industrial methods and genetically modified crops. Their fears about the increasing domination of big retail distributors were sharpened yesterday by the merger of Carrefour and Promodes, two French hypermarket chains. The Socialist-led Government sought yesterday to reassure farm unions that the resulting huge retailer—the world's second biggest—would not mean further pressure on small farmers.

The protest is being taken seriously by the Government as the European Union prepares to confront the United States in the next round of world trade talks, in the autumn. Opinion polls show huge public support for the farmers' goals. Noel Kapferer, a professor at a Paris business school, said that the campaign against McDonald's was the first sign of a European rebellion against American-imposed cultural uniformity. "Drinking Coca-Cola in the 1970s was to support the Vietnam War," he said. "Today consumers are rejecting the American way of life."

7. Editorial Cartoon About McDonald's in China, 2000

8. McDonald's Adapts to Local Culture, 1996

The folks at McDonald's like to tell the story about the young Japanese girl who arrived in Los Angeles, looked around and said to her mother: "Look, mom, they have McDonald's here too."

You could excuse her for being surprised that McDonald's was an American company. With 2,000 restaurants in Japan, McDonald's Japan, a.k.a. "Makadonaldo," is the biggest McDonald's franchise outside the U.S. The McDonald's folks even renamed Ronald McDonald in Japan "Donald McDonald" because there's no "R" sound in Japanese.

"You don't have 2,000 stores in Japan by being seen as an American company," said James Cantalupo, head of McDonald's International. "Look, McDonald's serves meat, bread and potatoes. They eat meat, bread and potatoes in most of the world. It's how you package it and the experience you offer that counts."

The way McDonald's has packaged itself is to be a "multi-local" company. That is, by insisting on a high degree of local ownership, and by tailoring its products just enough for local cultures, McDonald's has avoided the worst cultural backlashes that some other U.S. companies have encountered. Not only do localities now feel a stake in McDonald's success, but more important, countries do. Poland for instance has emerged as one of the largest regional suppliers of meat, potatoes and bread for McDonald's in Central Europe. That is real power. Because McDonald's is gradually moving from local sourcing of its raw materials to regional sourcing to global sourcing. One day soon, all McDonald's meat in Asia might come from Australia, all its potatoes from China. Already, every sesame seed on every McDonald's bun in the world comes from Mexico. That's as good as a country discovering oil.

This balance between local and global that McDonald's has found is worth reflecting upon. Because this phenomenon we call "globalization"—the integration of markets, trade, finance, information and corporate ownership around the globe—is actually a very American phenomenon: it wears Mickey Mouse ears, eats Big Mac's, drinks Coke, speaks on a Motorola phone and tracks its investments with Merrill Lynch using Windows 95. In other words, countries that plug into globalization are really plugging into a high degree of Americanization.

People will only take so much of that. Therefore, to the extent that U.S.-origin companies are able to become multi-local, able to integrate around the globe economically without people feeling that they are being culturally assaulted, they will be successful. To the extent they don't, they will trigger a real backlash that will slam not only them but all symbols of U.S. power. Iran now calls the U.S. "the capital of global arrogance."

People in other cultures cannot always distinguish between American power, American exports, American cultural assaults and globalization. That's why you already see terrorists lashing out at U.S. targets not for any instrumental reason, but simply to reject this steamroller of globalization/ Americanization, which has become so inescapable. (The McDonald's people have a saying: Sooner or later McDonald's is in every story. Where did O. J. eat just before the murder of Nicole? McDonald's. What did Commerce Secretary Ron Brown serve U.S. troops just before he died? McDonald's. . . .)

[413]

Chapter 13

McDomination:

The

Americanization

of Global Popular

Culture

(1950s to the

Present)

"You try to shut the door and it comes in through the window," says the historian Ronald Steel about globalization. "You try to shut the window and it comes in on the cable. You cut the cable, it comes in on the Internet. And it's not only in the room with you. You eat it. It gets inside you."

The only answer is multi-localism—democratizing globalization so that people everywhere feel some stake in how it impacts their lives. "McDonald's stands for a lot more than just hamburgers and American fast food," argued Mr. Cantalupo. "Cultural sensitivity is part of it too. There is no 'Euroburger.' . . . We have a different chicken sandwich in England than we do in Germany. We are trying not to think as a cookie cutter."

Source 9 from James L. Watson, "China's Big Mac Attack." Reprinted by permission of Foreign Affairs, *vol. 79 (May/June 2000), pp. 120–124, 134. Copyright 2000 by the Council on Foreign Relations, Inc.*

9. McDonald's in the People's Republic of China, 2000

Looming over Beijing's choking, bumper-to-bumper traffic, every tenth building seems to sport a giant neon sign advertising American wares: Xerox, Mobil, Kinko's, Northwest Airlines, IBM, Jeep, Gerber, even the Jolly Green Giant. American food chains and beverages are everywhere in central Beijing: Coca-Cola, Starbucks, Kentucky Fried Chicken, Häagen-Dazs, Dunkin' Donuts, Baskin-Robbins, Pepsi, TCBY, Pizza Hut, and of course McDonald's. As of June 1999, McDonald's had opened 235 restaurants in China. Hong Kong alone now boasts 158 McDonald's franchises, one for every 42,000 residents (compared to one for every 30,000 Americans).

Fast food can even trump hard politics. After NATO accidentally bombed the Chinese embassy in Belgrade during the war in Kosovo, Beijing students tried to organize a boycott of American companies in protest. Coca-Cola and McDonald's were at the top of their hit list, but the message seemed not to have reached Beijing's busy consumers: the three McDonald's I visited last July were packed with Chinese tourists, local yuppies, and grandparents treating their "little emperors and empresses" to Happy Meals. The only departure from the familiar American setting was the menu board (which was in Chinese, with English in smaller print) and the jarring sound of Mandarin shouted over cellular phones. People were downing burgers, fries, and Cokes. It was, as Yogi Berra said, déjà vu all over again; I had seen this scene a hundred times before in a dozen countries. Is globalism—and its cultural variant, McDonaldization—the face of the future?

American academe is teeming with theorists who argue that transnational corporations like McDonald's provide the shock troops for a new form of imperialism that is far more successful, and therefore more insidious, than its militarist antecedents. Young people everywhere, the argument goes, are avid consumers of soap operas, music videos, cartoons, electronic games, martial-arts books, celebrity posters, trendy clothing, and faddish hairstyles. To cater to them, shopping malls, supermarkets, amusement parks, and fast-food restaurants are popping up everywhere. Younger consumers are forging transnational bonds of empathy and shared interests that will, it is claimed, transform political alignments in ways that most world leaders—old men who do not read *Wired*—cannot begin to comprehend, let alone control. Government efforts to stop the march of American (and Japanese) pop culture are futile; censorship and trade barriers succeed only in making forbidden films, music, and Web sites irresistible to local youth.

One of the clearest expressions of the "cultural imperialism" hypothesis appeared in a 1996 *New York Times* op-ed by Ronald Steel: "It was never the Soviet Union, but the United States itself that is the true revolutionary power. . . .We purvey a culture based on mass entertainment and mass gratification. . . .The cultural message we transmit through Hollywood and McDonald's goes out across the world to capture, and also to undermine, other societies. . . .Unlike traditional conquerors, we are not content merely to subdue others: We insist that they be like us." In his recent book, *The Lexus and the Olive Tree*, Thomas Friedman presents a more benign view of the global influence of McDonald's. Friedman has long argued in his *New York Times* column that McDonald's and other manifestations of global culture serve the interests of middle classes that are emerging in autocratic, undemocratic societies. Furthermore, he notes, countries that have a McDonald's within their borders have never gone to war against each other. (The NATO war against Serbia would seem to shatter Friedman's Big Mac Law, but he does not give up easily. In his July 2, 1999, column, he argued that the shutdown and rapid reopening of Belgrade's six McDonald's actually prove his point.)

If Steel and his ideological allies are correct, McDonald's should be the poster child of cultural imperialism. McDonald's today has more than 25,000 outlets in 119 countries. Most of the corporation's revenues now come from operations outside the United States, and a new restaurant opens somewhere in the world every 17 hours.

McDonald's makes heroic efforts to ensure that its food looks, feels, and tastes the same everywhere. A Big Mac in Beijing tastes virtually identical to a Big Mac in Boston. Menus vary only when the local market is deemed mature enough to expand beyond burgers and fries. Consumers can enjoy Spicy Wings (red-pepper-laced chicken) in Beijing, kosher Big Macs (minus the cheese) in Jerusalem, vegetable McNuggets in New Delhi, or a McHuevo (a burger with fried egg) in Montevideo. Nonetheless, wherever McDonald's takes root, the core product—at least during the initial phase of operation—is not really the food but the experience of eating in a cheerful, air-conditioned, child-friendly restaurant that offers the revolutionary innovation of clean toilets.

Chapter 13

McDomination:

The

Americanization

of Global Popular

Culture

(1950s to the

Present)

Critics claim that the rapid spread of McDonald's and its fast-food rivals undermines indigenous cuisines and helps create a homogeneous, global culture. Beijing and Hong Kong thus make excellent test cases since they are the dual epicenters of China's haute cuisine (with apologies to Hunan, Sichuan, and Shanghai loyalists). If McDonald's can make inroads in these two markets, it must surely be an unstoppable force that levels cultures. But the truth of this parable of globalization is subtler than that.

How did McDonald's do it? How did a hamburger chain become so prominent in a cultural zone dominated by rice, noodles, fish, and pork? In China, adult consumers often report that they find the taste of fried beef patties strange and unappealing. Why, then, do they come back to McDonald's? And more to the point, why do they encourage their children to eat there?

The history of McDonald's in Hong Kong offers good clues about the mystery of the company's worldwide appeal. When Daniel Ng, an American-trained engineer, opened Hong Kong's first McDonald's in 1975, his local food-industry competitors dismissed the venture as a nonstarter: "Selling hamburgers to Cantonese? You must be joking!" Ng credits his boldness to the fact that he did not have an M.B.A. and had never taken a course in business theory.

During the early years of his franchise, Ng promoted McDonald's as an outpost of American culture, offering authentic hamburgers to "with-it" young people eager to forget that they lived in a tiny colony on the rim of Maoist China. Those who experienced what passed for hamburgers in British Hong Kong during the 1960s and 1970s will appreciate the innovation. Ng made the fateful decision not to compete with Chinese-style fast-food chains that had started a few years earlier (the largest of which, Café de Coral, was established in 1969). The signs outside his first restaurants were in English; the Chinese characters for McDonald's (Cantonese *Mak-dong-lou*, Mandarin *Mai-dang-lao*) did not appear until the business was safely established. Over a period of 20 years, McDonald's gradually became a mainstay of Hong Kong's middle-class culture. Today the restaurants are packed wall-to-wall with busy commuters, students, and retirees who treat them as homes away from home. A 1997 survey I conducted among Hong Kong university students revealed that few were even aware of the company's American origins. For Hong Kong youth, McDonald's is a familiar institution that offers comfort foods that they have eaten since early childhood.

Yunxiang Yan, a UCLA anthropologist, hints that a similar localization process may be underway in Beijing. McDonald's there is still a pricey venue that most Chinese treat as a tourist stop: you haven't really "done" Beijing unless you have visited the Forbidden City, walked around Tiananmen Square, and eaten at the "Golden Arches." Many visitors from the countryside take Big Mac boxes, Coke cups, and napkins home with them as proof that they did it right. Yan also discovered that working-class Beijing residents save up to take their kids to McDonald's and hover over them as they munch. (Later the adults eat in a cheaper, Chinese-style restaurant.) Parents told Yan that they wanted their children to "connect" with the world outside China. To them, McDonald's was an important stop on the way to Harvard Business School or the MIT labs. Yan has since discovered that local yuppies are beginning to eat Big Macs regularly. In 20 years, he predicts, young people in Beijing (like their counterparts in Hong Kong today) will not even care about the foreign origin of McDonald's, which will be serving ordinary food to people more interested in getting a quick meal than in having a cultural experience. The key to this process of localization is China's changing family system and the emergence of a "singleton" (only-child) subculture. . . .

WHOSE CULTURE IS IT, ANYWAY?

Is McDonald's leading a crusade to create a homogenous, global culture that suits the needs of an advanced capitalist world order? Not really. Today's economic and social realities demand an entirely new approach to global issues that takes consumers' perspectives into account. The explanatory device of "cultural imperialism" is little more than a warmed-over version of the neo-Marxist dependency theories that were popular in the 1960s and 1970s— approaches that do not begin to capture the complexity of today's emerging transnational systems.

The deeper one digs into the personal lives of consumers anywhere, the more complex matters become. People are not the automatons many theorists make them out to be. Hong Kong's discerning consumers have most assuredly not been stripped of their cultural heritage, nor have they become the uncomprehending dupes of transnational corporations.

In places like Hong Kong, it is increasingly difficult to see where the transnational ends and the local begins. Fast food is an excellent case in point: for the children who flock to weekend birthday parties, McDonald's is self-evidently local. Similarly, the Hong Kong elders who use McDonald's as a retreat from the loneliness of urban life could care less about the company's foreign origin. Hong Kong's consumers have made the "Golden Arches" their own.

One might also turn the lens around and take a close look at American society as it enters a new millennium. Chinese food is everywhere, giving McDonald's and KFC a run for their money in such unlikely settings as Moline and Memphis. Mandarin is fast becoming a dominant language in American research laboratories, and Chinese films draw ever more enthusiastic audiences. Last Halloween, every other kid in my Cambridge neighborhood appeared in (Japanese-inspired) Power Ranger costumes, striking poses that owe more to Bruce Lee than to Batman. Whose culture is it, anyway? If you have to ask, you have already missed the boat.

Chapter 13

McDomination:

The

Americanization

of Global Popular

Culture

(1950s to the

Present)

QUESTIONS TO CONSIDER

Earlier in this chapter, you were instructed to divide the nine pieces of evidence into three groups, one to correspond to each of the chapter's central questions. Remember that a piece of evidence may fit into more than one group, since it may help you to answer more than one of the central questions.

The first question was how McDonald's gives us insight into the process of cultural globalization. Which pieces of evidence help you answer that question? In what ways is the Norwegian tray liner (Source 1) helpful? What *other poster* does the poster in Source 1 bring to mind? Why did Queen Elizabeth II make a brief stop at a McDonald's restaurant (Source 3)? What did she order from the McDonald's menu? What is the central point of the *London Times* story about the queen?

On another note, how can you explain the enormous popularity of McDonald's in East Asia, and specifically in China (Sources 2, 4, and 9)? From the Background section of this chapter, you already know the demographic, economic, and cultural changes in the United States that contributed to McDonald's growth and success in that nation. Do the sources offer any indication that similar shifts are taking place in East Asia as well? It has been said by some people that in certain places Ronald (or Donald) McDonald is more recognizable than Santa Claus.

To whom does McDonald's market its products? How does McDonald's marketing strategy in Hong Kong and China (Sources 4 and 9) explain globalization? What do these sources *omit* (see Source 7)? What do all of these sources tell us about the recent history of the People's Republic of China?

As to the benefits and liabilities of the globalization of popular culture, again one might concentrate on China (Sources 2, 7, and 9). In China, has globalization had any benefits at all? What things have *not* changed? Many French farmers, led by Jose Bové, saw only the liabilities of the "McDonaldization" of French culture. What are those liabilities (Source 6)? According to McDonald's, what were the benefits to French farmers (Source 6, but, by inference, see also Source 1)? Why did the Bermuda government bar McDonald's (Source 5)? According to Thomas Friedman (Source 8), do the benefits of cultural globalization outweigh the liabilities, or vice versa? Where does Thomas Watson (Source 9) stand on that question?

The story on Bermuda (Source 5) reported that Bermuda had "struck a blow against American cultural imperialism." Where do your other sources (especially Sources 2, 3, 6, 8, and 9) stand on that issue? To what extent should people preserve their own culture and traditions by keeping out other cultural influences? Are cultures that permit the intrusion of other cultural influences ultimately doomed? What comparisons or accommodations are possible (see especially Source 9)?

EPILOGUE

Although other nations besides the United States have become more aggressive in exporting aspects of their own popular culture (especially Japan, with Pokemón, Godzilla, etc., and Great Britain), in many ways the globalization of popular culture is really the globalization of *American* popular culture. So powerful and ubiquitous had that trend become that in 1998, international bankers used the price of a Big Mac in Moscow (15.50 rubles) as a way to establish the exchange rate for Russian currency.[21]

In Budapest, Hungary, the "proper fashion statement" for young people at Budapest discos is a pair of Levi's blue jeans and an "American" T-shirt.[22] In Beijing in August 2000, Marvel Comics' Stan Lee (who had a hand in creating Spider-Man, the Incredible Hulk, and the X-Men) was the honored guest at a banquet of leading Japanese and Chinese cartoonists and animators (". . . if anything can bring countries together, it's cartoons"—Lee).[23] In Germany, a private firm is marketing what it calls "The American Dream," assistance (for a fee) in getting a United States green card (see photo).

21. *London Times*, September 1, 1998.

22. *Fortune*, December 31, 1990.

23. *New York Times*, August 31, 2000.

The U.S. government is now distributing
   By lottery
55,000
Green Cards
Chance of winning almost 1 in 15!

Free application forms:
0180-5110511

Never again problems with visa, job search, or a longer U.S. stay: The Green Card gives you the right to reside in the U.S. and to work there. Without restrictions and without reference to what your profession is!

(*Courtesy of The American Dream*)

Simultaneously, many nations have been able to incorporate aspects of the new global culture without having their own native cultures or traditions suffer. According to Sami Zubaida and Richard Tapper, in Turkey "there is evidence that the presence of establishments like McDonald's may actually be contributing to a revival of old-fashioned foods [such as kebabs, fried aubergine, cheese borek, baklava, and simit] which have been in danger of disappearing."[24] As Thomas Watson pointed out in Source 9, "People are not the automatons many theorists make them out to be." Is cultural homogenization a blessing? A curse?

24. Sami Zubaida and Richard Tapper, eds., *Culinary Cultures of the Middle East* (London: University of London Press, 1994), pp. 73, 75.

[420]

Both? Neither? And in the United States, too, popular culture is changing, in part influenced by immigrants from Asia and Latin America who bring their languages, music, and traditions *with them.*

And just as many people increasingly embrace parts of American popular culture through films, television, music, e-mail, the Internet, etc., so also Americans enthusiastically seek—and find—things from elsewhere to enrich their own culture. Indeed, some observers warn that what may come to pass will *not* be the Americanization of global culture, but rather a globalized culture of the "haves," often set against the diverse traditional cultures of the "have nots"—what Thomas Friedman characterized as the "Lexus and the olive tree."[25]

As global economics, pan-national movements, international migration, world demography, *and the globalization of popular culture* increasingly affect all of our lives, we will need a world understanding and a global perspective of these historical trends and events. Toward that understanding, we hope this volume has made a contribution.

25. Thomas L. Friedman, *The Lexus and the Olive Tree: Understanding Globalization,* updated and expanded ed. (New York: Anchor Books, 2000).